133024

Bristol
Polytechnic
14 NOV 1989
Libraries

UWE BRISTOL Polit
WITHDRAWN
LIBRARY SERVICES

320.941
LEY

Bristol
Polytechnic

MATTHIAS
LIBRARY

...ics in Britain

WITHDRAWN

Politics in Britain
From Labourism to Thatcherism

Revised Edition

COLIN LEYS

VERSO

London · New York

First published by Heinemann Educational Books, 1983
First published by Verso in 1986
This revised edition published by Verso 1989
© Colin Leys 1989
All rights reserved

Verso
UK: 6 Meard Street, London W1V 3HR
USA: 29 West 35th Street, New York, NY 10001-2291

Verso is the imprint of New Left Books

British Library Cataloguing in Publication Data
Leys, Colin
Politics in Britain : from Labourism to
Thatcherism.– Rev ed.
1. Great Britain. Politics
I. Title
320.941

ISBN 0–86091–240–X
ISBN 0–86091–954–4 pbk

Library of Congress Cataloging in Publication Data
Leys, Colin.
Politics in Britain : from Labourism to Thatcherism / Colin Leys.
– Rev. ed.
p.   cm.
Includes index.
ISBN 0–86091–240–X : $50.00 (U.S.). – ISBN 0–86091–954–4 (pbk.) :
$16.95 (U.S.)
1. Great Britain–Politics and government–1945– 2. Social
classes–Great Britain. I. Title.
JN231.L49   1989
941.085–dc19   88–36543
                              CIP

Printed in Great Britain by Bookcraft (Bath) Ltd
Disc Conversion by Columns Typesetters of Reading

Contents

Preface to the
Revised Edition

This book was originally conceived in the late 1970s because there seemed to be a need for a general introduction to politics in Britain which would focus on what was at stake there; namely the fate of capitalist industrialism, liberal democracy, and the socialist alternative. Today it seems strange that there existed a need for such a book, since the 1980s have made all this so clear, and critics of both right and left have declared that the book contains nothing but conventional wisdom. I fear that this is to exaggerate the progress made by conventional thinking, but I would be content if it were so, and in this spirit I have revised the text by taking the story up to the spring of 1988, updating the material in Parts II to IV, and taking note of some important recent contributions to the literature. I have abandoned the conclusion, since it is no longer necessary to insist on the significance of the political transformation that Britain has been undergoing. But I have not changed the book's main line of argument, which I think events have shown to be broadly sound. In preparing this edition I have again received valued help from the Advisory Research Committee of Queen's University and again benefitted from the efficiency and kindness of Bernice Gallagher and her colleagues in the Department of Political Studies at Queen's University.

PART I

1

British Politics and Political Science

The dominant postwar tradition of texts on British politics defined politics in a distinctive way. What it discussed was not so much politics as the institutions through which a particular segment of political life – parliamentary party competition and the conduct of government – is carried on. What is more, these institutions were to a large extent not so much critically analysed as celebrated – even though, from the 1960s onwards, the celebration was increasingly tinged with doubt and anxiety.

The basis of this tradition was the political standpoint from which most of these books were written – the standpoint of the political 'establishment' of MPs, civil servants, judges, journalists, media commentators and others, which the authors of these books shared. Politics, from this point of view, is what goes on in the arenas in which, broadly speaking, the political establishment play leading, controlling, managing roles. Among the large reaches of politics excluded from this definition are the activities of the workers, towards whom the establishment feel a sincere condescension, mingled with irritation and some hostility for the part which the workers have played in calling into question the viability of the economy on which the parliamentary and governmental system depends.*

* Condescension towards the leaders of trade unions, with their limited education and shiny suits, is seldom far below the surface: see for instance, Richard Rose, *Politics in England*, Little Brown, Boston 1980, p. 230: 'as picturesquely described by Ernest Bevin, the Labour Party grew out of the bowels of the trade union movement.' Michael Frayn caught the angle of vision perfectly in his satirical essay, 'A Perfect Strike'; 'It shouldn't be an unofficial strike, needless to say, because the public knows that if it had any justification at all, it would have been taken up by responsible trade union leaders. But that's not to say it should be official – it confirms the public's worst fears about union leaders to see them irresponsibly recommending strike action just when they seemed to

In spite of this irritation and hostility, however, few authors of political textbooks thought to broaden their conception of politics so as to include the activities of the workers, let alone considered the bearing of these activities on the development and fate of the political system, or reconsidered the bearing of the system on the fate of the workers.

By contrast this book seeks to make such issues central. It interprets British politics as referring to the contemporary struggles of the British people as a whole to determine their historical fate. It also assumes that the chief purpose of studying politics is to play a more effective part in politics. For this purpose it seems important that political knowledge should be as reliable as possible, which in turn implies the need for a definite and appropriate method of enquiry. In particular, it is necessary to understand politics as part of the wider social whole, and also to view it as a historical process. Perhaps surprisingly, these aims offend against certain rules that have been established in orthodox 'political science'.

Commitment and Objectivity

Many 'political scientists' subscribe to the doctrine of 'value freedom' according to which the student of politics should try to put aside his or her commitments, in order to be able to look at the facts objectively, instead of seeing only what he or she wants to see.*

Even for someone with definite political ends in view this sounds like good advice, but it is in fact misleading.

The essential mistake involved is that 'facts' do not exist 'out there', waiting to be 'seen'. There is an observable reality; but the concepts we employ in observing it help to determine what, given the reality, the 'facts' are held to be. If we look at Whitehall, using the concept of 'elites', we will tend to arrive at different facts from someone who uses the concept of 'classes'. Being objective, then, cannot be a question of

---

be adopting a sensible and cooperative attitude. I feel sure, too, that strikers have suffered in the past by unfavourable comparison on television with the employers' representatives. Somehow, the employers have always seemed better dressed; they've shown more signs of having a public school education and a good accent. Is this simply poor personnel selection on the strikers' part? Or does it suggest some deeper failing?' (in R.M. Blackburn and A. Cockburn, eds, *The Incompatibles*, Penguin, Harmondsworth 1967, p. 161).

* The doctrine of 'value free' social science is attributed to Max Weber, especially in his speech 'Science as a Vocation' (H.H. Gerth and C. Wright Mills, eds, *From Max Weber*, Routledge, London 1952, pp. 129–56), although it is doubtful if Weber can be interpreted in this way.

'ridding oneself of preconceptions' (we cannot look at the world and see 'facts', without prior concepts), but is a matter of not cheating – not refusing to see what one's own (pre)conceptions suggest reality is like; and certainly, seeing if other people's conceptions make better sense of it.

But is this more likely to happen if one has no commitments, or if they are weak? There seems no reason to think so. Bias may lead to correct conclusions, as well as to false ones; and Hugh Stretton argues rather convincingly that a strong commitment to some particular social goal will (other things being equal) make a social researcher more anxious to be right than one who is indifferent to the practical implications of what he or she is studying.[1] Of course, other things may not be equal; commitment may be accompanied by a blind zeal which swamps the scientific impulse. In practice, however, so-called 'value free' research has not been notable for its objectivity, nor committed research for the lack of it.

In any case, no one is free from commitments, least of all in politics, and they are never 'set aside'. The most 'value free' text has a standpoint – the author's location in society, in terms of culture, education, occupation, gender, class, nationality, and so on – which affects and colours how he or she defines politics, what kinds of explanation are pursued or excluded, and so on. A few examples of books on British politics will illustrate this point.

Professor Richard Rose's *Politics in England* (written mainly for North American students) is perhaps the clearest example of a text that is intended to be value free.[2] It defines British politics as electoral party politics, conceived of as a complex piece of machinery. The task of the student is to understand *how* it works – its different working parts, its varying modes of operation, and so on;[3] not *why* the machine is constructed the way it is, and works the way it does, let alone what it produces and does not produce, or who benefits and who loses from all this.

For example, the 1980 edition of Rose's book made the following points about Mrs Thatcher: she was one of four women cabinet ministers between 1964 and 1979, and the first woman Prime Minister; she first took office after winning an election, in which her opinion poll rating was lower than that of her opponent, Mr Callaghan; she aimed to be an 'active' Prime Minister; her father was active in local politics; her cabinet contained few businessmen and three peers. This completed the information offered about Mrs Thatcher. The radical change in the Conservative Party's direction which her election as leader in 1975 represented, its profound significance for the internal polarisation of both major parties under the growing stress of the economic crisis, were not mentioned, let alone studied. In the 1986 edition, more information was provided about Mrs Thatcher: there was a very brief discussion of the economic difficulties to which Mrs Thatcher's 'conviction politics' were a response (in the opening review of 'the constraints of history' within which the machine must operate) and there was information on the various ways in which the first two Thatcher governments tried to modify the machine. But the prevailing impression given is that these changes are quite limited, as all change tends to be; a view which most people, not to mention those who had become permanently unemployed, *or* those who had become very rich, during the 1980s, might well find strange. This is not to say that Rose is wrong: the things he has selected for study have often changed less than most (although he sometimes seems to underestimate the significance of the changes he does report). It is rather that his conception of politics tends to exclude the major changes that most people – including Mrs Thatcher herself – not unreasonably think have been big and important.

The fundamental reason for Rose's curious principle of selection is that he is not studying politics with a view to changing anything, but playing an academic game called 'comparative politics' (the gist of which, as Bernard Crick aptly remarked, is that 'what cannot sensibly be compared can usefully be contrasted') – and, moreover, playing it by American rules. These rules not only define politics very narrowly, as electoral and pressure group competition between 'elites', but also restrict explanation to a very narrow role (why a machine works as it does calls for a wider explanation than the question of how it works).

The rules also call for information to be presented as if it were capable of being explained as manifestations of established generalisations or laws based on observed behavioural regularities. Hence it is almost always given in the present tense and, where possible, in a quantitative form, as a sign that it is (or might be) explicable as an instance of such laws ('Members of Parliament are much more likely than voters to differ along party lines'). History enters in only as a constraint on the possible courses of action of the country's 'governors'. The historical forces actually at work, of which these 'governors' are a part, the historical options confronting the entire population, are not discussed, since Rose is not proposing to study politics in England to assist the reader to engage in making history. He conceives of himself as a social scientist, contemplating the parties and their projects from a vantage-point independent of any of them. Yet party-neutrality is not value-neutrality. Behind the appearance of 'value freedom' in Rose's work (as in virtually all works of this kind) there lies a clear 'establishment' outlook, as one can easily see from paying attention to such things as the book's *obiter dicta* on economic policy, to its tenderness towards senior civil servants (more qualified by 1986 but still notable) and to the fact that ordinary people figure in it only as 'machine-readable' data. It is also noticeable that the political machine – the 'system' – is not seen as including the trade unions, except as elements of the Labour Party, and as 'pressure groups'; and industrial struggle is not seriously discussed, even though it was directly or indirectly responsible for the fall of every government in the 1970s.*

Most British authors have been sceptical about the doctrine of value freedom but they have mostly adopted the same narrow definition of British politics, and held roughly the same view of it. A good example is Professor John Mackintosh, a Labour MP from 1966 until his untimely death in 1978. Mackintosh's view of politics was much more real, especially when he was drawing on his experience as a frustrated backbencher. Yet, in spite of the title of his book, *The Government and Politics of Britain*, 'politics' entered into it only in the form of party politics, and only in so far as it affected the 'system' of government – the Prime Minister, state and citizen, parliament, Whitehall, local government – which was his central concern.[4] 'The first objective for a student of politics', Mackintosh declared, 'is to try and discover where power lies within the system'. By 1977, he had concluded, none of the parties' current concerns, which reflected those of the voters, implied any clear direction of change for 'the system', but had to do with 'the product of government, the level of taxes, welfare benefits and wages, the degree of unemployment and the standards of the public services' – all of which, strange as it seems,

---

* Another effect of this approach is to play down the question of whether the generalisations made are valid. They are not meant to stand the test of practice, so much as to be items in examination questions. As a result, in spite of Rose's preoccupation with facts, the book contains many judgements that seem very debatable, and some apparently obvious contradictions, that do not seem to trouble the author. To take one example: 'Innovations promoted by followers of Jeremy Bentham's rationalistic philosophy led to a large, bureaucratic, and effective civil service. England's constitutional bureacracy was capable of organising everything from the economic saving of candle ends to prototype laws of the modern welfare state' (p. 16); 'the bias of the senior civil servant is . . . toward the status quo' (p. 83); 'by comparison with many specialists outside government, they often lack knowledge of the substance of the problems confronting them' (p. 87); 'Whitehall . . . prizes critical rather than constructive intelligence' (p. 107); 'the language of Whitehall mandarins often obscures rather than sharpens analysis' (p. 109); 'the fact that Whitehall's leaders have their hands on the tiller of the ship of state is not evidence that they can steer it in any direction they wish; the aim may simply be to keep afloat' (p. 110). It is to say the least not easy to discover what the significance of these vaguely critical remarks is, especially since it is not clear that Rose thinks that an active state-led reconstruction of British society and the British economy is called for, even if his value-free stance rules out his favouring any particular *kind* of reconstruction.

BRISTOL POLYTECHNIC
ST. MATTHIAS LIBRARY
FISHPONDS

Mackintosh clearly felt lay *outside* 'government and politics' as he defined it. He offered plenty of glimpses of party politics, but no description, let alone analysis, of the forces animating them. In publishing a posthumous sixth edition of the book in 1983, Professor Richards was obliged to add a new section on the 'attitudes of the parties' to the last chapter, which documented some of the great upheavals that were occurring: but it was symptomatic that while these changes were too radical to ignore, they could not be integrated into an account which presented the core of politics as a machine which by its nature continues fundamentally unchanged.*

Although as an MP Mackintosh was sensitive to party differences and took clear positions in relation to them, his book was intended less for those who want to engage in politics in order to change the world, than for those who were prospective recruits into the British educated elite and needed to know how 'the system' presently worked, and if possible in what ways it was changing, so as to be able to take their places *in* it – as civil servants, journalists, teachers, local councillors or even MPs. His prime concern with establishing where power lies, and how the system might be changing in that respect, corresponds to this.

Different as they are in many ways, Rose and Mackintosh have in common an underlying 'pluralist' conception of politics. This is the counterpart of the restricted conception of politics as the electoral competition between the parties, and the relations between Whitehall and 'pressure groups'. The core of the 'system' is seen as an essentially neutral apparatus which a multitude or 'plurality' of groups seek to influence or control. Even though he was a Labour MP Mackintosh did not present politics as essentially a struggle between the interests of labour and capital, or the political system as having been shaped (as it undoubtedly has) by the needs of capital in its effort to constrain, deflect or absorb the political power of the working class.

This conception distinguishes the work of both these authors from one other that may be briefly cited here, Peter Calvocoressi's *The British Experience 1945–75*. Although the title makes no such claims, Calvocoressi's book does offer an introduction – and a sophisticated and engagingly written one at that – to modern British politics – or at least to the *policies* that have resulted from these politics.[5] Significantly,

---

* Professor Richards incorporated Mackintosh's final sentiments into the last pages of the sixth edition. While the full import of the Thatcher government's programme was not as clear in 1983 as it later became, a wider conception of politics and a different theoretical approach would surely have avoided the general conclusion that 'there may be increasing doubt whether politics and the politicians matter as much as we used to think' and that 'Mrs Thatcher's government had a firm Commons' majority and was expected to make some changes that would reverse the previous direction of affairs' but had not done so (pp. 245–6).

it is a historical essay, even though its focus is hardly less recent than that of the two 'political science' texts we have discussed; also significantly, a great deal of it is about economics. Calvocoressi feels no inhibitions about discussing what is central to politics in modern Britain (he is not playing 'political science'). Nor does he hesitate to identify the major forces at work in British politics today, seeing here an evident continuity with the past – capital and labour, employers and unions, property and the people. Moreover Calvocoressi thinks that the purpose of studying politics is to influence them.

At the same time, his standpoint entails certain limitations. It is the standpoint of the middle-class liberal intellectual with social-democratic sympathies. Calvocoressi identifies himself with what he sees as a historic trend towards a 'caring' society – which, he holds, is the essence of socialism. On the other hand, he distances himself a little from those who have, in his words, sought most actively to serve as the 'national conscience', feeling that it is 'foolhardy' to give precedence to social outlays over industrial recovery; Britain must, he implies, reverse its priorities here – temporarily, no doubt. But, equally, he does not identify himself with the interests of capital (especially not with financial capital, for which he entertains a particular dislike). From this standpoint he sees a need to transcend the 'crude conflict' between labour and capital by means of 'a more fruitful partnership between employers and employed' which must involve giving workers 'more responsibility and involvement' (but not, apparently, ownership).[6] In other words, a foretaste of what would become the central themes and impulses of the Liberal and Social Democratic Party Alliance from 1981 to 1987; ideas which already exhibited the central problem, namely a fatal detachment from the principal protagonists, leading to what critics of the Alliance would later call a politics of 'wish fulfillment'. In the case of Calvocoressi, the result was a degree of retreat into celebration – though of the British people, not the political system. They are congratulated for being a 'steady people', who have neither panicked nor 'bolted after precipitate panaceas', whose 'democratic instincts remain intact' (although Britain also, he notes, 'prefers the few to the many').[7]

But who in 1988, let alone in 1979, could claim to see the way forward, apart from Mrs Thatcher and other 'conviction politicians' of the far right? In terms of relevance Calvocoressi's work stands the test of time well. It is the way in which its conclusions are determined by the author's standpoint, not their validity, which is at issue here. It also shows how every author's standpoint is reflected in a framework of concepts which determines what are the facts that the author sees, what is defined as politics, what is seen as needing explanation and what kinds of explanation count. Given this, the problem of objectivity cannot be solved by not having a standpoint but only by adopting one which requires objective knowledge, and by trying to work out a conceptual framework capable of yielding it.

Politics, Economy and Society

One of the peculiarities of most general books on British politics is that politics is discussed largely in isolation from the economy and (to a lesser extent) the society. The reasons for this are ultimately political. The separation of social studies into separate 'sciences' was part of the broader movement, begun in the 1920s, to give the study of society a 'professional' status by disengaging it from partisanship. The separation of 'political science' from 'economics' and 'sociology' only made sense if you could define separate spheres of activity in such a way that they were, in fact, largely uninfluenced by each other. This is one of the reasons why the political scientists' definition of politics tends to confine it to the machinery of the 'political system'; and this in turn only makes sense if the purpose of being a political scientist is not primarily to acquire knowledge useful for engaging in political struggles. For anyone who does want such knowledge, the separation of the study of politics from that of economics or social change of all kinds is as absurd as the restriction of the meaning of 'politics' to its machinery.

Most general political 'science' books on Britain implicitly recognise this by devoting a chapter or two to what they call the 'social context' or 'foundations' of British politics. The idea here is that the 'political system' does not actually stand quite alone; it is flanked by a 'social system' and sometimes also by an 'economic system'. Interestingly enough, the relation between these 'systems' and the 'political system' always seems to be unidirectional – the political system is influenced by the social system (by linguistic or regional difference, the 'class structure', 'culture', etc.) or by the economic system (the level of prosperity, the distribution of wealth, and so on) but not the other way round.* This is not so surprising when one considers that in order to examine the effects which the 'political system' has on the other 'systems' one must begin with an analysis of the political forces operating in it – their character, strengths, aims and tendencies – which has been ruled out of the proper purview of political science.

* In the numerous books and articles on the analysis of politics in terms of 'systems' the 'outputs' of the 'political system' are always supposed to be of equal importance with the 'inputs' but the best that can be said of this literature is that it is unutterably jejun

The most striking recent example of this approach – and an interesting one because it is peculiarly explicit – is Samuel Beer's *Britain Against Itself*.[8] Beer, the doyen of American students of British politics, put forward an interpretation of the 'discontented, quarrelsome, unsteady, ineffective, self-defeating seventies' which repudiated all explanations in terms of factors arising outside the political machinery itself; according to Beer, the problem was primarily 'a failure of the choice mechanism'. Politics had been 'collectivised' to the point where a multitude (a 'plurality') of organised groups were the sole effective political actors. This meant that governments confronted a plethora of competing demands for short-term benefits, which made it electorally risky to attend to long-term needs; and the same collectivism also accelerated the 'decomposition' of the class structure, so that the party leaderships could not rely on a solidly loyal class vote if they stood up to pressure-group demands. To make matters worse, there was a 'collapse of deference', arising from 'the romantic revolt' of the 1960s, and manifested in a 'new populism' – the rise of student protest, unofficial strikes, the Labour left, the new right, and so on. It is an engaging account, written with panache: but it takes the separation of 'the political system' from other 'systems' to its ultimately absurd limits. Like most political scientists who acknowledge the importance of the other 'systems' for the 'political system' Beer focuses only on the social/cultural system, and totally excludes economics;* the influence of the social/cultural system on the political system is seen as very great, but not the other way round, so that Beer is obliged to state that the sources of change in the social/cultural system are in the end simply unknowable.[9] In any case, the apparently total exclusion of economics from the analysis was disingenuous. Politics in Britain had been about nothing else for two decades. The idea that the plurality of collective groups whose conflicting interests were paralysing the 'choice mechanism' were doing so out of a merely mechanical (and in the end mutually self-destructive) impulse was quite implausible. Beer's thesis was actually a rather arcane version of the neo-conservative argument: restore the market. He did not believe that Mrs Thatcher would succeed, however: he thought that the ideas of the Social Democrats and the Liberals ran 'closer to the grain of political reality'.[10] While in some long-term sense this could still be true, as a medium-term prediction it was very wide of the mark. Part of the reason for that was the refusal to analyse the way in which the economic and political

---

* Very few political scientists writing on Britain have given a serious account of the economy in its relation with politics: for an outstanding recent exception see Peter Hall, *Governing the Economy: the Politics of State Intervention in Britain and France*, Oxford University Press, New York 1986.

crises of the 1960s interpenetrated each other at every turn.

It is not enough, then, to recognise that politics does not take place in a vacuum – that it is related to the economy and to society, as the language of 'systems' acknowledges; a radical break with this whole way of looking at the matter is required. Politics is indeed distinguishable from economics and social life – but it cannot be understood as a distinct 'field' of activity, occurring in a separate realm or region of its own. It needs to be grasped, rather, as an aspect of all social relations (including economic relations), the aspect of conflict and struggle. It is present in the workplace just as much as it is in elections, and is equally, if less obviously, active in the school system, the courts, the police, the pattern of housing, the scale and distribution of social services, the tax system – not to mention the structure of the family and the whole realm of 'culture'.

Does this mean, then, that elections, parliament, and party government are also merely aspects of economics, social structure and culture? This would certainly be a severe oversimplification, but a more fruitful one than the conventional view – that these are the arenas where politics more or less exclusively 'occurs'.

Such a view may seem to make the study of British politics impossibly complex. It is certainly hard to comprehend the complexity of any social whole, especially one as large and as ancient as Britain's, even if we are only seeking a provisional, practical understanding of some of its central features. But there is no reason for presuming that this complexity is impenetrable.

History

Politics, besides being seen as an aspect of the social whole, must obviously have a strong historical dimension. This does not mean that political generalisations are impossible. Political struggles in different times and places do resemble each other in many respects but each is a unique blend of elements derived from what has gone before, determining what can be done in the present and hence what may eventuate in the future. We need knowledge which embodies the lessons to be gained from studying the unique pattern of development of the particular country's politics on which we want to have some effect.

But this is not an argument for politics being studied as history. Historians are trying to understand the past: we want to understand the past in order to analyse the present and influence the future. Historical knowledge is indispensable to the study of politics, but not a substitute for it. It must be combined with knowledge of the present which can be acquired by various means not available to historians, including taking part in politics; and with comparative knowledge, based on the analysis of similarities and differences between various contemporary situations. Our conceptual framework must permit the combination of these different kinds of knowledge. Ahistorical approaches (the kind characterized by being written largely in the present tense) cannot hope to grasp what is happening, what questions have been historically posed, or what developments are possible. On the other hand, a purely historical understanding, that is not systematically integrated with knowledge of other contemporary situations, or of the dynamics of the immediate situation in which we are involved, is liable to be inconclusive (Calvocoressi is perhaps a case in point). The relation between historiography and the sort of knowledge called for here is indicated by Pierre Vilar in a discussion of Marx's own relation to history:

> In 1854 Marx received from the *New York Tribune* a request for some articles on recent Spanish *pronunciamento* – the very archetype of a banal 'event'. What did he do? *He learned Spanish* . . . Soon he was reading Lope and Caldéron and at last he could write to Engels – 'now I'm in the middle of Don Quixote!' The great and good Spanish anarchist militant Anselmo Lorenzo was astonished by Marx's Hispanic culture when he met him in 1871; admiring, if somewhat out-classed, he described it as 'bourgeois'. Nevertheless, in his series of articles of 1854–6, Marx had given an historical vision of Spain of which only the 20th century has been able to appreciate the full lessons – one which encompassed all the major features of Spanish history, without a single absurdity, and which in certain judgements on the War of Independence has yet to be improved upon. There was a genius at work here, admittedly. But also his method . . . . In order to write about one military escapade he did not 'write a history of Spain'; but he thought it necessary to *think Spain historically*.[11]

A relevant contemporary example is the series of essays written in the early 1960s by Perry Anderson and Tom Nairn, the best known of which is Anderson's 'Origins of the Present Crisis' – 'a sustained attempt to develop a coherent historical account of British society', as E.P. Thompson called it.[12] What Anderson and Nairn proposed was a new understanding of the long-term formation of the class of capital and the working class in Britain, the corresponding peculiarities of the British state, and the distinctive features of the British version of bourgeois ideology, all of which were brought together to explain both the long-term decline of the British economy, and the peculiar paralysis which inhibited either a left or a right response (see Chapter

3). Even sympathetic critics found some of the authors' judgements sweeping and questionable, yet it is hard to deny that these essays set the agenda for much of the whole contemporary debate about the nature and causes of the British crisis. It could even be argued that Anderson and Nairn grasped and articulated the existence of a crisis in a way that has hardly been surpassed more than two decades later. The important point to note, however, is that their intention was not to write the history of the previous three hundred years, but to quarry it, using new concepts and asking different questions, for information which would help explain the *present* crisis. They wanted to 'think' the present crisis 'historically'.*

The Role of Ideas

What is one to make of the role of ideas in politics? The changes that have occurred in British political ideas since 1945 have been remarkable. In the 1950s, for instance, both major parties publicly

---

* Anderson's and Nairn's thesis was restated by Anderson in a major retrospective article ('The Figures of Descent', *New Left Review* 161, 1987, pp. 20–77) in which he drew on a great deal of recent historical work (notably including Geoffrey Ingham's *Capitalism Divided? The City and Industry in British Social Development*, Macmillan, London 1984) and tried to ground the original argument more closely in the distinguishing characteristics of the British experience of capitalist development. His account of the formative years in the nineteenth century particularly stressed: the exceptionally long-lived social and political power of landowners; the great wealth and high social status of financiers, compared with manufacturers; the limited scope of state economic activity, compared with other industrialising states; the failure in 1832 of the new middle class to achieve a franchise wide enough to sustain an 'autonomous bourgeois party'; the subsequent colonisation of the reformed state apparatus by an anti-bourgeois elite; the weakness of the industrial bourgeoisie, both technically compared with their German or American competitors, and politically compared with the City; and the emergence of an industrial working class with a relatively high level of industrial organisation, and a relatively low level of independent political consciousness. This article was scathingly criticised by Michael Barratt-Brown in 'Away with All Great Arches: Anderson's History of British Capitalism' (*New Left Review* 167, 1988, pp. 22–51). The nub of Barratt-Brown's criticism is that Anderson underestimates the strength of manufacturing capital and misrepresents the City's interests as purely commercial, whereas what it defends are the interests of *international* capital, including manufacturing capital. Barratt-Brown, like Thompson in his attack on the original thesis (see note 16), makes some useful corrections to errors and overstatements in Anderson's case; but he is far from demolishing its most important arguments as he, with A. Callinicos (in 'Exception or Symptom? The British Crisis and the World System', *New Left Review* 169, 1988, pp. 97–106) seem to think. It remains clear that British manufacturers, and the culture of manufacture, have been technically and politically weak in Britian, relative to their counterparts in the main competing economies, and this has been constantly reflected in the state and state policies, which in turn have aggravated the weakness. See also C. Leys, 'Thatcherism and British Manufacturing: a Question of Hegemony', *New Left Review* 151, 1985, pp. 5–25.

supported full employment and a steady improvement in social services. By 1980, however, the Conservatives had openly, and the Labour Party tacitly, abandoned both of these commitments. Similarly, in 1950, Fascism was still something which the most popular war in modern British history had been fought to destroy. But by the 1970s neo-fascists were politically active in most large cities in Britain. In 1950 a 'Marxist' was either a communist – that is, a member of the Communist Party of Great Britain – or, possibly, a member of an obscure Trotskyist group; in either case, the representative of a politically irrelevant tendency. By the 1970s, 'Marxism' of some sort was quite commonplace among politically conscious students and people of broadly 'radical' persuasions everywhere.

What produced these far-reaching shifts in ideas, and how did they in turn affect political developments? We will not get much help in answering these questions from the concept of 'political culture' adopted by the behaviouralists. 'Political culture' is defined by Rose as 'a more or less harmonious mixture of the values, beliefs and emotions dominant in society'.[13] It is usually treated as something possessed in common by whole populations; and although it is generally presented as exercising a large (if vague) determining effect on political life, it seldom seems to have any determinants of its own. It plays much the same explanatory role in this sort of political science that the concept of 'national character' played in an earlier literature.

A more useful concept is that of ideology.[14] What is meant by ideology here is any set of social ideas that becomes part of the operative assumptions of the political practice of a particular social group – whether a majority or a minority. For this to happen, at least two requirements have to be met. The ideas must be to some extent effective: that is, they must correspond to some degree to people's practical experience. Secondly, the social origins of the ideas must be lost to view. For example, liberalism was historically the product of the rise of new propertied classes from the seventeenth century onwards, corresponding to their needs and to the reality of the new social order they were creating. Considered in abstraction from these origins (which systematisation by philosophers such as Locke made possible) liberalism had a wider and more compelling appeal than it would have had if its class origins had remained apparent. And so long as the political interests of the new middle classes and the workers could be reconciled within it, liberalism was able to achieve an ascendancy which is still formidable. But this ascendancy was never total, and new conflicts arose to undermine it. Irish colonialism generated nationalist ideas, the rise of organised labour generated socialist ideas, the backlash of imperialism generated racist ideas. Each of these subsequently achieved a measure of influence, wider or narrower and of longer or shorter duration, according to the effects of economic and social changes and the course of political struggles in which these ideas themselves played significant roles. Undoubtedly, this is an intangible and complex area of enquiry.[15]

It is difficult to know, in general, what determines the emergence of particular systems of ideas, and why some and not others succeed in penetrating the practical consciousness of important segments of the population. But there is no doubt that this process plays a crucial part in politics, not least in the rhythm of the development and resolution of crises which is such a prominent aspect of modern British politics.

Method and Standpoint

The methodological ideas just discussed – focusing on the social totality, trying to think the present historically, and seeking the social origins and the effects of ideas – contradict the tenets of much orthodox political science, and not by chance. They are among the methodological tenets of the materialist interpretation of history. But the theoretical basis of historical materialism, or Marxism, has itself never been more in dispute than now; and in following some of its methodological precepts no claim is being advanced for the theoretical or predictive achievements of historical materialism in general (although these are undoubtedly more impressive than vulgar anti-Marxism understands). It is rather that these ideas seem necessary in order to make sense of what has been happening. The reader must decide how useful is the system of concepts employed – and, perhaps, whether it deserves any less to be considered 'scientific' than other conceptual frameworks which others have not hesitated to call political 'science'.

As for the standpoint of this book, its aim is to be democratic and socialist. Maintaining this standpoint consistently is difficult, yet the more one contemplates the British situation today, the harder it becomes to avoid the conclusion that a fundamental choice between democracy and authoritarianism, and between some form of socialism and an increasingly unproductive, and/or socially costly, capitalism, is being posed. At the least, we must seek an understanding relevant to that choice.

At the same time, this understanding must be concerned with the present for its own sake, as well as with the future. What E.P. Thompson said of historians applies at least as strongly to students of contemporary politics:

history cannot be compared to a tunnel through which an express races until it brings its freight of passengers out into sunlit plains. Or, if it can be, then generation upon generation of passengers are born, live in the dark, and die while the train is still within the tunnel. An historian must surely be more interested than the teleologists allow him to be in the quality of life, the sufferings and satisfactions, of those who live and die in unredeemed time . . . any mature view of history (or of contemporary actuality) must in some way combine evaluations of both kinds – of men as consumers of their own mortal existence and as producers of a future, of men as individuals and as historical agents, of men being and becoming?[16]

It is a truism that the goals people struggle for are seldom achieved, at least not in their lifetimes, and not in the form they hope for. On the other hand, people are constantly striving for future goals. It should not be too much to ask that studies of politics should reflect the pathos and drama of both aspects of the human condition, though it often seems to be.

Notes

1 H. Stretton, *The Political Sciences*, Routledge, London 1969 pp. 155–7; see also his admirable discussion of 'bias' and 'values' on pp. 412–18.
2 R. Rose, *Politics in England*, 4th revised edition, Little, Brown, Boston 1986.
3 Ibid., p. 8.
4 The sixth edition revised by Peter G. Richards, was published as *Mackintosh's The Government and Politics of Britain*, Hutchinson, London 1984.
5 P. Calvocoressi, *The British Experience*, Pelican Books, Harmondsworth, 1979.
6 Ibid., pp. 111–12 and 115.
7 Ibid., p. 177.
8 S.H. Beer, *Britain Against Itself: the Political Contradictions of Collectivism*, Norton, New York 1982.
9 Ibid., p. 148.
10 Ibid., p. 219.
11 'Marxist History, a History in the Making: Dialogue with Louis Althusser', *New Left Review* 80, 1973, pp. 104–5.
12 'Origins' was first published in *New Left Review* 23, 1964, pp. 26–53; the description is from Thompson, 'The Peculiarities of the English', *Socialist Register*, 1965, p. 311.
13 Rose, p. 117.
14 The best overall introduction to the question of ideology is perhaps J. Larrain, *The Concept of Ideology*, University of Georgia Press, Athens 1979.
15 For a brilliant example of the analysis of ideology in the British context, see S. Hall et al., *Policing the Crisis*, Macmillan, London 1979.
16 E.P. Thompson, 'The Peculiarities of the English', *Socialist Register*, pp. 358–9.

Britain in
Crisis

A hundred and fifty years ago, when the industrial revolution was at its height, people in Britain had no doubt that the country was in the grip of powerful forces which were drastically changing its economic, social and political structure. The breathtaking accumulation of wealth, the dramatic expansion of the industrial towns, impressed themselves on contemporary observers as 'great and extraordinary facts', 'almost miraculous,' 'unparalleled in the history of the world'.[1] By 1840, the industrial revolution was almost universally recognised as 'probably the most important event in world history, at any rate since the invention of agriculture and cities'.[2] And later generations have had no difficulty in recognising that the industrial revolution also produced a new class of capital, and a new working class, or that the relationship between these classes had become, by the end of the nineteenth century, the central axis of British political life.

It is also well recognised now that from about 1870 the revolutionary forces which wrought all these changes slackened in Britain, while gathering strength in Germany, the USA, Belgium and subsequently elsewhere. It was not just that other countries also became industrialised, eventually reducing the British share of world trade and world production to one more in keeping with her population size (from nearly 25 per cent at the end of the 1920s – the peak – to about 14 per cent by 1945).[3] From the moment that foreign industrial competition began to be seriously felt, contemporaries became aware that Britain could not meet it, in one field after another. Had it not been for the growing volume of imports paid for out of profits and interest on British overseas investment and lending, and for the advantages which British exports enjoyed in empire markets (Tables 2.1, 2.2), the relative decline of Britain's economic power would have been much more rapid, and might well have produced a social and political crisis severe enough to lead to a radical reconstruction of the economy in an atmosphere of national emergency.[4]

As it was, Britain's relative decline was protracted. It was only towards the end of the last, and greatest, upswing in the world cycle of capital accumulation (i.e., the long boom which ended in 1970) that her real weakness became fully apparent. Britain's manufacturing competitiveness was now shrinking below the level needed to maintain the real level of national income, to the point where one sector of industry after another was driven out of business without significant new sectors arising to take their place (Table 2.3). The resulting trade deficit was closed by periodic 'packages' of deflationary economic

Table 2.1   How overseas investment income offsets Britain's trade deficit
1831–1931

	Balance of visible trade	Overseas investment earnings	'Invisible' trade	Current account balance	Proportion of visible trade gap covered by overseas investment earnings
1821	− 78.1	+ 3.9	+ 13.1	− 1.1	21.5%
1851	− 22.6	+ 10.4	+ 22.6	+ 8.0	46.0%
1871	− 46.0	+ 39.5	+ 82.4	+ 66.9	85.8%
1891	−122.1	+ 94.3	+ 99.6	+ 67.0	77.2%
1911	−121.2	+177.3	+146.8	+190.9	146.2%
1931	−407.0	+170.0	+134.0	− 37.0	41.7%

Source: B.R. Mitchell and P. Deane, *Abstract of British Historical Statistics*, Cambridge University Press, Cambridge 1962, pp. 333–5 (with bullion and specie movements excluded).

Table 2.2   Shares of major British exports going to empire markets 1870–1934

	1870	1880	1890	1900	1913	1929	1934
Textiles	26.6	36.8	37.2	39.9	43.9	42.2	44.2
Iron & iron goods	21.7	31.2	33.5	36.7	48.2	51.4	55.3
Machinery	19.0	18.3	24.6	22.3	32.5	43.5	51.2
Locomotives	16.0	67.5	27.8	49.5	58.6	43.8	65.3

Source: W. Schlote, *British Overseas Trade from 1700 to the 1930s*, Blackwell, Oxford 1952, pp. 166–7.

policies to curb the demand for imports and, theoretically, to encourage exports, although this served to aggravate the growing unemployment arising from industrial closures. Living standards finally stopped growing and then, for two years in the mid-1970s, and again in the early 1980s, actually fell, to the accompaniment of many signs of social strain.

There is, however, a striking contrast between the general readiness to recognise the revolutionary social forces which made Britain into an industrial capitalist country, and the general reluctance to recognise these same forces at work when their action is, so to speak, negative. The logic which propelled the new classes of capital and labour onto the front of the political stage as the agents of Britain's world economic and political dominance had now begun to drive Britain towards a different, less comfortable, destiny. People readily acknowledge that in the nineteenth century politics was about the coming to power of the capitalist class, and the reconstruction of the entire framework of economic policy, fiscal policy, educational policy, the national and local state structure, culture, etc. in conformity with the interests of that class. The same people, however, have often found it difficult to accept that the time has come when politics is about the necessity of a comparable upheaval. Yet while this thought may be unwelcome, it is not unthinkable. Just as the nineteenth century was a period of radical reconstruction, based on the triumphs of British capital, the late twentieth century is also a period of far-reaching social and political change, based on its defeats.

In the mid-1960s, the predominant view was that Britain's problems could be solved by extensive reforms – in the way the government 'managed' the economy, in fiscal policy, in the internal organisation of the civil service, in education, in the organisation of corporate industrial capital, and so on. This idea, which Harold Wilson so successfully articulated when he was elected to the Labour Party leadership in 1963, had been thoroughly discredited by the end of his first administration in 1970 (though just why these reforms were either impracticable, or irrelevant, is seldom explained).

Following this disappointment the anxiety increasingly felt by political commentators expressed itself in several alternative forms. One was to suggest that the British are, after all, a non-materialistic people, who prefer the 'quality of life' to high living standards, so that after a period of adjustment they will be content to live more modestly and things can go on much as before. If growth proved 'a will o' the wisp' it would indeed be comforting if the workers proved relatively satisfied, as Calvocoressi suggested, with 'pottering about in their gardens and watching football', while the middle classes were predominantly occupied with 'music, theatre, art exhibitions, rescue

Table 2.3 Some effects of Britain's declining manufacturing competitiveness 1951–1980

	1951	1961	1971	1974	1975	1976	1977	1978	1979	1980
British share of world exports (%)	21.9	16.4	10.9	8.8	9.3	8.7	9.3	9.5	9.7	10.2
Foreign share of domestic sales manufactures (%)	n.a.	n.a.	18.0	23.0	22.0	23.0	24.1	24.0	25.5	25.8
Foreign share of domestic sales of vehicles (%)	0	n.a.	12.0*	23.0	26.0	29.0	34.0	36.0	41.0	41.0
Real personal disposable income (index: 1975=100)	53	73	88	101	100	99	95	106	114	115
Unemployed (millions)	.214	.376	.775	.605	.921	1.274	1.378	1.376	1.307	1.665

*excluding tractors and motorcycles

Source: National Institute Economic Review, Economic Trends, Monthly Digest of Statistics, Department of Employment Gazette.

archaeology and buying and borrowing books'.[5] Another reaction was to celebrate industrial decline itself. It was positively good, according to the American journalist Bernard Nossiter, that Britain's dark satanic mills should close; instead, the British people would turn more and more to selling to foreigners *services* in the provision of which they have, as a nation, special skills.[6]

These ideas were – unfortunately perhaps – unrealistic;* but they do betray these authors' real anxiety: if the major classes, and perhaps especially the workers, who have less margin for sacrifice, were not content with non-material things, and if the 'deindustrialisation' of Britain continued, then the moderation, gradualism and civility which they saw as the pre-eminent virtues of British politics were unlikely to survive. In other words, the political struggle might enter a very different phase. And this is, indeed, still the central issue of contemporary British politics, which makes the study of British politics important not just for the British alone, but for any capitalist industrialised country which falls too far behind in the industrial race.

To understand this we must try to understand the causes and nature of the 'crisis'. What is the 'logic of relationships' which for more than a century has been pushing Britain steadily towards the margin of survival in the world of industrial competition? Since unlike, say, Australia or Canada, Britain cannot export primary commodities (with the short-run exception of oil), or even feed her own population, she must (*pace* Nossiter's vision of a nation of producers of television shows or hand-crafted pottery) export manufactured goods. At the end of the so-called deindustrialisation process there lies, for a large portion of the population, nothing but unemployment and growing poverty. And as these people cannot be relied upon (*pace* Calvocoressi) to potter contentedly in their gardens while this occurs, the process of 'deindustrialisation' entails the risk of a general political crisis.

One reason why so many people continued for so long to celebrate the British political system, rather than analyse the new circumstances

---

* The main reasons why a switch of resources to services is not a solution to Britain's economic problem are: 1. Services are on a much smaller scale than manufacturing. For instance, to offset a drop in Britain's share of world manufacturing exports of one percentage point in 1976, Britain's share of world exports of services would have had to increase by 3.3 percentage points – from 9.7 per cent to 13 per cent of the world total, an increase of more than a third. 2. The world market for services cannot be expected to grow very fast and Britain already has a large share of it. 3. The services which earn foreign exchange mostly do not employ many people (tourism is an important exception but for obvious reasons has some finite limits to its growth). Most of the increase in service employment since the 1960s has been in non-trade (i.e. public sector) services. (See J.R. Sargent, 'UK Performance in Services', in F. Blackaby, ed, *De-industrialisation*, Heinemann/NIESR, London, 1979, and T. Sheriff, *A Deindustrialised Britain?*, Fabian Research Series 341, London 1979).

which have undermined it, is possibly a reluctance to believe that what has happened elsewhere could happen in Britain. For the new circumstances in which Britain finds herself are less novel than many people like to suppose. A process of economic 'involution' and political polarisation, culminating in authoritarian regimes more or less heavily reliant on terror, occurred in successive countries in Latin America in the 1960s and 1970s, and notably in Chile and Uruguay in 1973, both of which had long democratic traditions. It would be superficial to draw too close a parallel with the experience of these countries;* but it is equally superficial (if very British) to suppose that Britain could never undergo its own version of this fate, that for Britain something will always turn up.

The belief that 'something will turn up' seemed, of course, to be almost miraculously confirmed by the discoveries of oil in the North Sea, starting in 1968, followed by massive increases in the world-market price of oil. By 1980 North Sea production was already equivalent to all Britain's oil requirements. Yet by this time North Sea oil was also just beginning to be seen as at best a modest economic blessing, and at worst as an economic disaster. No major industrial reconstruction financed by oil revenues, or linked to oil technology, had yet been put in hand or was even being seriously planned. The exchange value of sterling rose sharply because of the strong overall balance of payments caused by oil exports (and savings on oil imports). This made manufactured exports dearer, and imports cheaper. The result was to accelerate the closure rate of British manufacturing companies. Now North Sea oil was 'killing our industry'.[7]

But North Sea oil had warded off a *political* crisis. In 1979, the deficit on Britain's visible trade account (the gap between the cost of imported goods and the value of exported goods) was £3.2 billion, in spite of oil production worth about £6 billion. Without North Sea oil output, the visible trade deficit might well have been £5 billion and the overall balance of payments could have been in deficit to the tune of £4.5 billion.[8] This would have led at once to a payments crisis and – by one means or another – to a drastic reduction of national consumption. Admittedly these figures are abstractions. No deficit of that magnitude would have been allowed to build up. Long before it was reached, more modest cuts would have been imposed. Yet, on this point, the behaviour of the Callaghan government in the year 1976 is extremely instructive.

* Yet Chile and Uruguay, together with Argentina, had relatively high per capita incomes by world standards immediately after the Second World War; Uruguay had had constitutional democratic government from 1903, and Chile from 1932. After two decades of economic stagnation or regression, and mounting political crisis, the military seized power and made these countries bywords for barbarity.

At that stage, North Sea oil production was only worth £0.9 billion per annum, and the overall visible balance of trade deficit for 1976 was about £3.9 billion.[9] There was a flight of capital out of sterling. To halt the fall in the value of the pound, the government turned to the International Monetary Fund for a loan. The conditions attached to this loan (like all IMF loans) involved severe cuts in government spending and, therefore, in public consumption. There was strong opposition to it within the Labour Party. But Denis Healey, then Chancellor of the Exchequer, said that the alternative would be 'policies so severe that they would lead to riots in the streets' – i.e., so severe as to jeopardise the government's ability to govern at all. The IMF loan was repaid early, by April 1979 – partly out of government revenues from North Sea oil – by which time oil production had also largely closed the visible trade deficit, which by 1979 had risen to £2.4 billion.[10]

So North Sea oil, whatever its long-run economic effects, tided the existing party-parliamentary political system over a reef on which it might well have foundered in the late 1970s. Thanks to North Sea oil, the belief that the politics of the 1950s could somehow be restored was still surprisingly widespread among British political commentators in the early 1980s;* even though oil output would eventually decline from the late 1980s onwards, by which time, unless a radical reconstruction of manufacturing industry had been put in hand, the balance of payments gap would have to be closed by cuts in living standards even larger than those that had so alarmed the government in 1976.

The Concept of Crisis

Part of the reason for the widespread unwillingness to confront the reality of the crisis was perhaps that the word itself had been so overworked in the course of the previous two decades. As Tom Nairn remarked, with only slight exaggeration, 'since 1910 it has all been "crisis", save for those few years in the fifties when we had it so good (a slogan invented, characteristically, just when it had become plain that the post-war UK boom was over and we would soon be back to crisis as usual)'.[11] Can the concept of crisis be given a reasonably clear and precise meaning?

---

* Those who were converted to monetarism could perhaps be considered to have become convinced of the 'impossibility of going on in the old way', but many of these soon became disillusioned by the early economic policy failures of Thatcherism and turned back with renewed enthusiasm to the idea of 'centre option'. It is hard to believe that this would have seemed plausible by 1981 had Britain's short-term problems not been so greatly alleviated by North Sea oil.

The most systematic recent attempt to do this was made by Jürgen Habermas.[12] Borrowing (cautiously) from systems theory, Habermas tried to establish a model of society which would allow us to understand a social crisis in the sense in which medicine understands a crisis in an illness (as a turning-point at which the patient either recovers or dies) or dramatic criticism understands a crisis in the life of a character – the principal difference being that, there, the crisis is experienced as such, and consciously (though not necessarily rationally) participated in by the character concerned, a dimension of obvious relevance to social crises.

A major difficulty faced by all attempts to apply systems theory to social life is that the 'boundaries' of social organisms are not precise. It is seldom easy to know whether a society has changed in such a fundamental way that we must say that the old society has been *replaced* by a new one. Habermas suggested that this problem could be solved by focusing on the 'constitutive tradition' of a society; usually, at least in retrospect, its members know when the tradition that gives it its identity has been broken (e.g., post-revolutionary French society understood that the revolution had effected a very definite break from the old regime). Such breaks, Habermas argued, occur when a society ceases to be able to learn how to deal with changes (external or internal) which threaten to break its constitutive tradition. The capacity of a society to learn is given by the way in which its general principles of organisation determine (a) its control over 'outer nature' (i.e., its scientific, technological and organisational capacity) and (b) its 'integration of inner nature' (roughly, the aptitudes, values, personality types, etc., which are fostered by it).

On this model, liberal (competitive) capitalist societies evolve from crisis to crisis. This is because their principle of social organisation leads periodically to economic slumps which put in question the key social relations on which they are based – private ownership and the class system. 'Organised' or state-regulated capitalism has learned how to prevent production crises by means of a state economic sector, state economic planning, the substitution of bureaucratic for democratic decision-making, and 'corporatist' wage-fixing. But the tendency to economic crisis that is inherent in any system of production for profit remains. But now it is manifested in the form of fiscal crises, or crises of economic planning; or as crises of administrative capacity ('rationality crises'); or as 'legitimation crises' (when the state has difficulty in justifying new policies necessitated by the new tasks it must take on); or as 'motivation crises' (due to the erosion of traditional values necessary to the maintenance of capitalism – for instance traditional family values).

Habermas's discussion succeeds in giving some precision to the concept of social crisis. As he points out, the fact that a 'crisis consciousness' develops does not mean that a society is objectively in a crisis. He sets out, however, a plausible model of the way in which objective changes may put in question the survival of society as its members recognise it. In the case of Britain, both elements are discernible: a general sense of crisis, at least among the middle classes from the late 1960s onwards, and a variety of indicators of at least severe deficiencies of production, administrative capacity, legitimation and motivation.

But the model does not help to explain why crises occur *where* and *when* they do. The tendencies it outlines are generic to all advanced capitalist countries. Why did Britain enter into a general crisis (combining most of Habermas's 'crisis tendencies') when most other advanced capitalist countries did not? To explain this, a historical analysis of the specific sources of the crisis in Britain is needed. Moreover, in Britain's case it is not an underlying tendency to overproduction, but to underproductivity, that is central. Habermas's model is, in fact, a checklist of possible sources of crisis in advanced capitalist countries in general. While it has some relevance to Britain, it does not seem to touch on what is most distinctive about the one advanced capitalist country which had actually entered a general crisis at the time Habermas was writing.

An alternative approach to the analysis of crises is that of Antonio Gramsci, who defined a general or 'organic' crisis (a 'crisis of authority' or 'crisis of the state') as a dissolution of the ideology that secures the consent of the mass of the population to the existing order.[13] In Gramsci's view, philosophy, a more or less coherent and critical system of ideas, becomes an ideology when it becomes an 'implicit premise' of men's practical lives, reflected in their language, 'commonsense' (what people see as being 'the ways things are') and 'popular religion' or folklore (popular articles of faith, precepts for living). A philosophy that expresses the interests of the ruling class (for example the 'possessive individualism' of English liberal philosophy) becomes an ideology and binds the masses to the established order when it penetrates popular consciousness in this way. A 'crisis of the state' occurs when this cement breaks down, when 'the great masses have become detached from their traditional ideologies, and no longer believe what they used to believe':[14]

> the content of the crisis is the ruling class's hegemony, which occurs either because the ruling class has failed in some major undertaking for which it has requested, or forcibly extracted, the consent of the broad

masses (war, for example), or because huge masses . . . have passed suddenly from a state of political passivity to a certain activity, and put forward demands which taken together, albeit not organically formulated, add up to a revolution. A 'crisis of authority' is spoken of: this is precisely the crisis of hegemony, or general crisis of the State.[15]

At this point the 'historic bloc' of social classes that was once bound together by a unifying ideology under the leadership of the ruling class dissolves and must be either reconstructed or replaced through a fresh political initiative. The old dominant class, Gramsci suggests, is the first to respond, and generally restores control by means of a new philosophy, new men and new programmes; but an opportunity also arises to prevent this, to create a new 'historic bloc' under the leadership of a new, more popular alliance of classes.

Gramsci does not offer a theory of why organic crises occur, although the examples he gives in the passage cited above apply rather well to Britain, the first to the 1970s (after fifteen years in which successive governments had failed to produce the economic recovery for which they had repeatedly sought wage restraints, and imposed deflations), and the second to the period before 1914 (when the labour movement had moved out of its passive attachment to liberalism). But what Gramsci does is to make the concept of *general* crisis historically concrete. What is at stake is not a passive and intangible 'constitutive tradition' but an actively constructed ideological hegemony, that can be both analysed and contested. This idea (which underlies the work of Anderson and Nairn referred to in the previous chapter) allows us to make a preliminary clarification of the British situation as follows. Britain has known two general crises in the twentieth century, one before 1914, and a second which began in the 1960s and is still unresolved. The causes of these crises must be established by historical analysis: it will be argued that they are fundamentally the same.

The more specific crises – budget crises, sterling crises, and the like – which precede and accompany these general crises, are 'steering' problems which are perceived as crises by those specifically concerned with them (in the Treasury or the banking system, for example) when it is realised that they cannot be resolved by the adjustment mechanisms available but will require other, politically expensive policy changes, such as new taxes, redistribution of wealth, or deflation. They are seen as crises to the extent that the dominant class realises that these costs represent a long-term threat to their hegemony. The distinction between crises in specific sectors and general or organic crises is obscured by media hyperbole, but it must be kept clearly in view if the dynamics of the contemporary general crisis in Britain are to be understood.

Britain's Recurring Crises

The first essential is to recognise that the crisis which set in during the 1960s, and has still to be fully resolved, is not the first of its kind. The 'vast, insanely repetitious literature of self-censure and prophecy' which poured forth following the 'sterling crisis' of 1961 and shattered the complacency of the 'affluent years' of the previous decade, made the problem seem novel. But it had all happened before, and a comparison of the more recent literature with that of the earlier crisis is instructive.

In the early 1960s the problem was largely defined by the Labour Party, which had by then been in opposition for ten years. Because the party was divided on the question of further public ownership the leadership sought an explanation and a solution within the framework of the 'mixed economy' as it already existed. The essence of the problem, according to Harold Wilson (elected leader of the party in 1963) was first, a lack of planned and state-directed industrial investment (thanks to the Tories' lack of interest in the technical problems of an advanced industrial economy); and second, incompetence in the management of much of the private sector (a management recruited largely on the basis of private education and connections, not on merit, and one ignorant of, and indifferent towards, science and technology). In fact, by 1964 there had been no significant change for nearly fifteen years in educational provision, central or local government organisation and recruitment, the conduct of parliamentary business, or the management of the economy. So, understandably, there was widespread enthusiasm for Wilson's proposed reforms.

The reforms were of two kinds: reforms which would directly attack the shortcomings of state economic management, such as the setting up of a new growth-oriented Department of Economic Affairs to plan the economy (following the much-envied example of France); and reforms – especially in education and in the recruitment of civil servants – which would tend to put policymaking and management in the hands of technically proficient people, regardless of their social origins. The key idea in Wilson's diagnosis of the problem was *technology* – a cornucopia of new marvels, the benefits of which had been denied the British people by a lax government of overprivileged amateurs. In this spirit a wide range of reforms was put in hand after the Wilson government took office in 1964.

But by the end of the 1960s it was obvious that the diagnosis and the solution had been hopelessly shallow. Even if the state machine had been thoroughly 'modernised' and put exclusively in the hands of people with degrees in economics, science and engineering – and in reality the reforms attempted seemed frustratingly feeble – it now appeared very doubtful if the state could do much to solve the basic problems which the sixties had thrust on the public's attention. In spite of a National Plan, wage controls, subsidies, mergers and very large tax concessions, company profits declined by roughly 50 per cent between 1964 and 1970, while inflation accelerated from 3.3 per cent to 6 per cent, unemployment rose from 1.5 per cent to 2.6 per cent, and days lost in strikes increased from 2.3 million to 10.9 million.[16]

Wilson's complaint that his government had been 'blown off course' only reinforced this impression.* Problems beyond the reach of any governmental machine – problems having to do with the structure of the economy, with the relationship between employers and unions, or with the collective national psychology ('the will to work', 'insularity', etc.) – now came to be seen as fundamental. The alternative prescription of the Conservative leader Edward Heath – that efficient management and a hard-working labour force could be secured only through the maximum exposure to market competition – expressed and reinforced this change of view, which soon came to be generally accepted. In fact, popular commentary subsequently became fixed with mesmeric intensity on these apparently intractable 'attitudes'. The Labour Party blamed the bosses and the Conservatives blamed the workers, but most people thought that there were faults on both sides: the problem was that no one could offer a convincing plan for eliminating them. The left wing of the Labour Party called for more state control of company policy-making, and more worker-control; the right wing of the Conservative Party called for reducing the role of the state and letting market forces 'slim down' the economy until only those firms remained which could survive internationally, and only those workers had jobs who were prepared to work as hard as their German or Japanese counterparts.

Most people doubted if either formula would lead to an industrial renaissance, but seemed to have no better ideas. Very few were willing to contemplate the possibility that any effective 'solution' to the economic problem might call for a fundamental political transformation. Those who did were the small extra-parliamentary left, who were committed to socialist revolution, and the more powerful emerging ultra-right, who publicly wondered if Britain was still 'governable' –

---

* Wilson used this expression in reference to the seamen's strike of May 1966, which he blamed for the government's economic difficulties. The phrase stuck because it captured both the sense of failure which attached to his whole administration, and his readiness to blame everything but his own policies.

BRISTOL POLYTECHNIC
ST. MATTHIAS LIBRARY
FISHPONDS

i.e. if democracy might not have to be 'curtailed' in the interests of efficiency.

A more common reaction was to hanker after a political 'moratorium', a non-party interlude, conceived of either as an agreement to put the economy in the hands of some kind of technocratic elite, or as a 'government of national unity', an all-party coalition of patriots. The technocratic alternative was advocated by the Hudson Institute in its 1974 report, *The United Kingdom in 1980*, which urged that 'economic policy should become the province of a new national six-year plan [i.e., covering a period longer than the life of one parliament] under the aegis of the state; . . . we would stress an apolitical, or better still supra-political nature for this plan'. The plan was to become

> the province of Britain's best economists and administrators and engineers, all serving the nation in a self-conscious spirit of ambition (for the country) and enterprise. Those working for the plan . . . should come in time to see themselves as a new elite – not an arrogant technocratic bureaucracy beyond political control, but one committed to the restructuring of Britain and to its regeneration . . . what we are asking, then, is that in a new spirit of practicality the best brains of Britain be put to the task of analysing the society's economic needs, articulating regional plans, industrial plans, and long-range goals for the country as a whole, in contrast to the drift, evasion and sentimentality that has characterized economics in Britain at least since 1945.[17]

The alternative of a 'government of national unity' was proposed in 1974 by the Liberal leader, Jeremy Thorpe, shortly before the defeat of the Heath government, and again by right-wing Labour leaders in 1978 shortly before the defeat of the Callaghan government.

In all of this, history was repeating itself with some precision. After the Paris Fair of 1867 had shown that British industrial design was lagging seriously behind that of its new competitors in a disturbingly large number of fields, Matthew Arnold published a celebrated report, *Higher Schools and Universities in Germany*, which suggested that the proportion of the British population receiving higher education was less than half that of France or Prussia. There followed a series of educational commissions which confirmed the dramatic shortcomings of British education, and especially scientific education, and recommended extensive reforms. These recommendations went largely unheeded. In 1902 there were at most 1,500 chemists in British industry compared with 4,000 in German industry.[18] According to Hobsbawm, 'Britain in 1913 had only nine thousand university students compared to almost sixty thousand in Germany, . . . only five day students per ten thousand (in 1900) compared to almost thirteen in the USA; . . . Germany produced nine thousand graduate engineers per year while in England and Wales only 350 graduated in *all* branches of science, technology and mathematics with first- and second-class honours, and few of these were qualified for research'.[19] Indeed, as late as in 1913 only 208,000 British children (roughly five per cent) received any secondary education whatever, let alone any higher education, technical or otherwise.

British exporters found themselves squeezed out of foreign markets, and as foreign manufacturers began to penetrate the British domestic market 'the newspapers were full of gloomy talk about Britain's stagnating exports, lost markets and technological obsolescence, contrasted with Germany's superiority in business methods, salesmanship and industrial research'.[20]

The immediate historical background also bore some striking similarities to the situation after 1960. Just as the 1939–45 war had left Britain in a sellers' market for manufactures for the next fifteen years, so overseas wars (the American civil war of 1860–65, and Prussia's wars with Denmark, Austria and France from 1864 to 1871) had temporarily injured American and French production, helping British suppliers and fostering complacency. The Great Depression of 1873 to 1896, however, curtailed demand just when German and American productivity was rising very rapidly. Again, there is an obvious parallel with German, French and Japanese productivity growth in the 1950s and 1960s, and the onset of the world depression in the 1970s. The resulting conflict between capital and labour, in which employers sought to cut wages and 'dilute' labour (introducing new equipment manned by less skilled and lower-paid workers) also paralleled the industrial conflicts of the 1960s and 1970s.

The earlier situation likewise produced a 'vast literature of pessimism and alarm' (which eventually degenerated into a war hysteria against Germany).[21] In 1901–2 *The Times* ran a series of articles on 'The Crisis in British Industry' which foreshadowed all the complaints against the trade unions, as the chief cause of the crisis, that were to be made again (and not least in *The Times*) in the 1960s and 1970s; while a parallel literature – including the evidence given to a succession of commissions of inquiry from the 1880s onwards – pinpointed exactly the same shortcomings of British management that were also to be rediscovered half a century later.

The unions were charged with 'restriction of output' (later called restrictive practices), opposition to machinery (later called opposition to new technology), interference with management (later called interfering with management 'prerogatives'), interference with 'free' labour (later this was the question of the 'closed shop' and 'intimidation') and fomenting disputes (later attributed to 'agitators').

Manufacturers were charged – again, in the words of contemporaries – with having become 'too supine and easy-going', 'content to follow mechanically the lead given by their fathers'. It was said that they 'worked shorter hours, and they exerted themselves less to obtain new practical ideas than their fathers had done'. They were amateur:

> very often there is no planning at all; it is left to the operative and rule of thumb. Generally there is some planning of a rough and ready kind, but some of the most famous works in the country are in such a state of chaos that the stuff seems to be turned out by accident . . . There can be no doubt that the most serious cause of new methods and new machinery not being rapidly adopted is to be found in the general absence of accurate technical knowledge . . . on the part of the responsible chiefs of the majority of big printing houses . . . The capable man rising from below has much greater difficulties in his way (than in the USA), difficulties which are the result of centuries of prejudice and class interest.[22]

These views, and others which were to become familiar again after 1961, were advocated most consistently by the so-called National Efficiency movement. Just as the would-be reformers of the 1960s looked enviously at France, the would-be reformers of the early 1900s looked at Germany, and also Japan, both of which had defeated apparently much larger military opponents (Prussia had defeated Austria and France, Japan had defeated Russia), while Britain could hardly subdue the tiny Boer Republic in two and a half years of spectacular military and logistical incompetence. The National Efficiency movement indicted not so much industry alone, as the national character: the lack of the dedication, purpose, plan, discipline, and thoroughness which the leaders of the movement felt were characteristic of the Germans and the Japanese. A fundamental change of 'attitudes' was called for; a drastic expansion of public education and a planned shift of emphasis from the humanities to science and technology, directly linked to industrial needs; an overhaul of the machinery of government, local and central; a reduction of the power of the cost-conscious Treasury, and measures to make government more dynamic; a professionally trained civil and military elite, drawn from the talented in all ranks of society, in place of an upper-class stratum of ill-educated amateurs.[23]

As if this comprehensive preview of the themes of the 1960s and 1970s were not enough, the National Efficiency movement also manifested impatience with the party politics that seemed to frustrate these rational and urgently needed changes. Where the Hudson Report of 1974 proposed a new 'responsible elite, ambitious for their country', the National Efficiency movement seventy years earlier called for political power to be shared with, if not given to, 'experts', and for the introduction of businessmen and business methods into public policy-making. The movement questioned whether party politics were even compatible with national survival. Like Jeremy Thorpe in 1974 and Roy Jenkins (the former Labour Chancellor) in 1979, Liberal leaders in the first decade of the century, who shared the National Efficiency outlook and who saw the improbability of realising any significant part of it under the regime of either major party, sought an 'all-party' peacetime National Government.

History rarely repeats itself with the almost derisive fidelity that we see here. What it tells us in unmistakable terms is that we are dealing with something *systemic* – a syndrome towards which the whole society is periodically driven by the pattern of forces at work within it. It is remarkable that those researchers who have been most anxious to ground social science on regularities have been so uninterested in this one.

In the years after 1900, Britain's industrial weakness led to a crisis that was social and political as well as economic: a crisis of defence strategy; a crisis of order in industrial relations; a challenge to the authority of the elected government by the right wing in the House of Lords, and in the officer corps of the army, over the issue of Home Rule for Ireland; and a challenge to its legitimacy by the direct-action wing of the Suffragette movement. This accumulating crisis was suspended by the outbreak of war in 1914. The war and inter-war years saw a series of adjustments and compromises which gave a new lease of life to the old system. But the underlying causes of the crisis were not removed. When one considers how much the world had altered by 1960 it is almost awe-inspiring to reflect how, in Britain, nothing essential seemed to have changed at all, either in the forces that led to crisis, or in the British people's perceptions of their situation.

Explaining Britain's Crises

What accounts for this relentless regression? To try to explain the crisis of the late twentieth century is obviously to try to explain the manifestations of a tendency well over one hundred years old. This means that the explanation must be historical, and – since we are looking at the long-run behaviour of a whole society – must be based on a theory of the 'social whole'. But most of the theories of the crisis which have been advanced over the years since 1961 have been neither.

A good example of an ahistorical explanation is the widely accepted
theory that Britain's problems have been caused by excessive overseas
commitments, causing a perpetual balance of payments problem,
leading to constant recourse to deflationary policies and hence
underinvestment in manufacturing. This theory has many variants: one
stresses the British predilection for overseas rather than domestic
investment; another blames primarily overseas military commitments;
and so on. Although these tendencies have played a part in Britain's
economic problems, an historical perspective shows that they are
secondary. Britain's relative decline set in long before there was a
significant threat to the balance of payments, at a time when there was
sufficient capital to support both domestic and overseas investment,
and it continued after North Sea oil temporarily removed the threat to
the balance of payments in 1980.

In general ahistorical theories always pose a new question in the
process of answering one. If the balance of payments constraint, for
example, is important, how did it arise? If British management is
inefficient, how did it come to be inefficient? If the problem is that
trade union organisation is heterogeneous and decentralised, why did
it develop in that way, and why has it remained so? If government
economic policy-making has been inept, what caused this and why
does it continue?

Ahistorical theories usually also disregard the uniqueness of each
social totality. Theories of Britain's problems have been largely
positivist; they rest on the general assumption that explanation consists
in finding causal connections between social 'factors' that can be
isolated and which, underneath the uneven flow of events, exist in all
societies. A good example of the 'comparative method' used by
positivists is cited by Anthony Peaker in his *Economic Growth in
Modern Britain*.[24] In order to see whether the rate of economic growth
was related to the level of investment, an OECD study plotted the
average annual rate of growth for the period 1960 to 1970 against the
average annual percentage of national income invested, for twenty
countries. Britain had the lowest percentage of national income
invested (16 per cent) and the second lowest rate of growth (3 per
cent); West Germany had one of the highest levels of investment (23.5
per cent) and one of the highest rates of growth (5 per cent). But
several countries had higher growth rates than West Germany, with
much lower levels of investment, and Portugal, with a level of
investment little higher than Britain's, had one of the highest rates of
growth of all. There is a relationship between investment and growth,
but it is not straightforward and is unreliable. To put it another way, in
some countries raising investment seems to raise the growth rate, but

in others it does not, or does so by very little. In the language of positivism, it is, then, the particular way investment combines with other 'factors' in each country which we need to know.

To take another example, from the late 1960s onwards it was fashionable to blame Britain's industrial weakness on the unions, and especially on strikes. Peaker also compared the level of strike activity in Britain with those of its principal trade competitors, and established that the number of strike days per 100,000 workers was not significantly higher in Britain. However, the hostility of unionised workers towards government policies of wage control at the end of the sixties was so obvious that Peaker felt it *had* to be relevant. Perhaps, he suggested, the absence of a class party, such as the socialist or communist parties of the continent, meant that in Britain the workers' 'strong proletarian spirit' could not be 'dissipated' through politics, and so was channelled through industrial confrontation, to the advantage of Britain's manufacturing competitors.[25] As so often, when positivist explanations fail, they are replaced by thinly disguised restatements of establishment demonology.

In general, the basic presupposition of positivist explanations – that causes are knowable only from statistical relationships – rules out causes that are unique to particular places and particular periods of time. As a result, the economic literature, in particular, which is largely founded on this methodological prejudice, has been singularly unrewarding in diagnosing British problems.

Hobsbawm's Interpretation

A large step forward was taken in 1968 by Eric Hobsbawm. Hobsbawm proposed a theory which was above all historical, and the essence of which was that Britain's problems were – precisely – unique. On the other hand, Hobsbawm rejected the view that a satisfactory theory must be based on a conception of the social whole. For him, 'economic explanations of economic phenomena are to be preferred, if they are available'.[26] This was to lead to severe difficulties. The phenomenon of decline was not more economic than social or political, and Hobsbawm's attempt at disciplinary apartheid proved self-defeating.

His main thesis was that the circumstances which enabled Britain to be the first country to industrialise, and so gave her a unique advantage, proved a serious disadvantage when later industrialising countries, led by Germany and the USA, began to compete in world markets for manufactures, especially in the science-based, mass-consumption goods phase of the industrial revolution. Britain's primacy in the two earlier phases – the mechanisation of textile production, and the capital goods boom of the mid nineteenth century – had been based, Hobsbawm argued, on imperial power, which opened up foreign markets for Britain by force of arms and secured abundant sources of raw materials and cheap foodstuffs abroad. It had also rested on the existence of an already proletarianised labour force, and a landowning class much more committed to trade and more involved in agricultural modernisation, as well as being much less socially exclusive, than its continental counterparts. These two features, in particular, fostered the rapid expansion of a stratum of manufacturing entrepreneurs, with few social pretensions, who could make common cause with large segments of the landed ruling class, who, themselves, also profited from, and increasingly participated in, the industrial revolution. The technology of the first phases of the industrial revolution was relatively simple: the capital barriers were relatively low, with the result that England's industrial supremacy rested, in fact, on a patchwork of small firms and plants, usually in family ownership, employing a largely unskilled and certainly ill-educated workforce.

When Britain began to face serious manufacturing competition these features of the economy which had facilitated its early start turned into liabilities. The large-scale, technologically advanced German and American chemical, steel and electrical goods plants, setting out to make new products for mass markets, had few British counterparts. British manufacturing was still heavily based on the old staples – cotton textiles, iron and steel, railway materials and steam engines. The switch to the new industrial products and new technology was difficult for firms without the necessary technical expertise or large capital resources. Smallness of scale also militated against adequate borrowing. Innovations were often unprofitable without complementary new inputs from other sectors, but these were also technically backward. Worst of all, the new competition coincided with the Great Depression of 1873 to 1896. The real value of British manufactured exports grew by only 1.6 per cent per annum during these years while imports of manufactures grew by 4.5 per cent per annum.[27]

British manufacturing was 'subjected to a terrible beating' – but no drastic overhaul was put in hand, for two main reasons. One was that British capital had been invested abroad in growing quantities from about 1815 onwards, but especially after 1850. Indeed, by 1870 more was being invested abroad than in Britain.[28] On the other hand, from 1870 onwards more was received in interest on profits from abroad than was invested abroad. This income increasingly cushioned the balance of payments against the pressures of foreign manufacturing competition. Second, 'empire' markets absorbed British manufactures which could no longer be sold in the industrialised countries, so that the effect of the Great Depression 'was, alas, not great enough to frighten British industry into really fundamental change'.[29]

After World War I, the oldest sectors of the economy progressively collapsed. The worldwide depression, culminating in the 'slump', was, in Britain, the story of the permanent contraction of these industries and the waste of the lives of the families who depended on them.

The grimy, roaring, bleak industrial areas of the nineteenth century – in Northern England, Scotland and Wales – had never been very beautiful or comfortable, but they had been active and prosperous. Now all that remained was the grime, the bleakness, and the terrible silence of the factories and mines which did not work, the shipyards which were closed.[30]

The crisis of the thirties forced both business and government to take action. Free trade was abandoned, and a process of cartelisation and mergers was encouraged to give fewer, much larger firms protected shares of the home markets. But little structural or technological modernisation was put in hand. Instead, 'Britain became a non-competing country at home as well as abroad'.[31] This became painfully obvious in the 1960s when the technological and organisational weakness of British industry was once again exposed to foreign competition.

Hobsbawm's thesis – which is much richer than can be indicated in this bare outline – is thus that the fundamental cause of Britain's decline was the structural legacy of its early start, coupled with the proposition that 'in a capitalist economy (at all events in its nineteenth-century version) businessmen will be dynamic only insofar as this is rational by the criterion of the individual firm, which is to maximize its gains, minimize its losses, or possibly merely to maintain what it regards as a satisfactory long-term rate of profit'.[32] A radical reconstruction of the manufacturing economy will only be undertaken if this is rational for all, or at least the major, individual firms. But the existence of 'empire' markets, and after 1931 the existence of a protected home market, gave enough of them an easier alternative. What would have been collectively rational for all the firms in a sector was often not rational unless all acted in concert, which no mechanism existed to ensure as long as a traditionally 'adequate' profit could still be made on the basis of the old investment, and financial capital could find more profitable investment abroad.

It is a powerful and important argument. But is it as plausible as it looks? The most obvious question it raises concerns the mysterious failure of any government to intervene and become 'the pacemaker of change and the force driving the economy forward'.[33] Hobsbawm's explanation for this is that 'Britain, the first of all "developed" economies, found it hard to think in the terms which came so naturally to backward nations trying to catch up advanced ones, to poor ones trying to become rich, to ruined ones trying to rebuild, or even to those with a continuous tradition of technological pioneering'.[34]

But this is to ignore some rather major difficulties. For one thing, the wartime government of 1940–45 intervened successfully to reconstruct British agriculture to make it the most efficient in Europe. Why did this not extend to manufacturing, especially after the crisis had fully re-emerged in the 1970s? It is true that 'British socialists thought of the public sector as an engine for achieving a redistribution of incomes and a measure of social justice, or more vaguely (and in contrast to profit-making capitalism) a "public service"' – rather than as an instrument for forcing necessary changes in the private sector.[35] But why did they think like this? Since the price of the failure of 'business' to modernise itself was largely paid by the working class, why did British socialists not come to think in other terms? And, more generally, why was the pressure on the economy not 'desperate enough' when unemployment was above 10 per cent for so many of the years between the World Wars?

Hobsbawm's answer seems to be that habits of *mind* learned in the early nineteenth century persisted for more than a hundred years after experience should have suggested scrapping them – a rather 'idealist' position for a Marxist historian. We surely need an explanation of the determinants of 'government' action – or inaction. This, in turn, obviously involves understanding how social classes form and organise themselves – what entities like 'business' actually are and how they are related to 'government', through parties, elections, pressure groups, money, etc.; how such apparently influential political ideas as the Labour Party's view of the 'public sector' are formed and maintained; and how much independent effect they have. Further, such an explanation points to the need to distinguish 'governments' from the *state*, a much broader phenomenon, interacting with *civil society* in a much more continuous and structured way than 'governments'.

Another set of puzzles arises from Hobsbawm's view – for which there is good evidence – that British businessmen were not always profit-maximisers. According to economic theory, both classical and Marxist, this should lead to bankruptcy. Why it did not, or not immediately, may be partly explained by such special factors as the availability of empire markets, but there is still a puzzle: why were many British businessmen content with less than the highest possible rates of return? It seems that many of them compared the cost of new investment with the cost of the capital they had already laid out, and chose to go on accepting the existing rate of return from past investment, rather than seek a higher rate of return by risking new capital outlays. This, of course, is contrary to capitalist rationality, which says that seeking the highest rate of return is the only long-term way to stay in business. If British capitalists often thought like this – which seems to be the case – it is important to explain it, and such an explanation can hardly be confined to the sphere of economics. It is a question of why British capitalists thought in this way, while American, German, or Japanese capitalists did not.

To take one further problem in Hobsbawm's account, there were important conflicts within the class of property. The City of London regularly opposed manufacturing industry, for example, over the exchange value of sterling, the level of interest rates and free trade versus protection, as Hobsbawm points out. What determined the outcomes of these conflicts? Why did the re-establishment of overseas investments receive the priority it did after 1945, rather than a programme of state-directed industrial investment at home, and with a Labour government in office? The answers to these questions are not self-evident, nor are they to be found in the economic logic of capitalism alone – or at least not a single logic, operating uniformly within every individual national economy.

Hobsbawm rightly rejects 'simple sociological explanations' of Britain's economic decline, but a purely economic explanation, however sophisticated, is also inadequate.[36] What is needed is to combine the primarily economic–historical analysis of Hobsbawm with primarily sociological, cultural and political analyses, such as those of Anderson and Nairn, so as to try to link the different aspects of the social whole. No brief outline can hope to deal adequately with the problem; but if we are to 'think British politics historically' the attempt needs to be made.

Notes

1 Cited by Asa Briggs in *The Age of Improvement*, Longmans, London 1959, p. 18.
2 Eric Hobsbawm, *The Age of Revolution*, Weidenfeld and Nicolson, London 1962, p. 29; see also p. 52: 'And both Britain and the world knew that the Industrial Revolution, launched in this island by and through the traders and entrepreneurs, whose only law was to buy in the cheapest market and sell without restriction in the dearest, was transforming the world. Nothing could stand in its way.'
3 See Eric Hobsbawm, *Industry and Empire*, Penguin, Harmondsworth 1969, Table 26.

4 For the general importance of the empire, especially the new empire, for the British economy at the turn of the century, see the first chapter of R.D. Wolff, *The Economies of Colonialism*, Yale University Press, New Haven 1974.

5 Calvocoressi, *The British Experience*, Penguin, Harmondsworth, 1979, p. 228. The reference to growth as a 'will o' the wisp' is from R. Rose, *Politics in England*, Little, Brown, Boston 1980, p. 4.

6 Bernard Nossiter, *Britain: A Future That Works*, Deutsch, London 1978, esp. pp. 191–201.

7 Malcolm Crawford in the *Sunday Times*, 20 July 1980.

8 OECD *Economic Surveys: United Kingdom*, February 1980, p. 19; *Economic Trends*, No. 214, HMSO, London December 1979, p. 77. The figure of £6 bn is approximate and includes the value of natural gas production as well as oil. The actual impact of oil and gas production on the balance of payments is impossible to gauge precisely because so much else would have been different if this production had not existed.

9 *Economic Trends* No. 296, HMSO, London June 1978, p. 75; *Economic Surveys: United Kingdom*, February 1980, p. 19. In 1976 a surplus was achieved in the non-oil trade balance (for the first time since 1971) so the trade deficit was wholly due to oil imports, the need for which was clearly going to be eliminated by 1981 at the latest. The flight from the pound was thus a largely speculative and political movement.

10 *Survey of Current Affairs* 9/4, May 1979, p. 130; OECD *Economic Surveys: United Kingdom*, February 1980, p. 19.

11 T. Nairn, 'The Future of Britain's Crisis', *New Left Review*, 113/114, 1979, p. 44.

12 J. Habermas, *Legitimation Crisis*, Heinemann, London 1976. A similar general model, richly illustrated from a variety of national experiences, but especially that of the USA, is A. Wolfe, *The Limits of Legitimacy: Political Contradictions of Contemporary Capitalism*, Free Press, New York 1977.

13 A Gramsci, *Selections from the Prison Notebooks*, (Q. Hoare and G. Nowell Smith, eds), Lawrence and Wishart, London 1871; see esp. pp. 210, 275–6 for summaries of Gramsci's concept of crisis.

14 Ibid., p. 276.

15 Ibid., p. 210.

16 On profit rates see A. Glyn and B. Sutcliffe, *British Capitalism, Workers and the Profits Squeeze*, Penguin, Harmondsworth 1972, pp. 58–69.

17 Hudson Institute, *The United Kingdom in 1980: The Hudson Report*, London 1974, pp. 115–16.

18 According to a contemporary estimate by Sir James Dewar, cited in A.L. Levine, *Industrial Retardation in Britain 1880-1914*, Weidenfeld and Nicolson, London 1967, p. 71.

19 Hobsbawm, *Industry and Empire*, p. 182.

20 G.R. Searle, *The Quest for National Efficiency*, University of California Press, Berkeley 1971, pp. 73–4.

21 R.J.S. Hoffman, *Great Britain and the German Trade Rivalry 1875–1914*, University of Pennsylvania Press, Philadelphia 1933, p. 94.

22 All these quotations from the turn-of-the-century literature are from Levine, pp. 58–9 and 73.

23 Searle, esp. pp. 80–3 and 86–92.

24 A. Peaker, *Economic Growth in Modern Britain*, Macmillan, London 1974, pp. 37–8.

25 Ibid., pp. 70–1.

26 E. Hobsbawm, *Industry and Empire*, p. 187.

27 W.A. Lewis, *Growth and Fluctuations 1870–1913*, Allen and Unwin, London 1978, p. 118.

28 Hobsbawm, *Industry and Empire*, p. 192.

29 Ibid., p. 191.

30 Ibid., p. 208.

31 Ibid., p. 218.
32 Ibid., p. 187.
33 Ibid., p. 264.
34 Ibid., p. 270.
35 Ibid., p. 270.
36 For a similar argument see M.J. Wiener, *English Culture and the Decline of the Industrial Spirit, 1850–1980*, Cambridge University Press, Cambridge 1981, Appendix, pp. 167–70.

3

The First Crisis

Even if some of the structural constraints which Britain's early start imposed on her manufacturing sector seem less absolute than Hobsbawm implies, one thing is clear: speaking generally, British capitalist manufacturers never did compete successfully against other *capitalist* manufacturers. What they did was to overwhelm *pre-capitalist* production everywhere; and it was the comparative ease of this victory, rather than the commitment of capital to particular sectors, such as textiles or railways, or to particular forms of business organisation characteristic of early capitalism, that led to later problems.

Until the last years of the nineteenth century, British capital still depended very heavily on labour-intensive production, working long hours at a much more intensive pace than pre-capitalist manufacture.[1] British manufacturing employees were also concentrated in larger production units, subject to a more complex division of labour, producing more standardised products than non-capitalist producers. Their products *were* also technically more advanced, and they were increasingly assisted by power-driven machinery. But as Raphael Samuel has shown, the degree of mechanisation was quite modest, even in the most mechanised sectors, such as textiles and engineering. Growth in machine-production had led to the creation of innumerable new tasks performed by hand, and some of the most important industries, including coal, construction and agriculture, were barely mechanised at all. For instance, the expansion of coal output from about 40 million tons in 1855 to about 275 million in 1911 was accomplished by expanding the labour force from 200,000 to 1,200,000 helped by 70,000 pit ponies – that is, with virtually no increase in productivity.[2] To a large extent, British supremacy was still based on 'the formal subsumption of labour under capital'; the replacement of independent artisan production by wage employment, but without a radical change in the labour process.

Other countries – notably Germany and the USA – could develop their own industries initially by protecting their internal markets against British goods. But to compete with Britain in world markets they had to leapfrog Britain's stage of industrial development by heavy expenditure on superior technology, new products, and new methods of marketing to generate demand for them ('capitalist production sui generis').[3]

It was when this began to happen – from the late 1860s onwards – that British manufacturers started to lose ground. In the last phase of the Great Depression (from 1891 to 1896) the problem began to assume major proportions, mainly in the form of a more or less rapid eclipse of British goods by German goods in prime markets. After 1892 Germany outstripped Britain as a supplier of manufactures to Eastern Europe and Greece, after 1894 to the Low Countries and Russia, and finally, after 1910, to Italy and France. Germany also built up a strong trade surplus with Britain itself and sold more finished manufactures than unfinished goods to Britain, while Britain's (smaller) exports to Germany contained more unfinished goods than manufactured products.[4] By 1910 the German shipping magnate and commercial leader, Albert Ballin, could comment:

> the British can really no longer compete with us, and if it were not for the large funds they have invested, and for the sums of money which reach the small mother-country from the dominions, their saturated and conservative habits of life would soon make them a 'quantité négligeable' as far as their competition with us in the world's markets is concerned.[5]

The years immediately before the Great War were experienced as years of crisis. Real wages fell, neither party had an answer to the industrial problem, and from 1910 onwards the authority of the state was increasingly rejected, by the Irish, by the Suffragettes, and by a growing minority of anarcho-syndicalists in the labour movement. The scale of industrial conflict rose to a pitch not equalled before or since – apart from the General Strike of 1926 – while in 1913 senior army officers questioned the government's authority to impose Home Rule on Ulster.

The outbreak of war superseded the crisis of authority. Only when the relief afforded by the two wars, income from foreign investments, empire markets and domestic protection had at length all been exhausted, did British industry finally confront its nemesis. The question remains, why was so little attempt made to reconstruct British industry when its competitive weakness first appeared? Why should the spate of official and unofficial enquiries and reports on industrial efficiency at the turn of the century have had so little effect?[6]

As Hobsbawm pointed out, other governments used the state as an engine of industrial growth. Why did British governments not do the same? And, while many industrial capitalists in Britain may have become so complacent, or so infected with pre-capitalist values, as to prefer modest and vulnerable profits to risk-taking for growth, it is hard to believe that all of them were like this; that, at a time when capital was abundant and cheap, the situation should not have been modified by the initiative of at least a few enterprising capitalists who would have seen the opportunity to borrow on a big scale, and to leapfrog both domestic and foreign competitors by moving into still more advanced and capital-intensive production.[7]

Industrial Class Struggle

These questions lead directly into the politics and sociology of the class struggle. Sir Arthur Lewis comes close to the heart of the matter when he points out that, given that in 1913 British wages were about half the level of US wages, it should have been greatly to the advantage of British manufacturers to adopt American technology – if they could have got as much output from it as US manufacturers did. Yet, in those industries where American technology had been adopted (for instance the English boot and shoe industry, which converted to US-made machinery in the 1890s), British output was far lower.[8]

> British entrepreneurs were under heavy pressure in the last quarter of the century since the economy had turned unprofitable. American methods were fairly widely known. If entrepreneurs had expected them to yield the same output in Britain as in the USA, they would most probably have adopted them.

In the last analysis, Lewis attributes the fact that they did not do so to the 'lower work pace of the British workers'. Given this, he says, 'it is easy to see that the main reason why the British employers did not adopt the American technology was that it was not as productive for them as it was for American employers'.[9] On the other hand, Lewis also notes that the American factory was much more rationally organised – 'a more "scientific" place than the British factory'. There is also the question of whether the rate of work of British workers was proportional to their 50 per cent lower wages. If British workers had agreed to work twice as hard, might they have expected the employers to pay them twice as much?

The key to the perennial problem of which is the chicken and which is the egg in the relationship between management and labour in Britain is the historical development of the political relationship between capital and labour at this moment of history. For a hundred years the profitability of British capital had depended primarily – though not, of course, exclusively – on the extraction of as much work as possible from the labour force, for as small a wage as possible. This had not prevented real wages from gradually rising, as productivity gradually improved after the mid-century and trade union organisation spread; but it had not generally been necessary to seek a solution to the problem of profitability by raising productivity through technological innovation. When trade was poor, employers sought wage cuts and resisted the reduction of working hours, rather than contemplate new investment. The natural consequence was growing defensive solidarity on the part of the workers.

When the industrial 'climacteric' of the 1890s arrived, after more than twenty years of depression, wage cuts, lock-outs and strikes, workers and employers were moving rapidly towards a new phase of conflict. The employers organised themselves to try to break the power of the rapidly expanding trade union movement by means of lock-outs and court actions. A series of court judgements, culminating in the Taff Vale decision of 1901, stripped away much if not all of the financial and legal security that the unions were supposed to have been granted in the legislation of 1871–6. The employers succeeded, in the short run, in crushing the socialist militants in the unions and in curbing the duration and effectiveness of strikes ('the employers organised their forces, fought and won');[10] but they also finally precipitated the labour movement into forming its own political party, the Labour Party, and created new opportunities for the spread of socialist ideas.

If the labour movement had been crushed, matters would have been different. But after 1867 both Conservatives and Liberals depended on working-class votes, and no such conclusive defeat was ever possible or indeed contemplated. To a much greater extent than in Germany or the USA (where, said Arthur Shadwell in 1909, 'employers hate and dread the unions'), unions had an accepted place in British industry in spite of the struggles of the 80s and 90s. By 1911, 18 per cent of the employed population were members of trade unions and manufacturers were having to deal with ever better organised employees. To secure from these workers, after thirty years of increasingly fierce conflict,

American levels of output premissed on British wages, was politically out of the question. Whatever the rationality of this or that particular industrialist might incline him to do, the British working class was already too strong, and too antagonised, for the American (or German) option to be generally profitable. A complete transformation of political, social and ideological relations would have been necessary to break up the, by now, hardened pattern of capital–labour relations. But this was not 'practical politics' in the circumstances of the time.

The Contradictions of Party Politics

The main reason why this was not practical lay in the constraints imposed on the two major parties: both represented elements of capital but both were now competing for the votes of the workers – a situation which resulted from the peculiar historical evolution of the British capitalist class. As Anderson and Nairn pointed out, the British capitalist class was formed by a fusion of the rising mercantile and industrial interest with the old landed interest. How this fusion should be interpreted theoretically is a matter of dispute. Anderson sees it as beginning with a struggle – the English revolution – *within* the old landed aristocracy, between elements which were committed to capitalist accumulation (mainly in farming, but also in trade) and those which were not, and culminating in a decisive victory for the former: 'the landed aristocracy had, after a bitter internecine struggle, become its own capitalist class'.[11] This class of largely agrarian capitalists succeeded in keeping purely mercantile (and later, purely industrial) capital in a politically and socially subordinate position, which in Anderson's view accounts for the failure of British industry or governments to respond energetically to the industrial crisis from the 1890s onwards.

E.P. Thompson, on the other hand, considers that the fusion which occurred started earlier, and that while aristocratic *manners* prevailed, no distinctive aristocratic *interest* did, and so this cannot explain the failure of British capital to rationalise itself in the twentieth century.[12] Yet there is agreement that the English landed class not only increasingly became capitalist farmers, but also grew increasingly involved in mining ventures, railway-building, merchant banking, urban real estate investment and eventually, via the joint stock company, in the whole range of capitalist enterprise, including manufacturing; and that, for their part, 'new' men of wealth bought landed estates and sent their sons to be educated with the sons of the gentry at the new 'public' schools.

This fusion produced distinctive social, ideological and political results. The one that matters here is political. In the early nineteenth century neither the Whig nor the Tory parties, though dominated by landowners, excluded representatives of new wealth. Sir Robert Peel, the Tory leader, was the son of a self-made manufacturer, and Gladstone, a Peelite who became leader of the Liberals, was the son of a slave-owner. In addition, fear of revolution after 1879, and fear of English working-class strength after 1815, tended to drive new and old wealth together politically. The result was that both political parties came to represent broadly the same class, the class of property.

So long as only the propertied class had votes, this was not inconvenient. It allowed conflicting elements and tendencies within the class of property – commercial, financial, agricultural, manufacturing, professional, high church, dissent, pro-temperance and pro-publican, pro-imperial and 'little England' – to find organisational expression. But when the vote had to be extended in 1867 and 1884 (producing an electorate 60 per cent of whom were workers) this arrangement became highly problematic. To win elections the parties had to compete for working-class votes. They could only continue to serve the interests of property if they could find a way to combine them with the interests of the workers.

This imposed tremendous strains on the party leaders, torn between the class demands of their main supporters and the need to win votes. The difficulty was more acute for the Liberals, who saw themselves as the natural party of the workers, but their difficulty was made immeasurably worse by the Irish problem.

In Ireland colonial oppression and underdevelopment had produced an irreversible popular commitment to nationalism, while in Britain the increasingly powerful working class could no longer be denied the vote. Because of the Act of Union it was difficult, if not impossible, to withhold the extension of the franchise from Ireland and this permitted the Irish nationalists to capture 82 seats at Westminster in the elections of 1885, and thus to hold the balance of power between Liberals and Conservatives. From then on they could either be repressed, at increasing risk to liberal values throughout the United Kingdom, and probably at increasing economic cost; or 'home rule' for Ireland, as demanded by the nationalists, was ultimately inescapable. Gladstone recognised this and chose to preserve liberal values by accepting home rule. The anti-home rule or 'unionist' section of the Liberal Party, including Joseph Chamberlain and a number of his radical supporters, left the party and allied themselves with the Conservatives. A significant body of electors followed them. The Liberals paid the price of being excluded from power (thanks to

Conservative control of the House of Lords, rather than to electoral unpopularity alone, it must be said) for the best part of twenty years (the Conservatives were in office from 1886 to 1892 and 1895 to 1905).

During that time the Liberals could accomplish nothing for the British working class, while the Conservatives were under correspondingly less compulsion to accomplish anything for them, and showed increasingly little interest in doing so. Eventually – and reluctantly – a majority of the trade union leadership became convinced that they must seek independent representation for labour in parliament, and the Labour Representation Committee was established in 1900.

The more creative politicians of both parties at this time sought to reattach the workers to capital in ways that might conceivably have facilitated economic modernisation. Joseph Chamberlain, from the Conservative and Unionist side, advocated social reforms financed out of tariff revenue, and Lloyd George, for the Liberals, promoted social reforms financed out of taxes on wealth. Chamberlain's campaign for protection was the more relevant to the needs of British manufacturing. His scheme of 'tariff reform' would have ended half a century of free trade and reserved the British home market – still second only to that of the USA – for British manufactures; though in view of the failure of British companies to undertake radical investment programmes when protection was finally reintroduced in the 1930s it seems rather unlikely that Chamberlain's project contained the seeds of a radical restructuring of British industrial capital. In any case the electorate consistently rejected protection until 1931. No wonder that the 'National Efficiency' school dreamed of an all-party government which would entrust economic policy to 'experts'.

Class, State and Culture

The distinctive way in which capitalism was established in Britain also gave rise to other factors. Two in particular are often cited: the special role of the City of London, and the specific nature of the British state.

Britain's dominance in world trade and its role as a source of international loan capital had made the City of London the pre-eminent banking, exchange, shipping and insurance centre of the world before the First World War. Since the early nineteenth century it had also had a special relationship with and influence in the Treasury. The City was also where large fortunes were most likely to be made, and where old landed families were more prone to establish an interest.[13] As a result, the City of London, and the wider financial and commercial interests with which it was linked, were much better connected to the Conservative Party – which after 1886 drew into its ranks nearly all the landed interest, and after 1914 virtually all other capital as well. Thanks to the decline of the Liberals after 1918, this influence undoubtedly played an important part in the preference subsequently given to free trade and a strong pound over the needs of British manufacturing.*

As for the state, it was *structured* in a fashion that reflected the originality of the bourgeois revolution in Britain.[14] Unlike countries where state power had to be used to achieve the 'forced' industrial growth necessary to catch up with Britain, in Britain many features of the pre-capitalist state were carried over into the nineteenth century and beyond. The common element, Nairn suggests, was the 'represent-ative patrician' nature of the state apparatus: it was to an exceptional degree *composed of* the landed class and the gentry, serving as magistrates, and supplying both the members of parliament and the leading policy-makers in the principal departments of state. This remained the case after the introduction of entrance examinations for all grades of the whole civil service from 1870 onwards, which was a house-cleaning operation *within* the traditional upper class based in London, intended to exclude the middle class from the higher civil service by confining access to Oxford and Cambridge graduates, but selecting these on the basis of merit. John Vincent remarks:

> The canons of Peelite administration might as well have been applied to another planet for all the provinces knew of them. If people in Sheffield were affected at all by competitive examinations for the Civil Service or abolition of purchase in the army, it was through their sense of justice, not of interest.[15]

As the state apparatus expanded, recruitment to it was developed on class lines; policy-making remained the preserve of Oxford and Cambridge graduates who had received a classical education in public schools – schools originally created, it should be remembered, to *remove* 'the sons of shopkeepers from the taint of trade', not to interest them in trade. The state apparatus was thus not merely organisationally ill-adapted to become an agent of industrial recon-

---

* Why the City's influence should have continued to dominate even post-war Labour governments' policies is a more complex question (see Chapters 4, 5, 9 and 11). In 1977, for example, the Labour Prime Minister, James Callaghan, in a secret meeting with two other cabinet ministers, the Permanent Secretary of the Treasury and the Governor of the Bank of England, decided to let sterling appreciate in spite of the adverse consequences this would have for manufactured exports (B. Sedgemore, *The Secret Constitution*, Hodder and Stoughton, London 1980, pp. 14–15).

struction, but had a trained incapacity for that task.* The national preoccupation with industrial decline was articulated by independent researchers and publicists like Shadwell, Hobson and Williams, and taken up by editors and some MPs; it does not seem to have greatly exercised Whitehall.†

These cultural tendencies also affected the manufacturing class directly, as both contemporary and later critics remarked. Manufacturers were not only themselves largely ignorant of science, they were indifferent to the importance of investing in it. They employed relatively few scientists or engineers, and rarely gave those they did employ much influence in company policy; nor did they demand a major expansion of scientific and technical education. The effects were plain to every British visitor to German factories, where not only was the entire enterprise organised so as to take the most rational advantage of recent knowledge, but the technical training of the workers was strongly stressed:

> A deputation of employers and workmen went to the Continent in 1895 to visit German and Belgian iron and steel industries. They sought an explanation for the successful progress of these competitive plants, and what they learned must have been to many little short of startling. In Germany it was shown how much greater was the care taken to give the rank and file of men sound technical education, while young men of special promise were even sent to technical colleges for several years study at the expense of their employers. The consequence was that the German manufacturers had the advantage of employing a body of men who thoroughly understood the technique of their work.[16]

In the same spirit, the Germans invested heavily in their sales forces, understanding the need to create new markets for new products, in contrast to 'the glaring scarcity of British commercial travellers, and the ineffective endeavours to supply their place by lavish distribution of prices and catalogues – generally printed only in English.'[17]

The class of manufacturing owner-managers, though never composed of more than a 'minute fraction' of wholly self-made men, had once energetically propagated the *myth* of the self-made man and condemned the aristocratic ideal as idle and parasitic.[18] By 1900, after three

---

* As late as 1890 the Board of Trade was not considered a senior cabinet office, and political offices such as the Secretaryships of the Board of Education and Local Government, which were crucial to any industrial reconstruction, were even less well paid or prestigious.

† A significant contrast is provided by Whitehall's keen interest in the health of the working class considered as potential army recruits, which led to an otherwise uncharacteristic early policy of providing meals for working-class schoolchildren before the Great War.

generations of success, middle-class education and social acceptance, they had compromised significantly with aristocratic culture and had acquired a prevailing conservatism and complacency about their long-established business methods.[19] This even included a tendency, especially startling to Americans, to enforce a socially determined upper limit on workers' pay lest workers might cease to 'know their place', even if paying more *might* have secured a more than compensating increase in output.[20]

The Crisis in Ideology

The way in which economic interest, political alignments and cultural orientations interacted so as to preclude any effective response to the onset of economic decline was complex. For instance, although the interest of the City lay in free trade against protection, 'it remained firmly Conservative; in contrast Lancashire and the West Riding reverted to their traditional liberalism in the wake of [the Conservative Party's commitment to] Tariff Reform – which was designed to benefit British manufacturing'.[21] The City, which had attached itself to the Conservative Party in its imperialist phase during the 1880s, maintained this attachment after 1903 in spite of Chamberlain's conversion of the party rank and file to protection, relying on its great influence with the party leadership and the Treasury to resist this move. Similarly, even though increasing competitive pressure from abroad and the growing strength of organised labour were pushing the cotton manufacturers towards the Conservative Party, they chose to remain loyal to the Liberals and to the cause of free trade, on which the textile industry's fortunes had been built for sixty years.

This is a good example of the need to distinguish between the different chronological rhythms peculiar to different aspects of political life. The attachment of the cotton manufacturers to the Liberal cause proved extraordinarily enduring, thanks to their identification with free trade (the banner under which they had finally imposed their interest against that of the landed classes in the 1840s) and with the party which had expressed so many of their distinctive values – the right to religious dissent, temperance, economy and utility – for half a century. Conversely, the attachment of the City of London to the Conservatives, though quite recent and owing little to specific Conservative doctrines or policies, also proved remarkably strong. Chamberlain's Tariff Reform programme might have been expected to push the textile interest towards the Conservatives, and the City back to the Liberals, but their actual behaviour corresponded to a different logic, operating at the level of ideas and attitudes.

In fact, the first crisis was also a general crisis of ideology: tariff reform, socialism, women's emancipation and Irish nationalism simultaneously assaulted the orthodoxies of free trade, private property, male supremacy and English chauvinism. The list of dissonant themes could easily be extended: it signifies a crisis of 'hegemony' – a crisis of confidence in ideas which had hitherto provided all classes with their general understanding of the 'way things (naturally) were'.

These hitherto prevailing ideas were liberal ideas. The basis of their dominance had been laid down by about 1850, after free trade had triumphed over protection and ushered in half a century of reform aimed at completing the transformation of the corrupt and parasitical old state apparatus into one serviceable for a market-oriented industrialising society. But, simultaneously, the state began to soften the impact of industrialism on the working class. During the previous twenty-five years, the political consciousness of the workers had progressed rather rapidly through three phases – beginning with backward-looking efforts to reverse the catastrophic impact on their lives of 'political economy' (as the new doctrine of the market was known), followed by a phase of enthusiasm for the Owenite vision of replacing capitalism by a giant workers' cooperative, and ending with the campaign for the People's Charter – a mass political movement with an increasingly class-conscious left wing. This last development was accelerated by a decade of depressed trade and by bad harvests.

Eventually the state authorities' confidence that they could maintain control declined to a critical level. The adoption of free trade eased the confrontation by reducing food prices. The lifting of the previous ban on machinery exports in 1842, and measures to make it easier to export capital, permitted the profit rate to be increased without intensifying the exploitation of industrial workers. In this situation a start could be made in regulating factory safety (in 1844) and limiting working hours (in 1847); then the franchise was extended to (male) workers (in 1867 and 1884) and legal protection was given to trade unions (in 1871 and 1875–6). Finally, elementary education was extended to workers' children (in 1870 and 1876) and some of the worst abuses in the sale of food and drugs and in workers' housing and sanitation began to be brought under control (from 1875 onwards).

The main vehicle of this liberalisation was the Liberal Party; but the Conservatives under Disraeli were also forced to conform to it, under pain of being permanently excluded from power, so that it was the Conservatives who carried out both the franchise extension of 1867 and the social reforms of 1875. The *political* logic of liberalism could thus be summed up as regulating capitalism, to secure the class cooperation needed to make the extension of democracy safe for private property. This strategy was a complete success. In 1848 in London 150,000 special constables had been enrolled, troops and artillery dispersed at strategic points, and civil servants armed, to confront the workers massing at Kennington for what proved to be the last Chartist rally. In 1868 the same workers – or their sons – voted for the first time, and most of them voted Liberal.[22]

The acceptance of liberalism, the creed of the new middle class, by both the working class and the landed class during these years – its emergence as a 'hegemonic' ideology – rested on the degree of convergence which government policy succeeded in establishing between life as people experienced it, and life as liberal doctrine painted it. Good harvests in the 1850s, and slowly rising productivity in most sectors of the economy, reinforced the prospect of accommodation with industrial capitalism which the regulation of hours and safety held out to the workers.

In place of the Chartist agitation with its 'physical force' wing and revolutionary undercurrents, led largely by self-employed tradesmen and artisans outside the authority structure of the factory, there emerged the 'new model' craft unions of the 'labour aristocracy', the foremen and pacemakers in the factories.[23] These new unions were dedicated to 'responsible' bargaining, looked on strike action as evidence of failure, and acted much more as self-financing insurance societies to protect their members against sickness and unemployment than as fighting organisations. This corresponded perfectly to the new liberal conception of industrial class society, and for two crucial generations after 1850 the leaders of the 'new model' unions also served as new models of working-class life – thrifty, sober, religious, cautious and respectable. It was these men whose leadership led Gladstone to pronounce the workers 'fit to come within the pale of the constitution' and who mostly rewarded his confidence by supporting the Liberal Party.

Working-class militancy was not completely extinguished after 1848; the extension of the franchise after 1867 was also due to revived mass agitation, and militancy was to appear again in renewed industrial struggles throughout the Great Depression. But for thirty years after 1848 it was subordinated to class collaboration. During this formative period the basis of 'labourism' (the defence and advancement of the interests of labour within capitalism, as opposed to socialism, which looks to the replacement of capitalism) was laid. By the end of this period labourism had acquired a specific electoral form, the 'Lib–Lab' alliance, whereby the leading trade unionists endorsed the Liberals in return for the adoption as Liberal candidates of a number of representatives of 'labour', and the inclusion of some 'Lib–Lab' MPs in Liberal governments.*

The 'hegemony' of liberalism would have been impossible without the reforms introduced from the 1840s to the 1870s. Through them working men (if not women) were assured such benefits as the cheapest possible food (through free trade), a measure of protection from the crudest forms of exploitation at work and degradation at home, freedom to defend their interests against employers, a degree of protection in the courts, and an equal voice in elections. In these important respects, life appeared to be as liberal doctrine described it and to offer the prospect of modest but progressive improvement for the conscientious and hardworking breadwinner. This in turn sustained the 'popular religion' of self-improvement within the framework of working class culture – the friendly society, the 'co-op' shop, the colliery choir, the workingmen's club, the chapel and the pub.

But while reforms made the ideological hegemony of liberalism possible, it did not come about spontaneously. As John Foster showed in his remarkable study of Oldham, the reforms were accompanied by energetic efforts on the part of local employers and property owners, the national parties, the press, Sunday school organisers, Orange Lodge leaders and the like, to re-establish their cultural authority over the working class. It is this which explains the *speed* with which the working class not merely abandoned the militant radicalism of the Chartist movement, but positively embraced the liberal creed. In 1855 an ex-radical in Oldham replied to a speech by Bronterre O'Brien, the former Chartist leader, in the following remarkable terms:

> Mr O'Brien had told them that their conditions were as bad or worse than Russian serfs, but he would ask him to point to a page in history where Russian serfs could meet and discuss public questions as they were doing that night (hear, hear and cheers) – where Russian serfs could eat white bread and good and wholesome food. Mr O'Brien might talk about the slavery and depression of the people in this country, but when the time had come for their freedom they would get it. Look at the enlightenment they could obtain by a liberal press, and by the right of public meeting obtained by their brave and noble fathers (cheers).[24]

---

* The first Lib–Lab MPs were elected in 1874. The first Lib–Lab MP to join a Liberal government was Henry Broadhurst in 1885; the first Lib–Lab cabinet member was John Burns in 1905.

But by 1900 the hold of these ideas over the workers had been severely weakened. The Great Depression had undermined their foundations in many ways. Class collaboration in industry was called in question when, over a twenty-year period, employers responded to falling profit-rates by cutting wages and employees responded with rising levels of industrial action. It was even more fatally damaged when the courts, responding to the employers' offensive, began to strip away the trade union rights which had appeared to be enshrined in the legislation of 1870 and 1875–6. From 1889 onwards the ascendancy of the craft unions and their 'Lib–Lab' leaders began to be challenged by the new mass-membership unions of unskilled workers, unions which were much more responsive to the socialist propaganda of the Social Democratic Federation (formed in 1883), the Socialist League (1884), the Fabian Society (also 1884), Robert Blatchford's newspaper *Clarion* (founded in 1891) and the Independent Labour party (founded in 1893).

Events were soon to show that the ideal of class collaboration was too strongly embedded in the consciousness of most labour leaders to be easily or quickly displaced by socialism. But they rejected the Liberals' idea of the basis for such collaboration. They wanted a state which would redress the inequality of power in industrial relations and provide workers with social security and social services, and they no longer trusted the Liberal Party to achieve this – an attitude which the Liberals' record in office after 1906 did little to change. The social legislation which they introduced – including schemes for old age pensions, national health insurance and unemployment insurance – was too limited in scope and conceded too slowly to cause the labour leaders many second thoughts about the necessity of an independent party of labour.

As for Ireland, the basis for the ascendancy of liberalism never existed there. The franchise simply gave the Catholic majority means to express their rejection of a system of alien rule that had been illiberal in essence from the first. Similarly with feminism; middle-class women agitating against sex-discrimination in the law (especially concerning prostitution and marriage) and in education, and working-class women organising for the first time against 'sweated' labour, found that there was still a paling round the constitution and that they were outside it. Liberalism was thus called in question by workers (especially the unskilled majority), the Catholic Irish and an articulate and determined minority of women. By 1910 'liberal England' was already dying.[25]

There was a conservative response to the crisis of liberal hegemony – the ideology of imperialism. Although primarily identified with the

Conservative Party, imperialism captured an important wing of the Liberals, and some leading socialists too. It appealed to the insular, xenophobic and chauvinist (including anti-Irish) elements in British popular culture. It asserted the existence of a national interest above the interests of class, and a national destiny to govern inferior races. The 'aristocratic, amateur and normatively agrarian' social ideals of the imperialists received an enormous reinforcement from the popular success of imperialism as a political strategy down to 1900, especially in the public schools, which prospered and multiplied as never before. As Anderson pointed out, imperialism gave a new lease of life to the most archaic elements in the culture of the British capitalist class, just when their disappearance seemed overdue:

> with the agrarian depression of 1870s, the traditional base of the land-owning class lapsed. Thus, just at the moment when the atavistic values of the landed aristocracy appeared mortally threatened, imperialism rescued and reinforced them.[26]

The ideology of imperialism temporarily eclipsed that of liberalism, rather than displaced it, but it seriously aggravated the problems of the economy. It reinforced the external and trading orientation of the state, and tended to perpetuate industrial weakness by securing temporary export refuges in empire markets. (It no doubt also reinforced the passion of the middle class for creating as much social distance as possible between themselves and the workers, which expressed itself in ideas such as that already referred to of a 'proper' ceiling on workers' wages, the final eradication of which may yet be one of the significant accomplishments of Thatcherism.) Liberalism rested on economic prosperity. Imperialism helped to undermine that prosperity. After the Great War liberal ideas progressively ceased to be the ruling ideas of Britain.

The crisis was interrupted, and to some extent resolved, by the war, which suspended internal conflicts, allowing national unity to be reasserted as the supreme value and at the same time clearing the way for compromises that had been unattainable in peacetime – votes for women, independence for a partitioned Ireland, a grudging recognition that the power of organised labour necessitated granting at least some consultative status on economic issues to the leadership of the Trades Union Congress. The defeat of Germany and the imposition of war reparations, the retention of empire markets and continued receipts of overseas income gave British industry a respite and permitted the growth of new, science-based consumer industries like those already developed in Germany and the USA. But the causes of the crisis remained, in the structure and social relations of British industry, the nature of the class forces developed in the previous century, and the character of the British state. The advent of a new crisis was only a matter of time.

Notes

1 Raphael Samuel, 'Workshop of the World', *History Workshop*, 2, Spring 1977, p. 8 and passim.
2 Samuel, ibid., p. 21; Neil K. Buxton, *The Economic Development of the British Coal Industry*, Batsford, London 1978 p. 55; H.S. Jevons, *The British Coal Trade*, Kelley, New York 1915, p. 116.
3 Marx, *Capital* Vol. 1, Penguin, Harmondsworth 1976, p. 1,035. Marx's distinction between the 'formal' and 'real subsumption of labour under capital' is crucial to understanding the British experience; see pp. 1,019–38.
4 R.J.S. Hoffman, *Great Britain and the German Trade Rivalry, 1875–1914*, University of Pennsylvania Press, Philadelphia 1933, pp. 114 ff.
5 Cited in ibid., p. 97.
6 The average annual rate of growth of the stock of capital per worker for the whole economy of the UK 1870–1970 was 1%; the corresponding figures for other countries were: France (1913–70) 2.6%; W. Germany 1.9%; Italy (1882–1970) 2.5%; Japan 2.7%; USA 1.8%; see A. Maddison, 'The Long-Run Dynamics of Productivity Growth', *Banco Nazionale del Lavoro Review*, June 1977, cited in A. Glyn and J. Harrison, *The British Economic Disaster*, Pluto Press, London 1980, p. 37.
7 On the availability of capital see W.A. Lewis *Growth and Fluctuations 1870–1913*, Allen and Unwin, London 1978, pp. 115–16. ('There is no evidence that entrepreneurs experienced a shortage of capital in the home market'.) H.W. Richardson, however, in 'Over-Commitment in Britain before 1930' (in D.H. Aldcroft and H.W. Richardson, eds, *The British Economy 1870–1939*, Macmillan, London 1969) thinks there may have been some shortage, though not a severe one. On the psychology of industrial investment at this time see A.L. Levine, *Industrial Retardation in Britain 1880–1914*, Allen and Unwin, London 1967, pp. 122–5.
8 Lewis, pp. 123–6. 'In the mid-1930s, in boots and shoes, where British and American factories were using almost exactly the same machinery, American output per hour exceeded the British by about 80 per cent' (p. 126).
9 Lewis, p. 127.
10 Arthur Shadwell, *Industrial Efficiency*, Longmans, London 1909, p. 556.
11 P. Anderson, 'Origins of the Present Crisis', *New Left Review*, 23, 1964, pp. 17, 26–53.
12 E.P. Thompson, 'The Peculiarities of the English', *Socialist Register 1965*, pp. 311–62, esp. 314–30.
13 D.W. Rubinstein, 'Wealth, Elites and the Class Structure of Modern Britain', *Past and Present* 76, August 1977, passim. Over a third of all millionaires who died in Britain between 1900 and 1914 made their fortunes in the City of London (p. 105).
14 T. Nairn, 'The Twilight of the British State', in *The Break-Up of Britain*, London 1977, esp. pp. 14–32.
15 J. Vincent, *The Formation of the British Liberal Party*, Penguin, Harmondsworth 1972, p. 113.
16 Hoffman, pp. 240–41.
17 Ibid., p. 85.
18 H. Perkin, *The Origins of Modern English Society 1780–1880*, Routledge, London 1969, pp. 225 ff.
19 On 'the gentrification of the industrialist', see M.J. Wiener's survey, *English Culture*

and the Decline of the Industrial Spirit 1850–1980, Cambridge University Press, Cambridge, 1981, especially Chapters 2, 5, and 7.

20 Levine, pp. 77–8.
21 Rubinstein, pp. 123–4.
22 On this transformation see P. Corrigan and D. Sayer, *The Great Arch: English State Formation as Cultural Revolution*, Blackwell, Oxford 1985, Chapter 6.
23 J. Foster, *Class Struggle and the Industrial Revolution*, Methuen, London 1974, Chapters 6–7.
24 Quoted by Foster, p. 242. Dangerfield's analysis has been taken up in a stimulating collection of papers, *Crises in the British State*, edited by M. Langan and B. Schwartz, (Hutchinson and Centre for Contemporary Cultural Studies, London 1985), which considerably extends our knowledge of 'the first crisis'.
25 Cf. G. Dangerfield, *The Strange Death of Liberal England*, London 1936.
26 Anderson, p. 23.

4

Labour and the
New Political Order

The second crisis was separated from the first by four decades. Two world wars and a decade of slump had effected far-reaching changes in the economy, the parties, the state and social life. New 'science-based' industries had been established and they provided some compensation for the continued decline of the old staples of textiles, coalmining and shipbuilding. The new consumer-goods industries were concentrated in the Midlands and the South-East. London became, for the first time in its history, a major industrial centre.*

Private and public suburban development, based on new urban road-transport systems, drastically altered the geography of work and leisure. The Victorian slums of London, Glasgow, Nottingham and elsewhere had at last been largely cleared. Radio increasingly displaced newspapers, and was in turn increasingly displaced by television, as the popular source of news. Labour shortages in the two wars, and the rapid growth of semi-skilled non-manual work, had drawn women back into the productive labour force on a large scale. Secondary education of some sort had belatedly become universal and university education virtually free. There was full employment and a comprehensive system of social security. People could be forgiven for supposing that the economic problems that had caused such anxiety at the turn of the century had vanished along with horse-drawn traffic and

* And perhaps for the last time. Through the 1970s London's manufacturing industry declined far more rapidly than in the country as a whole. Between 1971 and 1982, jobs in London's manufacturing industry fell from 1.2 million to 660,000, a fall of 44 per cent, compared to a national decline of 25 per cent. This decline was especially concentrated in parts of inner London, though after 1979 it spread throughout the capital (paper given by Michael Ward, Chairman of the GLC Industry and Employment Committee to a seminar on public/private cooperation of the Chartered Institute of Public Finance and Accountancy, 21 June 1982).

Liberal governments. The ascension of Queen Elizabeth II to the throne in 1952 was greeted as the dawn of a new Elizabethan Age. In reality, it was the prelude to the final crisis of the age of Victoria.

Yet, for those who looked there were plenty of signs already between the wars that the new industries suffered from similar weaknesses to those of the older ones: the problem seemed to be social or political, not simply one of obsolete economic sectors alone. Britain's share of the expanding world market for new products such as electrical goods, cars, radios and scientific equipment fell, while the shares of the USA, the Netherlands, Germany, Canada, Sweden and Switzerland rose. A contemporary observer wrote:

> Today what is really important and significant in England is not the depression of the depressed industries, but the relatively small progress made by the relatively prosperous. It is the growing, not the decaying, which require watching.[1]

Moreover, Britain did not suffer from any special handicaps which could explain this relative failure as being due to adverse external forces:

> Disorder and prosperity, depreciating and appreciating exchanges, tariffs and dumping, subsidies and prohibitions may all in fact have proved damaging; but there must surely have been some special reason connected with the *internal* economy which rendered them more disastrous to the United Kingdom than to other countries.[2]

The protective tariff established in Britain after 1931, and state encouragement for mergers during the 1930s, did not help matters. The new cartels took advantage of protection to raise prices but not to modernise. 'Britain became a non-competing country at home as well as abroad.'[3] The Second World War postponed the consequences by removing the Axis economies from the world market for nearly fifteen years. On the other hand, it also wiped out Britain's overseas investments. After the war, exports had to cover more than 80 per cent of imports, rather than the mere 55 per cent of pre-war days when interest and dividends from overseas investments were still abundant. Moreover, the post-war General Agreement on Tariffs and Trade progressively reduced the permitted level of protection of Britain's home and colonial markets, while British exporters' informal advantages in the latter were eroded by the process of decolonisation. By 1960, Britain's prosperity was no longer underpinned by advantages accumulated from the nineteenth century. Once foreign competition revived, British industry would suffer a relentless economic contraction unless and until its productivity could be raised to match that of its chief competitors.

The years after 1914 had been used not to modernise the economy, so much as to construct a new political order, with a new dominant ideology, which preserved the old social and economic order in all essentials. As a result, when the special conditions affecting international competition in manufactures ended, at the beginning of the 1960s, the economy was no more able than before to meet the competition from more efficient economies, and the country moved steadily towards a new crisis.

The key element in the new political order was the incorporation of the labour movement – both the trade unions and the Labour Party – into the state. From the time of the First World War, trade union leaders began to be accorded (however grudgingly, and as far as possible only symbolically) recognition as a legitimate and substantial political force. The terms of this recognition were that they should confine themselves to purely industrial questions and pursue industrial aims 'responsibly': that is, that they should accept the legitimacy (and by implication the permanence) of the private ownership of industry. Similarly, the Labour Party, emerging in 1923 as the second largest party in parliament, was entrusted with the government of Britain's privately owned economy – on condition that in office it showed no inclination to get rid of it.

Economic and political conditions in the inter-war years allowed this modification to the political order to be undertaken with a minimum of risk. The unions, though much stronger as a result of the war, were constrained by chronic unemployment, and the Labour Party, though twice winning enough seats to form a government (in 1923–4 and 1929–31), never had an overall parliamentary majority, and could therefore be dismissed from office by the combined votes of Conservative and Liberal MPs if it showed signs of adopting policies dangerous to private property.

After an initial period (1918–22), during which the wartime coalition of Conservatives and Liberals was prolonged into peacetime, the Liberal Party, having split into two factions around the rival leaders Lloyd-George and Asquith, declined to a parliamentary rump. Those elements of capital which had so far remained loyal to the Liberals now transferred their allegiance to the Conservatives as the only party still capable of resisting socialism. The Conservative leadership, however, understood that the only safe way to do this was to oblige the labour movement to renounce socialism in the sense of anything but the pursuit of moderate reforms within capitalism.

Fortunately for them, the Labour Party's leader Ramsay MacDonald had long advocated this, although he also talked in vague rhetoric of a socialist future. Like the Fabians, who saw the problem as one of 'educating the ruling class to socialism', MacDonald's idea of socialism involved above all a convergence of opinion between workers and the middle class on the necessity of a regulated, humanised and 'mixed' economy, with 'municipal socialism' (enterprises run by local government, plus local social services) at the base, and central government planning and some state-owned industry at the top, leading to a progressive decline of class differences. Socialism, he argued, would appeal to the rich as well as the poor,

> because it brings order where there is now chaos, organisation where there is now confusion, law where there is now anarchy, justice where there is now injustice. Socialism marks the growth of society, not the uprising of a class. The consciousness which it seeks to quicken is not one of economic class solidarity, but one of social unity and growth towards organic wholeness.[4]

And although a left wing of the party strongly disagreed, believing that socialism meant confronting a fundamental conflict of interest between capital and the working class, most trade union leaders and most of their members tended to agree with MacDonald, if more prosaically. In practice, they believed in pressing for further reforms within capitalism, and maintaining the Labour Party in parliament as an instrument for this purpose. They therefore backed MacDonald in his efforts to allay the fears of those middle-class voters who had hitherto voted Liberal and whose support he considered essential on both philosophical and practical grounds. From the first he determined on an ostentatiously 'moderate' and 'constitutional' line by opposing the party's militant wing (whom he called 'our wild men'), publicly abjuring the use of industrial action for political ends, and when first in office in 1924, demonstrating that the party was 'responsible' by proposing no socialist measures or administrative innovations.

This policy came to a head in 1926, when the party was again in opposition. The TUC called a General Strike in support of the coalminers' resistance to wage cuts of up to 40 per cent. The Labour Party leadership supported the strike ambiguously and reluctantly, the TUC retreated, the general strike was called off unconditionally after only nine days and the miners' strike was eventually broken. The Conservatives passed a Trade Disputes Act in 1927 which outlawed 'sympathetic' strikes and the TUC formally resolved to revert to the policy of collaboration with employers which had been begun during the war. The second minority Labour government of 1929–31 (again led by MacDonald) conformed to the same logic, seeking to win long-term electoral support by confining itself to very limited reforms which Liberal MPs would support.

This strategy was momentarily called in question by the ignominious end of the 1929–31 Labour government, when MacDonald agreed to head a so-called National Government, consisting almost exclusively of Conservatives and Liberals, to implement cuts in social security payments that his own party and the TUC had rejected. In the subsequent election of October 1931 Labour's parliamentary representation was reduced to 52 seats – almost back to the level of 1906. The Labour Party Conference now resolved not to take office again without proposing 'definite socialist legislation' on which it would stand or fall. For the moment this change of policy seemed fairly academic. In the 1935 election the Labour vote recovered, but not its share of seats, and the slump weakened the trade unions still further.

The situation changed rapidly, however, with the coming of the Second World War. Full employment restored union membership, and the need for national unity dictated that the Labour Party should be brought into the wartime coalition on much more equal terms than in 1916. Key ministries were held by Labour leaders, including Ernest Bevin, General Secretary of the biggest union, the Transport and General Workers Union. The popular mobilisation required by total war also meant that extremes of inequality, and the persistent unemployment of the inter-war years, had to be repudiated. Popular aspirations for a more secure, and above all 'fairer' society now had to be reckoned with. Years of socialist propaganda, and the threat of fascism, had converted a wide segment of middle-class opinion to the need for change. Keynes's strategy of regulating effective demand so as to maintain high levels of employment suggested that social-democratic policies were compatible with capitalism and might even be necessary for its survival, and the success of the war economy seemed to prove that it was practicable. The new political order, incorporating the labour movement, thus eventually led to a general acceptance of many of the main tenets of social democracy: that capitalism could and should be made acceptable to 'ordinary people' by being regulated, humanised, and made to support a comprehensive system of social security.

This was the basis of Labour's 'landslide' victory in the first post-war election of July 1945, on a programme of public ownership of a number of key industries and a new system of state-provided social welfare. But the scope of the consensus was limited, even on the Labour side. The fiasco of 1931 had really convinced the party's leaders that when they next took office they must be effective, not that they must be socialist, and four years of coalition government during the war had reinforced this view. They actually opposed the resolution of the 1944 Annual Conference which committed the Labour Party to a package of specific measures of nationalisation, although unlike later Labour leaders they accepted it when it was overwhelmingly passed on a vote.

Similar reservations were felt among the trade union leadership. The unions had lost almost half their members between 1921 and 1934 and, with over two million unemployed throughout most of the 1930s, they had been able to do little more than try to minimise wage cuts for those remaining in jobs. Full employment during and after the war restored union membership, and real wages rose substantially, but the union leaders had been deeply scarred by the Depression and opposed any measures that might jeopardise the prosperity of the remaining private enterprise sector. Most of them were more hostile to communism than to capitalism (Ernest Bevin, who became Foreign Secretary in 1945, was one of the most militant champions of the Cold War). Experience with the wartime system of economic controls had shown that unemployment could be avoided, and upon this they were determined to insist. They were also committed to nationalising those industries which in private ownership could no longer pay the employees a living wage. But there was no inclination to go further; nor – on the other hand – did many trade union leaders envisage the possibility that full employment might strengthen the working class to the point where capital's profitability might be fatally eroded.

The Labour leadership thus saw themselves as having a mandate not for socialism, but for the ideals of the war years – full employment, social security and 'fair shares'. This permitted the progressive wing of the Conservative Party to embark on a campaign to convince their own diehards that it was both safe and necessary to accept the new order. Their success led to a 'consensus' on the main elements in Labour's social-democratic package to which all parties adhered, in broad terms, until the end of the 1950s.

Implementing the Consensus 1945–51

The Labour Prime Minister Clement Attlee – 'a very modest little man, with a great deal to be modest about', Churchill is supposed to have said – was well suited to the task that he and his senior colleagues had set themselves, having served as party leader since 1933 and as Deputy Prime Minister in the wartime coalition. His government inherited three major assets from the war. First, the plan put forward in 1942 by the Liberal economist Sir William Beveridge, providing for universal insurance against sickness, old age, widowhood and unemployment, and for family allowances. The 'Beveridge Plan' gave concrete expression to what most people wanted. Beveridge himself energetically promoted it and, in spite of Churchill's opposition, many Conservatives became persuaded of its political necessity. Support was also overwhelming for the Labour government's National Health Act of 1946, enabling it to be carried in spite of opposition from a majority of doctors. Second, the government inherited an elaborate framework of wartime economic controls, from state allocation of raw materials to manufacturers to the direction of workers into jobs, and including the rationing of food and clothes and the control of all prices and rents. This allowed the government to manage the transition from military to civilian production without significant unemployment or economic dislocation. Third, the government inherited a vast, unfilled international demand for virtually anything Britain could export.

The party's 1945 pledges were rapidly redeemed. With regard to nationalisation, the Bank of England, the coal mines, the railway and canal companies, the power and gas companies and all road haulage were transferred to public ownership by 1948. Most of the iron and steel companies were also 'nationalised' in an Act of 1949, but in this case the strength of the industry's opposition to the measure (many steel companies, unlike the coal mines and the railways, were still profitable) combined with reviving Conservative Party morale and faltering purpose in the cabinet to delay the implementation of the Act until 1951. Shortly afterwards (in October 1951) the Conservatives returned to power and in 1953 legislated for the companies to be sold back to their former owners.

The effect of the nationalisation measures was that, in 1950, nationalised industries produced roughly 20 per cent of total GDP, and employed 9 per cent of the workforce. This gave the state an important measure of direct influence in the economy through the investment, pricing and employment policies of these industries.

However, the long-term political implications were two-edged. First, nearly all the industries nationalised, including many of the steel companies, were declining industries, and most were victims of long-standing neglect by their former owners. The compensation awarded to the former owners was probably excessive. Certainly neither the railways nor the coal mines were able both to service the compensation debt, and to find from profits the investment funds needed in order to stay competitive; they could not break even 'taking one year with another', as the legislation envisaged. The problem grew worse, especially after 1951, as successive governments limited the nationalised industries' ability to borrow for investment, and directed the railways, the Electricity Board and the Coal Board to keep down their prices, and the state-owned airlines to buy expensive British-made aircraft. The result was that nationalised industries became identified in the public mind with 'loss-making', which was in turn ascribed to inefficiency, and were then forced to become more 'productive' by drastically contracting.

Second, the nationalised industries were established as public corporations, with boards appointed by the relevant minister and drawn predominantly from the former private boards of management. Consumer councils were set up, but these were not elective either, and had no powers. In short, 'nationalisation' was not 'socialisation'. So far from acquiring a new sense of identification with the state, the workers in the nationalised industries found themselves prime targets of successive governments' attempts to control wages, since the state could, as their employer, apply downward pressure on their wages without passing special legislation. From the mid-1950s to the 1960s the incomes of public sector employees, including most nationalised industry workers, grew more slowly than the incomes of workers in the private sector.

Third, the Conservatives, aided by large anti-nationalisation advertising expenditures by the private sector, made 'nationalisation' the focus of an intense ideological campaign to limit any further socialist advance.[5] This campaign was successful. The record of performance of the nationalised industries, within the constraints imposed on them by the Labour legislation of 1946–9 and the subsequent policies of Conservative governments, provided no basis for the development of popular support. Opinion polls registered a steady loss of public support for nationalisation, to the point where, in 1959, the Labour leader Hugh Gaitskell sought, though unsuccessfully, to expunge from the party's constitution any further commitment to nationalisation. In spite of Gaitskell's formal defeat on this issue, the Labour Party never subsequently returned in practice to the view that the 'common ownership of the means of production' was a valid objective in its own right.

The other half of the Labour government's programme was the establishment of the 'welfare state' through family allowances (introduced in 1945) and the National Insurance Act of 1946, which provided against loss of livelihood from unemployment, sickness, industrial injury, maternity, death of the breadwinner or retirement; and through the National Health Act (also of 1946) which made medical services freely available to all. These were pioneering reforms, ahead of all other western countries at the time.

They too, however, had some serious limitations, the most

important being their undemocratic character. The new services were administered by civil servants; there was no attempt to involve the public directly in their provision. They were administered bureaucratically, however valuable they were, and when, later, the service provided gradually declined, members of the public were slow to realise what was happening, and then did not feel personally responsible, or capable of getting things put right. The result was that thirty years on (by the early 1970s) the percentage of national income spent on social services in Britain was below that of the other West European industrial countries, while the absolute level of spending per capita was very much lower still.[6] A second weakness was that the contributory element in the funding of both National Insurance and the National Health Service was a flat rate, which fell most heavily on the poor. Combined with a not particularly redistributive tax system, the effect was that 'the "welfare state" provide[d] for wage earners to finance the bulk of their own social security. Redistribution between classes [was] very limited.'[7]

The fact that the tax system was not very redistributive contradicts a popular myth, strongly propagated until well into the 1970s, that the post-war Labour government also brought about a great reduction in income inequality. Between 1938 and 1949, the share of total personal income received by the richest 1 per cent of the population fell from about 15 per cent to about 10 per cent, but this resulted from wartime tax changes; afer 1949, only a minor further reduction in post-tax income inequality occurred; the income share of the poorest 50 per cent scarcely changed at all.*

In fact, the Attlee government was quite orthodox in its economic policies. Any temptation it might have felt to be otherwise was curbed by its need to close the massive balance of payments gap (caused by the loss of income from foreign assets sold to finance the war, and by pent-up demand for raw material imports) before an American loan for post-war reconstruction was exhausted in 1949. It was able to do this only by imposing an extreme 'austerity' programme on the population (continuing to ration food, clothing and other necessities), by a big devaluation of the pound in 1949, and by securing the unions' agreement to exercise restraint in wage demands from early 1948 until September 1950. The balance of payments deficit on current account (i.e., in traded goods and services) was closed in 1949.

By that time, however, the government's energy, as well as its will to further reform, had been exhausted. Although the Labour vote rose

* The figure may overstate the redistribution that did occur: see the 7th Report of the Royal Commission on the Distribution of Income and Wealth (Cmnd 7595 of 1977), p. 7.

substantially in the election of 1950 (to 13.2 million from 12 million in 1945), the Conservative vote recovered to 12.5 million (see Table 5.1). Labour's big majorities in urban working-class constituencies meant that it had more 'wasted' votes, and its majority in parliament fell to five seats. The leadership was divided over the rearmament programme called for by the USA afer the outbreak of the Korean war. The political initiative was allowed to pass back to the Conservatives, who won a majority of 20 seats in the election of October 1951.

The Age of Affluence 1951–60

The Conservatives were to hold power for thirteen years, until 1964, winning three successive elections (1951, 1955 and 1959), a political feat without precedent.* This was made possible by an equally unprecedented rate of economic growth which was maintained throughout the 1950s. Output rose about 35 per cent between 1951 and 1961; real average earnings by some 2.7 per cent a year. This was fundamentally due to the 'long boom', the worldwide upturn in the accumulation cycle which lasted from the 1940s until the late 1960s. It was also due to the temporary absence from world markets of the export production of the major economies most severely dislocated by the war – the German, Italian, French and Japanese.

Thanks to this, the Conservatives were able to preside over years of rising wages and relatively high profits (over the decade as a whole profit rates were approximately 15.5 per cent).[8] This made it easier for them to accept Labour's social-democratic legacy, including the 'mixed economy' – a label which suggested a change in its basically capitalist nature which had not in fact occurred – and the welfare state. Nothing was added to either, but with only a few exceptions – notably the steel industry, and the profitable parts of the road haulage industry – there was no attempt to put the clock back. Thanks to the boom, too, unemployment remained minimal (at no time was it above 2 per cent between 1951 and 1964), and the Conservatives proved as eager to avoid industrial conflict as any Labour government – in fact, almost more so. Their claim was that the good times were due to the merits of private enterprise – capitalism had overcome its former limitations, and the Conservatives had shed their indifference to the interests of labour. Harold Macmillan, who became Conservative leader and

* The Liberals had won the successive elections of January–February 1906, January–February 1910 and December 1910, but in the two 1910 elections they failed to win overall majorities, whereas the Conservatives increased their majority in both 1955 and 1959.

Prime Minister in 1957, campaigned in 1959 on the slogan 'Life's better with the Conservatives. Dont't let Labour ruin it.'* The voters were enjoying the new lifestyle of cars, television, household appliances and package holidays in Spain, which their rising incomes made possible. They were helped to make up their minds politically by 'giveaway' budgets before the elections of 1955 and 1959. The Conservatives ended the decade with an overall parliamentary majority of 100.

Upon his retirement in 1955 Attlee was succeeded as Labour leader by Hugh Gaitskell, an Oxford economist who believed strongly that the mission of the Labour Party was to humanise capitalist society, not to reform it out of existence. Gaitskell was also influenced by Labour Party theorists and sociologists who believed that the class struggle as it had existed for more than a century and a half was now over, and that the workers were becoming middle-class in outlook as they grew richer. Mark Abrams's book, *Must Labour Lose?*, argued that it must, so long as it remained the party of nationalisation, which was no longer popular; while Tony Crosland, in *The Future of Socialism*, held out the vision of a prosperous capitalist economy paying for an increasingly generous, enlightened and meritocratic welfare state.

Gaitskell threw his influence against all proposals for further nationalisation. His attempt to expunge Clause 4 of the party's constitution (which commits the party to 'common ownership' of the means of production) was defeated by a combination of the party's left wing with 'traditionalists' who were not keen on further nationalisation but (like the German Social Democrats in the famous 'Bernstein debate' at the turn of the century) were fearful of the consequences that such a symbolic renunciation of socialism might have for party morale. This struggle, and a parallel left–right struggle in 1960–61 over the issue of nuclear disarmament, worked to the Conservatives' electoral advantage.

In spite of the atmosphere of prosperity, the 1950s were later seen as years of fatal illusion, in which the Conservative government maintained an international posture beyond Britain's reduced means and ignored the growing relative weakness of the British economy. Britain's rate of growth, while high by her own historical standards, was no longer high enough. At the same time as Britain's output rose by 35 per cent, between 1951 and 1961, France's rose by nearly 100 per cent, Germany's and Italy's by 200 per cent, and Japan's by 400 per cent. This was not just a question of the other countries starting from a smaller base. Their growth rates rested on very high rates of

---

* Churchill retired in 1955 and was succeeded by the Foreign Secretary, Sir Anthony Eden. Eden resigned in 1957 after the fiasco of the Anglo-French attack on the Suez Canal.

BRISTOL POLYTECHNIC
ST. MATTHIAS LIBRARY
FISHPONDS

investment and productivity growth. Between 1955 and 1965, as their manufacturing production began to return to world markets, the British share of world manufacturing exports fell from 20 per cent to 14 per cent.[9] Thanks to a simultaneous fall in the prices of raw material imports, the balance of payments remained positive for most of the decade, but vulnerability to speculation against sterling (due to the financial markets' recognition of Britain's growing relative industrial weakness) led to packages of deflationary measures in both 1955 and 1957 – the 'stops' of the 'stop-go' cycle, as the Conservatives' alternation between deflation and expansion came to be called.

Given the weakening industrial base, Conservative policies during the 1950s became more and more unrealistic. Leaving economic policy to a succession of six different Chancellors of the Exchequer, none of them with economic training, the Conservatives pursued international policies based on the idea that Britain was still a 'first-class' power. These policies included the maintenance of British forces in the Far East and in Germany, and the effort to maintain an independent British nuclear weapons system. The average level of defence spending throughout the decade was close to 9 per cent of GNP, compared to the 3 to 5 per cent of Britain's main economic competitors. From the same illusion flowed the costly and futile attempt to over-throw Egypt's President Nasser by the attack on the Suez Canal in 1956, and the initial, short-sighted and costly decision not to join the European Common Market at its formation in 1958. Few would now dispute the judgement of Samuel Britain that this great-power illusion was

> the common factor behind our failure to join the European movement when we could have got in on our own terms, the crippling of the economy in the Korean armament drive, the failure to fund the sterling balances after the war, the long delay in rethinking both the international role of sterling and its exchange parity, the investment of large resources in a series of military and aerospace projects, many of which had to be cancelled before completion, and the growth of overseas defence commitments.[10]

Reality did begin to force itself on the attention of the Conservatives before the end of the decade. In 1959 Macmillan recognised the strength of African nationalism and appointed a Colonial Secretary, Iain MacLeod, who was willing and competent to arrange a rapid programme of transition to independence. Formally, at least, the British Empire was liquidated. Macmillan also accepted that it had become impossible for Britain to finance an independent nuclear missile system and that she must therefore buy one from the USA (with the obvious political dependence which this involved). In 1961, following the same logic, and with strong encouragement from the Americans, he accepted the need for a realistic alternative to the increasingly unreliable 'sterling area' as the basis for British commerce, and belatedly sought admission to the European Common Market (only to be rebuffed by de Gaulle).

These were radical departures from traditional Conservative interests and attitudes. It would have taken exceptional management and good luck to have induced the party, already humiliated by Suez, to accept them in the way that it had previously accepted the domestic legacy of the Attlee government. Even so, it might have been possible, had the economy been strong enough to sustain a new national role for Britain as one of Europe's prosperous middle-rank powers. But the 'consensus' years had diverted attention from the underlying causes of the country's industrial deficiencies.

As a result a second crisis began, and led, like the first, to a steady deterioration in the authority of governments and the state, and to a progressive weakening of popular support for the dominant ideas of the political order built up over the previous four decades. For twenty years after 1945 the Conservatives had not dared, and mostly had not wished, to advocate restoring high unemployment, dismantling the welfare state or ending public ownership of the principal nationalised industries; any more than the Labour Party had seriously advocated any significant extension of public ownership or new measures of popular control of industry. Over the next twenty years, this consensus disappeared, and a new political order had to be created again.

Notes

1 A. Loveday, *Britain and World Trade*, Longman Green, London 1931, p. 160.
2 Ibid., pp. 170–71 (italics added).
3 E. Hobsbawm, *Industry and Empire*, Penguin, Harmondsworth 1969, p. 218.
4 B. Barker, ed., *Ramsay MacDonald's Political Writings*, Allen Lane, London 1972, p. 93.
5 J. Leruez, *Economic Planning and Politics in Britain*, Robertson, London 1973, p. 201.
6 I. Gough, *The Political Economy of the Welfare State*, Macmillan, London 1979, p. 79.
7 J. Westergaard and H. Resler, *Class in a Capitalist Society*, Heinemann, London 1975, p. 66.
8 A. Glyn and B. Sutcliffe, *British Capitalism, Workers and the Profits Squeeze*, Penguin, Harmondsworth 1972, p. 66, Table 33.
9 *National Institute Economic Reviews*, Statistical Appendices.
10 S. Brittan, *Steering the Economy*, Penguin, Harmondsworth 1964, p. 493.

5

The Paralysis of
Social Democracy

From 1961 onwards British politics became dominated once more by the country's economic problems. Britain's share of world exports of manufactures fell persistently (from 15.7 per cent in 1961 to 9.5 per cent in 1978), while foreign manufactures increasingly penetrated the British domestic market, reaching 25.6 per cent of total domestic sales (nearly 60 per cent, in the case of car sales) by mid-1979. The overall rate of profit (before tax) fell from 14.2 per cent in 1960 to 4.7 per cent in 1978. Investment remained static, falling further and further behind the levels of competing economies abroad. By 1978, productivity in manufacturing was little over half the German level.

The immediate result was a succession of increasingly severe 'sterling crises'. As the relative decline of exports and growth of imports kept tending to push the current account into deficit, holders of sterling speculated against the pound, reasoning that a devaluation would be needed to close the gap, and hoping to make a profit by forcing the authorities into it. Governments – Conservative until 1964, then Labour – resisted this, by using their reserves of foreign exchange to buy pounds, and by deflating the economy so as to reduce the level of demand for imports. This aggravated the unemployment which was already being caused by the closure of unsuccessful companies. As a result, between 1961 and 1979 manufacturing employment fell by 20 per cent – a loss of 2.1 million jobs. Whole sectors of manufacturing disappeared – from motorcyles (in which Britain in 1950 had led the world) to a large part of the home appliances sector – while others such as shipbuilding, cars and even steel were threatened. Unemployment rose from 0.3 million (1.5 per cent) in 1961 to 1.4 million (7 per cent) in 1978. Manufacturing output rose only slowly in the 1960s, and hardly rose at all in the 1970s. Inequality was rediscovered, with a vengeance.

By the early 1970s it turned out that some 23 per cent of the population were too poor to take a full part in the normal life of the community.[1]

Workers – the unionised rank and file – were not prepared to accept unemployment and downward pressure on wages without a struggle, and thanks to the 'affluent' fifties, when sometimes more job vacancies were recorded than job-seekers, they had become well placed to resist. In return for sustained production, management, especially in engineering, had conceded a substantial measure of shop-floor influence over the labour process. This influence was channelled through the shop stewards, directly elected by the workers in each 'shop'. As the 1960s progressed, rank and file resistance led to 'unofficial' – i.e. non union-endorsed – strikes, usually lasting less than three days and often only a few hours, which came to account for 95 per cent of all strikes. Thanks to this, real wages of manual workers still increased on average by 2.5 per cent a year throughout the 1960s, only a little below the 2.7 per cent achieved in the 1950s.[2] Manufacturing companies could not pass all this on in price increases because foreign firms, with superior productivity, were underselling them. As a result, investment fell further and further behind the levels achieved in competing economies. Although governments – most notably the Labour government of 1964–70 – provided subsidies, resulting in some increase in investment (financed, in effect, out of revenues from personal income tax), the results were not impressive.

The failure of successive governments to reverse these trends led to a marked loss of electoral support for the two major parties. In the 1959 election the Labour and Conservative parties between them had taken 93.2 per cent of the vote; by October 1974 their combined share of the vote was down to 75 per cent, or only 55 per cent of the total electorate (see Table 5.1). This reflected more than loss of confidence in the parties' leaderships. The social-democratic values to which even the Conservatives had subscribed during the 1950s were losing some of their authority. The parties themselves, faced with the intractable problem of economic decline, became increasingly polarised. Political currents previously considered 'extreme' – the market-oriented doctrines of the 'new right' and the more radical socialist views of the 'Labour left' – gained ground in the parties outside parliament, and in the case of the Conservatives, captured control inside the parliamentary party as well in 1975. The authoritarian strand in the Conservative Party became more pronounced; the narrowly parliamentary approach of the Labour leadership was increasingly rejected by the party's activists. Outside Northern Ireland there were no outright challenges to constitutional authority comparable to those of 1910–14; but the state increasingly prepared for them.

Table 5.1   The decline in the major parties' vote 1945–1974

| | Percentage of votes cast | | | Labour and Conservative vote as percentage of electorate | | | |
	Labour	Conservatives	Others	Lab	+ Con	=	Total
1945	47.8	39.8	11.8	36.1	+ 29.8	=	65.9
1950	46.1	43.5	10.4	39.8	+ 37.7	=	77.5
1951	48.8	48.0	3.2	40.2	+ 39.6	=	79.8
1955	46.4	49.7	3.9	35.6	+ 38.2	=	73.8
1959	43.8	49.4	6.8	34.5	+ 38.7	=	73.2
1964	44.1	43.4	12.5	34.0	+ 33.4	=	67.4
1966	47.9	41.9	9.7	36.1	+ 31.7	=	67.8
1970	43.0	46.4	10.7	31.0	+ 33.3	=	64.3
1974 (Feb)	37.1	37.9	25.0	29.1	+ 29.9	=	59.0
1974 (Oct)	39.2	35.8	25.0	28.7	+ 26.2	=	54.9

New Aspects

As late as 1980 few people saw the crisis in such a serious light. This was partly because of the time span which separated this crisis from the earlier one, making it hard to recognise it as a recurrence of an old syndrome, and partly because of some novel aspects.

The most obvious of these was that after 1970 the British crisis was compounded by a worldwide accumulation crisis. The reasons for the end of the long post-war boom are complex. The exhaustion of the impulse of technological innovation provoked by the Second World War is usually considered a basic, underlying cause. The advent of Japanese competition in all the most advanced sectors of production also cut into accumulation in the USA and Europe. Spare capacity emerged, and spare investible funds, leading to a strong movement of manufacturing capital towards cheap-labour, anti-union regimes such as Taiwan and Brazil. This aggravated the problem of maintaining growth rates in Europe and the USA, a problem further exacerbated by the oil-price increases after 1973. By the end of the 1970s virtually all the industrialised economies were experiencing reduced growth rates, rising unemployment, inflation and in some cases balance of payments problems as well. What distinguishes the British experience, however, and underlines more clearly than anything else its 'endogenous' nature, is that in Britain the new crisis had already begun in the 1960s

– a decade of unparalleled prosperity for the rest of the industrialised world. The worldwide accumulation crisis of the 1970s did not cause the British crisis, but it did make it worse.

Another novel aspect of the crisis was the changed nature of manufacturing capital in Britain. It had become extremely centralised, and to a very significant extent internationalised. In 1910, the largest hundred manufacturing companies had accounted for less than 15 per cent of total output. By 1970 they accounted for about 50 per cent, and by 1980, about 60 per cent.[3] Fifty of these same hundred companies were multinational, and fifty accounted for more than a quarter of Britain's visible exports.[4] By 1979 American-owned firms alone accounted for 19.5 per cent of Britain's visible exports, and 31 per cent of all British exports were transactions between different branches of single companies – that is, intra-firm transactions.[5] At the same time, British multinational companies owned a disproportionately large share of world assets, and made a third of their profits from overseas operations.

As Stuart Holland pointed out, the rise of this 'meso-economic' sector (in between the 'macro-economic' level of the whole economy and the 'micro-economic' level of the individual firm) rendered obsolete a good deal of conventional wisdom about state economic management. Profit-accounting, transfer pricing and the sheer scale and complexity of the operations of the major companies make them almost impossible to inspect, monitor or police. A large part of the manufacturing sector had become increasingly immune to state efforts to control prices, to regulate the supply of credit, to tax corporate profits, or to affect economic growth by exchange rate changes. Much of the failure of successive governments in the 1960s and 1970s to accomplish any of their economic goals was due to more fundamental causes, but some of it was due to the growing difficulty which any government would have experienced in controlling an economy which had increasingly become a mere 'location' in the global division of labour of corporate manufacturing empires – and an increasingly unattractive one.

There is a crucial contradiction between the fact that Britain ranks first in the European top 500 with 140 firms yet has an economic performance lower than and worse than any of our main European competitors. The reason lies substantially in the extent to which such leading multinationals have written Britain off as the main location for their expansion, and are shunting investment and jobs in modern industry abroad.[6]

This affected both Labour and Conservative governments in different ways. Labour governments seeking more control over private-sector investment policies, for example, could find themselves either ultimately impotent in face of corporate control over markets, information and investment funds; or, if they were to make determined efforts to break this control, they could face a crisis of 'business confidence', and a threatened or actual capital flight.*

Conservative governments, on the other hand, seeking to strengthen 'market forces', would find that this tended to accelerate the decline of the already too weak *national* (as opposed to multinational) sector of the British economy. Yet, without a national economy, a national party of capital risks the loss of its electoral base. The fact that the Conservative Party's representation in the House of Commons after the 1979 election was overwhelmingly concentrated in constituencies south of the Trent was a painful reminder of this.†

Yet – and here was the most striking novelty of the new crisis – the state itself had enormously expanded. In 1910 total state expenditure had been 12.7 per cent of GDP. By 1975 it was 57.9 per cent (including transfer spending). By 1977, the public sector (central and local government and public enterprises) employed almost 30 per cent of the labour force.

The expansion of the state, combined with the growth of monopoly in the private sector, accounted for a good deal of the inflation that accompanied the stagnation of output. Since hyperinflation on Israeli or Chilean lines was judged socially and politically unacceptable, even Labour governments hesitated to try to use the state as an instrument of further economic expansion. The scale of state employment also complicated the problem of wage levels in general. Wage demands in the state sector encountered only the political limits set by governments' will to resist, and by the mid-1970s this will had been weakened. At the same time, the greatly enlarged state seemed no more suited or inclined than it had ever been to initiate and carry through a radical reconstruction of the economy.

---

* A well-publicised threat of a capital flight was that of Pilkingtons, the glass manufacturers, after the October 1974 elections. Private investment abroad during the years 1975-78 inclusive was equal to 31 per cent of gross investment in Britain by industrial and commercial companies.

† In 1979 the Conservatives won only 75 (32 per cent) of the 235 seats in Northern England and Scotland, the lowest share in any general election won by the Conservatives since 1951; conversely, they won 186 (85 per cent) of the 219 seats in England south of the Midlands, excluding London (D. Butler and A. Sloman, *British Political Facts*, Macmillan, London 1980, p. 213).

Perceptions of the Crisis

These new features of the crisis, and the extensive changes that had occurred since the First World War, made it hard for people to recognise it for what it was. As a result, they ran through the gamut of the earlier diagnoses, as if discovering them for the first time: trade union restrictive practices and strikes, amateurism and conservativism in management, technical and scientific backwardness, poor design and poor salesmanship, inadequate scale of production, party competition for votes, excessive overseas investment, an overvalued pound.[7] Some of the diagnoses were new. For instance, the tendency to blame excessive overseas investment, an overvalued pound or the 'stop-go' oscillations of government policy reflected a much greater realisation of the conflict of interest between manufacturing and financial or commercial interests than had existed sixty years before. Another new diagnosis was that there were 'too few producers', that is, too many state employees – a version of the neo-conservative reaction to the growth of the state.[8]

By now it should not be necessary to belabour the point that most of these diagnoses were not wrong – on the contrary most of them are essentially correct. For example, a comparative study of British and foreign automobile production by the government's Central Policy Review staff in 1975 suggested that relative to US and European plants British plants were overmanned. But, it added, 'even when manning levels are virtually identical and the capital equipment, model involved and plant layout are the same, the output of production lines in Britain is about half of that of continental plants'. The report seemed to imply that the fault lay with the workers: 'In other words, with the same power at his elbow and doing the same job as the British worker, a continental car assembly worker normally produces twice as much as his British counterpart.'[9] In fact, capital per employee in the British car industry as a whole was much lower than in Europe or the USA, and British plants were also too numerous, and produced too many engine types and a poorly balanced range of models. Another study showed that American-managed firms in Britain were more profitable than equivalent British-managed firms.[10] The truth was that management was less competent *and*, partly because of this, workers worked less efficiently (and perhaps less hard) than elsewhere. No one factor, or a few factors taken in isolation, contained the key to the problem. It could only be understood as the consequence of a total historical process.

By the 1960s, the relationship between capital and labour in Britain had been modified in many ways, but not in essentials: on the one hand, a class of capital still deeply attached to many pre-capitalist values, and on the other, an organised working class deeply sceptical of any suggestion that any advantage that they might concede to the employers would actually advance their own long-term interests. What was new in the 1960s was that the workers had acquired the strength to resist any increase in the level of exploitation, when such an increase had finally become essential. To maintain its existing competitiveness – let alone improve it – in face of rapidly rising productivity in other countries, big increases in the productivity of British manufacturing were required. This implied massive increases in investment. *The Times*, in 1973, suggested £20 billion. But whatever the figure, the implication was for investment on an unprecedented scale. This in turn implied the need for vast increases in profits. Would the workers be willing to leave these to the shareholders? In any case, part of these sums would have to come from profits on the basis of existing investment levels, that is, by tax changes in favour of profits. The conditions which permitted capital in Germany, France or Japan to impose an initially high level of exploitation (i.e., the gap between value added and wages) on the workforce did not exist in Britain – even if British management had had the necessary technical and managerial sophistication. British workers were too well organised, and they were no longer much impressed by the 'work ethic' which had been so assiduously preached to them in the nineteenth century (any more than British management seemed to have been, at least since the turn of the century). As the President of the National Union of Mineworkers, Joe Gormley, put it to the 1979 Labour Party Conference: 'The British people were not made to work' – a sentiment rather unlikely to have been expressed by his opposite number in Germany, the USA or Japan.

On the other hand, the British working class in the 1960s was no more ready to vote for a party seriously committed to an entirely new economic order than it had ever been. Whatever dreams it may once have entertained of building a transformed, egalitarian society – such as the Owenite movement of the 1830s had envisaged, for instance – had long been forgotten. The working-class consciousness which emerged after the defeats of the early nineteenth century was 'corporate', not 'hegemonic': it was a consciousness of the distinct interests of the workers as workers – as at most an historic *underclass*. This remained broadly true in the 1960s.[11] So the contradictions between the need of capital to move to a higher level of exploitation, and the determination of workers to prevent this, presented itself as something to be resolved within the existing political framework

defined by the Conservative and Labour Parties. It took two decades
to discover that this was impossible.

State-led Modernisation – the Wilson Reforms

Harold Wilson, who became Labour leader in 1963, had opposed
Gaitskell's efforts to delete Clause 4 from the party's constitution. This
maintained his reputation as a man of the left, but his grounds were
pragmatic, if not cynical: 'We were being asked to take Genesis out of
the bible. You don't have to be a fundamentalist to say that Genesis is
a part of the bible.'[12] Wilson consistently resisted efforts to commit the
party to new measures of public ownership. Instead, he laid stress on
modernisation and technology within the existing 'mixed economy'. He
attacked the Conservatives as a party led by aristocratic amateurs,
ignorant of the scientific and technological requirements of the modern
world, who had presided for 'thirteen wasted years' over an economy
whose management cadres were similarly recruited on the basis of class
and connections, not merit; without planning, without reform, without
keeping up with the times. Instead, he offered a vision of a society run
by its men of talent. In a much-quoted speech to the Labour Party
Conference in October 1963, after his election as party leader, he said:

> We are redefining and we are re-stating our socialism in terms of the
> scientific revolution . . . the Britain that is going to be forged in the white
> heat of this revolution will be no place for restrictive practices or out-dated
> methods on either side of industry.[13]

The passage illustrates very well the thrust of Wilson's appeal – to
'both sides of industry' against incompetence, not to the working class
against capital. Wilson understood that the consensus was endangered
by industrial weakness. He offered to do what was necessary to
remedy it. He answered the need to reassure people that, after all, 'no
one need be defeated in the class war because no war was being
fought. Capitalism could provide affluence for the working class while
at the same time preserving the gains of the well-to-do'.[14] In the
October 1964 election, the Labour Party campaign based on this theme
at last secured electoral victory – though with only the barest majority
of four seats.

   Wilson's analysis of the economic problem was that it was due to a
lack of central planning based on a commitment to growth (the French
planning system was particularly identified as a model); to production
on too small a scale; and to a generally archaic structure of state

policy-making and business management, hostile to innovation and closed to lower-class talent. Promising to accomplish more in a hundred days than the Conservatives had done in thirteen years, Wilson quickly set in motion a comprehensive set of reforms. He established a new Department of Economic Affairs, charged with producing a National (five-year) Plan and promoting long-term economic growth, to offset the 'dead hand' of the Treasury, with its traditional preoccupation with short-term policy, balancing the books and maintaining the value of sterling; an Industrial Reorganisation Corporation, with substantial funds to subsidise corporate mergers; fiscal policies designed to encourage high levels of investment; and a wide range of institutional reforms designed to modernise the structure of the state.

These included reforms of the civil service, based on the report of a commission of inquiry (the Fulton Commission) which recommended the abolition of the hierarchy of 'classes' into which the policy-making cadre had been divided at the turn of the century, and measures to permit 'specialists' – technically trained officials – to rise into the senior ranks. There were also measures to replace the separate grammar, secondary modern and technical school system of secondary education by all-ability 'comprehensive' high schools; and to break the older universities' status monopoly by sharply increasing the number of degree-granting institutions, including the former Colleges of Advanced Technology (which became universities), the Polytechnics and the Teacher Training Colleges. Parliament was also to be reformed, to give new standing committees oversight of policy-making in government departments; an ombudsman, rejected by the Macmillan government, was established in 1967; the Official Secrets Act was to be amended, in the interests of more 'open' (and hence more efficient) government; and a major review of local government organisation was begun.

The same spirit of innovation was shown in social policy. Besides re-establishing traditional Labour priorities (for instance, by restoring the priority in house-building to one favouring publicly owned housing for rent, over private-sector housing for sale) the government introduced a capital gains tax (long since established elsewhere) and a separate corporation tax, and planned for the introduction of income-related pensions based on graduated contributions. All in all, it was a stunning contrast with the era of Churchill and Macmillan. Early in 1966, in spite of the multiple economic difficulties which had been encountered, Wilson called an election, correctly judging that people had been convinced that his government understood the problems facing the country and had an effective formula for tackling them. In that election, in March 1966, Labour's majority (which had fallen from four seats to one through a by-election defeat) was increased to 96.

But the voters were to be disappointed. The economic measures – especially the tax relief and subsidies to industry, and the programme of mergers promoted by the Industrial Reorganisation Corporation – did not lead to an increase in productivity relative to Britain's competitors. It is doubtful if these measures – or any measures that did not touch the central relationships between capital and labour – could have achieved much. But they were never really given a chance. To succeed, they needed a climate of expansion. This was the core assumption of the National Plan produced by the new Department of Economic Affairs in September 1965. It assumed a target rate of growth of 4 per cent per annum, resulting in a 25 per cent increase in national output between 1964 and 1970. But by the time the Plan was published, the economy was being fiercely deflated in order to prevent a new sterling crisis forcing a devaluation of the pound. In fact the government spent its entire period in office cutting back domestic demand, not expanding it. Output grew by 14 per cent, not 25 per cent; and gross investment grew by 20 per cent, not the 38 per cent forecast in the Plan, so that there was no question of increased productivity relative to other countries arising from this source.[15] In fact, British productivity grew 30 per cent between 1963 and 1970, French and German 50 per cent, and Japanese over 100 per cent (see Table 5.2).

The immediate reason for this failure was the attempt to maintain the exchange rate of the pound on an industrial base that had already become too weak to support it. When Labour took office in 1964, the exchange rate was still US$2.80, the rate fixed in 1949. But Labour also inherited a current account deficit of £402 million in the balance of payments (the visible trade deficit was £545 million, offset by a surplus of £143 million in invisibles – earnings from shipping, banking,

Table 5.2 Output per person-hour in manufacturing 1963–1970

	1963	1964	1965	1966	1967	1968	1969	1970
Japan	100	111	118	129	151	170	196	223
France	100	107	111	118	124	133	148	157
Germany	100	110	113	116	126	137	144	147
UK	100	106	110	114	118	125	127	131
Canada	100	106	110	114	118	125	129	131
USA	100	104	107	110	112	115	118	122

Source: National Institute Economic Review, Statistical Appendices.

insurance services, etc.). If this gap was not closed, a devaluation would be inevitable. Foreign holders of sterling, seeing the new government's first budget (which fulfilled election pledges to improve the level of social security benefits), judged that it would not cut back home demand enough to close the balance of payments gap, and a flight from sterling began.

The US government urged Wilson not to devalue the pound, fearing that it would force a devaluation of the dollar as well. Wilson, in any case, seems to have thought that the 1949 devaluation had hurt the Labour Party's image as an 'effective' manager of the economy, and was opposed to a further devaluation. In his conviction that bad economic management by the Conservatives was such an important part of the problem, he failed to realise – as did most of his ministers and advisers – the seriousness of the underlying weakness of British manufacturing. There followed a series of piecemeal efforts to defend the pound by borrowing. When this did not work, the government was forced to deflate. Finally, in 1967, it was forced to devalue anyway (from US$2.80 to US$2.40 – a 15 per cent drop); and then, in order to ensure that this was not challenged by further speculation, still further deflation was required.

The result was a disaster. The 'technological revolution', which – if it was to be more than rhetoric – depended on accelerated economic growth, was stillborn. Planning, in the words of one of the National Plan's authors, was 'many months dead already, or murdered' by the end of 1966.[16] The 'pacemaking' Department of Economic Affairs itself was abolished in 1969. A large foreign debt had been incurred in the futile defence of the pound, which had to be repaid before revenues could be applied to the increasingly massive task of economic reconstruction. The other social goals of the government suffered equally. The comprehensivisation of schools had to be tackled without building any new schools. The hospital service, starved under the Conservatives – not a single new hospital had been built in their thirteen years in office – continued to be starved.

Most serious of all, from a political point of view, the government set itself to try to save company profitability, and to satisfy its foreign creditors, by curbing wage increases. In the years from 1948 to 1950 the Labour government had secured voluntary wage restraint from the union leadership. Now, expectations were very different, and the unions had less control over their members. After an attempt to rely on voluntary agreement in 1964, legislation was passed in 1965 (partly in response to American pressure) to give the government powers to delay any wage settlements that exceeded a permitted 'norm'. In 1966, the powers were extended to permit the imposition of a general wage-freeze, followed by legal ceilings on all wage increases. Finally, in 1968, seeing that these controls could not be maintained, Wilson proposed legislation on American and Canadian lines, which would, in effect, have outlawed unofficial strikes and compelled the balloting of union members before strikes could be held, on pain of heavy financial penalties against the unions.

Throughout all this the unions, aware that price controls (which had also been instituted) were ineffectual, and that dividends, too, were barely curtailed in practice, grew more and more resistant.[17] In 1969 they finally threatened to withdraw their support from the government if the new proposals (embodied in a White Paper called *In Place of Strife*) were taken any further. Wilson and the minister responsible, Barbara Castle, were forced to retreat. The contradiction between the Labour Party's legitimacy as a representative of the interests of labour, and the Wilson government's attempt to try to save British manufacturing capital, was thus brought into the open.

The attempt to deal with the economic crisis by deflation and wage controls not only cost the Labour Party votes; it also led to a politicisation of industrial struggle. Nine per cent more working days were lost in the sixties than in the fifties, though this was nothing compared to what was to follow in the seventies (Table 5.3). The industrial front acquired a new political salience; the Wilson government, as it was drawn deeper and deeper into the defence of British capital, found itself more and more frustrated by the unwillingness of the workers to make the sacrifices asked of them. A succession of

Table 5.3 Working days lost in strikes 1951–1980

	1951	1952	1953	1954	1955	1956	1957	1958	1959	1960
Million days	1.7	1.8	2.2	2.4	3.8	2.1	8.4	3.5	5.3	3.0

	1961	1962	1963	1964	1965	1966	1967	1968	1969	1970
Million days	3.0	5.8	1.8	2.3	2.9	2.4	2.8	4.7	6.8	11.0

	1971	1972	1973	1974	1975	1976	1977	1978	1979	1980
Million days	13.6	23.9	7.2	14.7	6.0	3.3	10.1	9.4	29.5	12.0

Source: Monthly Digest of Statistics, CSO, London.

councils, commissions and boards, appointed (at five-figure salaries) to pronounce on the 'justice' or otherwise of workers' pay claims for sums in the order of £100 or so a year, succeeded only in disposing of any lingering illusion that wages were determined in some 'natural' fashion. In the 1960s the workers lost some of the 'profoundly attractive innocence' which Professor Chapman had found in them only a few years before.[18]

The Labour government's eventual subordination of all its other goals to the defence of the capitalist economy led to the emergence of new political forces. The student movement, growing out of the nuclear disarmament campaign and opposition to the government's support for the American war in Vietnam, challenged the whole range of established attitudes, and helped the development of new left-wing organisations, both reformist and revolutionary. Left-wing intellectuals, alienated from the Labour Party, joined more radical groups such as the International Socialists or the International Marxist Group, or the women's movement.

At the other political pole there was the growth of racism. Starting in the mid-1950s, a rapid influx of immigrants from the West Indies, South Asia and East Africa occurred. By 1970 1.2 million British people were of 'new Commonwealth and Pakistan' origin. Conservative and Labour leaders allowed themselves to be frightened by racist agitation into competing with each other to demonstrate their readiness to cut down the flow, passing the Commonwealth Immigration Acts of 1962 and 1968. This in turn encouraged the activities of the neo-fascist groups who, in 1966, formed the National Front.

Another development which compounded the crisis was the collapse of authority in Northern Ireland. The system of social, political and economic subordination of the Catholic minority by the Protestant majority in the six counties of Ulster had been connived at for over forty years by Labour as well as Conservative governments. The social-democratic consensus stopped short at the Irish Channel. On the other hand the provisions of the welfare state, which had been gladly adopted by the Unionist government in Belfast (since it was subsidised from Whitehall), had made the Catholics less insecure, and given new educational opportunities to their children. In 1968, partly inspired by the civil rights movement in the USA, the Northern Ireland Civil Rights Association, largely led by educated Catholics, challenged the status quo by demanding equal rights for all, including Catholics. The challenge was met by repression, leading to the intervention of the British army and to a revival of Irish Republican Army activity in the province, inaugurating what quickly became a bitter and intractable new phase in Ireland's two-centuries-old civil and colonial war.

The crisis in Ulster was not a result of the crisis in the economy, but was closely linked to it. Belfast had participated in the earliest stages of the industrial revolution and was now particularly affected by the decline of old staple industries such as shipbuilding and textiles. Unemployment in Northern Ireland was the highest of any region of the United Kingdom, and it affected Catholics most. The Catholic challenge to Protestant domination, especially in the form of discrimination in state employment and housing, reflected this. And the weakness of the British economy precluded any attempt to resolve the problem by large-scale investment programmes.

There were also significant centrifugal tendencies in Scotland and Wales. In England the decline in support for Labour and Conservatives was matched by a revival of support for the Liberals, but in Wales, and especially in Scotland, it was the nationalist parties which chiefly gained (see Table 12.1). By the late 1970s the nationalist trend was to play a fateful part in breaking up the post-war political order.

Unable to deal with the economic crisis at home, the government also found itself less and less able to act effectively abroad. The most dramatic example of this was its inability to impose its will on Ian Smith and the white settlers in Rhodesia when they made their Unilateral Declaration of Independence in 1965. At that time Labour had a majority of three in the House of Commons, and for this reason alone Wilson could not have intervened militarily even if he had wished to. Instead, he made the mistake of boasting that economic sanctions would bring down the illegal regime in 'weeks rather than months', while Smith, knowing this boast to be empty, refused the various face-saving compromises which Wilson subsequently offered. Both men, however, underrated the long-run strength of the Zimbabwean liberation movement, which eventually settled the issue by force of arms in 1980.

Wilson's general foreign policy differed little from Macmillan's. In 1968 the decision was finally taken to withdraw all British troops 'east of Suez'. As the timing shows, it was a decision taken more on financial grounds than for its own sake. And in 1967, Wilson (reversing his position, as Macmillan had done earlier) made his own application to join the European Common Market. This, however, de Gaulle vetoed once again in May 1968, maintaining that Britain was not yet ready to become a member of the European community. In retrospect, it is hard to fault this judgement, especially since Wilson's unswerving support for US policy in Vietnam made it clear that Britain's so-called 'special relationship' with the USA was increasingly that of a client.

There were redeeming elements in the record of the Wilson years. The laws covering divorce and abortion were liberalised, capital punishment was abolished, and the well-intentioned attempt to promote 'equality of educational esteem' through the comprehensivisation of secondary schools was pursued. There was also an expansion of university education (which, exceptionally, was maintained against the general trend of spending cuts). Not everything ended in failure. It was true that unemployment was rising, but for those in employment the end of wage controls and the defeat of the proposed new law to curtail strike action led to a recovery in wages in 1969–70 which substantially made good the relative losses imposed by controls in the previous years. And from the point of view of the City of London, the government's deflationary policies had finally closed the balance of payments gap.

Labour's defeat in the June 1970 election was, in fact, by no means a foregone conclusion. Shortly before the election the opinion polls suggested that Labour would win. But the gap between the government's economic performance and its promises was too wide. Wilson's rhetoric about harnessing science to socialism had proved too hollow. Labour Party membership had declined precipitously. At the last moment, the balance of opinion turned away from the general line of continuity with the past, which Wilson had maintained, and towards the 'new conservatism' propounded by the Conservative leader Edward Heath.

Notes

1 P. Townsend, *Poverty in the United Kingdom*, Penguin, Harmondsworth 1979, p. 273. An even larger proportion were poor, or on the 'margin' of poverty, by the state's own poverty-line criteria.
2 D. Robinson, 'Labour Market Policies', in W. Beckerman, ed., *The Labour Government's Economic Record*, Duckworth, London 1972, p. 313, Table 9.1.
3 S. Holland, *The Socialist Challenge*, Quartet Books, London 1975, pp. 49–50. Holland cites a forecast that by 1985 the proportion would be 66%.
4 Ibid., p. 76.
5 'Ninety-four firms account for half Britain's exports', *British Business*, 3 July 1981, Table 3.
6 Holland, pp. 77–8.
7 A list of the sources for these views in the sixties and seventies would be very long. Early examples are H. Thomas, ed., *The Establishment*, Blond, London 1959; B. Chapman, *British Government Observed*, Allen and Unwin, London 1963; M. Shanks, *The Stagnant Society*, Penguin, Harmondsworth 1961; M. Nicholson, *The System*, Hodder and Stoughton, London 1967.
8 R. Bacon and W. Eltis, *Britain's Economic Problem: Too Few Producers*, Macmillan, London 1976.
9 Central Policy Review Staff, *The Future of the British Car Industry*, HMSO, London 1970, p. 83.
10 J.H. Dunning, 'US Subsidiaries in Britain and their UK Competitors', *Business Ratios*, No. 1, Autumn 1966.

11 See especially T. Nairn, 'The English Working Class', *New Left Review* 24, March/April 1964, pp. 43–57, and 'The Nature of the Labour Party', in P. Anderson and R. Blackburn, *Towards Socialism*, Fontana, London 1967, pp. 159–217.
12 Quoted in A. Sked and C. Cook, *Post-War Britain*, Penguin, Harmondsworth 1979, p. 207.
13 D. Butler and A. Sloman, *British Political Facts 1900–1979*, Macmillan, London 1980, p. 253.
14 V. Bognador and R. Skidelsky, *The Age of Affluence*, Macmillan, London 1970, p. 10.
15 R. Opie, 'Economic Planning and Growth', in W. Beckerman, ed., *The Labour Government's Economic Record*, pp. 174–5.
16 Opie, p. 177.
17 On price controls see L. Panitch, *Social Democracy and Industrial Militancy*, Cambridge University Press, Cambridge 1976, pp. 129, 160 and 210; on dividend controls see pp. 114, 140 and 154.
18 B. Chapman, *British Government Observed*, Allen and Unwin, London 1963, p. 56.

6

Into the New Crisis

After the Conservative Party's defeat in the 1964 election many party activists and MPs felt that, in effect, Wilson's charge that it was led by an amateur, backward-looking elite contained an uncomfortable element of truth. There was a growing distrust of the party's traditionally upper-class leadership – the 'magic circle', the former Colonial Secretary Iain Macleod called them – including Macmillan himself, and his successor Sir Alec Douglas-Home. Home had become Prime Minister and leader of the party in 1963 on the basis of advice tendered to the Queen by Macmillan (when he had to resign from ill-health) after informal consultations within the party leadership. It was decided that from now on the leader should be elected by the Conservative MPs. Home stood aside and in the election held in July 1965 the choice fell on Edward Heath.

Heath, like Wilson, had been President of the Board of Trade. He had also been Macmillan's negotiator in the abortive Common Market application from 1961 to 1963, and was very much a 'European' and a 'technocrat'. Like Wilson too, 'Heath's abiding commitment was to the ideology of growth'.[1] But where Wilson hoped to achieve modernisation through active state intervention, Heath sought it through competition – through reducing state intervention, curbing monopolies, allowing the market to weed out backwardness and reward innovation.

The later sixties also saw a more fundamental right-wing movement than Heath's 'competition policy' gaining ground inside the Conservative Party. Enoch Powell, Heath's 'shadow minister' for health, shared his enthusiasm for the market and for cutting back the state, but went much farther in calling for denationalisation, an end to state intervention in industrial disputes, and strict control of the money supply to control inflation. He also combined this with a nationalist campaign against entry into the EEC, and a racist campaign against immigrants, both of which proved popular themes. In 1968 Heath dismissed him from the shadow cabinet for his most notorious speech, a veiled invocation of racial violence ('As I look ahead, I am filled with foreboding. Like the Roman, I seem to see "the River Tiber foaming with much blood" ').* But the new monetarist, nationalist, racist rejection of the post-war consensus which Powell expressed found a keen response on the authoritarian right wing of the party. These currents converged with Heath's more limited 'competition policy' at a pre-election strategy conference at the Selsdon Park Hotel in Croydon in January 1970 which committed the party to many of the 'new right' policies, including the abolition of universal social security payments and legislation to curtail trade union powers. Wilson commented: 'Selsdon Man is designing a system of society for the ruthless and the pushing, the uncaring . . . his message to the rest is: "you're out on you own".'[2]

The story of the next decade is the story of how at first Selsdon Man was defeated, because the consensus had not yet been weakened enough, and of how from 1974 to 1979 the consensus was then further eroded in a second unsuccessful attempt by Wilson and his successor, James Callaghan, to rescue Britain's competitive position without challenging the balance of power between capital and labour. Finally, the way was opened for a new, much more radical Conservative attempt to break with the past under the leadership of Margaret Thatcher.

The Heath Initiatives 1970–74

Heath's strategy was straightforward. Having prepared the ground with de Gaulle's successor, Pompidou, he reapplied for admission to the EEC in 1971. Also in 1971, to prevent the inevitable 'sterling crisis' choking off his strategy for economic expansion, he abandoned the fixed exchange rate and allowed the pound to 'float', thus reducing sterling's role as an international reserve currency, and overcoming one of de Gaulle's former objections to British entry. Britain finally entered the EEC in 1973.

Secondly, he set about dismantling much of the apparatus of state economic intervention created during the Wilson years – the Prices and Incomes Board, the Industrial Reorganisation Corporation, the system

---

* Powell received 105,000 letters of congratulations within a few days of this speech (Andrew Gamble, *The Conservative Nation*, Routledge and Kegan Paul, London 1974, p. 121).

of investment grants. Thirdly, the budgets introduced by the Conservative Chancellor, Anthony Barber, during the government's first eighteen months shifted the burden of taxation substantially away from companies and the richer tax payers and onto the working class – to the tune of about £2 billion, or some 12 per cent of total revenue. Combined with a reduction in the subsidy given to council house rents (under the Housing Finance Act 1972) and an increase in the charges made for medical care, the class character of the new fiscal policy was unmistakable. It helped to restore declining company post-tax profits, and was supposed to restore incentives to entrepreneurship.

But it also exacerbated the unions' hostility to the fourth main element of the Heath programme, the Industrial Relations Act of 1971. This Act, which came into force in 1972, introduced the North American pattern of legal regulation of industrial conflict by imposing punitive financial sanctions on registered unions whose members took industrial action other than by prescribed procedures. These provided for compulsory 'cooling-off' periods and strike ballots before strikes could be called, and imposed severe penalties for taking industrial action against an employer while an existing contract was in force. Unions were free not to register under the Act, but then they lost their legal immunity from civil actions by employers for breaches of contract. Under the Act, unofficial strikes became either illegal or vulnerable to civil suits; so did 'sympathetic' strikes, the ultimate expression of the solidarity which was the British labour movement's historic source of strength.*

The government's idea was that, having altered the balance of power in favour of employers, it should stand aside from industrial relations and let the 'law of supply and demand' determine the level of wages. It therefore began by abruptly terminating the consultative arrangements between Downing Street and Congress House (the TUC headquarters) which had been established since the war. On the other hand, as a major employer, it set itself to resist all wage claims by public-sector workers above the level it considered in line with the growth of productivity.

But the labour movement's massive opposition to the Industrial Relations Act became the prime cause of the Heath government's eventual defeat. The Trades Union Congress advised all its member unions not to register under the Act and expelled thirty-two small unions which did so. The militancy displayed against the Act was due

---

* Sympathetic strikes had been banned by the Trades Disputes Act of 1927 passed by the Conservative government after the General Strike in the previous year. Repealing the 1927 Act had been one of the first acts of the Attlee government in 1946.

partly to the comprehensive nature of the threat – the unions were in
no doubt that if the Act prevailed, the balance of advantage would
shift decisively to the employers – and partly to the build-up of rank
and file confidence, expectations and organisational experience during
the previous two decades. Militancy had been increased by the Wilson
government's wage controls and by rising inflation, and was now
intensified by the Heath government's fiscal policies (especially by
measures directly affecting workers, such as increased council-house
rents, increased charges for school meals and cuts in subventions to
areas of high unemployment).

The outcome of this struggle showed that, when the unions and their
members were united, they were stronger than the government. In a
strike in January and February 1972 – just before the 1971 Industrial
Relations Act came into force – the mineworkers forced the
government to concede a wage increase three times as big as the Coal
Board's 'final' offer. This strike also revealed extensive public
sympathy for the miners – a sign of life still left in the 'consensus'
which was to cost Heath dearly two years later. Similar confrontations
with the railwaymen and the dockers later in 1972 – the latter bringing
the country to the verge of a general strike – in effect made the
Industrial Relations Act a dead letter within three months of its
introduction. A year later, the Director-General of the Confederation
of British Industries, Campbell Adamson, publicly condemned the Act
as having been responsible for the drastic deterioration in industrial
relations which had marked the Heath years.

The strength of the labour movement forced a radical shift in policy.
Heath's strategy called for an economic expansion if 'market forces'
were to produce the investment boom needed to bring about a radical
improvement in productivity. But expansion would be jeopardised if
large wage increases led to rapidly rising prices, rather than increased
profits and investment. The strikes in the first half of 1972 showed that
the Industrial Relations Act was powerless to prevent this. In the
summer of 1972, therefore, the TUC leadership was suddenly recalled
to Whitehall for discussions on a new voluntary policy of wage
restraint. When these discussions failed, the most comprehensive
system of legal wage controls yet seen was enacted by Parliament in
November 1972. This was a dramatic departure from the philosophy
of the market. It was also keenly resented by the unions, contrasting as
it did with the spectacular gains awarded to the well-to-do in the
Barber budgets of the previous two years.

There now began a dramatic convergence of forces, each indicative
of a different side of the contradiction in which the Heath strategy was
caught. Internationally, the long boom came to an end in 1970.

Competition in world markets for manufactured goods became more intense, and exports harder to sell. 'Hot' money flowed into commodity markets, pushing up commodity prices and causing a sharp increase in Britain's import bill and hence aggravating an inflation already accelerated by expansionary budgets. Retail prices rose on average by 8.4 per cent a year from 1969 to 1973, twice the rate of the preceding four years; the prices of exports were forced up likewise. The expansion also sucked in imports on an unprecedented scale.

The combined result was a haemorrhage in the balance of payments. The 'visible' balance moved from a surplus of £261 million in 1971 (inherited from Wilson's deflationary policies) to a deficit of £722 million in 1972. This was cushioned by an 'invisibles' surplus of £875 million, to leave a modest overall current surplus. To avoid having to halt the economic expansion needed to defend a fixed exchange-rate against speculative selling, the pound had been 'floated'. But in 1973 the visible balance showed a deficit of £2,383 million (only half of which was due to the increase in oil prices following the Egypt–Israel war in October), and the overall current balance was just under £1 billion in deficit. Even with a floating exchange rate, there could now be no question of further expansion. That November, an emergency deflationary budget was introduced. The 'dash for freedom' was over.

Meantime the government was chagrined to find that manufacturers failed to respond to its policies by increasing investment. Real manufacturing investment in each of the years of the Heath government stayed more or less constant, at a level slightly below that of the last years of the Wilson government. As Heath complained to the Institute of Directors in 1973:

> The curse of British industry is that it has never anticipated demand. When we came in we were told there weren't sufficient inducements to invest. So we provided the inducements. Then we were told people were scared of balance of payments difficulties leading to stop-go. So we floated the pound. Then we were told of fears of inflation and now we're dealing with that. And still you aren't investing enough.[3]

But companies voted with their profits, and it was not a vote of confidence in the Heath strategy. Between 1970 and 1973 the volume of direct investment abroad tripled.

Even the policy of cutting back the state had to be abandoned. The Conservatives had particularly set their face against using the state to subsidise failing concerns. The 'competition policy' dictated that inefficient companies should be weeded out to make way for efficient ones. But the government's celebrated commitment 'to gear its policies to the great majority of the people, who are not lame ducks' was broken, in 1971, by the decision to salvage Rolls Royce by nationalising it. In face of the lack of response by industry, the government also felt obliged to return to a system of investment grants and, in 1972, established an Industrial Development Executive, which bore a striking resemblance to Wilson's Industrial Reorganisation Corporation, abolished in 1970.

Heath's 'U-turn', back to the essential strategies of the sixties, resulted, ultimately, from the fact that the electorate was not ready to accept the consequences which a consistent application of 'social market doctrine' to British conditions would have entailed – namely, an industrial recession on a scale not witnessed since the 1930s. Heath himself was also unwilling to accept these consequences (as his subsequent attacks on Thatcher's economic policies demonstrated). When confronted by serious political or social costs, his attempt to revert to the 'corporatist' approach of the previous decade (i.e. seeking to secure union compliance in wage controls through their incorporation with business representatives in consultative economic policy machinery) reflected his strictly qualified commitment to the new conservative creed.

The Egypt–Israel War of October 1973 (which led to a doubling, and later quadrupling, of the price of oil) coincided with the start of Stage 3 of the government's wage control programme, which set a ceiling of seven per cent on wage settlements for the coming year. In November the coalminers, judging that the sudden improvement in the prospects for coal (relative to oil) presented a unique opportunity for them to recover some of the ground in pay which they had lost in relation to other skilled workers since 1946, began an overtime ban to enforce pay claims of between 22 and 46 per cent (depending on the category of worker). Heath responded by declaring a state of emergency under which a variety of measures were taken to conserve coal stocks, culminating at the New Year in a national three-day working week. The TUC nervously sought a compromise, but the miners pressed on and voted for a strike, whereupon Heath called an election for February 1974.

Opinion poll evidence suggested a good deal of public scepticism about the need for this confrontation. What the election result indicated above all was a lack of enthusiasm for both the Conservative and the Labour Parties, both of which lost votes, while six million votes (19 per cent) went to the Liberals, and 600,000 to the Scottish National Party (22 per cent of the Scottish vote). Labour won four more seats than the Conservatives, but had no overall majority. The Liberals, however, declined to keep the Conservatives in office. Heath was obliged to resign and Wilson returned to office as leader of a

BRISTOL POLYTECHNIC
ST. MATTHIAS LIBRARY
FISHPONDS

minority government with Liberal support.

Heath remained leader of the Conservatives for another year. But after losing twenty more seats in the election of October 1974 (called by Wilson in an attempt to secure a parliamentary majority) he paid the penalty by being replaced by Margaret Thatcher, his former Minister of Education, in a leadership contest in February 1975.

Thatcher's victory was seen at the time in largely personal terms – particularly as a revenge by backbenchers offended by Heath's notorious aloofness – as well as an instance of the well-established rule that Tory leaders may not lose more than one election. Heath had lost three, including the election of 1966. But the right wing of the Conservative party in parliament were also opting for a leader who represented a more aggressive brand of right-wing Conservatism, reflecting more faithfully the prejudices on hanging, race, 'communism in the unions', 'welfare scroungers' and the like, which were entertained by their suburban supporters – and, as Thatcher herself shrewdly understood, by large numbers of workers too. Under the Wilson–Callaghan administrations which followed her election as leader, the remaining credit of the social-democratic consensus dwindled still further, while the Conservative Party was being prepared, under Thatcher's leadership, for a right-wing initiative more doctrinaire, radical and unpredictable in its outcome than anything in the party's previous history. Selsdon Woman was to prove a great deal more deadly than Selsdon Man.

The 'Social Contract' 1974–79

Wilson, in contrast to Heath, had retained his leadership of the Labour Party after the 1970 defeat without serious challenge. Responding to the industrial militancy of the rank and file of the party and unions, the 1971 party conference had adopted a more far-reaching programme than anything it had entertained since 1945, including 'a socialist plan of production, based on public ownership, with minimum compensation, of the commanding heights of the economy'.[4] At Wilson's insistence this was later watered down by the National Executive, although the tone of party statements remained radical. The 1974 manifesto pledged 'a fundamental and irreversible shift in the balance of power and wealth in favour of working people and their families'. Nationalisation, however, was promised only for shipbuilding, the aircraft industry and the docks (all ailing sectors). The private sector was otherwise to be brought within the ambit of state planning only by means of selective share purchases by a National Enterprise Board, and by 'Planning

Agreements' between the state and individual large companies. The party also proposed to introduce a measure of 'industrial democracy' in the largest firms.

Tony Benn, who had become the leading spokesman of the party's left wing, declared at the party's 1972 conference: 'the crisis that we inherit when we come to power will be the occasion for fundamental change and not the excuse for postponing it'. But the party was not converted to this view, and when Wilson took office again in February 1974 it had not come to power. It was a minority government, holding office with Liberal and Nationalist party support. It was also a government confronted with a catastrophic balance of payments deficit, inflation accelerating towards twenty per cent and the pent-up frustration of a labour movement more mobilised than ever before – but not, for the most part, any more committed than before to fundamental social and economic change. Wilson, for his part, was as committed as ever to the view that the only realistic goal for Labour was to find an agreed basis for reviving the ailing capitalist economy. The immediate problem was that organised labour was not willing to see profits restored at its expense without any quid pro quo. Heath had deliberately abandoned the institutionalised and regular consultation between the state and the leaderships of organised labour and capital that had been so characteristic of the later fifties and sixties. Wilson now made Labour's special ability to repair the government's relationship with the unions the cornerstone of his policy and of his electoral appeal.

The key phrase in this exercise was the 'social contract', adopted by the party and the TUC to denote the set of understandings between the state, capital and labour on the basis of which the state could look for the labour movement's cooperation with its policies, and which Heath was charged with having destroyed. Wilson undertook to repair the 'social contract' so that the voluntary support of the unions could then be obtained for a new 'incomes policy'.

The immediate necessity was to settle the miners' strike. This was done by accepting the recommendations of the Pay Board, to which Heath had sent the miners' claim before the election, and which gave the miners what they had asked for. The restoration of the 'social contract' was then put in hand. First, trade union rights were restored by a Trade Unions and Industrial Relations Act which repealed the 1971 Industrial Relations Act, and extended the principle of the closed shop, and an Employment Protection Act, which was meant to improve job security by tightening up on unfair dismissal and providing compensation paid by the employer for many categories of redundant worker. A commission was also set up (the Bullock Commission) to make recommendations for 'industrial democracy'.

Second, the 'social wage' – collectively consumed services and social security benefits – was to be increased. The 1972 Housing Finance Act, which had raised council-house rents, was repealed; state pensions and widows' benefits were raised and better indexed against inflation; the tax burden was shifted (slightly) back toward the rich; and price controls were established and prices of some essential foods subsidised. The government later undertook to increase the 'social wage' each year in real terms.

Third, a National Enterprise Board was established to invest public funds in companies in profitable sectors; the nationalisation of shipbuilding and aircraft production was embarked upon. 'Planning Agreements' with the largest firms, covering their employment and investment plans, were to be made by the Department of Industry, headed by Benn.

Having outlined this strategy for securing trade union cooperation and state-directed industrial recovery, Wilson called an election in October. The result was equivocal. The Labour vote actually fell slightly, but the Conservative vote fell further, by 1.4 million, and the Liberals also suffered a setback (see Table 5.1). Labour emerged with an overall majority of three seats, too small for a reliable 'working' majority. But in an effort to head off the Scottish National Party's challenge in Scotland (a traditional Labour stronghold) the party had promised to legislate for a Scottish Assembly with devolved powers. The SNP, with 30 per cent of the Scottish vote in October, and eleven MPs, calculated that an Assembly could be used as a stepping stone towards real independence, and so decided to support the government. The Welsh Nationalists, with three MPs, and the Liberals with thirteen, also gave qualified support. (The devolution offer extended to Wales too, although Welsh opinion was much less strongly nationalist – see Chapter 12.) The government could govern, on this basis – if it could resolve the immediate economic crisis.

By the end of 1974 the rate of inflation was 23 per cent, and over the twelve months from July 1974 to July 1975 it rose to more than 26 per cent. Over the same period money earnings rose nearly 28 per cent. Meantime the current balance of payments deficit for 1974 was no less than £3.6 billion (on visible trade alone it was £5.2 billion, offset by a surplus of £1.6 billion on invisible trade). The deficit was covered partly by the inflow of funds for investment by foreign companies in the North Sea oilfields, and partly by short-term foreign loans. By May 1975, however, it was clear that a final crisis was not far off. Labour's claim to be able to deliver union cooperation in stabilising the economy was now to be tested.

The initiative was taken by the one man who had the real authority to do so: Jack Jones, leader of the two million workers in the Transport and General Workers Union. He proposed a voluntary agreement to restrict wage claims in 1975–6 to a flat rate maximum of £6 per week, with no increase in incomes over £8,500 per annum – an agreement that would hurt the lowest-paid workers least. This was accepted by the government and the TUC and implemented with remarkable fidelity. (To anticipate, it was followed by a further agreement for 1976–7, to limit claims to a maximum increase of 4.5 per cent or £4 per week, and in 1977–8, although the unions declined to enter into any further agreement, many of them conformed in practice to the government's wish for a ceiling of 10 per cent. Estimates of the effects of this restraint vary, but it is generally agreed that over the years 1975–7, manual workers as a whole experienced a cut in real income of between 7 and 8 per cent compared with 1974; a loss which was largely made up, however, in 1978.)

On this basis Wilson hoped to get some industrial recovery, and foreign support for interim measures to cover the balance of payments deficit. But this was too optimistic. For one thing the world trade recession (after a temporary revival in 1971–3) severely limited the prospect of any recovery of exports. Secondly, the level of public consumption implied in the social contract was higher than foreign creditors thought the economy could afford. Thirdly, there was a general loss of 'business confidence', focused largely on Benn, the left-wing Secretary of State for Industry.

To meet these reservations, the government introduced deflationary measures in November 1974, and began to redistribute the tax burden away from company profits again. In June 1975, taking advantage of a national referendum decision in favour of remaining in the EEC (on somewhat modified terms), Wilson also removed Benn, who had led the campaign for a 'no' vote, from the Department of Industry to the Department of Energy. This spelled the end of any attempt to use the National Enterprise Board or Planning Agreements to extend public ownership or public participation in the economic policy-making of the large-firm ('meso-economic') sector. The only novel elements in Labour's approach to the industrial crisis were thus abandoned in favour of the familiar and self-destructive policy of deflation, just as the National Plan had been abandoned in 1965–6.

In March 1976, Wilson retired, professing himself confident that things were on course for a recovery, and was succeeded as leader and Prime Minister by his Foreign Secretary, James Callaghan. But by this time it was clear that foreign capital was not yet convinced that the balance of payments gap would be closed, and a movement out of sterling began which took the value of the pound down from US$2.02 in January 1976 to US$1.63 in September (it had been US$2.60 at the end of 1971). A devaluation on this scale entailed all sorts of new and intractable problems. To reverse it by a corresponding scale of deflation would, thought Callaghan and the Chancellor of the Exchequer, Denis Healey, court political instability (see Chapter 2, p. 24). The only remaining option – short of abandoning the capitalist system and declaring the whole economy public property, which could not have been further from their thoughts – was to seek a transitional foreign loan. In June 1976, a $5 billion loan was obtained from foreign central banks, but for only six months.

By September, with $1.5 billion of this loan used up, the government accepted the need to seek a longer-term loan from the International Monetary Fund, even though this would inevitably entail drastic deflationary policies.[5] At the same time, the government lost its parliamentary majority as a result of a series of by elections. It was sustained in office only by the SNP for the sake of the Scotland Bill, and by the Liberals for the sake of electoral 'credibility' as a party able to influence events – a strategy which eventually led, in March 1977, to an official 'pact' between Callaghan and the Liberal leader, David Steel.

From this point onwards, the Callaghan government's policy was almost entirely subordinated to the deflationary goals set by the IMF, although Healey also became convinced of their necessity. By 1978–9 total government spending had risen 11 per cent over the 1973–4 level; but this was largely due to increased spending on debt interest, unemployment pay (the number of people unemployed had risen from 600,000 in 1974 to 1.5 million in 1978), and subsidies to employers to maintain employment. Plans to expand provision in other fields were cut back, and in some areas spending was reduced below 1973–4 levels.[6] The 'social wage' also stagnated, increasing by only 0.3 per cent in real terms over the whole period 1974–9. The National Enterprise Board made no acquisitions except to prevent various large enterprises, such as Ferranti and British Leyland, from collapsing with the consequent loss of large numbers of jobs and long-term industrial capacity. The only Planning Agreements concluded were with the Chrysler Corporation, at the time of the government's attempt to induce the company, by a large loan, not to close its Scottish subsidiary in 1975 – and with the National Coal Board! The Bullock Commission's recommendations in 1977 for a system of trade union representation on the boards of directors of all large firms were strenuously opposed by the Confederation of British Industry and later dropped.

As for industrial recovery, it was further away than ever. British exports continued to expand more slowly than the volume of world trade; British productivity continued to rise more slowly than that of France, Germany or Japan. Manufacturing output fell by 6 per cent in 1974–5 and rose by only 4.4 per cent from 1975 to 1979. By the end of the decade 'deindustrialisation' had become a large and ominous reality. In Northern Ireland, which had passed under direct rule from Whitehall in 1972, nothing could be done, except, possibly, with massive expenditures, but these were out of the question. Likewise, nothing was done about the scandal of racial discrimination in jobs, housing and in other fields.[7] The only clear accomplishments of these years were, first, that the Labour government approached the end of this decade, like the last, with its inherited balance of payments deficit more or less eliminated – partly thanks to the level of deflation (i.e., unemployment and idle plants leading to fewer imports), and partly because of rapidly growing North Sea oil production; and second, that inflation had eventually fallen back to 9.5 per cent, little more than its pre-1974 level. The situation had been stabilised – but at the cost of a more or less complete social stasis.

It now fell to the unions, for the third time in a decade, to destroy the fragile (and increasingly opportunistic) political balance. The patience of many workers – especially the lower-paid – was wearing thin. The recovery which had been so often promised in return for their sacrifices seemed more remote than ever. In 1978, the TUC refused Callaghan's request for a fourth year of wage restraint. In September, when all commentators judged that he would be well advised to call an election, he instead called for a new wage ceiling of 5 per cent, a call which was rejected by the Labour Party Conference. Meanwhile the workers at Ford (UK), which had declared profits for 1977 of £246 million, judging (not unreasonably) that most of this would not be invested in Britain but would be remitted to Detroit, demanded a wage increase of 30 per cent. After a strike lasting seventeen weeks, they accepted 19 per cent. The dam now broke in a series of large-scale strikes throughout what also proved to be one of the coldest winters in living memory. The low-paid public sector unions were particularly involved, from ambulance drivers to street-cleaners and school janitors. The snow lay in Regent Street, with no one to to clear it away. Rubbish accumulating in normally wholesome districts was not collected. Schools were closed.

While the 'winter of discontent' continued, referenda were held in Scotland and Wales on the proposed devolution of powers from Westminster. Opponents of devolution inside the Labour Party had joined with Conservatives to amend the Scotland Bill to the effect that unless at least 40 per cent of the whole Scottish electorate voted 'yes', the government would not be bound to establish a Scottish Assembly. On 1 March 1979, 52 per cent of those voting voted 'yes', but they constituted only 33 per cent of the electorate, and Callaghan reasonably judged that this did not warrant implementing the devolution scheme. The SNP members of parliament vented their frustration by deciding to support a motion of no confidence moved by Margaret Thatcher later in March. The Liberals had also abandoned the 'pact' with Labour in 1978 after Labour MPs had voted against the use of proportional representation for elections to the European Parliament (which Liberals had seen as an important precedent for a future change in the British electoral system). So the vote of no confidence was carried against the government, and an election was called for May.

Thatcher, aided by a media campaign which suggested mounting middle-class hysteria, attacked the unions and argued, effectively enough, that Labour's claim to be able to secure union wage restraint was empty. The state, she declared, was a rigid, overgrown and parasitic obstacle to economic recovery, not an instrument of prosperity or welfare. She promised to cut income tax as well as state spending and adopted a position on immigration that was seen as explicitly racist. The result was a massive swing of 2.2 million votes to the Conservatives (including an 18 per cent swing among skilled manual workers), producing a Conservative majority of forty-one. The SNP paid the price of their pique, being reduced from eleven MPs to two. In the accelerating development of the crisis, the moment of 'Thatcherism' had arrived.

Notes

1 A. Gamble, *The Conservative Nation*, Routledge and Kegan Paul, London 1974, p. 91.
2 D. Butler and A. Sloman, *British Political Facts*, Macmillan, London 1980, p. 254.
3 *The Times*, 8 June 1973.
4 1971 Labour Party Conference Report.
5 On the operation of the IMF see Cheryl Payer, *The Debt Trap*, Penguin, Harmondsworth 1974.
6 See A. Glyn and J. Harrison, *The British Economic Disaster*, Pluto Press, London 1980, p. 121 for an analysis of the figures.
7 See D.J. Smith, *Racial Disadvantage in Britain*, Penguin, Harmondsworth 1977.

The New Conservative Project
of Margaret Thatcher

The failure of the 'social contract' as a basis for economic recovery had finally driven British politics towards a radical realignment. For the first time the leadership of a major party was committed to a project which went to the heart of the relationship between capital and labour. Thatcher had long subscribed to the individualist, anti-state, anti-union, anti-egalitarian views of her party's right wing. Shortly before her election as leader she also adopted the 'social market' and monetarist economic doctrines to which her friend and counsellor Sir Keith Joseph had recently been converted. Unlike the 'competition policy' of Edward Heath, Thatcher's vision included drastically curtailing, if not dismantling, the welfare state, as fast as electoral considerations allowed; effecting the decisive reduction in trade union power from which Heath had drawn back after the failure of his 1971 Industrial Relations Act; reducing the power of any and all institutions seen as representing 'socialism', from the BBC to Labour-controlled local authorities; and overcoming social and cultural resistance to a new order based on hard work, inequality, and the firm imposition of authority in the workshop and in the streets, by means of 'firm government' and an ideological crusade lasting, if necessary, for a decade or more. Whether realistic or not, the new strategy had a coherent logic. Unlike Heath, its proponents were not only ready to accept the social costs of restoring 'incentives' by creating mass unemployment, but judged that the public could be persuaded to accept them too.

The ideological movement which 'Thatcherism' represented was as important as its economic policies, and perhaps more so. Some observers argued that its long-run significance would lie primarily in the extent to which it succeeded in completing the break-up of the amalgam of ideas which composed the post-war social-democratic consensus (Fabian faith in the state, Keynesian commitment to full employment, and Liberal commitment to social security); and only secondarily in what it achieved through economic policies in office. The campaign to link the pro-market, anti-state doctrines of Thatcherism to popular Conservative themes such as the call for 'law and order' versus 'crime' and 'terrorism', 'the family' versus 'vandalism' or 'permissiveness', 'hard work' versus 'welfare scroungers', and so on, certainly gave it more popular appeal than the Labour Left's advocacy of the Alternative Economic Strategy (see pp. 108–9) which had no such 'populist' dimension.

Moreover, the 'consensus' values which it attacked had by now been seriously undermined. The Labour Party could no longer deliver material rewards to the workers when in office; the credibility of the Fabian, full-employment welfare state had been seriously impaired. The state which people encountered as school parents or state employees, or when they were retired, unemployed, or sick, often seemed patronising, bureaucratic and mean, rather than an instrument of the popular will. The working class itself had been undergoing some profound changes, too, as we shall see in Chapters 8 and 9. The 'common style of proletarian life' of the 1930s and 1940s, with which the welfare state had been so intimately linked, had begun to break up. For both these reasons commitment to the 'welfare state' was no longer 'second nature', as it had been for the previous generation. It was no longer unthinkable for workers to be hostile to the state; it had at length become possible, Thatcher realised, to fight an election campaign on a platform explicitly *attacking* equality. This was the essential basis of the radical transformation in British politics that was ushered in by the general election of June 1979.

In this election the Conservatives won 43.9 per cent of the vote and 339 seats, giving them an overall majority in the House of Commons of 43. In 1983, with a slightly lower share of the vote (42.4 per cent), they raised their majority to 144. In 1987, with 42.3 per cent, their majority was 102 (see Table 7.1). Mrs Thatcher had always maintained that it would take at least two parliaments for her programme for reversing Britain's decline to take effect. Thanks to the weakness and divisions of the opposition, she not only secured a third term: a fourth and even a fifth were not out of the question. The 1980s became the decade of Thatcherism, and it was not impossible that the 1990s would be another.

The question of how the crisis would be resolved was thus settled decisively against the project of the Labour left, who ended the decade of the 1980s marginalised and discredited. It was also settled against

Table 7.1   General Election Results 1979–1987

| | Votes Cast | | | | | |
| | 1979 | | 1983 | | 1987 | |
	m.	%	m.	%	m.	%
Conservative	13.7	43.9	13.0	42.4	13.8	42.3
Labour	11.5	36.9	8.5	27.6	10.0	30.8
Liberal	4.3	13.8				
Liberal–SDP Alliance			7.8	25.4	7.3	22.6
Plaid Cymru	0.1	0.4	0.1	0.4	0.1	0.4
SNP	0.5	1.6	0.3	1.1	0.4	1.3
Others	1.0	3.3	1.0	3.2	0.8	2.6
Total	31.2	100.0	30.7	100.0	32.5	100.0

| | Seats Won | | |
	1979	1983	1987
Conservative	339	397	376
Labour	269	209	229
Liberal	11		
Liberal–SDP Alliance		23	22
Plaid Cymru	2	2	3
SNP	2	2	3
Others	12	17	17
Total	635	650	650

Source: Keesings Contemporary Archives.

any renewal of 'consensus' politics: the Labour Party failed to retain enough electoral support outside the old industrial heartlands, while the Liberal–SDP Alliance (formed in 1981 – see pp. 249–55 below) failed to secure enough electoral support at the centre of the political spectrum to establish a significant 'third force' in parliament. The opportunity to try to resolve the crisis was given exclusively to Mrs Thatcher and her supporters in the Conservative Party.

Testing Time: June 1979–December 1981

The first two and half years of office were critical in determining whether Mrs Thatcher would be able to carry out her project. During

BRISTOL POLYTECHNIC
ST. MATTHIAS LIBRARY
FISHPONDS

this time she had to secure acquiescence in the social costs of switching to a 'market-based' economic strategy, both among the electorate and within her own party.

This meant, above all, an early and severe deflation, which would force companies to cut costs and become more efficient while driving up unemployment and lowering the trade unions' ability and will to resist reduced manning levels and changed working practices. The ostensible rationale for deflation was the attack on inflation, which neo-conservatives everywhere identify as the prime enemy on both moral and economic grounds. The chosen weapon was to be control of the money supply. In practice, the government never succeeded in meeting its own monetary targets: the real weapons of choice were cuts in public expenditure and interest rate and exchange rate management. The precise effects of government economic policy in the years 1979–81 are disputed; probably the best estimate is that government policies caused between two-fifths and a half of the total increase in unemployment during this period (an increase of 1.35 million, to a total of 2.4 million by the end of 1981).[1] Maintaining the base interest rate at 17 per cent for almost twelve months from the autumn of 1979 raised manufacturers' costs and led to a steep rise in the exchange rate of the pound, and hence a drastic loss in competitiveness for most British exports; this accelerated the spate of factory closures and contributed substantially to the 14 per cent drop in manufacturing output that occurred between 1979 and 1981.

Meanwhile exchange controls were lifted, and not surprisingly, in these circumstances, led to a dramatic exodus of capital: the total value of British privately owned assets abroad rose from £6.3 billion in 1979 to £24.3 billion in December 1981. This led to an increase in the flow of interest and dividends back into Britain, partly offsetting the growing deficit in the non-oil balance of trade caused by the continuing competitive weakness of manufacturing; but the funds that had been sent abroad were funds that might otherwise have been invested in Britain to remedy that weakness. The government's view was that the outflow of funds showed that this last alternative would not have been good economics: the market had shown that investing these funds in Britain would have been a waste of resources.

Besides the drastic increase in unemployment, other early economic measures of the Thatcher government were also bound to be unpopular. A large increase in value-added tax, to raise more revenue from indirect taxation, contributed to a big increase in inflation in the short run (up from about 9 per cent in May 1979 to a peak of 21.9 per cent in May 1980, before falling back to 12 per cent in December 1981); and by this means and others successive budgets transferred the burden of taxation away from the rich and towards the poor (see Table 7.2). The salaries of most civil servants were de-linked from those of comparable personnel in the private sector and in effect frozen, while the police and the armed services and judges received large pay increases in line with the government's pledge to 'strengthen law and order'.

The initial public spending cuts fell largely on capital expenditure, followed by reductions in the number of civil service jobs (from 732,000 to 599,000 between 1979 and 1981) rather than in the level of social security benefits;[2] although savings were also gradually made in these (for instance by indexing pensions to the level of inflation rather than to real earnings, so that pensioners' real incomes no longer kept pace with the living standards of the rest of the population), the government at first refrained from any direct attack on social security or the main institutions of the welfare state. As a result, the share of state spending in total GDP actually rose instead of declining, due to the rapid rise in unemployment pay and the decline in GDP. It was not until 1987–8 that the proportion of GDP spent by the state fell below the 43 per cent that it had reached under Labour in 1978–9.

The costs of the new strategy were largely borne by the unemployed, not the population as a whole. The question for the government was thus whether the cabinet, Conservative backbenchers and the Conservative rank and file would remain steady long enough for the return to permanent unemployment of over 10 per cent to become accepted. In 1980–81 this battle was fought and won by Mrs Thatcher and her cabinet allies against other cabinet ministers in charge of the big spending departments, and especially against the more prominent 'Heathmen', or 'wets', of whom she still had at least half a dozen in her cabinet. In fact in the summer and autumn of 1980 she failed to

Table 7.2 Incidence of income-tax changes 1979–1987

Earnings	£ per year	Average tax rates* (%)	
	1987	1979	1987
Half average	5,800	13.9	16.3
Average	11,600	26.0	25.5
2 × average	23,200	30.5	28.5
5 × average	58,000	51.6	43.5

* For a married man with two children, taking account of national insurance contributions and child benefits.

Source: Economist May 23 1987.

persuade the cabinet to support further spending cuts on the scale she and the Treasury wanted; to compensate for this she called for and got a severely deflationary budget in March 1981, when unemployment had already passed two million.

This was the testing time. Mrs Thatcher's leadership was not initially popular within the parliamentary Conservative Party; she was seen as having become leader through a bold coup, made possible by Heath's refusal to stand down and the reluctance of his senior colleagues to stand against him, rather than through any established claim to the succession. Her determination to face down opposition to her tough economic stance at first relied heavily on the party's traditional support for its leader when in office, and on the fear of the consequences of another Labour government. Even so, Thatcher's repeated insistence that 'there is no alternative' began to lose its rallying power as unemployment reached 1930s levels and as riots broke out in a dozen inner cities in July 1981, following pitched street battles with the police in London's Brixton and Liverpool's Toxteth. In October the President of the Confederation of British Industry voiced the discontent of the large manufacturing companies that were suffering huge losses under the government's interest rate and exchange rate policies, although this was quickly muted by others in the Confederation's leadership. In the same month the Conservative Party Conference also showed itself deeply unhappy, as public opinion polls registered intense dissatisfaction with the results of the deflation, and with Mrs Thatcher personally (in the December 1981 Gallup Poll only 25 per cent approved of her as Prime Minister, the lowest level of any premier since 1945).

But in January 1982 public opinion began to move the other way. While people still said unemployment was the most important problem facing the country, they gradually ceased to hold the government responsible for it. Levels of unemployment which had been considered 'unthinkable' (the official level was 10.3 per cent by December 1981, and would peak at 12 per cent in the autumn of 1985 – the reality was closer to the male unemployment rates of 12.8 per cent and 14.3 per cent at these two dates) slowly came to be accepted as inevitable, if not yet taken for granted.[3] As the worldwide economic recovery began in 1983, led by the 'military Keynesianism' of the Reagan administration in the USA (i.e. high levels of military expenditure financed by unprecedented budget deficits), and accelerated in 1983–4, the real disposable incomes of those in work began to rise too – achieving, ultimately, an average annual increase of 3 per cent over the years 1982 to 1987, the highest ever achieved over a similar length of time.

In retrospect, it seems likely that by April 1982 the government's danger-point had already been passed. The psychological and moral map of British politics had already begun to be redrawn. The 'winners' – the employed, in general, and the higher-paid, including skilled manual workers, in particular – began to endorse the philosophy of individualism. It worked for them, while the 'losers' – the 2.8 million unemployed and their families, the low-paid, whose taxes had risen, the single-parent families and the sick and the elderly, dependent on reduced state benefits – all came to be seen more and more as unfortunates, who deserved sympathy (perhaps – the neo-conservative condemnation of 'welfare scroungers', single mothers, and the like, found some popular response) but whose needs could no longer be the test of government policy: they were not *productive*.

This shift in public thinking would take another five years to become fully apparent, and would not be more than that – a shift – during the 1980s. Even in 1987 a large majority even of Conservative voters expressed themselves to pollsters as being in favour of more state spending on social services, even if it meant higher taxes. The social-democratic values of fairness and collective responsibility for meeting basic needs were far from being wholly rejected. But in 1983 only 27.6 per cent of voters voted for the Labour Party, the only party that consistently stood for this policy, and 42.4 per cent continued to vote for the Conservatives, who were committed to cutting taxes, not improving services.

Mrs Thatcher's success in winning second and third terms probably owed a great deal to her very inflexibility: her insistence on the necessity of her policies ensured that however unpopular they were, the debate took place on ground chosen by her. This was strikingly illustrated in a series of departures from the style of government that had been familiar throughout the consensus years: in Northern Ireland, where in 1981 ten hunger strikers in the Maze prison were allowed to die rather than be granted any concessions: in the 1981 riots, where the government refused to hold social conditions in the inner cities responsible, stressing only the need to repress criminal behaviour; and not least in the handling of industrial disputes.

Whereas previous governments, including Heath's, could be relied upon to try to mediate in prolonged major strikes, in order to minimise the cost to the economy, the Thatcher government stood aside and allowed a series of strikes to run their course, such as the engineering workers' strike in August 1979, or the two-month strike at the British Steel Corporation in early 1980. Tactical retreats were executed, most notably in order to avoid a coal strike in 1981: but by 1982 the level of strike action was falling dramatically, along with union membership, as unemployment rose. The government's legislation to limit union powers – the Employment Acts of 1980 and 1982 – reinforced but did not cause this trend: 'flying pickets' (sending union members from one part of the country to join mass pickets in another), which had been the miners' key weapon in 1972, were made liable to civil action by employers, along with sympathy strikes and secondary action (such as the refusal by members of another union to handle the products of a company whose workers are on strike), and several other practices based on the British labour movement's most important traditional asset – political solidarity. But that solidarity was weakening anyway. Unlike Heath's ill-fated Industrial Relations Act of 1971, the 1980 and 1982 Employment Acts and the 1984 Trade Union Act (which regulated the unions' internal affairs and limited the closed shop) were designed to overcome opposition by taking only a few steps at a time, rather than all at once. But even they would not have been so feebly opposed if they had been introduced in 1971. The militancy of those years was gradually forgotten. The TUC called for a 'Day of Action' (a one-day general strike) on 14 May 1980, to protest against the government's policies, including the first Employment Act. The response to this call for token action was very modest (less than a million workers stopped work).

Meanwhile, in her ultimately successful efforts to reduce Britain's budgetary contribution to the EEC, Mrs Thatcher's intransigence was seen in action on behalf of the whole nation. While the Falklands War in April–June 1982 was to display these qualities to much greater effect, the image of the 'iron lady' had been established well before it. The vision of the future painted by Mrs Thatcher might be narrow, commercial, tasteless and unfeeling – 'a cross between Victorian England and today's Japan located somewhere in Esher' as Peter Riddell put it – and propounded in disagreeably hectoring tones, but it was consistent. As voters contemplated their options, they might not share her certainties, but they could be increasingly sure that she would continue to subscribe to them.

By contrast, the opposition was deeply divided, and presented no clear alternative vision of the future. Following its defeat in 1979 the Labour Party entered on an acute internal struggle between its left wing, led by Benn and supported by a majority of the party's constituency activists, and the centrist social democrats in the parliamentary party's leadership.

While the new right had been coming to power in the Conservative Party in the 1970s an opposite tendency had been gaining ground in the Labour Party. The failures of the Wilson government in the sixties, and the militancy of the union rank and file, led to the adoption of much more radical policies by party conferences after the 1970 defeat. Out of these emerged an 'Alternative Economic Strategy' (AES) which gradually crystallised as the left's response to the crisis of the economy. Its essential elements were economic expansion, led by increased state expenditure; a reduced working week of 35 hours, to spread employment; nationalisation of some 25 major companies and all banks, with planning agreements (reinforced by industrial democracy) for the rest of the large-firm sector; and import controls, to permit expansion without precipitating a new balance of payments crisis (most observers agreed that British manufacturing was now so weak that even the large contribution of North Sea oil would not be enough to avert a payments problem in any large-scale reflation). Prices would also be controlled, but not wages. Most of the strategy's supporters also advocated withdrawal from the EEC in order to recover the freedom of action necessary to implement this strategy. This latter argument had been defeated in the 1975 referendum, and in office after 1975 Wilson, Callaghan and Healey had also abandoned the other elements of the strategy; but it became the common platform of the various 'left' tendencies in the party and was reasserted by a large majority at the 1979 Party Conference following the election defeat.

Among the AES's many problems the most obvious was that it assumed that a Labour government would be able to secure from the private sector (through competition from 'selectively' nationalised firms, through state control of investment funds and through planning agreements plus worker representatives on boards of directors) what the private sector had not given to Heath – namely, massive new investment. Moreover, this would be expected to happen in the context of controlled prices (but not wages) and, presumably, revived trade union strength. As critics to the left of the Labour Party pointed out, this seemed to assume away the problem caused by lack of 'business confidence' in the past. Only experience could show whether it was indeed all wishful thinking, whether the strategy really implied going beyond a state-led mixed economy to a wholly state-owned, socialist economy – and whether political support for this could be secured.

Up to 1981, however, its advocates inside the Labour Party were less concerned with such problems, critical as they were, than with the problem of how to ensure that any such alternative strategy would ever be put to the test of experience – how to ensure that, in future, a Labour government would not abandon any radical strategy adopted by the party conference. Seeing the history of the party as a series of such 'betrayals', the Labour left – its ranks swollen by a new influx of activists into the party, including Marxists of various tendencies – concentrated most of its energy after 1975 on a struggle to make the parliamentary wing of the party more accountable to the party outside parliament. In this they were aided by a growing impatience among many trade union activists. In 1979 the Conference finally endorsed two of the three internal reforms for which the left had been pressing: the National Executive would have final control over the content of election manifestos (rather than the leader alone); and Labour MPs would be required to submit to 'reselection' by their constituency parties between general elections. In September 1980 the Conference also decided that the party leader himself would no longer be chosen by the Labour Members of Parliament, but would be elected by an electoral college in which constituency and union representatives would also take part. The precise formula for the electoral college was to be determined at a special conference at Wembley in January 1981.

Faced with this development, in October 1980 Callaghan announced his retirement, with a view to allowing a 'moderate' leader to be chosen by the MPs under the existing rules. The leading candidate was Denis Healey, the former Chancellor of the Exchequer, whose choicest invective was apt to be reserved for the party's left wing (they must, he said, be 'out of their tiny Chinese minds'). MPs hesitated to plunge the party into the struggle which this intransigence portended and chose instead Michael Foot. Foot was a former leader of the party's left-wing Tribune Group, lukewarm towards the EEC, committed to unilateral nuclear disarmament, and broadly sympathetic to the Alternative Economic Strategy. On the other hand he was a passionate 'parliamentarian' who was not identified with the left's drive for extra-parliamentary control. Before the Wembley special Conference the National Executive adopted a compromise proposal put forward by Foot for an electoral college, according to which half the delegates would be MPs. But the Conference adopted a formula which gave 40 per cent of the delegates to the unions, 30 per cent to representatives of the constituency parties, and only 30 per cent to the MPs.

The stage was thus set for a trial of strength between left and right within the party. The reselection process made no dramatic impact in the short run. Much more dramatic was the decision by Tony Benn to contest the annual election (provided for under the party's rules) for the deputy leadership, an election which was covered by the new electoral college rules. The deputy leadership was a largely symbolic office whose incumbent, chosen by the Labour MPs in 1980, was Healey. Benn was narrowly defeated, after a bruising and deeply divisive campaign lasting through the summer of 1981.

Throughout this struggle Foot exercised no effective leadership and the point of choosing him as a compromise candidate was entirely lost. Not only did the Benn–Healey contest divide the party in the most public way, but a still more damaging split within the party had meantime occurred when in January 1981, following the Wembley Conference, four former Labour ministers – Roy Jenkins, Shirley Williams, David Owen and Bill Rodgers – announced their intention of forming a new Social Democratic Party.

Coming from the Labour Party's right wing, the 'Gang of Four' saw little future for themselves in the party's leadership under the new constitution. On the other hand, given the unpopularity of the government's policies in 1981, and what they saw, with some justice, as the equal lack of popular support for the ideas of the Labour left, they judged that they had nothing to lose, and perhaps everything to gain, by making a bid for the political 'centre ground' in a radically transformed party system. Foot's ineffectual leadership offered no countervailing force, and so the SDP was officially launched in March 1981. By the end of the year it had attracted twenty-four sitting Labour MPs, and one Conservative, and had acquired two additional MPs through by-election victories in Croydon and the Liverpool suburb of Crosby in November, to make a total of twenty-seven. Almost as soon as the party was formed it entered into an alliance with the Liberals, with a view to combining the existing Liberal vote with whatever votes the SDP could attract from Labour. By December 1981 50 per cent of all voters were telling opinion polls that they would vote for the Alliance. While this proportion fell back to 33 per cent by February 1982, this was still the same level of support as Labour's, and clearly implied the possibility of a third party breakthrough.

Faced with this threat, the trade union leadership determined to put an end to Labour's inner-party conflict. At another special conference, in January 1982 at Bishop's Stortford, Benn agreed not to contest the deputy leadership again, while the right wing agreed to accept the 1980–81 constitutional changes. However, the spectacle of the conflicts, as reported by media which seemed as hostile to Labour as they were enthusiastic about the Alliance, had given an incalculable advantage to Thatcher. Even if the Falkland Islands had not been invaded, she might well have been in a position to win an election as early as the autumn of 1982, had she been so inclined. The Falklands War, however, converted a probability into a certainty.

The Rewards of Populism: January 1982–June 1983

On 2 April 1982 Argentine forces occupied the Falkland Islands. Lord Carrington, the Foreign Secretary, resigned. A military task force was assembled and despatched to the South Atlantic. Less than three months later, after more than 1,000 people had been killed, and at a cost to the Treasury of £1.6 billion, the 1,800 residents of the islands were once again subject to British rule. In economic terms it was a Pyrrhic victory. The islands were a colonial company sheep estate, surviving by paying very low wages to the indigenous workforce which was, as a result, steadily contracting (the post-war population was expected to drop to 1,000, and there were already more Falkland Islanders in Argentina than in the Falklands). To defend the islands now required a garrison of 4,000, at an estimated cost of over £400 million per annum (not counting the cost of repairing war damage, or a further £100 million which it was proposed to spend on economic development). The diplomatic costs were also severe: the support obtained from the countries of the European Community had to be paid for (as became clear when the 'Luxembourg compromise' on the EEC budget was overridden at Britain's expense in May), while Britain's position in Latin America deteriorated severely.

But in Britain the result was a dramatic reversal of the Conservatives' political fortunes. In the opinion polls support for the Conservatives rose to over 50 per cent in June. In the local government elections held in May the Conservatives made substantial gains – unprecedented since 1945 for a government in mid-term – which were followed by an equally unprecedented by-election victory in Mitcham and Morden in south London.

This remarkable reversal of fortunes was due to Mrs Thatcher's skilful exploitation of the issues raised by the war. Dipping deep into the well of frustrated national pride and nostalgia for a lost imperial past, she presented herself and her governnent as the defenders of freedom against tyranny in the tradition of Churchill. Critics of the war, including Benn and a handful of Labour left MPs, were vilified as traitors, as were television producers who did not identify themselves unambiguously with the cause for which 'our boys' were fighting. Military success gradually overcame an initial public reluctance to endorse the shedding of blood; and with the final victory, the 'Falklands factor' became a formidable electoral asset. The media obsession with the war was reinforced by a succession of publicity dramas – official visits from the Pope and President Reagan and the birth of a son to Princess Diana – followed by a series of receptions for returning heroes attended by the Prime Minister and Prince Charles: a protracted visual celebration of nation, church and crown.

To say that Conservative confidence was restored by the Falklands War would be a great understatement. While dismissing talk of a snap election (which the evidence suggested would produce a Conservative landslide), Thatcherite leaders talked of 'an irreversible shift in the balance of the economy, as represented by the private sector' which another Conservative victory would make possible. The Chancellor of the Exchequer foreshadowed a policy of zero pay increases and a new programme of privatisation.

From the middle of 1982, also, the economy began to feel the benefit of the worldwide trade expansion. Profits recovered with the increase in domestic and export sales. Plant closures and layoffs slowed down. Unemployment stabilised at three million in 1985 and real personal incomes (for those in work) began to rise again. The government introduced new programmes to give 'job training' to unemployed workers. Output per person-hour in manufacturing rose sharply in 1981–2, due partly to the closure of the least efficient plants, partly to reduced 'overmanning', and partly to the more efficient use of the workers who remained. Although total output and incomes were well below what they probably would have been without the 'squeeze', people in work began to feel better off again.

In the meantime Thatcher had purged her cabinet of some of the leading 'wets' and prosecuted her programme with growing confidence. The programme of 'privatising' nationalised industries and council houses was accelerated. Privatisation had not been a major plank in the party's 1979 platform, and the earliest sales were relatively modest in scale, mostly relating to medium-sized companies that happened to be state-owned, not to the big industrial monopolies taken into public ownership by Labour between 1946 and 1951. However, the Chancellor of the Exchequer, in his search for ways to reduce the budget deficit, found the proceeds of these early sales useful (see Chapter 14, pp. 330–32); and by 1983 the government was beginning to envisage a programme of selling off virtually the entire state-owned sector at the rate of some £4–5 billion a year until the early 1990s. Not only would this allow for tax cuts sooner than would otherwise have been possible, it would also reduce the political influence of the trade unions involved, whose members would no longer be able to imagine that the government would help meet their wage demands by means of subsidies; and if the shares were priced low enough, privatisation might also create millions of grateful new shareholders, and at the same time make it virtually impossible for a future Labour government to contemplate renationalisation.

The sale of council houses to their tenants at substantial discounts (related to their length of tenancy) was motivated by a straightforward wish to create a new property-owning segment of the working-class electorate, while simultaneously weakening one of the bastions of traditional Labour support, the council housing estate. By mid-1983 about 315,000 houses had been sold, giving their new owners a chance to share in economic growth through the equity in their houses (and in the government's tax spending through mortgage interest relief), a chance that had hitherto been denied to the working class. 'Popular capitalism' (a phrase coined by the Conservative Chancellor, Nigel Lawson, in 1982) ceased to be pure rhetoric.

Nonetheless the scale of the Conservative victory in 1983 owed much more to the weakness of the opposition, and especially the Labour Party, than to a conviction that Thatcherism was 'working' – i.e. securing the longed-for economic transformation of Britain. Although inflation was down (reaching what would prove to be its lowest level for years to come at 3.7 per cent in May 1983), evidence of a major long-term change was as yet lacking. But besides its disunity, the Labour Party was ill-led and lacked a persuasive economic policy. The Alternative Economic Strategy, with its emphasis on state-led expansion via extended ownership and industrial intervention, seemed to resemble too much the failed formula of the 1970s, and the party's leadership was unable to convince the public that its policies would not lead only to renewed inflation. The party's commitment to leaving the EEC, and to eliminating all nuclear weapons from British soil (a policy strongly criticised on the eve of the election by the former leader and Prime Minister, Callaghan), also hurt it; while Foot's tired and confused rhetoric had lost all power to convince. Labour's support melted away during the last weeks of the campaign, partly to the advantage of the Alliance, but chiefly to that of Mrs Thatcher, who was able, thanks to the evenly divided opposition, to win a massively increased majority (see Table 7.1) on a fractionally *lower* share of the vote.

Consolidating Thatcherism: June 1983–June 1987

Most commentators have remarked on the limitations and uncertainties of Thatcher's second administration. It was marked by only one high drama – the year-long confrontation with the coalminers from January 1984 to January 1985 – and by few measures of radical reform: and there were many errors and failures. The Conservatives' large majority was not an unmixed blessing either, since it made it less risky for dissenting opinion to emerge within the parliamentary party.

Moreover, the Labour Party wasted no time in trying to repair the worst of the damage it had suffered. Foot resigned as leader immediately after the election and the so-called 'dream ticket' of Neil Kinnock and Roy Hattersley, representing the centre-left and centre-right of the parliamentary Labour Party respectively, was overwhelmingly endorsed by all three components of the party's new electoral college in October 1983. Benn had lost his seat in the election (due mainly to a boundary change) and so was out of the running. Foot had been 70; Kinnock was 41, very much a professional politician, who promised to unite the party on a pragmatic basis and appeal effectively to the social-democratic values which a substantial majority of the electorate still appeared to support.

The government had little new legislation to propose. Its economic strategy consisted, after all, in allowing market forces to work. On the other hand, public support for the welfare state seemed to rule out extensive social reforms to introduce market principles in the field of social services. In the autumn of 1982 there had been a strong adverse reaction to a leaked document showing that the cabinet was considering transferring some medical services to the private sector. Mrs Thatcher was obliged to declare at the party conference that 'the National Health Service is safe with us'. And other 'welfare' institutions, such as the tax relief given on the interest paid on mortgages by home owners, or state grants for university education, were sacred cows of the middle-class Conservative electorate on whose support the government depended. A government proposal in November 1984 to replace university grants by loans provoked a revolt by Conservative backbenchers and was ignominiously abandoned.

The main measures of the second Thatcher administration were, then, largely continuations of earlier policies: further council house sales and the privatisation of new and larger nationalised industries; renewed efforts to control local authority spending, with which the government had been grappling with very limited success in the previous parliament; further trade union legislation (the 1984 Trade Union Act); extensions of the Youth Training Scheme and the Job Training Scheme; a Police and Criminal Evidence Act and a Public Order Act; and a measure to end the solicitors' monopoly of house conveyancing. In this situation it was possible to discern an opportunity for the opposition to regain the initiative; for Labour to appear once again as the party of reform and progress, forcing the Conservatives into the position of defending their still new and far from universally accepted market-oriented policies. This would be especially true, it seemed, if the government showed itself inept, arrogant or divided – as it proceeded to do, in a series of well-publicised incidents.

In retrospect, however, what is striking about these years is that a series of government errors, and the emerging impression that its reforming impulse was spent, failed to redound to the advantage of the opposition. Part of the reason must be that the government was riding an economic boom. The opposition, for its part, remained divided (both between Labour and the Alliance, and within each of these); while the Labour Party remained mainly in a posture of defending the status quo ante and failed to propose a convincing or attractive vision of an alternative future social order.

The Labour Party was caught in a double bind. Apart from considerations of loyalty to the labour movement that had created the party eighty years earlier, for the moment it could not avoid being, above all, the parliamentary voice of the working class in the old industrial cities, where the costs of the Conservatives' economic strategy were being chiefly borne – and the defender of all those who were dependent on the welfare state, with which the party was so strongly identified. Whatever else the party did, it had to try to defend the welfare state, in spite of all the shortcomings and contradictions which it contained. The trade unions would have insisted on this, even if the party leadership had not taken it for granted.

On the other hand, the party's activists were increasingly polarised towards the so-called 'far left' – which was in turn split between the 'old left', represented in different ways by Arthur Scargill, the President of the National Union of Mineworkers and his Deputy, Mick McGahey, or by the Trotskyist Militant Tendency, which controlled the party in Liverpool; and the 'new left', reflecting the radical-democratic outlook of the 'new social movements' (especially the women's movement and the anti-nuclear movement, and minority rights movements such as blacks, gays, single parents, tenants, etc.).

The party's commitments to the old working class and the welfare state obliged it to defend the past. No matter how valid this stance was, it hurt the party because the recent past was also a record of failure. The 'far left', on the other hand, tended to identify the party with ideas and currents which were genuinely radical and forward-looking, but which were out of touch with the sentiments of most voters – and lacked an adequate sense of the need to sustain a comprehensive political project, geared to what was electorally, fiscally and above all productively possible in Britain in the 1980s and 1990s. It was this defect which was captured by the lethal phrase, 'the loony left'.*

It was by no means impossible that the party could be extricated

* P. Jenkins, in *Mrs Thatcher's Revolution*, London 1987, pp. 143–4, has an entertaining list of the projects of various Labour-controlled councils which forms the basis for this jibe, including a scheme for promoting non-competitive cricket in schools. Note, however, that Jenkins does not assess the extent to which some of the sillier ideas he lists were actually supported by the councils to which they were proposed, and also includes some policies (such as, for instance, programmes aimed to reduce prejudice against homosexuals) which seem anything but loony, and whose inclusion raises questions about Jenkins's own values.

from this predicament, that the talent and energy of its activists could be harnessed, and the anxieties and hopes of its supporters mobilised, on behalf of a new long-term project of radical reform. But it clearly called for exceptional qualities of imagination and leadership, which it seemed doubtful that Kinnock, or for that matter any potential successor, possessed.

The Alliance faced different but no less serious difficulties. The Liberals represented a wide range of diverse views, loosely held together in a highly elastic party constitution, well suited to opposition, but ill-adapted to power. The leader, David Steel, disliked Mrs Thatcher and inclined towards an arrangement with Labour if the Alliance were to gain the balance of power in the House of Commons. The SDP, in contrast, was represented by only six MPs, only one of whom, David Owen, was a national figure (Jenkins, Williams and Rodgers having all failed to get elected in June 1983). The party increasingly became identified with Owen's personal views, and he not only differed from Steel on several major issues, and inclined more to Mrs Thatcher than to Kinnock, but transparently hoped to eclipse Steel in the event that the Alliance were to hold the balance of power in a future parliament. While support for the Alliance in the opinion polls fluctuated with the level of popular disenchantment with the Conservatives, it failed to establish an image of itself as an alternative government, but appeared more and more as what it in fact was – a disparate coalition of politicians, some of them talented and energetic, for whose services there was no longer an obvious use.

For, in spite of well-publicised and numerous mistakes and internal conflicts, damaging exhibitions of arrogance and occasional reverses, the government retained the initiative, and its policies gradually ceased to seem novel. This did not make them uncontroversial, let alone natural. But not enough voters wanted to venture back into the previous era, which already began to seem quite distant – at any rate, not with any of the available guides. 'Thatcherism', however morally uncomfortable and economically problematic it might seem, gradually became the reality, to be improved upon if possible, but otherwise to be lived with. Thus the years from 1983 to 1987 proved to be years of consolidation for Thatcherism, to an extent that belied the government's apparent difficulties, and the angry opposition it continued to arouse.

The privatisation programme gathered momentum. From 1979/80 to 1982/83 asset sales had averaged £440m per annum: in each of the next two years sales more than doubled; by 1986/87 sales were £4.4 billion and were projected to continue at about £4.5 billion a year until 1991. The proceeds of the sales were treated by the Treasury as current revenue and applied to reducing the Public Sector Borrowing

Requirement or budget deficit. Together with North Sea oil and gas revenues, and rising tax receipts due to expanding output, privatisation enabled the government to achieve its long-promised aim of reducing taxes from 1985 onwards, and to expand public spending at the same time (not as a percentage of GDP, but in absolute terms). The result was an old-fashioned pre-election government 'spending spree' in the years 1985–7: 'Indeed, it is perfectly fair to call 1987 the year of the Lawson boom, in the same way that the booms of 1964 and 1973 are associated with the names of Maudling and Barber.'[4] Another result of the expanded privatisation programme was that 'between 1979 and 1987 the proportion of the population owning shares increased from 7% to 20%':[5] an average of 10,000 per constituency (as the *Economist* noted), who would not be likely to vote Labour if the Labour Party stayed committed to renationalisation. Council house sales also continued at an acclerated rate, following a new Housing Act in 1984. By 1987 about a million houses had been sold, and the proportion of the population living in their own homes had risen to 66 per cent, compared with 52 per cent in 1979. Forty-four percent of workers who owned their own homes voted Conservative in 1987, compared with 25 per cent of council tenants.[6] After the 1987 election Mrs Thatcher did not hesitate to state the political implications, saying that 'just as we gained political support at the last election from people who had acquired their own homes and shares, so we shall secure still further our political base in 1991–2 – by giving people a real say in education and housing'.[7]

The reduction of trade union power continued. The 1984 Trade Union Act obliged unions to hold more frequent elections of their national officers, and also to ballot their members on strike action and on the continuation of their political funds (the aim of this was to make the Labour Party, which depended on these funds, more sensitive to the views of the unions' 'moderate' rank and file). The privatisation of some 40 per cent of the nationalised industries had also made large numbers of trade unionists into employees of private companies whose managers would, in theory, not hesitate to fight to win in disputes over manning levels, work practices and pay, because they now had to show a profit. (This argument was somewhat spoiled by the fact that the big nationalised monopolies, such as British Telecom, remained monopolies when they were nationalised, with no particular incentive to become more efficient.) And in 1983 the government appointed Ian MacGregor chairman of the National Coal Board, with a mandate to make the industry profitable; this meant, in effect, closing uneconomic pits and disregarding the procedural agreement that existed with the National Union of Mineworkers, which would prolong and generally limit such closures. In 1981 the NUM had threatened strike action to resist such a move, and the government had backed off. By 1984 it was ready.

The closures programme implied the end of most of the pit communities in Britain, and the final contraction of the once-powerful NUM to a position of relative insignificance within the labour movement. The NUM was divided, however, between areas where pits were threatened, such as Yorkshire, Derbyshire and South Wales, and those where the pits were profitable, especially Nottinghamshire. Arthur Scargill, the NUM President and prime mover in the flying picket tactic that had proved so effective in 1972, was determined to make the issue of closures into a decisive struggle. But he had not secured promises of support from the rest of the union movement, or from the Labour Party leadership, who were not convinced that the defence of every threatened pit community was a rational policy which they must endorse, or one which could and should be made into a test of strength with the government.

The strike began at threatened pits in south Yorkshire and Derbyshire, and spread by local action throughout the other coalfields; once begun in this way, it continued without a union-wide strike ballot, initially because the national leadership were unsure of winning one, and later (when it was clear from polls that there would be a majority for the strike) because it was seen as giving in to 'outside' pressure to do so. Striking miners instead tried to 'persuade' those still at work by mounting mass pickets, which were met with still heavier intimidation by the police, organised as a nationwide flying counter-picket by the National Reporting Centre established for the purpose following the lessons of the 1972 strike (see Chapter 15, p. 360). Support from other unions was mostly lukewarm and sporadic; the Labour leadership was caught between the need to show loyalty to a union with unique historical claims to such loyalty, and the need to avoid endorsing either the use of force by NUM pickets (which the media made a touchstone of political acceptability), or the aims of a strike which Kinnock saw could not be won. Kinnock was also unenthusiastic about Scargill and his politics, and remained effectively aloof from the struggle. As a result, the miners fought largely alone, in spite of the sympathy and practical support of thousands of individuals throughout the country, and eventually surrendered unconditionally in January 1985.

A much smaller but also highly publicised year-long strike by the two printworkers' unions, the NGA and SOGAT, against the Murdoch newspapers' decision to instal new printing technology at a new plant at Wapping, suffered a similar defeat in January 1986. By 1985 total union membership had fallen to 10.7 million from 13.2 million in 1979, faster than the decline in jobs, and strike activity was at its lowest level for twenty years. While the media still reported trade union news as union leaders conferred, arranged union mergers, and worked within the Labour Party for the return of a Labour government, they were no longer household names as they had been during the years of corporatism; they were no longer consulted by the government or had any influence on policy. According to Jenkins, only 1 per cent of the population polled by Gallup in 1987 considered union power the chief issue facing the country, compared with 73 per cent in May 1979.[8]

In its plan for destroying the institutional bases of 'socialism' the government's other chief targets were the Labour-controlled local authorities. What had begun (under Healey's chancellorship in the 1970s) as an attempt to control local government spending in line with state spending generally, developed into an increasingly confused and bitter struggle between successive Conservative local government ministers and Labour councils – especially those responsible for areas of acute inner-city need (see Chapter 15). The 1983 Conservative manifesto had promised the abolition of the six metropolitan councils established in 1972 and the Greater London Council, created in 1963, all of them Labour-controlled; this was accomplished by March 1986. By 1987, the government had also taken powers to control both the total level of spending and the level of the rates collected by the remaining local authorities. The blatantly political motivation of the destruction of local government autonomy aroused strong opposition, including protests from Conservatives who were unhappy about the relentless centralism of the Thatcherite 'strong state'.

Similar disquiet was touched off by several other government actions, such as the cabinet's decision in January 1984 to ban trade unions at the Government Communications Headquarters (GCHQ) at Cheltenham, which a high court judge (later overruled on appeal) found 'contrary to the principles of natural justice'; or the free use of the notorious Section 2 of the Official Secrets Act to prosecute civil servants for 'leaks' – notably in the case of Sarah Tisdall, a foreign office clerk jailed for six months in 1984 for leaking to the press the date of the arrival of Cruise missiles in Britain, and the government's plans for announcing it; and that of Clive Ponting, a Ministry of Defence official, tried but acquitted in February 1985 for having passed to an MP information on the government's concealment of the circumstances surrounding the sinking of the Argentine cruiser, the *Admiral Belgrano*, in the Falklands War. There was also the questionable manipulation of the media by the Prime Minister's office in January 1987, to discredit the Minister of Defence, Michael Heseltine, who was challenging her on the issue of whether Westland Helicopters, a British manufacturer facing bankruptcy, should be taken over by the American Sikorsky company, or a European consortium. Because of Heseltine's popularity with the media and the Conservative rank and file, this otherwise minor issue damaged Thatcher, who the public did not believe was telling the truth about it. Other setbacks included a very hostile public reaction to the revelation early in 1986 that the government was planning to sell Austin Rover and Leyland Trucks to Ford and General Motors, which led to the abandonment of the plan; and the widespread condemnation of Mrs Thatcher's decision to allow the USA to bomb Libya from bases in Britain in April 1986.

But although the opposition and the media saw the government as increasingly accident-prone, these incidents failed to cause it serious injury. Thatcher had progressively removed from the cabinet the so-called 'wets' inherited from the days of Macmillan and Heath, such as St John Stevas (dismissed in January 1981), Lord Soames and Sir Ian Gilmour (September 1981), Francis Pym (June 1983) and John Biffen (June 1987); while others retired (James Prior, in September 1984) or resigned (Lord Carrington, following the Argentine invasion of the Falklands in April 1982, and Heseltine, in January 1987). In their place she brought forward reliable 'dries' such as Norman Tebbitt, Leon Brittan, Nigel Lawson, Nicholas Ridley, and Cecil Parkinson. Some of these were unable to play the roles originally envisaged for them, but the 1983 election had also strengthened the Thatcherite wing of the party in parliament and ministerial replacements were increasingly available. The government was never in real danger of a schism in the parliamentary party – an attempt in May 1985 by some thirty 'wet' backbenchers, led by the former Foreign Secretary Pym, to form a Centre Forward group in opposition to the Thatcherite hegemony was promptly contained and neutralised – nor from widespread defection on the part of Conservative voters. Its standing in the opinion polls fell from a high of 45 per cent in September 1983 to a low of 30 per cent in January 1986, following the Westland Helicopters affair; but it climbed back again to 40 per cent by the end of the year, recovering the lead from Labour and maintaining it throughout the months leading up to the general election of June 1987.

This time the Labour Party under Kinnock fought a campaign widely praised for its 'professionalism' and suffered no repeat of the haemorrhage of support that occurred in 1983; but it failed to do more than recover some of the ground it had lost then, or reverse the long-term decline that had set in during the 1950s, and it particularly failed to recover votes outside the industrial and inner-city heartlands. The skilled workers who had first deserted to the Conservatives in 1979 failed to return. Even in London, the swing back to Labour was only

1.6 per cent, netting only 23 out of 84 London seats: outside London, in the whole of Southern England and East Anglia, Labour still had only 3 MPs out of a total of 176. Only in the north, where the swing was 5 per cent, and in Scotland, where it was 7.3 per cent, did Labour recover fully from 1983, confirming the party's continuing confinement in its old electoral ghetto.

A very self-critical postmortem ensued. At the party conference in October Kinnock was given a broad mandate to rethink party policy, as speaker after speaker acknowledged the lack of 'credibility' of the party's economic strategy. But it was obviously extraordinarily difficult to develop a new programme which would retain the support of the unions and the disadvantaged, while appealing in new ways to the prosperous working and middle classes in a situation increasingly defined by Thatcherite values and perceptions. A further problem was the party's anti-nuclear policy, to which Kinnock as well as most of the party's activists were committed, but which even Labour voters tended to reject. The problem was made worse by the pressing need to win the next election, if the party was to retain its image as a 'normal' party of government, when the fundamental necessity was to formulate and win support for a fresh vision of the future, a necessarily long-term undertaking.

The chief loser in 1987 was the Alliance, which fell back to only 23 per cent of the vote, and immediately began to disintegrate. The nuclear issue was a critical factor in the Alliance's defeat too, since Owen was strongly committed to a national nuclear defence policy, while the Liberals on balance opposed it. The antagonism between David Owen and David Steel also damaged the Alliance; and it was once again the victim of 'third party syndrome'. With the lapse of time since 1983, the party scene no longer looked so volatile. The 'new right' had been in office for eight years and so had ceased to alarm, while the 'far left' within the Labour Party had been marginalised. The vision of a mild, European-style party coalition, presiding over a European-style economic modernisation programme with a social-market doctrine like that of the German Social Democrats, had been eclipsed by the practical reality of Mrs Thatcher's *non*-social-market doctrine. The SDP platform, insofar as it could now be distinguished from the personal views of David Owen, seemed only to promise to do what Mrs Thatcher was already doing, but in a nicer manner. The gibe that the Alliance promised 'a better yesterday' had become painfully accurate.

This was some consolation for Labour, since if the Alliance broke up, Labour might hope eventually to recapture much of the anti-Thatcher vote, which was still an overall majority (57 per cent). But for the time being the result confirmed the Conservatives' strong hold on power, even with their relatively modest and unchanged share of the popular vote.

Second-stage Thatcherism: June 1987–April 1988

In the run-up to the 1987 election the government, and Mrs Thatcher in particular, had recovered their confidence and raised their sights. Urged on by the ideologists of the new right (many of whom had despaired, after 1983, of the government's capacity for any further radicalism), Thatcher inscribed in the 1987 manifesto three major targets for the next phase of her war against 'socialist monopoly': the remaining tenant-occupied council estates; the ability of Labour councils to spend rates levied on businesses and better-off home owners; and the state schools, which she saw as fiefs of local authority power and vehicles for the inculcation of 'socialist' values. Events were immediately to add a fourth target, the National Health Service, which was entering a financial crisis due to chronic and deliberate underfunding by the government over the previous eight years. There was, besides, a further instalment of the government's war on the unions.

This took the form of a new Employment Bill, introduced early in the new parliament. As with the earlier legislation, it did not create new offences to be punished by criminal proceedings but gave new legally enforceable rights to private citizens – in this case union members, who would also have a new commissioner to help them with funds and legal advice against their unions. Union members would have the right not to be called out on strike without a secret ballot, and not to be penalised for refusing to strike. Unions would not be immune from legal action by injured parties where they took industrial action to get or keep a closed shop, and employees would have a remedy against their employers if they were dismissed for not belonging to a union – in other words, unions would not be able to impose sanctions on strike-breakers and individuals would not need to join unions following a closed shop agreement. All top union officials would have to be elected by postal ballots of all members – a measure designed to reduce the influence of 'activists' (defined as those who bother to vote in elections held at the workplace or elsewhere).

Under the new Housing Bill run-down inner city council estates would be transferred to new Housing Action Trusts, charged with upgrading them and then transferring them to new, non-council owners approved by a new private sector Housing Finance Corporation. Tenants on other council estates would have the right to have ownership of their homes transferred to other approved landlords (as the Labour party pointed out, the bill did not give tenants of private property the converse right). The government argued that it would introduce competition in the rented housing market; councils managing their housing well would have nothing to fear.

Under a new Local Government Bill local authorities would lose their power to levy a rate on property. The proceeds of a new nationwide tax on businesses would be distributed on an equitable basis to all local authorities, as would a central government grant, for a total of 75 per cent of local authority revenue (80 per cent in Scotland and 85 per cent in Wales); the remaining 25 per cent (20 per cent in Scotland and 15 per cent in Wales) would come from a 'community service charge' to be levied on all residents, regardless of income (welfare recipients would have to pay 20 per cent of it). Councils would have power to increase this charge, but as it would fall most heavily on their least affluent electors, the government was fairly confident that the power would be sparingly used. This poll tax, as it was popularly called, aroused strong opposition, not only because of its inequity as a flat rate tax, and because it would leave local authorities with so little independent power; but also because many people, and not only in the Labour Party, feared the consequences of trying to trace and prosecute people who failed to pay such a tax. Various schemes were mooted to amend the proposal by 'banding' or graduating the tax, or varying the exemptions from it, but the government was determined to carry through its original plans.

The Education Bill was the most far-reaching of all. It proposed, first, that financial responsibility for each secondary school should be devolved onto its head and its board of governors, who would receive their state funding directly from the Department of Education and Science, cutting out the local authority; second, that there would be no limits on enrolment, so that popular schools could grow, while unpopular ones would contract; third, schools would be allowed to charge fees for 'extras' which in practice could extend to such items as equipment, books and materials; and fourth, any school would be allowed to 'opt out' of local authority control entirely by a majority vote of the parents. At the same time, the Bill provided for the Department of Education and Science to lay down a national curriculum covering between 80 per cent and 90 per cent of class time. Critics argued that the Bill would produce a hierarchy of schools, from declining schools in declining areas, where the parents could not afford 'extras', to expanding schools in middle-class areas, enriched by parental fees; eventually, it was suggested, some of these would (although the Bill's sponsors denied any such intention) not just opt out of local authority control, but go further and seek to become fully independent fee-paying schools, while retaining state funding through an extension of the 'assisted places' scheme. The Bill also envisaged the transfer of schools from the Inner London Education Authority to the various inner London boroughs at the latters' request; in February 1988 the government announced that it would amend this provision and abolish the ILEA, a pace-setter in education for over a century, in April 1990.

The National Health Service was not the subject of new proposals in the Conservatives' 1987 manifesto. Its emergence as an issue was due partly to a threatened nurses' strike at the end of 1987, which was about the level of NHS funding as well as nurses' pay, and partly to the emergence at about the same time of heightened media awareness of a crisis in hospital services and morale caused by underfunding. The government maintained that it was spending more than ever on the Service, which was true; but it was systematically below the level needed to maintain standards of health care, given rising costs and rising numbers of people needing care.[9] The government's aim in underfunding was to force the NHS to become more efficient, but comparisons showed that the NHS was already so much cheaper than the health services of other countries that it was very doubtful if there was any room for further cuts without accepting rising mortality and morbidity rates. The government had no prepared plan: it began a policy review in which it soon became clear that the 1947 principle of universal and free health care would eventually be abandoned. It was a measure of the consolidation of Thatcherism that what had been unthinkable in the autumn of 1982 – the break-up of the NHS – had become not only thinkable but likely by the spring of 1988.

The institutions of the welfare state thus turned out to be no longer untouchable. Under the banner of 'cost effectiveness' the National Health Service, the most sensitive of all the legacies of the Beveridge era, was to be at least partially dismembered; the egalitarian impulse behind the 'comprehensivisation' of the secondary school system in the 1960s was to be reversed; and the financial autonomy of elected local governments, and the principle of local taxation according to ability to pay, would become things of the past. So, too, would the role of local councils as providers of cheap housing for the working class. The ideals of 'universality', 'fairness', and 'caring', inherited from the reaction to the slump and the experience of the People's War, were increasingly devalued. It remained to be seen what Thatcherism would finally propose for those people – estimated in 1987 at over 8 million – who were living at or below the poverty line, and unlikely in most cases ever to rise above it: they would presumably still require some form of means-tested residual provision from state revenues. But it was already safe to predict that provision for the rest of the population would be gradually transferred from the state to privately funded insurance schemes in a growing range of social security fields. Mrs Thatcher was confident that 'having a say' in the quality of services they would receive by buying them on the market would make more people support the Conservatives; and she might well be proved right, so long as the state of the economy increased the real disposable incomes of those in work, so that they could afford to do this. The problem that would face her successors if and when this condition no longer held was another matter.

Notes

1 P. Riddell, *The Thatcher Government* (2nd edn), Blackwell, Oxford 1985, p. 91.
2 *Social Trends 1986*, p. 68.
3 *Employment Gazette*, November 1987.
4 T. Congdon, in *The Times*, 30 December 1987.
5 P. Jenkins, *Mrs Thatcher's Revolution: the End of the Socialist Era*, Cape, London 1987, p. 370.
6 D. Butler and D. Kavanagh, *The British General Election of 1987*, MacMillan, London 1988, p. 276.
7 The *Independent* 17 July 1987.
8 Jenkins, p. 369.
9 *Sunday Times*, 24 January 1988.

PART II

8

Capital and Labour

'You know, the shareholders have got the money to
buy shares. We haven't got it. So I suppose they have
to have them'.

(Worker at ChemCo)[1]

The warp and weft of British society consists of the relations between
the owners and the non-owners of its productive resources. These
relations are fundamental to the formation and nature of classes and
parties, and are implicit in almost every sphere of culture, sacred and
profane. But the way classes, parties and culture are based on and
refract the relation between capital and labour is complex. This
chapter seeks to outline the basic relationship at its most direct and
simple level.

Three broad phases of development in the relation between capital
and labour can be distinguished: the phase of competitive industrial
capitalism, from the late eighteenth century till about 1870; the phase
of monopoly capitalism, from about 1870 till about 1930; and from
about 1930 onwards, the phase of organised or state-managed
capitalism, which includes, from the 1950s onwards especially, the
development of multinational production. While it would be wrong to
ascribe exceptional importance to any one of these phases, the earlier
ones were politically formative, and so it is necessary to pay some
attention to them even though contemporary British capitalism
exhibits so many differences.

The first phase is important because it was the first, because it was
very prolonged, and because it was in certain respects *limited*.
Throughout the nineteenth century, the expansion of manufacturing
capital was primarily 'extensive' – that is, based on employing more

people in mainly unmechanised manual work. On this basis industrial output increased sevenfold between 1800 and 1900, when together with mining and building it accounted for 40 per cent of the national income. This proportion would rise to almost 50 per cent in the late 1950s, before declining again in face of the rise of the service sector.

Throughout this time – and especially in the two decades prior to the First World War – a large share of the profits from manufacturing was siphoned off for investment abroad. The vast holdings of overseas assets owned by British capitalists at the end of the century had been built up largely from the earnings of British manufacturing, especially before 1875.[2]

The urban working class came into being in the same prolonged and qualified process. By 1830, E.P. Thompson has argued, it was already 'made' (or rather, it had already 'made itself' through its resistance to exploitation and repression).[3] Yet in 1831, 28 per cent of all families were still engaged in agriculture; factory work proper was still largely confined to textiles and the north; divisions among workers based on religion, race (the Irish), income and skill, were severe, and prevailing ideas of how to remedy the workers' ills were confused and often impractical.

By 1870 artisanal self-employment was rapidly giving way to wage labour in all sectors, and the Great Depression of 1873 to 1896 accelerated the elimination of agriculture as a major area of employment (by 1901 it accounted for only 8.4 per cent of all employees). However, the small family firm, using relatively primitive technology, remained a characteristic form of industrial capital, and the highly differentiated workforce was still, in its majority, non-industrial. This was the situation when the formation of capital and labour into organised antagonists entered its decisive stage during the Great Depression, amid bitter struggles which were to leave an enduring mark on the organisation and attitudes of both.

Capital took refuge increasingly in monopoly – in empire markets, in tariffs, and in mergers and cartels – and at the same time employers organised in order to overcome union opposition to wage cuts and the 'dilution' of labour – i.e. the replacement of skilled labour by less skilled or unskilled labour (often female), using new machinery. Concentration of capital accelerated, as the depression eliminated weaker firms and bigger firms found themselves better placed to secure a degree of monopoly, which in turn favoured their growth at the expense of others. The older industrial sectors stagnated and finally began to contract, but not without protracted struggles in which the employers, organised into federations in particular sectors (such as coalmining), tried to survive by weakening the unions and cutting wages – struggles which dominated industrial relations before and after the Great War. The workers, in reply, organised themselves in large 'general' unions (embracing a great variety of occupations in a wide range of industries) with a strongly defensive ethic of class solidarity.

These structures survived into the third, and still continuing, phase with relatively few essential changes. In the period of 'organised' capitalism the oldest economic sectors contracted drastically and in key instances were nationalised (coalmining, railways, steel and shipbuilding). 'White collar', 'service industry' and state employment expanded, leading to changes in the balance of power within the trade union movement (but not, on the whole, to changed organisation or strategies). Trade unions followed the concentration of capital with a merger movement of their own, especially from the mid-1960s onwards; but they were not able to match capital's shift to the internationalisation of production. Capital became increasingly able to move production from one part of the world to another, independently of the geographical pattern of demand for products, and to determine independently where profits should appear to accrue; trade unions developed no corresponding powers. These changes had, of course, important political implications.

The Elements of Capital

The most significant recent changes within capital are the sharp increase in concentration, the emergence of new sectors and the decline of older ones, and internationalisation. In manufacturing alone, the largest hundred firms, which accounted for 16 per cent of net output in 1909, accounted for 42 per cent in 1975; and 100 firms owned 79 per cent of the net assets of all quoted commercial and industrial firms.[4] From the point of view of labour, four out of five workers now worked for firms with over 100 employees; less than a quarter of a million worked for firms with fewer than 20 employees. The 'meso-economic sector' was now paramount. Growth of investment and profits was greatest in the food, drink and tobacco sector, and in services and shipping. Not only did the old 'staple' industries decline, but all manufacturing began to decline relative to other sectors even before the dramatic deindustrialisation of the 1970s. The process of internationalisation was very rapid after 1950. By 1979, 31 per cent of British exports were 'intra-firm' transactions and British manufacturing and commercial companies were making over 10 per cent of their income abroad. Eighty-two per cent of all exports were

BRISTOL POLYTECHNIC
ST. MATTHIAS LIBRARY
FISHPONDS

due to multinational companies (of which two-fifths were foreign-owned).[5]

Throughout these developments, however, one crucial feature of British capital remained constant – the political dominance of financial and commercial capital. The special position of banking and merchant capital arose from their historical priority and their role in the export-based expansion of industry. The export trade was financed by merchant capital and depended on the power of the state, which was financed by banking capital through the public debt. As manufacturing industry expanded, so did the importance of banking and trade; sterling became the supreme international trading currency and London the centre of attraction for foreign investors and borrowers. The City of London, where the banks and insurance, shipping and trading companies were concentrated, became 'the most cosmopolitan element in British society' whose 'wealth and culture wore down the reluctance of the British upper classes to accept even the upper echelons of the Haute Juiverie'.[6] A job in the City – dealing largely with one's social equals and having no direct contact with production – became socially acceptable in a way that industrial management never did, or at least not until the age of the giant firm.

This reinforced the external orientation of British economic policy. The City's interest lay in maintaining a strong pound and freedom of movement for capital, and policies such as protection, devaluation and exchange controls, designed to assist industry, were consistently resisted. In the struggle over tariff reform, after 1902, the City had plenty of allies (in the trade and transport sectors, and among the working classes, who feared increases in food prices), but its later victories are more remarkable. In 1925 Britain went back on the gold standard at the 1914 rate of exchange; this seriously overvalued the pound and sounded the death-knell for many shipyards and textile mills as well as for a large part of the coal industry (still the largest single industry in terms of employment). Even new and relatively efficient manufacturing sectors were severely handicapped.

Bankers' lack of 'confidence' also destroyed not only the second, unlamented Labour government of 1929–31, but also the only production-oriented economic solution proposed (apart from Mosley's Fascism) for the economic problem at this time, namely the Macmillan Committee's proposals for making banks become long-term equity investors in manufacturing as they were in Germany.[7] After the Second World War the City's desire to restore British foreign investments and maintain sterling as an international reserve currency led to a persistently overvalued pound and to large outflows of investment overseas at times when domestic investment was increasingly inadequate.*

Eventually, as we have seen, the desperate condition of manufacturing forced a change and sterling was 'floated' in 1971. By this time, however, the whole international monetary system was in a state of flux and the City had discovered that when most currencies were 'floating', including the pound, it could make money as an international financial centre dealing in many other trading currencies.

But the other differences of interest between the City and industrial capital remained. After 1979, for example, the City adopted the tenets of monetarism with an enthusiasm based partly on its anxiety to cut inflation and maintain the value of sterling, but also on the fact that high interest rates, which formed a necessary element of monetarist policy, brought profits to the banks and attracted more foreign capital to London. In 1980 a sharp conflict arose between manufacturing industry and the City over interest rates. The Director-General of the Confederation of British Industry, Sir Terence Beckett, publicly criticised Mrs Thatcher for maintaining interest rates at a level that was threatening many manufacturers' survival. He was rebuked by various 'loyalist' business spokesmen, though the government did reduce interest rates in the March 1981 budget, and introduced a retroactive tax on some of the banks' windfall profits. This clearly revealed the conflict; but the overall effect of the Thatcher policies (including the lifting of all exchange controls), while theoretically designed to rejuvenate manufacturing, was to consolidate the City's dominance.

Given the relatively limited weight of the interests represented by the City in the economy as a whole (see Table 8.1), it may well seem unreasonable to explain the City's dominance over industry exclusively in terms of its special position in the social structure. But longstanding organisational factors were also at work. Since the 1830s there had been a close nexus between the City, the Bank of England and the Treasury.[8] The Bank, though nationalised in 1946, retains its real autonomy (the Thatcher government showed no inclination to privatise it), and represents the City's views to the Treasury more intimately and effectively than the CBI represents the views of manufacturing industry. Moreover, the dependence of successive governments on

* 'Official estimates of private long-term investment by Britain in the period 1946–64 gave a cumulative total in the overseas sterling area of £12,900m, or two-thirds of the total outflow of British private long-term capital, and £11,900m in the rest of the world put together. This investment in the sterling area was equivalent in money terms to the pre-war accumulation of British investment of the previous hundred years' (S. Strange, *Sterling and British Policy*, Oxford University Press, Oxford 1971, pp. 66–7).

Table 8.1   Shares of Gross Domestic Product 1959–1979

	% of GDP			
	1959	*1969*	*1979*	*1986*
Insurance, banking finance and business services	3.0	6.8	9.0	15.6
Distributive trades	12.6	10.6	10.5	14.0
Manufacturing	35.6	33.0	27.9	24.3

Source: Annual Abstracts of Statistics, HMSO, London.

foreign loans when dealing with chronic balance of payments deficits reinforced the City's views, At times like 1966 7, or 1976, foreign bankers' confidence was seen as holding the key to short-term political survival, and before North Sea oil came on stream this dependence was such that deference to City opinion tended to become axiomatic for Treasury policy-makers. This was critical for the decision, or 'non-decision', that was made about the use of the North Sea oil windfall. Labour envisaged, belatedly, a state-led and state-financed industrial modernisation strategy; the Liberals envisaged a special fund to lend to private industry for modernisation; the Conservatives in office used oil revenues to finance unemployment, allowing the manufacturing sector to contract to what the market judged to be its viable size.

What is striking, as one reflects on this pattern of events, is not just the strength of banking and commercial capital in determining policy, but also the political weakness of manufacturing capital. As its position deteriorated, so its opposition to policies oriented towards the interests of finance and trade stiffened, but it was notably unsuccessful in proposing a convincing industrial strategy of its own. With the exception of Chamberlain's imperial project the leaders of British manufacturing industry have not conceived of a *political* order in which productive capital would set state policy and dominate the national culture.[9] They have been more influenced by fear – fear of competition, fear of labour, and fear of the state. As Crouch commented in 1979,

any move against the City would undoubtedly mean, in the British political context, increased government involvement in investment, probably with a significant trade-union role. Industrialists feel much less threatened by the City, responsive after all to capitalist interests, than by government (especially a Labour one) and union intervention in the issue – investment –

And as Longstreth noted:

> The fact that the industrial sector is completely dominated by multinationals implies that it shares various immediate interests with finance, namely the desire to keep open the option of capital export, and has good reason to follow the City's lead in matters of industrial policy even if the consequence is erosion of the home base to some degree.[11]

It is even likely that, for many companies, the concept of a 'home base' was losing much of its former significance.

Compared with the difference of interests between money and manufacturing capital, other divisions have been of modest importance. The unhappiness of small business in the face of galloping concentration and the tendency of fiscal policy to be focused on the needs of big companies was an important factor in the emergence of Thatcherism. It led to panegyrics for small business at Conservative Party conferences, and to various measures of relief for small business in the budgets of 1979–81. It was very doubtful, however, if this would much affect the growth in the weight and influence of large companies.

The Organisation of Capital

Capital was represented by five main types of organisation: employers' federations; industrial and trade associations; the Bank of England; the Confederation of British Industry; and a cluster of research, propaganda and espionage organisations.

Employers' federations date back to the Great Depression days of 1873–96 and the attempt to defeat the trade unions. Periodically this endeavour is revived, for example in the unsuccessful attempt by the Engineering Employers' Federation to defeat the Amalgamated Union of Engineering Workers in a two-month confrontation in the late summer of 1979. But the federations lost their prime purpose when the Trade Disputes Act of 1906 gave the unions immunity from civil suits for economic losses caused to employers by industrial action. Their effectiveness was further undermined by the growth of plant-level bargaining, which reflected the uneven ability of employers to pay a nationally agreed wage, as well as the absence of industry-wide unions. However, the federations played a significant part in the initial formulation of the anti-union legislation of 1980–84, which went a long way to restore the legal advantages which employers had enjoyed over trade unions before 1906.

The Confederation of British Industry was formed in 1965 out of the former Federation of British Industry and the National Association of British Manufacturers, which had represented smaller companies. It was a merger strongly encouraged by the Wilson government and one which reflected the rapid advance of industrial concentration at that time. From the mid-1970s the CBI began to voice, with increasing urgency, the needs of industrial capital as a whole, and in purely organisational terms was well equipped to do so. With an annual budget of over £16 million it made constant representations to all the economic departments of state, collaborated with them in collecting economic statistics, and represented capital vis-à-vis labour on a large number of state advisory bodies. The weaknesses of the CBI – which, after all, presided over an industrial decline of unprecedented proportions in the years after its formation – sprang from the fundamental political shortcomings of British industrial capital, not from organisational inadequacy.

Even after 1979, the CBI refrained from attacking some policies, such as the maintenance of a high value for sterling, which handicapped British manufacturing exports and facilitated the penetration of the home market by foreign goods. CBI policy reflected the weight of the large multinational companies, of which a very important segment – notably the oil companies, and the manufacturers of 'packaged goods' with high import content, such as processed foods, for the home market – benefited from a strong pound. Similarly, the CBI declined to call for measures to oblige the banks to invest long term in manufacturing, or to prevent capital being invested abroad. The truth was that the CBI reproduced within itself the structural peculiarities of British capital which lay at the heart of Britain's industrial problem. It did not act as a voice for the single-minded pursuit of policies to construct an internationally competitive industrial complex in Britain.

The most consistent political thrust of capital, in fact, was expressed as much by the cluster of propaganda and union-breaking organisations which it financed as it was by the CBI. These fell broadly into two categories. Research and propaganda organisations, such as the Institute of Directors, the Institute of Economic Affairs, the Institute for the Study of Conflict, AIMS (of Freedom and Enterprise) and the Freedom Association, provided ideological support through conferences, pamphlets and other media; collectively they played an important role in developing and popularising the 'new right' and 'social market' doctrines which gained ascendancy in the late 1970s. Espionage and 'union-busting' organisations included the Economic League, Common Cause and British United Industrialists. These specialised in blacklisting union activists, infiltrating unions, financing court proceedings against unions and the like. One estimate put the finances provided by capital to this last group of organisations at a level greater than the combined funds of the Conservative and Labour parties in an election year.[12]

Labour

The nature and pattern of work, and hence of the workforce, altered with the changes in British capital. First, the workforce employed in farming went on declining until, by the end of the 1980s, only 210,000 people (including part-time employees), or less than 1 per cent of the workforce, were on the land, compared with 1,386,000 or 8.4 per cent in 1901. The virtual completion of the urbanisation process in Britain by 1900 helps to explain the peculiarly defensive solidarity of the British labour movement. Already by that time there was no agrarian alternative, in an economy which seemed decreasingly able to afford workers a decent existence. No fewer than 2.3 million people emigrated over the decade and a half before the First World War: but for most people it was clear that their situation could be improved only through collective political action to change the existing framework. This understanding lasted until the 1950s.

Second, major changes occurred in the employment of women. Broadly speaking, married women, who had begun to be withdrawn from productive work by the beginning of the century, were drawn back into it (or forced back through economic pressure) in the two world wars and from the 1950s onwards. Meanwhile, single women had moved out of domestic service (which in 1931 still accounted for 23 per cent of all women in employment), partly into unskilled or semi-skilled manual work (especially in the new service industries), but above all into clerical work (which accounted for about 40 per cent of all women workers by the end of the 1970s). By 1985, 62 per cent of married women and 73 per cent of single women were economically active, mainly in low-paid jobs and increasingly part-time; they accounted for 44 per cent of all employees in employment.

Third, there was a marked decline in 'manual labour'. This needs to be treated with caution. Although the figures suggest that the proportion of people in manual work fell from 77 per cent in 1931 to 52 per cent in 1981 (and the proportion of women alone from 76 per cent to 44 per cent over the same period), a significant part of the change is really a change from one kind of manual work to another, which is classified as 'non-manual' for reasons that are ultimately ideological.[13] This is obvious in the case of women junior clerical workers, whose work is hardly less manual or more 'mental' than that of most skilled manual workers, yet who are classified as 'junior non-manual workers'. Much of the shift was due to the growth of work of this kind, and the final disappearance of still essentially pre-industrial forms of manual work (some of them very skilled) which were relics of the earlier years of capitalism. Most of the new non-manual jobs were hardly 'middle-class' occupations.[14] On the other hand, there *was* also an increase in the share of supervisory and semi-professional work – between 1964 and 1983, for example, the proportion of the electorate classified as belonging to the 'salariat' rose from 18 per cent to 27 per cent;[15] and even where the new 'non-manual' work was 'low level', the change was a real one and had ideological and political consequences. The new work might be no less tedious – in fact it might be more tedious – but it was often less exhausting and usually carried with it better working conditions and slightly higher status. Moreover, much manual work itself had become less dependent on strength. A workforce that is nearly half 'white collar' and predominantly employed by large organisations *is* a different workforce from the old one in which 70 per cent were manual workers, working largely for small family firms, many of them as 'common labourers'.

Fourth, by 1978, 27 per cent of all workers were in the state sector. This was an ambivalent change. It freed an important segment of the workforce from direct dependence on private employment, yet at the same time increased the risk of divisions within the workforce, especially between workers paid out of taxes and those who were not. On the other hand, as state employment expanded, workers in this sector were particularly exposed to the efforts of successive governments to curb wage increases. From the sixties onwards some public-sector unions began to play the sort of militant role formerly played only by the big industrial private-sector unions (for instance, low-paid public sector workers played a large part in the 'winter of discontent' of 1978–9). The Thatcherite appeal to public resentment of the capitalist state could be, and was, extended to generate hostility between state and non-state employees. By 1988 the Conservatives' privatisation pro-gramme and cuts in public spending had reduced the number of people working in the public sector to about 22 per cent of the workforce.

Fifth, and last, there were important changes in the level and distribution of incomes. After 1945 there was a large increase in average real earnings, which sharply distinguished this period from the preceding fifty years. The increase has continued, for those in work, apart from short periods of stagnation in the late seventies and early eighties, despite Britain's lagging productivity. At the same time, poverty 'reappeared'.

The reasons for the re-emergence of a distinct group, 'the poor', were complex, but several major components stand out. First, there were people who were dependent on state pensions or social security payments which were fixed at a grossly inadequate level, such as retired workers and their wives; widows; sick or disabled workers and their families; and single-parent families (who now accounted for 13 per cent of all children). Second, there were the victims of unemployment – 2.5 million workers (9.5 per cent of the working population) and their families at the end of 1987 (down from 3.2 million or 11.6 per cent in mid-1986, but up from 1.3 million or 4.7 per cent in 1978, not to mention 0.6 million or 2.6 per cent in 1970), very unevenly distributed geographically.* Third, there were workers in low-paid, often poorly unionised jobs, mainly in low-productivity sectors such as catering, cleaning and distribution. What all these categories had in common was that their incomes were so low that they depended on 'supplementary benefits' provided by the state to bring them *up to* the official 'poverty level'. By 1985 the number of people living at or below this level had risen to just under 9.4 million and in 1984 20 per cent of all households were living almost exclusively on social security benefits, while a further 20 per cent depended on them for half of their incomes.

Speaking generally, it is clear that the changes outlined here implied major alterations in the consciousness and internal relations of the working class, and the need for major developments in union organisation and strategy. Before considering these issues, however, it is worth reflecting briefly on the nature of work, as it emerged in the age of organised, large-scale capitalism in the crucial industrial sector of the economy.

It is sobering to read the sociological evidence collected on this question by Huw Beynon and his colleagues, in a pioneering series of studies in the sixties and seventies. What they consistently show is how, in spite of so many changes, so little seemed to have changed in essentials. This was not so hard to understand, perhaps, on the production line at Ford's Halewood factory in Liverpool, where the workers were under pressure to speed up the work, but with fewer workers ('reduced manning ratios'), and where nothing had been done to reduce the alienation for which assembly-line work is so notorious. But what of ChemCo, one of the most modern chemical plants in Britain, with a 'New Working Agreement' to raise productivity, with

---

* For instance in the fourth quarter of 1986 unemployment was 6.6% in the South-East, 10.5% in the West Midlands, 12.7% in Scotland and 17.8% in Northern Ireland. The crisis, experienced as a disaster in some areas, was barely felt in others.

high wages by British standards – only 20 per cent below Dutch and German wages in 1967 – and with a 'cooperative' trade union branch? In the end the problem remained that 'nobody cared'. The work was still boring, noisy, sometimes dangerous and – for a surprising number of workers – often plain, muscular, heavy labour, that left you finished at forty-five. As Nichols and Beynon report: 'One worker – the only one at Riverside who refused to talk to us – summed up his job like this: "It's f------ awful. Just do it. That's all. Do it."[16] But many didn't do it, as waste, absenteeism, and general underperformance at ChemCo showed.

Of course, there were many people in Britain, as elsewhere, who liked their work, not all of them in creative or materially advantageous occupations. But not many of these worked for the 'hundred or so gigantic corporations' on which Britain's economic welfare ultimately depended. Among those who did, few were socialists. Many more were concerned only with what they saw as an inevitable and interminable struggle to limit, wherever possible, the stress and unpleasantness of their work, and to maximise their wages and security. It was under these conditions, even when they seemed little different from those in similar plants elsewhere, that British management seemed by and large unable to match the competition.

By 1987, this picture was undoubtedly changing, but how far and in what ways remained uncertain. Unemployment combined with anti-union legislation had reduced industrial militancy to a historically low level and management was also said to be improving in at least some important sectors of industry. The trade union movement was divided in its attitude to the new regime. But it was still difficult to imagine that industrial militancy would not revive in one form or another with any long-term recovery in employment; only then would it become clear whether a lasting change in the nature of work, and of the workers' reponse to it, had been achieved.

The Organisation of Labour

By 1979 (the peak year for union strength) 13.3 million workers, or 54.5 per cent of the labour force, were members of trade unions; most of them voluntarily, some because it was a condition of employment under closed shop agreements. The percentage was higher than in many other OECD countries, though lower than in Australia, Austria, Belgium, Denmark, Finland, Norway, Sweden and Norway (see Table 8.2). The rate of unionisation among men was much higher than for women. The unions were therefore strong, but not exceptionally so. By 1986 total union membership had fallen to 10.5 million or 38.6 per

Table 8.2 Trade union density in 17 advanced capitalist countries 1979–1985

Country	Density 1979 (%)	Density 1985 (%)	Change 1979–85 (% points)
Denmark	86	98	+12
Belgium	77	84	+7
Sweden	89	95	+6
Ireland	49	51	+2
Austria	59	61	+2
Norway	60	61	+1
Canada	36	37	+1
Finland	84	85	+1
West Germany	42	42	0
France	28	28	0
Switzerland	36	35	−1
Australia	58	57	−1
Japan	32	29	−3
Italy	51	45	−6
Netherlands	43	37	−6
United Kingdom	58	52	−6
USA	25	18	−7

Source: J. Kelly, *Trade Unions and Socialist Politics*, Verso, London 1988, p. 269, citing R. Freeman.

cent of the labour force, a decline almost twice as big as the fall in employment.

By 1979, too, the vast majority of trade unionists had become concentrated in a few, very large unions (see Table 8.3). A union merger movement that began in the sixties had reduced the total number of unions and made the big unions bigger still, while new giant unions emerged in the public sector (NALGO and NUPE). This process continued in face of the unemployment and anti-union legislation of the eighties. By 1984 6.7 million workers (61 per cent of all trade unionists) belonged to 10 unions having over 250,000 members each; 8.8 million (79.1 per cent) were in 21 unions with 100,000 or more members.[17]

These unions were overwhelmingly 'general'. At the end of the nineteenth century, when most of them took their modern form, British industrial capitalism was still in transition from using labour to do work which was still much like that of the pre-industrial era, to modern production based on constant revolutions in technology and hence in work. To organise the great majority of workers, who were

Table 8.3   Unions with over 250,000 members, 1962, 1979 and 1987
(first seven unions are in 1962 rank order)

	1962	1979	1987	Rank Order 1987
1. TGWU	1,318,274	2,072,818	1,337,944	1
2. AEU/AUEW	982,182	1,483,419	857,599	2
3. GMWU/GMBATU	786,138	964,836	814,084	3
4. NUM	545,329	259,966	(104,941)	12*
5. USDAW	351,371	462,178	381,984	7
6. NUR	308,050	—	(125,000)	11*
7. ETU/EETPU	252,851	420,000	336,155	8
8. NALGO	—	729,405	750,430	4
9. NUPE	—	712,000	657,633	5
10. ASTMS	—	471,000	390,000	6
11. UCATT	—	320,723	249,485	9
12. NUT	—	291,239	(184,455)	10*
Total members	4,544,195	8,187,584	5,775,314	
No. of unions	7	11	9	

* Excluded from total, as falling below threshold.

We have included UCATT as a marginal case, since it claims 515 members short of 250,000.

Source: K. Coates and T. Topham, *Trade Unions in Britain*, Fontana, London 1988, p. 64.

still largely unskilled, and employed in a wide range of diverse trades and establishments, the new unions could not – unlike those formed in the 1850s and 60s – consist of workers possessing specific craft skills. The unskilled labourer's 'only chance . . . was to recruit into one gigantic union all those who could possibly blackleg on him – in the last analysis every "unskilled" man, woman or juvenile in the country; and thus to create a vast closed shop.'[18]

On the other hand, the 'common labourer' *was* giving way to the partly skilled, partly specialised labourer, who could not, without loss, be replaced by a complete novice. So the general unions became, in fact, associations of 'quasi-industrial' unions in a great range of different industries, each local industrial branch enjoying a large measure of autonomy. Then, in the years 1906–14, renewed industrial conflict forced the general unions to organise, in addition, non-local 'trades' (categories of semi-skilled and skilled workers across the country), so that the unions became amalgamations of both 'quasi-industrial' and 'quasi-craft' unions. This process was greatly accelerated after 1918. Conversely, many of the skilled crafts which the earlier unions had organised were gradually displaced by technical change. The engineers' union, for example, originally a union of the 'labour aristocrats' of the steam-engine, gradually came to represent a much larger force of skilled and semi-skilled workers in the metal and machinery industries, through not before many semi-skilled workers in these industries had been organised into other, general unions.

As a result, no modern British union is industry-wide, covering all the workers in a single field of employment, and very few are still pure 'craft' unions. Most unions have members in many different sectors of the economy, and most plants have workers in several unions. The most characteristic effects of this have been:

(a) Wages and conditions are not determined nationally. There are national agreements (made between the leaders of unions and the various employers' federations and associations), but these set only national minima; plant-level bargaining sets the rates and conditions applicable to the unions' members in each particular plant, at whatever levels the companies can afford and the local union negotiators can secure. This tendency has become even more pronounced in the Thatcher years.

(b) In day to day industrial relations, each 'shop' or section of a factory has a shop steward, directly elected by the workers in that shop to represent them regardless of the different unions to which they may belong. Shop stewards are coordinated by 'convenors', and in the engineering industry, in particular, they constitute the effective voice of the organised workforce. In the mid-1960s, the heyday of rank and file militancy, the Donovan Commission found that there were about 350,000 shop stewards, operating 'below' the level of the unions' national, district and branch officials, and in many respects being more significant.[19] The power of shop stewards has been reduced by the decline in shopfloor militancy.

A second distinctive feature of British trade unionism, until the 1980s at least, has been its substantial freedom from legal regulation, which distinguished it sharply from the position of the unions in Germany, the USA and Canada, in particular. There was no such thing as either a statutory right to strike, or an illegal strike; if workers decided not to work, they simply stopped working, and from 1906 onwards employers could not sue them for damages caused by this. There was no legally prescribed bargaining route, nor was a union prohibited from taking industrial action during the period of an existing agreement. In short, union–management relations rested only on the relative strengths of the two sides – and their mutual dependence.

This freedom from state control originated in the Conservatives' and Liberals' competition for working-class votes at the end of the nineteenth century. But its survival also reflected the exceptional solidarity of the British working class in the past. Every time capital sought to reverse the liberalisation of industrial relations adopted at that time, it was eventually forced to return to it – with the Trade Disputes Acts of 1906 and 1946, the abandonment of the Wilson–Castle proposals in 1969, and the repeal, in 1974, of the 1971 Industrial Relations Act.

In the boom of the 1950s, labour was scarce, wages rose and so did union membership. In engineering, especially, workers wrested from management an unprecedentedly large measure of control over the labour process, significantly reducing 'management prerogatives' – the 'principles that are at stake when the foreman starts to allocate work and the steward retorts, "Hang on a minute. You tell us what's to be done and we'll decide who does it".'[20] This was achieved mainly through 'unofficial' strike action, which (unlike the typical 'wildcat' strike in North America) was not illegal but was simply not official, in the sense that union officials had not called for it. Unofficial strikes usually lasted for no more than a few days, but by the end of the 1960s they accounted for 95 per cent of all strikes in Britain. It was because of the effectiveness of unofficial strikes that the Wilson and Heath governments both made unsuccessful attempts to change the law. In the end it was only the unemployment induced by the Thatcher government, and the accompanying union legislation, which reduced strike action, including unofficial strikes, to a historically low level (see below, pp. 152–4).

The significance of strikes is debatable. Before 1979 it was commonplace to attribute Britain's economic problems to strikes, but a comparison with other countries does not support this unequivocally. Table 8.4 shows that more days were 'lost' through strikes in Britain than in most other EEC countries, but fewer than in the USA or Canada (where fewer, but much longer, strikes were the rule). In any case, as Hyman has pointed out, the real cost of days 'lost' through strikes is dubious. Other costs fall when workers are on strike, and lost production is often largely made up when the strike is over. Absences from work due to strikes are modest compared with absences due to illness (10 million person-days compared with well over 310 million due to illness in 1977, for example); or with days lost from industrial accidents, which are often due – as is much of the illness – to

CAPITAL AND LABOUR

145

Table 8.4   Strikes in Britain and elsewhere 1970–1979

| | *Working days lost through industrial disputes per 1,000 workers in mining, manufacturing, construction and transport* | | |
	1970–79	*1970–74*	*1975–79*
Canada	1,840	1,724	1,965
Italy*	1,778	1,746	1,810
USA	1,211	1,380	1,042
UK	1,088	1,186	990
Belgium	489	520	458
France	312	300	324
W. Germany	92	92	92
Netherlands	82	118	38

* Includes gas, electricity and water

Source: Department of Employment, *Employment Gazette*, 89/1, January 1981, p. 28.

inadequate safety precautions and poor working conditions, not to mention the days lost because of management inefficiency, which are not recorded at all.[21]

It is also important to note that, even in the most militant years, most workers were not involved in any strikes at all; for instance, in the years 1971–3, 83 per cent of all employees were not involved in any strike action.[22] Strikes were largely confined to industries in trouble, where workers were faced with redundancies, speed-ups or declining pay relative to other sectors, such as the coal industry (which accounted for no less than three-quarters of all stoppages throughout the 1950s), the docks and motor-vehicle industries in the 1960s, and low-paid public sector workers in the late 1970s. It is none the less clear that strike action in those years did limit the ability of particular sectors of capital to solve their problems by increasing the rate of exploitation of the labour force, even if the low productivity of British industry cannot plausibly be blamed on strikes.[23]

This fact underlay the intense hostility felt by capital towards the unions, a hostility reflected with growing intensity by the media from the mid-1960s onwards. The militancy of those years also meant that general programmes of wage control could not be made permanent, and that management generally lacked confidence that large increases in profits would follow from large-scale investments.

This situation gave rise to a widespread misunderstanding about the trade unions. Unions were widely judged to have 'too much power', whereas power lay with the unionised rank and file of a few industries where militancy and solidarity were at a high level, rather than with the unions themselves; the unions as such were in reality rather weak in several respects. Some commentators recognised this by urging legal changes to *strengthen* the unions, by making them *less* democratic and giving more power to their bureaucracies, who were judged more 'responsible' (i.e., more inclined to fall in with the wishes of management.* But even from a democratic standpoint the union structure inherited from the Victorian era contained major sources of weakness.

First, the organisation of 'general' unions did not correspond in a rational manner to the organisation of industry. This made it difficult for individual unions to formulate and successfully advance long-term demands for the development of the various sectors in which their members worked. Second, although they were unencumbered by the expensive staffs of lawyers required for negotiations by unions in North America, they tended to lack staff who could formulate the more complex bargaining strategies of, for example, the Swedish unions; this was partly owing to the fact that union dues were kept low (about two-thirds the level of the European average as a share of workers' earnings) by the need felt by unions to remain competitive with other unions recruiting in the same industries. The demands of British unions have, in fact, been in many ways more limited than those advanced by unions in the other OECD countries. Third, for these reasons British unions did not respond as effectively as they might to some of the changes in the nature and pattern of work outlined above. Women, for instance, remained poorly represented even in unions in which a large proportion of the members were women, and the Equal Pay Act of 1970, though passed as a result of union pressure, had limited effects.[†] The large numbers of new white-collar and state employees in the post-war era were mostly recruited

* For instance Ben Hooberman, later a leading member of the SDP, wrote in 1974; 'In order to strengthen the powers of decision-making in unions it may be necessary to restrict elections to senior union officers. The officials who represent the middle management of the union could then be appointed on the basis of merit rather than elected on the grounds of popularity. Their terms of engagement could give them reasonable job security and compensation should they be dismissed or declared redundant. In this way, officials would become part of the permanent governing machine of the union and freed from the hazards of the electoral system. They would carry out decisions without hestitation and have an interest in communicating and commending to the members in their regions the policies adopted by elected officers of the union'. (*An Introduction to British Trade Unions*, Penguin, Harmondsworth 1974, p. 29.)

† In 1978 only 8 out of 65 members of the National Executive Committee of the National and Local Government Officers union, the fourth largest union in Britain, were women, although women accounted for 40% of the membership. In a sample of unions investigated by the TUC in 1975 a third of the members were women, but only 3% of the full-time officials were women. Women's gross hourly earnings rose from 63.1% of men's in 1970 to 73% in 1979.

into unions, but much less effectively recruited into the 'labour movement', as is shown by the fact that, by 1977, nearly half of the 11.7 million workers whose unions were affiliated to the TUC were not affiliated to the Labour Party which the TUC had originally created. The unions, and particularly the 'broad left' alliance of activists within them, did take up the causes of women, the unemployed, pensioners, young people and other underprivileged groups, but at the end of the 1970s the union movement as a whole could not yet be said to have become an effective expression of the changes that had occurred in the workforce in the preceding decades. The movement's inability to respond effectively to the unemployment and anti-union legislation of the early 1980s had a good deal to do with this fact.

The problem was then aggravated by the effects of Thatcherite economic policies. Industrial employment fell, weakening the old blue-collar unions. Nearly all the net new employment of over a million jobs created during the Thatcher years down to 1987 were part-time, overwhelmingly low-skill jobs, and mainly filled by women, all of which features made them less easy to unionise. The differences in pay and circumstances between the roughly 16 million full-time, mainly male, workforce in employment, at one end of the spectrum, and the roughly 8 million mainly female, part-time and temporary workers at the other, created potentially serious new lines of division within the labour movement.[24] So did the critical distinction between skilled workers in the expanding 'high-tech' fields, and skilled workers in declining fields (exemplified by the competition between the electricians and electronic telecommunications workers, on the one hand, and the printworkers, on the other, for the new jobs created by technical change in the newspaper industry). And the gap between those in employment and those more or less permanently out of work posed yet another threat to unity.

These problems were not insuperable. They could even stimulate major advances. For instance, when the Conservative government passed legislation requiring the unions to ballot their members on the issue of whether they should have political funds for supporting the Labour Party (see below, p. 153), the unions were galvanised into action, and to the government's surprise and chagrin secured substantial majorities in favour of political funds in every case, including some unions that had not previously had one.[25] But the changes that were occurring in the labour market posed a serious threat, including even the possibility that the unions' coordinating body, the Trades Union Congress, would split, with the 'high-tech' unions (notably the electricians and electronic telecommunications workers, the engineers, joined by the Union of Democratic Mine-

workers, which had split from the NUM after the 1984–5 miners'
strike) forming a new trade union 'central' dedicated to collaboration
with capital via 'no-strike' agreements.

This risk arose because the Trades Union Congress, though it
enjoyed the strength that came from being – hitherto – a single centre
(unlike the situation in several other European union movements), and
had a competent secretariat, was not in a position to make good the
basic weaknesses of the unions themselves. It could act only within the
framework of a general consensus of its member unions' leaderships,
and had no powers over member unions other than the power to expel
(a power which could obviously only be used in exceptional
circumstances). Its 37-member General Council, elected at annual
TUC conferences and including most of the major trade union leaders,
was none the less a very important political body; the labour
movement as a whole could not be expected to accomplish much that
the General Council was not prepared to support. It was the Council
that had launched the General Strike on 3 May 1926, and called it off
on the 12th. Later, refusal by the Council to support cuts in the 'dole'
led to the collapse of the MacDonald government in 1931 and, in 1969,
its opposition killed the Wilson–Castle proposals for industrial
relations legislation and secured the eventual repeal of the Industrial
Relations Act of 1971. The Council's attitude to the struggles within
the Labour Party over the strategy to be adopted in the 1980s would be
no less crucial, and in this context it was seriously handicapped in
representing a movement whose organisation was in important respects
archaic. The solidarity which had been the secret of the labour
movement's strength in the past needed increasingly to be re-created
on new lines to which the unions were still very imperfectly attuned.*

Corporatism and its Overthrow

After 1918 the power of organised labour and large-scale capital forced
the state to deal with them more and more directly. The National
Employers' Federation, the Federation of British Industries (as it then
was), the TUC and major individual unions such as the AUEW and
the TGWU became more than 'pressure groups' seeking to influence

---

* The trade unions and the TUC were not the only organisations which represented
the economic interests of labour. There were, besides, the Cooperative movement,
which in 1979 still had 10.4 million members and 6.7% of all retail sales in Britain,
though it was by then in serious financial difficulties; and other supportive organisations
such as the Institute for Workers' Control and the Conference of Socialist Economists
(policy research and educational associations). These bodies could play, however, at best
a marginal and long-term role.

policy. 'Parliament *appeared* to be the home and parties the source of political power', but in truth 'great areas of national policy tended to become the prerogative of ministers and civil servants dealing directly with the organisations of the employers and the workers'.[26] This was the reality, and in the 1970s the oscillation of policy between an ever more desperate search for consensus on economic and social policy and the increasingly sharp rejection of consensus, led to a literature which for the first time tried to portray the working of the state in relation to the economy as it actually was, rather than as liberal theory imagined it to be.

What had emerged had obvious affinities with the doctrine of the 'corporate state' advanced by conservative thinkers in the nineteenth century and later adopted by Fascist regimes in Italy, Spain and Portugal. According to this doctrine the state recognises the different interests of which society is composed by fostering their organisation in separate nationwide institutions which both represent and control their members, and then provides a forum within which their complementary needs are harmonised. But since in reality the interest of capital and labour conflict, 'harmony' has in practice to be imposed. Actual corporate states have always been authoritarian. However, the dream of harmony has inspired 'corporatist' ideas among representatives of both capital and labour in liberal states too, including Britain.[27] What developed in Britain in practice was a 'quasi-corporatist' system of economic and social policy-making and industrial conflict management – a 'corporate bias' grafted onto the parliamentary structure.[28]

Before the 1960s, however, the graft remained relatively inconspicuous, for three reasons. First, it was largely a product of the two world wars, which required a national economic effort for which the labour movement's cooperation was indispensable. During the First World War the sacrifices called for from the workers – the ban on strikes, the 'dilution' of labour, wages which did not keep pace with prices, and the appalling losses on the front – were not matched by adequate control of either prices or profits. Consequently, the Shop Stewards' Movement flourished and radical and revolutionary socialist ideas spread. By 1916,

the TUC had . . . become the Government's only lasting insurance against the Shop Stewards' Movement and the terrifying combination of industrial and political unrest in wartime, clearly visible in Germany, Italy and France.

As a result,

by the middle of 1916 a new conception of trade unionism was becoming

current in England in which responsible and representative leadership was
seen to merit a role in the country's political life.[29]

This was indeed a major change, though its implications were not
thoroughly accepted until much later – no doubt because the origins of
corporatism had an 'exceptional' character, like so much else in
wartime. The peacetime continuation of the relationships established
in the war years, after much of the rest of the wartime machinery of
government had been dismantled, was seen as nothing remarkable.

Second, during most of the inter-war period the labour movement
was relatively weak. Between the 1926 General Strike and the general
election of 1935, trade union leaders adopted a broadly cooperative
attitude towards capital. In 1928, following the General Strike and the
Trade Disputes Act of 1927 (see Chapter 4), Sir Alfred Mond, an
industrialist and former Minister of Health, held talks with Ben
Turner, the Chairman of the TUC, which culminated in a proposal for
a consultative Industrial Council representing workers and employers.
This appealed to neither the employers nor the TUC, but in
subsequent meetings the TUC and the National Confederation of
Employers' Organisations 'set themselves to build their own form of
industrial cooperation – corporatist in a far more subtle and flexible
form'.[30] This was, essentially, a relationship of consultation which
enabled both sides to discover where conflict was likely to occur and
how it could best be avoided. It was not the sort of arrangement to
cause much anxiety to strict constitutionalists, but it laid the basis for a
much more significant joint exercise of power when prosperity
returned.

The third reason why corporatism remained relatively inconspicuous
was the modesty of trade union demands. Until the 1970s these were
almost wholly confined to wage levels and hours of work. British
unions were much slower than unions elsewhere to include even so-
called 'fringe benefits' among their demands, let alone demands such
as participation in management or specific investment policies on the
part of the employing companies. This reflected in part what Crouch
calls 'the Compromise':[31] in spite of their unique freedom from
statutory regulations (by comparison with other countries) British
trade unions did not challenge 'management prerogatives' (at least not
officially, even though plant-level bargaining from the 1950s onwards
undermined many management prerogatives in practice); and they also
accepted a strict separation between industrial action (the unions'
prerogative) and political action (the Labour Party's).

Nonetheless the machinery, and even more the informal practices,
had been put in place. When the Labour Party joined the war coalition

in 1940, Ernest Bevin, the General Secretary of the TGWU, became Minister of Labour and secured trade union agreement to another ban on strikes, supported this time by effective controls over profits and prices. The TUC and the employers formed a Joint Consultative Council which acquired 'the status of an unofficial Government department'.[32] The years 1945–51 saw a partial rift when the unions seemed, in the eyes of capital, to have acquired a privileged position, since 'their' party now had a large parliamentary majority. But this proved much more apparent than real, and after 1951, helped by historically high rates of growth, Conservative governments maintained the informal triangular relationship.

From now on, 'what had been merely interest groups crossed the political threshold and became part of the extended state'. [33] But this only became obvious with the renewal of the crisis. Now governments sought to control wages in peacetime. In return they once again had to try to control prices and profits, but now – in contrast with the war years – they had also to convince both unions and employers that the sacrifices were worthwhile. This meant inviting them to participate, or seeming to invite them to participate, in economic policy-making. This was the primary reason why, in 1962, the Conservative government under Macmillan established the National Economic Development Council, a high level consultative body representing the TUC, the CBI and the government. Its purpose was to plan economic development; its political significance lay in giving a formal role in long-term economic policy-making to these non-party, non-parliamentary organisations.

The pressure of the crisis quickly revealed the limits of corporatism, however. In 1916, under the exigencies of war, Lloyd George had been able to rely on TUC and Labour Party support when he suppressed the ILP newspaper and used force to break up the left-wing leadership of the Clydeside engineering workers. It is doubtful if this could have been repeated during the Second World War and it was certainly out of the question by the 1960s and 1970s. The trade union rank and file had become too confident and militancy was too widespread. Although wage controls were imposed by Labour in 1966 with TUC support, the government's abandonment of its plans for expansion and the ineffectiveness of price controls quickly led to mass discontent, culminating in the abortive effort to bring in legislation to control strikes in 1969. There followed the initial effort by Heath to dispense with corporatism; tripartite meetings of government, unions and employers largely ceased, except for the meetings of the NEDC (which had become somewhat ritualistic with the abandonment of Labour's planning initiative after 1966). Strikes were allowed to run their course without state intervention.

But the collapse of the Heath strategy, itself due to the advanced debility of British industry, inaugurated not merely a revival of corporatism but a fundamental change in its nature. By July 1972 Heath had decided that wages could not be left to the determination of the market in Britain – not even with the help of the Industrial Relations Act, which in any case threatened industrial conflict on an unacceptable scale. The TUC and CBI were once again summoned to Downing Street. This time, however, the unions had understood that if they were to give up their freedom to bargain for wage increases, they should demand substantial compensation in terms of social and economic policy. The TUC therefore 'put nearly every issue of socio-economic policy on the agenda'.[34] Their demands included reversing, or at least mitigating, the effects of most of the government's tax and social policies of the previous two years. This, of course, was a lot more than Heath was prepared to concede, and besides, he was in a hurry. In November 1972 he introduced a statutory wage freeze and followed it up with new legislation for long-term controls, resulting in a confrontation with the miners in the autumn and winter of 1973–4.

The next phase of 'bargained corporatism' (to use Crouch's term) was the 'social contract' of 1974–5, in which the unions not only obtained from the Labour government a significant quid pro quo for wage restraint *before* they began to restrain wage demands, but were able to have included in the 'contract' a broad range of social as well as economic policies. What is more, these policies included some which bore directly on the relationship of the, unions to the state. The Trade Union and Labour Relations Act and the Employment Protection Act, passed in 1975, did not refer explicitly to the corporatist structure itself but they consolidated its base by strengthening the legal position of labour vis-à-vis capital. On the other hand, they did not increase the political *power* of labour, which had always rested on solidarity and on the unions' autonomy from the state, not on legislative provisions. This became very clear when, in 1979, the Thatcher government came to power dedicated to the destruction of every vestige of corporatism: from June 1979 onwards, the unions were completely excluded from participation in the determination of economic policy, and the law was radically rewritten so as to remove most of the gains that the unions had won and maintained since 1906.

This was possible only on the condition that trade union solidarity could not be mobilised effectively against the government (and that a majority of the electorate supported the exclusion – which as opinion polls showed, they did). The main weapon used to weaken solidarity was the unemployment produced by the 1979–81 deflation. But new legislation, reinforced by anti-union court rulings, contributed greatly to this by making it harder for unions to win industrial disputes, making them less valuable to their members, and by making solidarity very costly.

Three acts – the Employment Acts of 1980 and 1982, and the Trade Union Act of 1984 – were the main legal instruments used, but as Coates and Topham point out, the readiness of judges to interpret union rights very narrowly, and especially to grant injunctions (enforced by huge fines and even the sequestration of a union's assets) against industrial action which an employer represents as actionable under the new laws, has circumscribed the unions' actions very tightly – while employers have become increasingly willing to resort to the courts as they have realised that the unions are less and less able and willing to retaliate.

The common theme of all these acts insofar as they related to industrial action was that they drastically narrowed the range of trade union actions which are immune to civil action in the courts. They did not create new criminal offences, and so did not in themselves bring the state into direct conflict with the unions, as the 1971 Industrial Relations Act did. But through the mechanism of court injunctions they made the judiciary into a (frequently willing) enforcing agency for employer interests.

The 1980 and 1982 Acts removed immunity from sympathetic strikes, secondary action, secondary picketing, and flying pickets (the key to the miners' famous victory in 1972). From now on industrial action was only immune from civil action for damages against the union if it was done by those employed at the workplace of those involved (it could not even be at another plant which was owned by the same company), conformed to the government's 'guide-lines' on picketing (which in effect barred mass pickets), and was wholly or mainly concerned with a trade dispute (i.e. if a judge ruled that it had a 'political' motive it was not immune). The 1984 Act added a requirement that a national ballot of all union members must be held within four weeks of the start of any industrial action, if it was to remain immune. The Employment Acts also went far towards neutralising the benefits to the unions of 'closed shops' (where an employer agrees to hire only union members) and making it hard to establish new ones, eroding an important foundation of employee solidarity in industrial disputes. The 1984 Act regulated trade unions' internal affairs by requiring direct ballots of all union members every three years for union executive members (i.e. indirect elections, which tend to give the final choice to union activists, were banned); and ballots every ten years on the question of whether a union should maintain a political fund, the basis of Labour Party finances (no equivalent law regulated company donations to the Conservative Party). Coates and Topham's summary of the overall results of the new legal regime is accurate:

> Fundamentally, the state no longer acts in its traditional role to support and reinforce collective bargaining as the norm. On the contrary, its interventions are solely concerned to produce the opposite condition of a fragmented and increasingly individualistic labour market. The courts have discovered new means of enforcement, including sequestration of union assets, and receivership, which have devastated union security in industrial disputes. Picketing has become ever more hazardous, as police powers and methods have developed to alarming proportions. We may now reasonably characterise British law and trade disputes as a condition of legal harassment of strikers, the like of which has not been experienced since the early nineteenth century, and which, in its degree, is unknown on the continent of Europe.[35]

The results can be seen in the decline of trade union membership (see p. 140 above) and in the marked decline in strike activity, punctuated only by the 1984–85 mineworkers' strike (see pp. 118–19 above). The 1986 strike figures were the lowest since 1956 (see Table 8.5). A strike by the National Union of Seamen against large-scale layoffs by P&O's European Ferries early in 1988 clearly showed where power now lay. An attempt at sympathetic action against Sealink, European Ferries' chief British competitor, was promptly crushed by court action, 872 P&O crew-members were dismissed and the NUS's assets were sequestrated. Another court issued an injunction against demonstrations by striking crew-members on the grounds that they were 'intimidatory'. The *Economist* commented at the time:

> Only the possibility of solidarity from dockers and shipworkers in continental Europe, beyond the reach of Mrs Thatcher's trade-union laws, leaves the outcome in doubt . . . The dispute has shown the devastating effect of Tory industrial-relations law . . . Without secondary picketing, the main way in which the TUC can offer hope to an embattled member has gone – and with it one of the main forces for cohesion among Britain's different unions.[36]

As unemployment started to fall after 1986 some trade union leaders, fortified by union mergers, began to appear more confident, but the new regime (which a majority of the public appeared to accept) remained a massive obstacle to renewed militancy; and as ACAS, the government-sponsored Advisory, Conciliation and Arbitration Service, reported, union density was falling, especially in the fastest growing sectors of the economy, and employers generally were increasingly

Table 8.5   Strikes 1978–1987

	No. of Strikes	Days lost
1978	2,471	9.4m
1979	2,080	29.5m
1980	1,330	12.0m
1981	1,338	4.3m
1982	1,528	1.5m
1983	1,352	3.8m
1984	1,206	27.1m
1985	887	6.4m
1986	1,053	1.9m
1987	901	3.5m

Source: *Employment Gazette* April 1988.

reconsidering their relations with unions, securing contracts restoring much greater management freedom and in some cases even managing to withdraw union recognition. With so much in flux, it would be a mistake to assume that the power of labour had been permanently reduced, let alone broken; but the days of union power based on mass action and political solidarity seemed unlikely to return soon.

Capital and Labour: an Assessment

In the pluralists' universe, capital and labour are merely 'factors of production' which, along with a multitude of other interests, act as 'pressure groups' of relatively equal strength: if anything, 'labour' was considered to have become, at least before 1980, more powerful than 'business'. Yet, as Miliband pointed out, in capitalist society capital is necessarily dominant.[37] He identified three basic sources of this dominance:

1. Capital's autonomous power of decision in the economy, based on its ownership and control of production and accumulated wealth, and the dependence of governments on 'business confidence' for investment, growth, and tax revenues;*

* In this connection the intensity of British capital's resistance to proposals for the industrial democracy is noteworthy. In 1973 the Labour Party promised to introduce a measure of industrial democracy when next returned to office. The majority report of the Bullock Committee (established by Wilson in 1975) recommended in 1977 giving workers and shareholders equal representation on the boards of directors of all companies employing 2,000 or more workers (some 738 companies in all at this time),

2. The strength which capital derives from its international character – the support given to it by foreign bankers, the IMF, and foreign governments; and

3. The social and financial advantages which capital enjoys – superior access to, and sympathy from, state officials and legislators, the ability to switch large financial resources into research, propaganda, the Conservative Party, lock-outs, etc.

Labour, on the other hand, lacks these advantages, including that of funds. (In spite of much disingenuous talk about the scale of trade union bank balances, in 1979 they amounted to only £27 per trade union member, however impressive the figures might be made to appear by adding them all together.)[38] Labour also suffers from certain inherent limitations noted by Anderson.[39]

1. Trade unions are an intrinsic part of capitalist society; by their nature they 'both resist the given unequal distribution of income within the society by their wage demands, and ratify the principle of an unequal distribution by their existence';
2. They have only one significant weapon, the passive, negative and sometimes unsuitably blunt weapon of the withdrawal of labour, compared with the many active, positive steps open to capital;
3. They are sectoral organisations, producing on their own only a 'corporate' consciousness (a consciousness of belonging to a particular economic group of workers, not to all workers at large) which not even their central body, the TUC, can easily transcend. As a result, labour tends to be more divided than capital.

But the root cause of labour's relative weakness is less organisational than ideological. It lies in the fact that 'capital' is ultimately the *system of relationships* which arises from the fact that most productive resources are owned by a very small minority of the population for

---

with a smaller number of additional directors chosen from outside the company by the workers and shareholders' representatives jointly. The CBI representatives on the Committee dissented and the CBI refused to discuss the main issues further. The Callaghan government allowed the matter to die. The only move in this direction was taken experimentally by the Post Office, a public corporation, and this was terminated at the end of 1979 'at the request of the Chairman and all the non-worker directors' (The *Economist*, 23 February 1980). It should be recalled that in West Germany, workers and shareholders have equal representation on boards which supervise the boards of directors of the largest firms (650 firms in 1976); in Norway, the workers elect a third of the directors of all companies with over 50 employees; in Sweden, the workers elect two directors of all companies with over 100 employees, and all decisions concerning the sale of the company, changes in production organisation, investments and most senior appointments are subject to negotiation with the unions.

whom most of the rest work.* This fact pervades every aspect of life (including the way in which the state-owned sector of production operates) and gives capital the advantage of being taken for granted, so that all actions that tend to conflict with the interests of capital are felt to be somehow improper, even by many of those involved in them.

The media – themselves largely part of private capital – play an important part in producing this effect, not least in the field of industrial relations itself, where television (watched by working-class adults for an average of 20 hours per week) presents 'both sides' – but (a) unequally – more coverage, and much more sympathetic coverage, is given to the management side; and (b) in a way which, by adopting an apparently 'neutral' (and by implication authoritative) standpoint, endorses the idea that there is a legitimate 'public' interest which the relationship between capital and labour serves.[40] This conception of neutrality endorses as natural the whole arrangement whereby most people are employees who must work for others. Media treatment of industrial relations in the 1960s and 70s, however, was not even consistently neutral in this sense; and this had something to do with the fact that the proportion of people willing to agree that 'the unions have too much power' rose from 54 per cent in the middle of 1968 to 74 per cent at the end of 1975, and that by the latter date even 66 per cent of trade unionists were of the same opinion.[41] (By 1987, however, the unions were no longer seen as a serious problem, and the proportion

---

* The basic facts about the ownership of capital are often obscured by discussions which focus on the question of the distribution of 'wealth', as for instance in the report of the 1975 Royal Commission on the Distribution of Income and Wealth. Stating that it had 'no axe to grind' the Commission focused primarily on the question of how 'fair' the distribution of wealth in Britain was – a question which a decade of wage controls had made politically sensitive. The Commission defined wealth as 'marketable assets' and even went on to show that if rights to pensions were included, the poorest 80% of the population owned 45% of the national wealth. However, even if pension rights are disregarded, most of the marketable assets counted as wealth were items such as dwellings, consumer durables, and personal savings which the owners cannot use as *capital*, i.e., cannot use to enable them to employ other people for profit. The core of personally-owned *capital* consists of farms, forests and non-residential real estate, the assets of small businesses and above all the assets of limited liability companies. Five per cent of the population owned 80% of all company shares; 1 per cent owned 54%. A much wider group of people owned a few shares, but this only blurs the edges of the central reality that capital is largely owned, and wholly controlled, by about 1 per cent of the population for whom two-thirds of the rest work. The ownership of company shares by pension funds is sometimes held to qualify this and it is true that by 1975 nearly 17% of company shares were held by pension funds. But as Minns has shown, these funds are largely controlled by the banks and are managed in the interests of the companies concerned; there is no indication that they have been or will be used to change either the control or the distribution of ownership of capital (R. Minns, *Pension Funds and British Capitalism*, Heinemann, London 1980).

of the public who were prepared to say that unions were, in general, 'a good thing', had recovered from the figure of 51 per cent in 1979, to 71 per cent – a proportion last seen in 1954.)[42]

But the ultimate source of the hegemony of capital is social relations themselves, the fact that most workers (including most trade union leaders) are socialised in homes where, for example, it is taken for granted that most of the children attend schools over which the parents have no control and which will prepare them to be wage workers; where women expect to be paid less than men, and to do the lion's share of the housework as well as their jobs; where the daily paper is a pro-business tabloid, and so on. The acceptance of capital, expressed in the quotation at the beginning of this chapter, originates in this experience, and is reflected and reinforced by the media.

Notes

1 T. Nichols and P. Armstrong, *Workers Divided*, Fontana, London 1976, p. 56.
2 S.G.E. Lythe, 'Britain, the Financial Capital of the World', in C.J. Barlett, ed., *Britain Pre-Eminent*, Macmillan, London 1969, pp. 40–1.
3 E.P. Thompson, *The Making of the English Working Class*, Penguin, Harmondsworth, London 1968.
4 S. Aaronovitch et al., *The Political Economy of British Capitalism*, McGraw-Hill, London 1981, p. 267.
5 *Economic Trends*, Supplement 1981, p. 172, and *Business Monitor*, May 1979, p. 85.
6 Lythe, p. 33.
7 F. Longstreth, 'The City, Industry and the State', in C. Crouch, ed., *State and Economy in Contemporary Capitalism*, St. Martins Press, New York 1979, p. 171.
8 G. Ingham, in *Capitalism Divided: The City and Industry in British Social Development*, Macmillan, London 1984, provides an important account of the formation of the City–Bank–Treasury nexus in the early nineteenth century; an account criticised, but not seriously challenged, by M. Barratt-Brown in 'Away With All Great Arches: Anderson's History of British Capitalism', *New Left Review* 167, January/February 1988, pp. 22–51, and by B. Fine and L. Harris, *The Peculiarities of the British Economy*, Lawrence and Wishart, London 1985, Chapter 20. On the contemporary role of the City see also J. Coakley and L. Harris, *The City of Capital*, Blackwell, Oxford 1983.
9 The CBI's Discussion Document, *The Will to Win* published in March 1981 could be regarded as an eleventh-hour attempt to outline an economic policy needed for industrial recovery, but it lacked a serious political dimension.
10 C. Crouch, *The Politics of Industrial Relations*, Fontana, London 1979, p. 157. See also C. Leys, 'Thatcherism and British Manufacturing: A Question of Hegemony', *New Left Review* 151, May/June 1985, pp. 5–25.
11 Longstreth, 'The City', p. 188.
12 See *Review of Security and the State 1978*, Julian Friedmann, London 1978, pp. 135–45, for an article on the Economic League in which this estimate is cited.
13 See T. Nichols, 'Social Class: Official, Sociological and Statistical', in J. Irvine et al., eds, *Demystifying Social Statistics*, Pluto Press, London 1979, pp. 158–9.
14 On this point, see J. Westergaard and H. Resler, *Class in a Capitalist Society*, Heinemann, London 1975, pp. 291–6.

15 A. Heath et al., *How Britain Votes*, Oxford 1985, p. 36.
16 T. Nichols and H. Beynon, *Living with Capitalism*, Routledge, London 1977, p. 200; see also H. Beynon, *Working for Ford*, Allen Lane, London 1973 and T. Nichols and P. Armstrong, *Workers Divided*, Fontana, London 1976.
17 K. Coates and T. Topham, *Trade Unions in Britain*, Fontana, London 1988, pp. 67-8.
18 E.J. Hobsbawm, 'General Unions in the British Labour Movement', in *Labouring Men*, Weidenfeld and Nicolson, London 1964, p. 181.
19 The Royal Commission on Trade Unions and Employers' Associations *Report*, HMSO, London 1968; Hyman, however, thought that there were about 200,000 (R. Hyman, *Strikes*, Fontana, London 1972, p. 45).
20 H. Beynon, *Working for Ford*, p. 145.
21 Hyman, pp. 33-4. It is also relevant that workers in most EEC countries tend to have longer holidays, besides working shorter hours, than British workers.
22 C.T.B. Smith et al., *Strikes in Britain: Manpower Paper No. 15*, Department of Employment, London 1978, p. 139.
23 On the general issue of scapegoating the workers see the excellent study by T. Nichols, *The British Worker Question*, Routledge and Kegan Paul, London 1986.
24 See C. Leadbeater, *Marxism Today*, April 1987.
25 Coates and Topham, *Trade Unions in Britain*, pp. 348-49.
26 K. Middlemas, *Politics in Industrial Society*, Deutsch, London 1979, pp. 309 and 327.
27 L. Carpenter, 'Corporatism in Britain 1930-50', *Journal of Contemporary History*, 1, 1976, pp. 3-25.
28 The best definition of corporatism as a structure of political management within advanced capitalism is in L. Panitch, 'Recent Theorisations of Corporatism: Reflections on a Growth Industry', *British Journal of Sociology*, 31/2, 1980, pp. 159-87. The term 'corporate bias' is from Middlemas (see note 26).
29 Middlemas, pp. 89-90.
30 Ibid., p. 209.
31 C. Crouch, *Class Conflict and the Industrial Relations Crisis*, Heinemann, London 1977, Chapter 3.
32 Middlemas, p. 279.
33 Ibid., p. 373.
34 Crouch, p. 243.
35 Coates and Topham, *Trade Unions in Britain*, pp. 315-16.
36 The *Economist*, 30 April and 7 May 1988.
37 R. Miliband, *The State in Capitalist Society*, Weidenfeld and Nicolson, London 1969, Chapter 6, 'Imperfect Competition'.
38 Certification Office for Trade Unions and Employers' Associations, *Annual Report of the Certification Officer 1979*, p. 49. The total was £269.9 million. The total political funds of the unions at the end of 1979 were £4.5 million.
39 P. Anderson, 'The Limits and Possibilities of Trade Union Action', in R. Blackburn and A. Cockburn, eds, *The Incompatibles: Trade Union Militancy and the Consensus*, Penguin, Harmondsworth 1967, pp. 263-80, reprinted in T. Clarke and L. Clements, eds, *Trade Unions Under Capitalism*, Fontana, London 1977, pp. 334-50.
40 Glasgow University Media Group, *Bad News* and *More Bad News*, Routledge, London 1976 and 1980.
41 *NOP Bulletin*, March 1969, and the *Economist*, 10 January 1976, reporting a MORI survey.
42 *The Gallup Political Index* 1988; courtesy of R. Whybrow.

9

Social Classes and British Politics

During the 'age of affluence' in the 1950s a rather strange argument was advanced, that this 'most class-ridden country under the sun' (as Orwell called it) was positively united by its class differences. The most characteristic example of this was held to be the 'deferential' working-class voter who voted for the Conservatives because he (or she) felt that the 'upper class' was bred to rule ('Breeding counts every time. I like to be set an example and have someone I can look up to').[1] In other words, British people were supposed to know their place in the class system and be satisfied with it. Less was heard of the merits of this amiable arrangement as the crisis unfolded after 1961. Still, the nature of the class system is far from obvious, and its political significance needs careful consideration.

The first essential is to establish what we mean by 'class'. For many writers, the existence of classes is simply a 'given' with which the parties must work, and so for them the social classes of Britain should naturally be described first (in so far as this is judged to be necessary at all).[2] But it is also possible to consider classes as at least partly the *products* of party competition, and as will be argued shortly, there are good reasons for doing so. 'Classes' are perhaps best thought of as expressing the constant *interaction* between socio-economic structure and political process, and between what is determined and what can be, and is, changed by human agency. This is a severe oversimplification; but it is less misleading than to present 'the class system' as something 'prior to' political parties. The significance of this chapter's location, between the discussion of the capital–labour relationship and the discussion of the parties, should be interpreted in this sense.

Conceptualising Social Classes

The word 'class' was first applied to British society when the industrial revolution began to produce large new categories of occupation which were unknown in the pre-industrial social order. Previously, there had been the gentry, and the 'common people', with merchants, bankers, clergymen, doctors, clerks, shopkeepers and the like constituting no more than well-understood qualifications to a social hierarchy still fundamentally based on land ownership. By the middle of the nineteenth century the new categories had become too important to be treated in this way. People spoke of the 'middle classes', those in between the landed gentry and the common people. The word was first used in the plural and was extended to the 'labouring classes' by polite society only later.[3] The Conservative Party leader Lord Salisbury, for example, wrote to Joseph Chamberlain as late as 1886 that the Conservative Party's 'strongest ingredients' were 'the classes and the dependants of class' – meaning by 'classes' only the *propertied* and their personal servants, tenants, clients, tradespeople, doctors, tutors, etc.[4] The reduction of the 'middle classes' to one 'middle class' and of the 'labouring classes' to one 'working class' in popular usage was the result of politics. It reflected the emergence of a labour movement which, by 1900, had developed an awareness of common interests uniting all wage-earners, and a corresponding tendency for all those who had any personal property to define themselves *out* of the 'working class' residentially, educationally and electorally.

So much for popular usage. Can we make anything more of the concept of class than a general descriptive category of this kind? The most common tendency has been to take popular usage and simply try to make it more precise. Society is seen as 'stratified', divided into layers according to different levels of esteem or status. These 'strata' are largely defined by occupation, and this is actually the meaning given to the term 'social class' in the censuses, producing a 'class structure' like the first one shown in Table 9.1.

As Nichols says, we can regard this as 'the nearest thing we have to an official definition of "social class"'.[5] It is noteworthy that not only are the categories of this 'structure' based on an official judgement of the degrees of esteem to be attached to the various occupations, but as Nichols also points out, in this classification, 'the owners of capital are lost to sight' – the 'class system' thus constructed completely *ignores* the capital–labour relationship.[6]

Still, this official judgement of degree of esteem is quite close to that which ordinary people make when asked by sociological investigators

Table 9.1   Social classes according to the Census,
and according to people's 'self-ratings', 1985

Census definitions	
I (professional) & II (intermediate)	21%
IIIa (skilled non-manual)	23%
IIIb (skilled manual)	22%
IV (partly skilled) & V (unskilled)	23%
Never worked/not classifiable	11%
'Self-ratings'	
Upper middle class	1%
Upper middle or middle class	24%
Upper working class	21%
Working class	48%
Poor	3%
Don't know/not answered	3%

Sources: R. Jowell and S. Witherspoon, eds, *British Social
Attitudes: the 1985 Report*, SCPR/Gower, Aldershot 1985,
p. 3; *Social Trends 1987*, p. 16.

to rank occupations according to their status; and the main contribution
of most sociologists to the question of social class in Britain has been
to try to refine the criteria according to which the ranking is done. For
instance, sociologists distinguish between so-called 'objective' bases of
'social class' – the 'factors' which determine what class people see
themselves as belonging to – and the 'subjective images' which people
have of themselves as belonging to a particular class. But the essence
of the former is, everyone agrees, occupation. So, although for some
purposes it is interesting to know that eleven out of twelve British
people assign themselves to either the 'middle class' or the 'working
class', it turns out that this is so strongly related to their occupational
status that this serves as a proxy for 'self-assigned class' for most
purposes. The data collected on this basis are not without value.
Striking differences in people's conditions of life are revealed by
classifying them in this way, as Table 9.2 shows.

The same is true of people's party preferences. The 1985 Social
Attitudes Survey found that people identified with parties along class
lines (defined in this way) as shown in Table 9.3. From the point of
view of someone wishing to spread higher education more equally, or
of a party organiser contemplating an election campaign, Tables 9.2
and 9.3 are useful starting-points. But, beyond that, two kinds of
problem immediately arise. First, what is the nature of the relationship?
For example, do skilled manual workers tend to vote Labour because

Table 9.2 Differences of condition by socio-economic group, 1985 (%)

	Chronic sickness men/women	Children aged 16–19 in full-time education
Professional	20	54
Employees & managers	27	46
Intermediate and Junior non-manual	26	45
Skilled manual and own-account non-professional	31	25
Semi-skilled manual and personal service	32 ⎱	20
Unskilled manual	34 ⎰	

Source: General Household Survey 1985.

of its record of concern for them or because they are more unionised than other kinds of worker? Second, what determines what occupations there are, how people are distributed among them, and what rewards and status they carry?

Sociologists have done a great deal of work on the first of these two questions, but very little on the second. Yet when answers to the first question have been found, the second still needs to be answered. Otherwise, explaining anything in terms of 'classes' is not very helpful – it simply refers us to the occupational status structure, which itself remains unexplained.

For this reason anyone who wants to explain politics in terms of class needs a concept of class that belongs to a general theory of social change, as the Marxist concept of class is meant to do. The basic idea of Marx was that classes are constituted by the relations of production

Table 9.3 Party identification by social class (census definitions) 1985

	Conservative	Alliance	Labour	Other parties & non-aligned
I and II (professional & intermediate)	51	16	22	5
III (skilled non-manual)	48	17	23	6
III (skilled manual)	31	10	46	9
IV & V (semi-skilled and unskilled)	25	11	52	7

Source: R. Jowell & S. Witherspoon, eds, *British Social Attitudes: the 1985 Report*, SCPR/Gower, Aldershot 1985, p. 7.

that are dominant in any given society – in a capitalist society, by the relations of ownership and control of the means of production that link the owners to the non-owners of capital. Marx failed to provide a definition of class, but Lenin defined it as follows:

> Classes are large groups of people which differ from each other by the place they occupy in a historically definite system of social production, by their relation (in most cases fixed and formulated in laws) to the means of production, by their role in the social organization of labour, and, consequently, by the dimensions and method of acquiring the share of social wealth that they obtain. Classes are groups of people one of which may appropriate the labour of another owing to the different places they occupy in the definite system of social economy.[7]

This definition is very general and does not particularly stress the aspect of antagonism between the principal classes which is so important in Marx's theory. It will serve, however, as an initial formulation. With this concept of class, classes appear as historical agents produced by the 'logic' of a specific economic and social system. Political action is then conceived of as expressing the interests which people see themselves as having by virtue of their class membership, and the results of these actions in turn react back on the development of the economy and society. This may not be a valid theory; but it is the *kind* of theory needed if 'class' is to be a useful explanatory concept, rather than a purely empirical concept that merely accepts, without further enquiry, the 'stratification system' found to be operative in a given society at a given time – especially when this means adopting uncritically the language of everyday life, according to which, as Nichols wryly remarks, 'there is a "middle class", with a "working class" underneath, and – a sort of bald class structure this – nothing on top'.[8]

The Role of Class in British Politics: Some Theoretical Questions

The Marxist concept of class presents some immediate problems when applied to contemporary Britain. It ought, for instance, to be able to explain political developments by showing that people act as they do because of their class interests. But the Marxian concept does not seem to predict the political activities of many people in Britain, especially the many workers who support the Conservatives. A second major difficulty is that modern capitalism does not differentiate people as clearly into antagonistic classes, one exploiting and the other exploited, as Marx often seems to have assumed. The growth of a 'new' middle class (or new middle classes) of professional, technical, supervisory and especially state-employed salaried workers, who appear to be neither exploiting nor – except in a rather abstract sense – exploited, seems to cast further doubt on the utility of the Marxian concept of class for the study of British politics (or the politics of any other advanced capitalist society, for that matter). Each of these difficulties must be considered in turn.

The first problem was, in fact, recognised by Marx, who conceived of a class as coming into existence as a result of the development of a given mode of production, but acquiring 'class consciousness' only gradually in the course of struggles with another antagonistic class. Marx, however, tended to assume that these struggles would inevitably reveal more and more clearly to the exploited class where its class interest lay, and how it was necessary to make a political revolution in order to satisfy this interest. The development of the British working class, a third of whom, after two hundred years of capitalism, do not see themselves as having a class interest opposed to the capitalists, and hardly any of whom are revolutionary, obviously casts doubt on the usefulness of Marx's class concept for explaining British politics.

Theorists have sought to deal with this problem in one of two main ways. One approach, exemplified by Giddens, is to retain the idea that classes are constituted by the relations of production, but to see their political significance as varying greatly, according to other aspects of each country's historical experience.[9] Giddens refers to this as differing degrees of 'class structuration'. Thus, a working class, for example, is more 'structurated' the less individual social mobility there is into and out of it, because this makes the life experience of its members more homogeneous. This 'structuration' is also strengthened by the sharpness of the distinctions drawn at work between operatives and technicians, or between workers and supervisors, and by differences in income and related benefits, especially those which tend to reinforce the residential segregation of classes. An example of this would be the difficulty most British workers experienced in the past in getting mortgages, so reinforcing the tendency for them to be concentrated in rented 'council housing'. These considerations seem relevant to the differences found between Britain and the USA or Canada, for example, in respect to the salience and usefulness of 'class' as an explanation of political life. British classes are relatively more 'structurated'.

Giddens also argues that the reason why the British (or any other) working class has at most a 'labourist', and not a revolutionary, consciousness is that once the transition to capitalist society is complete, and the industrial and political relationship between labour and capital has been institutionalised, the working class no longer has any experience of alternative modes of production which could give it a sense that any other system of production is historically *possible*. That is why, according to Giddens, revolutionary consciousness was characteristic of the European working class only in the first half of the nineteenth century ('the point of impact of post-feudalism and capitalist industrialism'); and why it tends to develop nowadays among workers in 'backward' countries where the contrast or contradiction between the potential of capitalist production technology, and the pre-capitalist relations of production which still prevail, generates painful paradoxes and a powerful sense of the possibility (as well as the desirability) of radical change. In Giddens's view, therefore, Marx's concept of class is broadly sound, but his theory of social change needs revision: in advanced capitalist societies like Britain's, the working class is not impelled to see itself as irreconcilably opposed to the capitalist class or to envisage a revolutionary alternative to capitalist society.

This approach, with its rather fatalistic political implications (to the effect that things in Britain could hardly be otherwise, and that no radical change can be expected), has two main weaknesses. First, it does not account for differences *within* the British working class in respect of class or political consciousness; and second, it tends to assume that capitalism is a much more *stable* system of production than it in fact is. In reality, the short- and long-term changes which are constantly occurring in the capital–labour relation, interacting with political leadership and organisation and the effects of ideological struggles, have affected the political significance of the class system in Britain in decisive ways. They have led to periods of confrontation and the spread of socialist ideas – including 'revolutionary' ideas of various kinds – as well as to periods of collaboration and consensus.

Recognition of these fluctuations has been one of the bases for the other approach to the problem of how far the Marxian concept of class can explain the realities of modern British politics. According to this view, while the economic division of labour and the relations of exploitation create classes, organisation and leadership are the key to their development as political 'agents'. Lenin adopted an extreme form of this doctrine at one point, arguing that a party of professional revolutionaries, including especially elements drawn from the 'bourgeois intelligentsia', was the decisive factor in determining whether a working class could progress beyond mere 'trade-union consciousness'.[10]

Lenin's view has been used to rationalise a long sequence of unsuccessful attempts at the revolutionary mobilisation of British workers since the formation of the Communist Party of Great Britain in 1920. Later theorists, however, have adopted a more democratic and nuanced position. A leading example here is Przeworski, who traced the way in which all the social-democratic parties in Western Europe have, in effect, been forced by electoral competition to become merely reformist parties and, eventually, to convert their own supporters into supporters of the capitalist system.[11] Przeworski sees this as neither more nor less than a political victory, won in the course of a century, by the capitalist class over the working class: as he puts it, classes are *formed* (i.e., given specific forms, not brought into existence – capitalism does *that* of its own accord) through struggles *about* classes. These are struggles that determine what it means to be a worker and who will see themselves as workers: all political struggles are 'class struggles' in this sense, even if the protagonists do not see themselves as acting as members of a class or upholding class interests, let alone consciously trying to determine the long-run balance of class power by affecting people's consciousness of class.

This approach has the merit of being historical, and it allows for more possibility of radical change than Giddens's sociological-structural view (while not being wholly inconsistent with it). In Przeworski's view, 'labourism' (not to mention Conservative voting) among British workers reflects a historic defeat which in new circumstances may be retrieved. It is not a 'generic' and permanent feature of capitalism as such. Przeworski is also well aware of the vulnerability of capitalism in general, and of individual national capitalist economies in particular, to crises. While he recognises that crises lead as easily to fascism as to socialism (perhaps more easily), he also points out that they are 'break' points in which the political significance of previous periods of class 'formation' is disclosed, and opportunities arise to form classes in new ways.[12] In other words, Przeworski modifies Marx's theory of the way classes affect policy, but not so much as to empty it permanently of all its original impact. In Przeworski's view, the interplay between the economic development of capitalism and the politics of capitalist countries such as Britain hinges on classes, but in a process of mutual interaction and with no predetermined outcomes.

What is attractive about this interpretation is that it retains the value of Marx's concept of class by keeping it located within a general theory of social change, but at the same time recognises that classes are the result, as well as the origin, of political action. The anonymous *Times* columnist understood this when he wrote the famous comment that Disraeli 'discerned the Conservative working man as the sculptor perceives the angel prisoned in a block of marble'. Disraeli, in other words, saw the possibility of *forming* the British working class into what it is today (with largely conservative views and considerable Conservative Party sympathies) very much as Marx imagined that the communists would (in his phrase) 'form the proletariat into a class' of a very different kind.[13] It is a realistic and useful concept of class, and we shall broadly use it in what follows.

The 'New Middle Class'

There remains, however, the second major problem noted earlier, the significance of the growth of the 'new' middle class or classes. This is actually a broader issue than whether modern capitalism has generated a new class in between the capitalists and the working class. Substantial differences of condition also exist between modern workers. For example, workers with technical qualifications employed in the control rooms of capital-intensive plants such as ChemCo have markedly different levels of income and conditions of work from those of most semi-skilled operatives, let alone unskilled manual workers. These differences have led some European sociologists, such as Mallet, to write of a 'new working class' which they consider potentially a vanguard of social change. Other sociologists, contemplating the growth of 'white collar' state and service industry employment, have seen this as evidence that part of the working class was being transformed into a 'middle class'.

Interpretations vary primarily according to whether or not one wants to retain the core Marxian idea that capitalism thrusts two principal classes into opposition to each other, and that this provides the long-term driving force of history. Giddens, as we have seen, rejects the last part of this theory and, consistently with this, considers that a 'basic three-class system' of an 'upper', 'middle' and 'lower' or 'working' class is 'generic to capitalist society'.[14] Just as he does not think that the conflict of interest between workers and the 'upper' class is enough to make the workers revolutionary, so he does not believe that the workers are, as Marx sometimes wrote, destined to become the 'vast majority'. Instead, the 'middle class' is more or less 'structurated' into a separate class with interests no more opposed to the capitalists' than to the workers'.

Marxist writers, by contrast, have tackled the problem in ways that stress the fundamental opposition between capital and labour, considering these 'new' elements as either actual or potential allies, or even members of the working class, in spite of their different conditions of work and life. All of these approaches focus attention on the relations of production, the ultimate basis of class, rather than on conditions of life, which they see as secondary.

Wright, for example, considers that besides the basic distinction between owning and not owning capital, which divides capitalists from workers, there are other differentiating factors generic to modern capitalism which affect class action and class consciousness: on the side of those who own means of production, how much they own – whether they own enough not to have to work themselves, or only just enough not to be self-employed, for example, and not enough to employ anyone to work for them; and on the side of those who own no means of production and must be employees, what skills or credentials they possess, and whether they dispose of 'organisational assets' (such as professional organisation, for example), either of which can separate them off from other employees and give them enhanced earnings, status and power.[15]

A similar approach is that of Carchedi. He sees employees in supervisory or managerial/professional roles as non-capitalists who, however, spend part of their time exercising the 'global function of capital', which includes the design and planning of profitable production and sales, and the coordination of tasks, as well as the imposition of authority on the rest of the workforce.[16] The extent to which a job involves this function is a question of degree; when it contains a substantial element of the global function of capital, its occupant tends to be a member of a 'middle class'. This is reinforced when the rest of the job is 'non-productive' – that is to say, when it does not contribute to the production of commodities which sell at a profit, as is the case with most state workers and also (in the opinion of most theorists) of commercial workers such as bank employees or supermarket staff.*

A sales manager in a large company is the clearest example of this middle class. The significance of the difference between Carchedi and Wright comes out clearly in Carchedi's further insistence that the process of capitalist production involves a constant search for ways to reduce costs by substituting cheaper labour for more expensive labour. The resulting 'dequalification' of jobs, or 'deskilling' as it is often called (following Braverman), means that, over time, the new middle class is subject to a constant process of 'proletarianisation'.[17] A hundred years ago a 'clerk' was a position of considerable status

---

* But not employees of state commercial enterprises such as the National Coal Board, which do produce commodities for the market. The distinction between productive and unproductive labour turns on the labour theory of value; work is only 'productive' when it produces surplus value, and this is judged important for class analysis by theorists who think that only workers who do this will find themselves fully exposed to the pressure on their wages and hours which employers subject to capitalist competition are driven to try to exert. For an explanation of the distinction, see Ian Gough, 'Marx's Theory of Productive and Unproductive Labour' New Left Review 76, 1972, pp. 47–72.

reflecting relatively scarce skills. Today this position involves low-paid routine work. Twenty years ago computer programmers were scarce and relatively highly paid. Today they are routine workers. Technical advance also constantly throws up new jobs of a 'middle-class' nature; Carchedi's point is that they are all vulnerable to this long-term erosion. According to him, the conditions of existence of the new middle class contain features which make it susceptible to alliance with the working class; white-collar unionisation of formerly 'middle-class' occupations such as bank employees and company technicians, and the growing militancy of such unions in the 1960s and 1970s, leading to their affiliation to the TUC, could be interpreted this way.

Evidently, these different conceptualisations have different political implications. We do not need to endorse any of them. They have been reviewed here mainly in order to show that the facts will bear quite a variety of different interpretations. Contrary to the assertions of many writers, to insist that a middle class 'exists' in Britain is not an empirical observation, but a political or ideological statement.* So is the claim that there is no such thing as a middle class. What we have is the *term* 'middle class', which has a perfectly obvious historical origin in the transition from the pre-capitalist to capitalist society, being used today as a more or less unconscious weapon in the ongoing struggle between capital and labour, to try to attach to the side of capital the various segments of the population which the development of the economy and the state differentiate out from the old core of manual workers.

The theories mentioned above are less incompatible with each other than their authors sometimes seem to think; each of them contains important insights. It may even be possible to systematise them into a single theory, but this task lies beyond the scope of the present discussion. We will simply try to draw on these insights, and to use them in ways which are consistent, in discussing some questions about class that have great practical importance for British politics.[18]

To sum up this part of the discussion, we conclude that it is first necessary to go beyond the empirically observed fact that people in Britain think in class terms, and to try to establish a concept of class that will help explain political action. Such a concept can be found in

---

* For example, Butler and Stokes writes as follows: 'In short, virtually everyone accepted the conventional class dichotomy between middle and working class. It is difficult not to see this as evidence of the acceptance of the view that British society is divided into two primary classes. This is much more than a sociologist's simplification; it seems to be deeply rooted in the mind of the ordinary British citizen.' (D.E. Butler and D. Stokes, *Political Change in Britain*, p. 46.)

Marxist theory, but it needs to be modified in order to detach it from some oversimplified and reductionist aspects of that theory. We have, then, two historically formed classes – capitalist and working classes – plus a succession of new social categories, constantly produced by the development of capitalist production and the state, which popular usage, encouraged by empiricist social science, once again calls 'the middle class'. These categories are often subject to pressures, especially 'dequalification', which tend to polarise them towards the working class; but they are also subject to pressures in the opposite direction (especially rising real incomes) and in addition, they are the object of constant political and ideological efforts to maintain and consolidate their sense of being apart from the workers and attached to capital. Similar efforts are directed towards the workers in even the oldest of working-class occupations, affecting how far they see themselves as working class, and what this might mean for them politically. The relevance of some of these ideas for the British experience will be considered in what follows.

The Changing Connotations of Social Class in Britain

On the one hand, it is clear that the struggle between capital and labour, sometimes open, sometimes partly concealed, runs through all British political history for the past two hundred years or more, and that this struggle has been reflected in popular perceptions of society as divided into classes with more or less conflicting interests. On the other hand, there is great variation in the extent to which people see a connection between class and politics (particularly politics defined as party politics). In the mid-1960s 86 per cent of working-class Labour supporters saw party politics as being about class interests, whereas about 65 per cent of 'middle-class' Conservative supporters saw party politics as having no connnection with classes or class interests.[19] Such differences are partly due to class interest itself: it is understandable that people in professional, managerial occupations which pay well and enjoy high status should deny that their support for the Conservative Party reflects any class interest. It is also due to the effects of party propaganda. In so far as the Labour Party stressed its mission as a champion of working-class interests, working-class Labour voters would tend to see politics in class terms.

In the late 1950s many sociologists, and many Labour Party strategists, considered that differences of *condition* between the classes

were narrowing, or even disappearing, to the point where any such
emphasis on working-class interests was becoming electorally risky.
Working-class life, they thought, was becoming more and more like
middle-class life. It was argued that the distribution of income and
wealth had become much more equal; that social mobility was
increasing (especially as a result of wider educational provision); that
increased absolute levels of income were permitting workers to adopt
'middle-class' living patterns (cars, television sets, holidays in Spain);
and that the growth of new 'middle-class' employment was in any case
reducing the working class's weight in the electorate. In addition, it
was argued, there was no real capitalist class left for the working class
to oppose. Shareholding had become widely dispersed, and separated
from management, which was salaried work and not directly animated
by the thirst for profit.

The empirical refutation of most of these ideas, which was notably
begun by Westergaard and consummated in his book with Resler,
Class in a Capitalist Society, can only be summarised here in the
briefest terms.[20] The distribution of income and wealth became more
equal during both world wars but after 1945 changed only slightly (in
the 1980s it became noticeably less equal again).* What little
redistribution of income there was occurred wholly within the top
half of the population, mostly within the top 20 per cent, and
ceased altogether by 1970. Individual social mobility exists, but mostly
across a limited range – from skilled manual work to supervisory work
being the most typical example of upward movement across the
politically sensitive manual/non-manual divide. This mobility is in any
event unequal – sons of higher-status fathers have more upward and
less downward mobility than manual workers – and is not significantly
greater than it was in the past. The idea that wider access to higher
education had changed matters was an illusion. In the first place, the
scale of the improvement was minimal – in 1979 a manual worker's son

---

* A government survey of personal incomes published in 1987 reported a shift in
income distribution between 1978–9 and 1984–5 'unprecedented in recorded British
economic history', according to the *Guardian* (18 December 1987). 'The top 10 per cent
of income earners have raised their share of total pre-tax income from 26.1 per cent in
1978–9 to 29.5 per cent in 1984–5, and their share of post-tax income from 23.4 per cent
to 26.5 per cent. This share now exceeds the combined total post-tax incomes of the
bottom 50 per cent of income earners, whose cumulative total fell from 26.2 per cent to
24.9 per cent by 1984–5 . . . Almost all the benefit (in post-tax income increase) has been
concentrated in the top 10 per cent, who have increased their gross pay much faster than
the rest of the population, and have disproportionately benefited from the surge of
profitability and dividends from British businesses. The slashing of top tax rates also
helped them'.

still had only one-eleventh as much chance of entering university as the son of a professional man or a manager. Secondly, the post-war expansion of professional and managerial employment, which called for more people with higher educational qualifications, benefited mostly 'middle-class' children. In fact, expansion of educational provision turned out not to have improved the chances of workers' children reaching such positions in the slightest degree.[21] The argument that absolute increases in workers' incomes leading to significant changes in their living patterns had some force, but invalid conclusions were drawn from it. For one thing, 'middle-class' living patterns were improving simultaneously – as workers bought houses and fridges, so the 'middle class' bought second homes and freezers. The gulf between manual workers' lives and those of non-manual workers, especially the higher-paid, remained clear and wide – not only in terms of a continuing and wide difference between manual workers' incomes and those of most non-manual workers, but also in terms of hours worked, the absence of any 'career' expectations for manual workers (especially their different 'earnings profile' with declining incomes in later life), shorter holidays, limited fringe benefits, harsher work discipline and dependence on wage bargaining, and a willingness to strike, to keep their incomes rising.[22] Higher earnings did not permit many workers to adopt a truly 'middle-class' lifestyle, but only certain elements or imitations of it.

The argument that manual work was giving way to non-manual work was more persuasive, though apt to be exaggerated. Much less convincing was the argument about shareholding and management. Westergaard and Resler showed that company directors were the group of shareholders with the largest holdings of shares of any elite group; and the judgement of Giddens 'that an overall homogeneity of value and belief and a high degree of social solidarity, as manifest in interpersonal contacts, friendship and marriage ties, is more noticeable than any marked cleavages' between owners and managers, would now be broadly accepted.[23]

As for the workers, more and more of them were employed by large companies where they confronted only paid managers, not owners. In some situations this probably did tend to make them less militant (for example, many of the workers at ChemCo, while expressing hostility to management, also regarded them as deserving their position and rewards by virtue of their qualifications, and saw the shareholders as remote individuals bearing no responsibility for company policy). But in other situations – for example, the car industry – the separation of ownership from management had no 'moderating' effects; and as small, owner-managed firms tend to be less unionised, the trend

BRISTOL POLYTECHNIC
ST. MATTHIAS LIBRARY
FISHPONDS

towards big companies and the separation of ownership from management had other effects which tended to increase class-consciousness, at least in its 'corporate' or 'trade union' form.

The announcement of the 'withering away' of class was, then, premature, to say the least. However, authors such as Westergaard, who did so much to demolish this fiction, tended to overstate the counter-argument. Although classes did not disappear, class relations were changing throughout the entire post-war period, in some respects radically. Some of the changes pointed out by the withering-away-of-class school were significant, although not in the way alleged. For example, the increase in the absolute real incomes of workers did not eliminate the distinction between manual workers and non-manual workers, but it did make manual workers feel richer. This had both negative and positive political effects. It encouraged a consumerist, leisure-oriented, 'privatised' and hence more individualistic outlook, which contributed to a decline in workers' interest in trade union and party activity; on the other hand it was accompanied by a *rise* in trade union membership, and, as we have seen, by growing rank and file power on the shop floor in some industries, and it raised expectations which mobilised people in support of various new collective goals.

Yet, while real wages had risen, real poverty had also increased, and it grew rapidly worse as the crisis advanced. By 1976, the proportion of the population living on or below the official poverty line (i.e., the level of income up to which Supplementary Benefits are paid) was 11.4 per cent, and the proportion with incomes no more than 20 per cent above this line – which most researchers in the field consider a more realistic measure of deprivation – was 18.6 per cent.[24] This gave rise to a new and profound division within the working class, as most of those in work were gaining, while this growing minority fell into poverty.* When we add together such changes – and the changes in the nature of work and the structure of

---

* The following definition of poverty given by the Supplementary Benefits Commission deserves reproduction: 'Poverty, in urban, industrial countries like Britain, is a standard of living so low that it excludes and isolates people from the rest of the community. To keep out of poverty they must have an income which enables them to participate in the life of the community. They must be able, for example, to keep themselves reasonably fed, and well enough dressed to maintain their self-respect and to attend interviews for jobs with confidence. Their homes must be reasonably warm; their children should not feel shamed by the quality of their clothing; the family must be able to visit relatives and give them something on their birthdays and at Christmas-time; they must be able to read newspapers and retain their television sets and their membership of trade unions and churches. And they must be able to live in a way, so far as possible, that public officials, doctors, teachers, landlords and others, treat them with the courtesy due to every member of the community.' (Cited by Coates and Silburn, *Poverty: The Forgotten Englishmen*, Penguin, Harmondsworth 1981, p. 257)

the workforce outlined in Chapter 8 – we find, not the 'embourgeoise-ment' of the working class, but a kind of dissolution or decomposition. The old 'matrix' of working-class life, which had included an increasingly automatic allegiance to the Labour Party, was breaking up. The changes of the post-war years had not made the workers 'middle class' but they had weakened the ties of tradition and place which underpinned the traditional sense of what it was to be 'working class'.[25]

Fewer were manual workers (which in itself involved some changes in outlook) and more owned their own houses (over 50 per cent of skilled manual workers and foremen by 1978).[26] Combined with slum clearance, this meant that fewer and fewer workers now lived in one of the old inner-city working-class districts with its close-knit community life revolving around the local football club, the local 'co-op', the local cinema, the local dance-hall and the local pub (or chapel). More had working wives, more owned cars and took holidays abroad. More worked for the state: this did not mean that they no longer needed trade unions to increase or maintain their wages, but their political context altered – they belonged to different unions, and when they were obliged to strike it often meant striking at the expense of other workers (as consumers of state services such as schools or hospitals or public transport), with divisive effects to which the unions often seemed insufficiently sensitive. Yet another new line of differentiation arose from immigration. An important minority of workers, mostly in low-paid employment, were now black, with different traditions and tastes, who were often the object of discrimination and the focus of racist agitation.

In other words, what had changed were many of the historical connotations of working-class life which had in the past furnished so many *badges*, by reference to which workers knew they were, and were known to be, members of the 'working class'. This was immensely important because it touched on what had hitherto been so distinctive about the British 'class system' – its *caste-like* character, the astonishing precision and fixity with which everyone was located in it by almost indelible signs of accent, dress and manner, imprinted on him or her by upbringing and experience.

This point must be briefly expanded, and brought together with the theoretical and historical interpretations offered earlier. What so impressed the North American visitor to Britain in the past was the pervasive and explicit recognition of class distinctions; what astonished the continental visitor was their prevailing acceptance. Historical circumstances in North America have led to a class system in which attributes of class origin play a comparatively inconspicuous role, leading to a degree of invisibility (low 'structuration' in Giddens's terms) which is reinforced by a powerful (dominant) class ideology that denies that classes exist. In Britain, on the other hand, the new propertied classes of the early nineteenth century were most anxious to acquire the badges of rank of the existing, explicitly stratified pre-capitalist social order, which thus received a new lease of life. In contrast with France or Germany, the British working class, after the defeat of its earliest radical initiatives, never gave its allegiance to a radical or revolutionary party but gradually moved from being the tail of (mainly) the Liberal Party to supporting 'labourism' and the Labour Party.

The explicit system of rank of the earlier agrarian social order was thus preserved, but infused with new content to form an unusually explicit system of class; while the antagonism which elsewhere accompanied a strong sense of class among the workers was, in Britain, unusually muted. The years after the Second World War saw a change in both dimensions. The British working class lost a good many of its former class badges, together with some of its faith in labourism. These changes worked in combination to the advantage of the radical right in the 1970s. Although the old class system had helped to preserve an obsolescent economy and an archaic state, the labour movement had also drawn strength from a working-class solidarity based on the sharp cultural demarcation of class boundaries. The loosening of the bonds of the old working-class culture provided an opportunity to redefine the 'classness' of the workers most affected by these changes. The working class did not begin to 'wither away'. It began to break out of its traditional mould and became susceptible of being 'formed' again in new ways*. The radical right – and some of

* The process has been poignantly portrayed by Trevor Blackwell and Jeremy Seabrook in their book *A World Still to Win*. In language closer to that of working people than the 'repellant and stultifying' language of social science (such as has largely invaded this chapter), they record the fruition and then the disillusion of the Welfare State; the failure of the Labour Party to perceive the causes and the depth of that disillusion; and how this left capital free to 'remake' the working class in a new, more individualistic pattern:

The Labour Movement felt it had delivered the working class. They knew very well what they had delivered it from; what they might be delivering it to was a speculation that rarely troubled . . . [the] representatives of a people whose loyalties were being successfully competed for elsewhere. . . . Socialism continued to see people as if their position as workers informed every aspect of their lives, while their own experience increasingly told them this was no longer the case, if it ever had been. As work took less traditional forms and people's employment became less constitutive of their identity, . . . the words 'working class' seemed to take on an archaic ring, and seemed to refer not only to decreasing segments of the population but also to a shrinking area of what mattered to people. What labour could not articulate, capitalism was able to speak readily to in its universal language of money, and labour's awkward silence was filled with the joyous ringing of capitalism's cash-tills. (*A World Still to Win: The Reconstruction of the Post-War Working class*, Faber, London 1985, pp. 78, 112–13.)

those who later formed the Social Democratic Party – realised this.[27] The electoral victory of Thatcherism demonstrated the enormous importance of their perception that a fresh opportunity had arisen to create a new kind of 'conservative working man'. It was a victory – not necessarily permanent, but a victory all the same – in the struggle between classes, *about* classes.

Some similar changes also occurred among the 'middle classes'. They were affected in somewhat contradictory ways by changes such as the growing necessity for white-collar workers to unionise, the continued dequalification of various traditionally middle-class occupations, the dilution of formerly high-status occupations (e.g. through the rapid expansion of the 'helping professions'), the encroachment of the working class on formerly middle-class preserves (driving, air travel, the grammar schools), and the effects of inflation. Such changes tended to polarise the middle classes, partly towards the labour movement, and partly towards anti-union and authoritarian positions. What changed least were the class associations of the capitalist class proper; their base in the public schools, the ancient universities, the army, the City, the Church of England, landownership and the honours system – although in the 1980s the Thatcherites found themselves in conflict with some of these institutions, especially the universities and the Church, thanks to the government's increasingly authoritarian and divisive policies.

Class and Party

Writers on the relationship between class and party in Britain have mostly been experts on electoral behaviour, who have accepted the sociological concept of class and who see the relationship between the parties and classes as a kind of fishing competition in which the parties compete to see which one can pull the most votes out of each 'stratum' of an electorate seen as 'stratified' in a pre-given way. These writers also tend to define politics as party politics, and party politics as a series of election campaigns. This approach is not very illuminating, and at worst, is quite misleading.

Butler and Stokes, for example, subjected the data from a series of surveys of electors' party preferences in the 1960s to a sophisticated quantitative analysis under the title *Political Change in Britain*. It fell to another specialist on elections, Ivor Crewe, to point out that even within their limited conception of 'politics' Butler and Stokes had failed even to notice the most dramatic changes that had occurred in the period they studied: the decline in the proportion of the electorate voting for either of the two main parties, the fall in turnout and the

increasing volatility of support between the major parties (all of which
are obvious *starting-points* for the analysis of political change pursued
in this book).[28]

Crewe also showed that the model which Butler and Stokes had used
to explain where their interest lay, namely in changes in the two major
parties' shares of the vote, was invalidated by the decline that had
occurred in support for both parties. For example, according to Butler
and Stokes, the main determinant of voting is the strength of each
individual voter's psychological identification with a given party, which
is strongly inherited from one's parents and grows stronger over a
lifetime. From this it ought to have followed that, as the electorate
came to consist more and more of people who had known only the
Conservative and Labour Parties in office, and fewer of whose parents
could have been Liberal voters, support for the two major parties
would rise; whereas the precise opposite had occurred. Butler and
Stokes, in fact, not only reduced the concept of class to a mere
occupational category, but also reduced the concept of voting to a
mere individual psychological reflex, largely independent of the course
of the political struggle.

The sort of study of which their work is a leading example
does illuminate some of the complex factors that enter into every
election outcome – the effects of the death of older voters, the
differing abstention rates of various categories of voter, differing
patterns of vote switching, etc. It can also shed light on the relation
between voting patterns and such things as trade union membership,
residence in a predominantly working-class constituency, and so on.
But if one ignores almost entirely the political events and changing
social forces in the context of which elections actually occur, one
cannot explain what actually happens in elections, let alone shed any
light on the real relationship between party and class.

It is not, therefore, in this literature that we can hope to find a
satisfactory analysis of the party–class relationship, even though not all
election specialists have such a narrow conception of politics.[29]
Because of their method (i.e., seeking to interpret statistical relationships between data on voting or statements of party support, and class
'indicators' such as occupation), all such studies use an empiricist, and
ultimately ideological conception of class. For illumination on the
relationship between class and party, the best sources by far remain
historical treatments of party politics, some of which will be referred to
in the following two chapters. However, a brief comment on the
pitfalls involved may first be appropriate.

In a class society, political parties clearly express class interests, but
the way they do so is complex. As we shall see in Chapter 10, the

Conservative Party undoubtedly represents and defends the interests of capital against the interests of labour, but it would be a serious oversimplification, and underestimation, to call it the party of capital. Similarly, the Labour Party was formed to promote the interests of labour but it defined these interests not only as including *everyone* who worked ('by hand or brain') but also – after 1926 if not before – as involving collaboration with capital. From its inception, the party was led mainly by professional men (most of the party's few women leaders came from the trade unions); it increasingly returned non-workers to parliament (especially after 1951); and when in office from 1964 onwards it accepted in practice the need to preserve profits at the expense of wages. So it is at least a serious oversimplification to call it 'the party of the working class' – even though it may continue to be seen in this light by the great majority of those who *see* themselves as 'working class'. Any attempt to *reduce* parties to their 'class base' necessarily suppresses these problems. How then should the relationship be understood?

Briefly, parties must first be distinguished from organisations which aim at defending the immediate perceived interests of particular groups (including classes or elements of classes). The point of a political party is to secure those interests by means of a much wider project:

> a party is not a trade union, not an employers' association, much less a professional association. A party's existence implies a transition from the defence of corporative* interests to the promotion of a specific project for society, and must be analysed in its direct relation to the question of power. Involved in a party is social space in its totality. A party undertakes not only the promotion of specific, multiple and heterogeneous interests, but also the reproduction of the totality of the social formation. In it unfolds the whole domain of hegemony, alliances and compromises.[30]

A party must, by its nature, formulate programmes for, and develop links with, numerous elements in society outside the class whose

---

* The term 'corporative' derives from Gramsci: 'A tradesman does not join a political party in order to do business, nor an industrialist in order to produce more at a lower cost, nor a peasant to learn new methods of cultivation, even if some aspects of these demands of the tradesman, the industrialist or the peasant can find satisfaction in the party. For these purposes, within limits, there exists the professional association, in which the economic–corporate activity of the tradesman, industrialist or peasant is most suitably promoted. In the political party the elements of an economic social group [a class] get beyond that moment of their historical development and become agents of more general activities of a national and international character' (*Selections from the Prison Notebooks*, ed. Q. Hoare and G. Nowell-Smith, Lawrence and Wishart, London 1971, p. 16).

interests fundamentally inspire it.* These programmes and links may take a great variety of forms, depending on circumstances. In the last analysis a party's record in office discloses its 'class character' – that is, the class interests it ultimately serves – but this must be interpreted with care. For example, did the Conservative Party's acceptance of the welfare state after 1951 show it to have acquired a working-class character? Did the Labour Party's economic policies from 1964 to 1970 mean that it had taken on a capitalist character? A proper analysis must be long-term, and have a necessary degree of sophistication.

Since a party must be concerned with 'the reproduction of the totality of the social formation', it must be ready on occasion to sacrifice some of the immediate economic interests of the social class or classes it represents. The occasions when parties do this are especially revealing. They show how the party leaders understand the party's raison d'être; what interests they judge to be central and what they consider ultimately dispensable. These moments are obviously fraught with danger for the leadership and can easily lead to personal defeats, as in the famous case of Peel's decision to repeal the Corn Laws in 1846. Another equally famous case, Roosevelt's adoption of the New Deal programme, turned out more fortunately for Roosevelt personally, though he was well aware of the risks: 'The rich may have thought that Roosevelt was betraying his class; but Roosevelt certainly supposed [reflecting in spring 1935, on the mounting opposition from business circles] . . . that his class was betraying him.'[31]

Przeworski makes the same point in his summary of the dilemma of social-democratic leaders as their programmes for a transition to socialism without revolution lead to economic crises:

> Faced with an economic crisis, threatened with loss of electoral support, concerned about the possibility of a fascist counter-revolution, social democrats abandon the project of a transition or at least pause to wait for more auspicious times. They find the courage to explain to the working class that it is better to be exploited than to create a situation which contains the risk of turning against them. They refuse to stake their fortunes on a worsening of the crisis. They offer the compromise; they maintain and defend it.[32]

This does not mean that party leaders' judgements are always correct. Mistakes are made, betrayals do occur. The point is rather that while

---

* For example, the Conservative and Unionist Party leader Lord Salisbury had feared in 1903 that if Chamberlain converted the party to free trade it would be transformed into a Conservative Party of the American or Colonial type, a party of manufacturers and nouveaux riches', which would be electorally perilous: see F. Halevy, *Imperialism and the Rise of Labour*, Benn, London 1951, p. 326.

parties do have objective relationships to classes of which party leaders are well aware, determining what these relations are is perhaps the most complex of all tasks of political analysis.

Secondly, in considering the relation between classes and parties, it is necessary to keep in view the point already made concerning the socially constructed nature of class, remembering that classes are the objects of party competition, something 'produced' by parties, as well as something pre-given. It is true that classes *are* pre-given, both in the sense that the relations of production are what they are at any given moment, and in the sense that classes have a form and content given to them by previous 'class struggles'. But classes are also constantly being 'reproduced' in new ways: materially, by economic and social changes which affect the occupational structure (e.g., the accelerated concentration of capital in the sixties or the deindustrialisation of the seventies), or people's living conditions (e.g., changing tax or housing policies); and ideologically, by policies and campaigns aimed at defining people in class terms in particular ways. The relationship between classes and parties is thus always a complex and dynamic process of interaction.

To anticipate briefly the following chapters, we may very schematically conceive of the relation between class and the major parties in Britain *before* 1960 as follows. Two-thirds of the manual workforce and their families had been successfully defined by the Labour Party and the trade unions, with the help of the distinctive character of working-class life, as members of the working class, committed to the Labour Party as the party of the workers. And about 20 per cent of salaried, white-collar and professional workers had been defined as Labour supporters on the basis of the party's championship of social reform, modernisation, equality of educational opportunity, etc. Conversely, the Conservatives had succeeded in defining a significant minority of wage-workers as either 'deferential' Conservatives, or as aspirant 'middle-class' Conservatives, on the basis of the fact that the Conservative Party also, at that time, subscribed to the post-war consensus on full employment and 'welfare'.

After 1960, however, the consensus gradually ceased to be compatible with economic growth, while the changes in the nature of the labour force weakened both parties' definitional grip on their respective segments of it. Both manual workers and the 'new' middle class threw up elements outside the established definitions, while the 'old' middle class became more and more impatient with the concessions entailed by the consensus. The emphasis shifted from the *maintenance* of established class allegiances to the *redefinition* of classes, and the articulation of new grounds for party allegiance. This shift was initiated by the Conservative Party, which far outstripped the Labour Party in this respect during the 1970s. But if we look more closely at some of the new social forces to which the Conservative initiatives were in part a response, we can see that the picture is more complex. It was not just an altered relationship between parties and social classes, and not just an opportunity for the Conservatives, which the crisis produced.

Classes and Other Political Forces

From the mid-sixties onwards some new elements became politically important in Britain, as in other advanced industrial countries: for example the women's movement, the student movement, the movement against racism, the gay liberation movement, the ecological movement. People were mobilised, as women against sexual discrimination, as blacks against racism, as villagers against new motorways and as town-dwellers against 'developers', to a degree which at least matched their mobilisation as workers against exploitation. What is the relationship between social class, the historic origin and continuing basis of the parties, and these new political forces, which almost wholly ignored – and were largely ignored by – the major parties?

Some observers have been inclined to see the new movements as evidence that politics were ceasing to be 'class-determined', becoming instead a matter of plural competing interests unconnected with social class, although as the seventies unfolded this seemed less plausible. Others have seen them as reactions to the failure of party politics to secure an electoral consensus for the policies needed to resolve the crisis of British capitalism, leading to more and more bureaucratic 'corporatist' forms of policy-making, intervening in more and more spheres of life.[33] Still others have seen the new groups and movements as evidence of the existence of generic conflict between state power as such and 'the people' – parallel to the conflict between classes but not reducible to it – a conflict which has become more acute as states have been forced to become larger and more bureaucratic.[34]

The most interesting analyses of this question turn on Gramsci's theory of hegemony. The ideological hegemony of the dominant class resulted, in Gramsci's view, from a process in which other groups had been actively enlisted in support of a general or national 'project' put forward by that class, in which they saw (or thought they saw) their own aspirations realised. This was more than a question of alliances; it involved a fusion of these different elements into an 'intellectual and moral unity'.[35] In the same way, Gramsci argued, the working class must establish its hegemony over various other social elements by putting forward policies, and a general conception of the future, which offered a genuine prospect of solving the varied problems they experienced and which brought them into conflict with the existing order.

From this standpoint, the emergence of new and radical political forces in Britain may be seen as evidence of the collapsing hegemony of the dominant class, which had either to be reconstructed or succumb to the counter-hegemony of opposing social forces. There are many indications that this theory is broadly correct. The 'Thatcherite' themes of family, law-and-order, racism, 'hard work' and the like appealed to popular reactions *against* these new movements, in language which tapped a large reservoir of traditional sentiment among ordinary people.[36] By contrast, the Labour Party's emphasis throughout the 1970s was almost wholly on economic issues of immediate concern to the workers as workers (with a strong bias towards male workers), and only very secondarily on issues such as personal security, racial or sexual emancipation or the environment. In short, the Labour Party did not respond as positively to these new movements as the Conservative Party responded negatively.*

In office, the Labour Party did pass laws in favour of equal pay for women (1970), against discrimination against women (1975), and against racial discrimination (1977), but in all of these it sought the line of least resistance between its own radical wing (and the demands of blacks and women) and the established order.[37] The legislation was weak and weakly enforced, and the party did not seriously take up the broader, less economic issues raised by the blacks' or the women's movements, let alone those raised by the environmentalists, the students, the gays, or the nationalists – a failure which cost it dearly.

This is not to say that a successful new progressive alliance could be built out of these new materials; but the old alliance between the working class, organised in the labour movement, and the liberal-minded wing of the intelligentsia, which had been the basis of Labour's past successes, was no longer capable of achieving any further advance on the left, whereas the potential of some of these new movements was

---

* It was the Liberals, with their 'anti-class' philosophy, rather than the Labour Party, who engaged with some of the new issues by taking up 'community politics' – working with ratepayers' and tenants' associations and claimants' unions – for primarily tactical reasons in the early 1970s, and found that it paid some handsome dividends, leading to their having the largest number of seats on Liverpool City Council in 1974 and a large share of the vote in local elections elsewhere. The National Front also engaged in 'community politics' of a different stripe, presenting the problems of the inner-city areas as being due to coloured immigration and the indifference to it of middle-class 'liberals' in city halls and at Westminster.

considerable. The women's movement is the most striking case in point.[38]

The subordination of women is as old as history and so, probably, is the record of women's resistance. What was novel about the women's movement in Britain (and elsewhere) in the late 1970s was its scale, comprehensiveness and historical awareness, and its organisational versatility. These features seem to be linked to the fact that, by the late 1960s, women had a higher participation-rate in paid employment than at any previous time this century, and a higher level of education (inferior to men's as it still was) than at any previous time in British history – while, at the same time, women continued to experience comprehensive social, sexual, cultural, economic and political subordination. Feminist activists now directed their attack on this whole structure, while for many more women practical struggles for reforms such as equal pay, equal job opportunities, day care facilities, etc., gradually disclosed the interconnectedness of all aspects of oppression. Women trade unionists, for example, found that the Equal Pay Act of 1970 (which made it illegal to pay women less than men for doing similar work) did not help so long as most women were confined to jobs that men did not do at all; and employers, sometimes with trade union connivance, went to great lengths to segregate women's and men's work more thoroughly in the five years that they were allowed for making 'adjustments' between the passage of the Act in 1970 and its implementation in 1975.

> Equal pay was seen to be meaningless without equal opportunity [i.e., to hold 'men's' jobs]. Equal opportunity was seen to be meaningless unless women were given the chance to take their opportunities. To do so women needed equal education and training. They also needed the right to control their fertility, to choose when or whether to have a child. If they chose children, they needed paid maternity leave to protect their jobs and good child care facilities to enable them to continue work after having a child. To be equal meant being equal in terms of sick pay, pensions, social security and tax; it meant having the right to sign a hire purchase form without the husband's consent. In fact the logical argument led to the demand for equal citizenship.[39]

In 1981, it seemed to many people that the women's movement was destined for yet another eclipse. The trend to more equal pay had halted in 1977 and subsequently began to go into reverse. By the mid-1980s women's wages had fallen back to 68 per cent of men's in manual work, and 61 per cent in non-manual work. Unemployment induced by the Thatcher policies eliminated women from jobs faster than men, partly because of the cuts in the public sector where so many women worked. Women occupied the great majority of the new jobs created in the 1980s, but these were overwhelmingly service-sector and part-time jobs, and the average number of hours worked by women fell to an average of 18 per week (and those working less then 16 hours had no employment protection).[40] The cuts also reduced or eliminated the few publicly provided services which enabled mothers to work (day nurseries, nursery schools, cooked school meals). At the other end of the scale women were still largely excluded from senior positions in the civil service, from government advisory bodies, from trade union offices (even in unions most of whose members are women) and from parliament.[41] And a strong Conservative campaign to revive the ideology of the family threatened to reverse the progress made in the previous decade in raising public consciousness of women's oppression and their right to equality.

But this reckoned without the width of the gap that had opened up between the dominant sexist ideology (which conceals, minimises or justifies women's subordination) and women's practical experience. Documentation and analysis of women's oppression was improving rapidly and growing numbers of women were becoming aware of it and angry about it. Moreover the social basis of the ideology of motherhood as a vocation was being steadily eroded; the 'typical family' (of male breadwinner, unwaged wife and two children) so often referred to by judges, wage negotiators, and the drafters of social security regulations now accounted for only 5 per cent of all families. It seemed improbable that women would allow their new demands to lapse indefinitely.

The Labour leadership remained, in general, unresponsive. The five women's seats on the party's National Executive Committee continued to be filled by the 'block vote' at the Annual Conference – a vote cast overwhelmingly by men. Individual women have played important roles in the party, but no serious steps have been taken to achieve equality of representation for women at all levels in the structure, or to commit the party to national policies to advance women's rights in all spheres. In short, Labour was not yet a feminist party, and for a party of radical change this remained a radical weakness.

The problems faced by the various minorities such as blacks and gays, and single issue groups like the ecologists, posed similar challenges. Government policies in the 1980s aggravated their problems (for instance the notorious Section 28 of the 1988 Local Government Act which prohibited the teaching of 'the acceptability of homosexuality as a pretended family relationship, or the policy of encouraging development in formerly protected 'green belts'). The 'broad left' inside and outside the Labour Party had begun to realise that important as issues of employment and production were, they did not exhaust the urgent concerns which many people felt. They were also beginning to recognise that feminist, ecological and other demands, while they were unlikely to be satisfied within the existing hierarchy of status and reward, would not be automatically satisfied under socialism either, *unless* socialism were explicitly defined so as to meet them. Some of the needs to which these demands responded – for instance, the needs of many tenants and squatters and low-paid workers – had a clear basis in class relations. But more often there remained an important distinction between the needs people felt as workers and their needs as women, blacks, environmentalists, or whatever. Not all progressive demands can be reduced to class interests, and what is more, not all are necessarily compatible with the immediate 'corporate' interests of workers. To take two examples, real equality for women in pay and access to jobs would be likely to increase male unemployment in the short run, and pollution controls, too, can cost jobs.[42] The potential offered by the emerging social movements of the 1970s for a new and radical programme was great, but to exploit it would call for a higher order of imagination and political skill than the leadership of the late 1980s had yet exhibited.

Conclusion

The distinctive features of the British class system can be identified only if we first clarify what we mean by 'class'. Having rejected the reduction of the concept of class to that of *stratum*, because it at best describes popular ideology at a particular moment, without enabling us to explain anything, we must face the difficulties involved in the alternative, Marxian concept of class. These difficulties can be partly resolved if we conceive of social classes as sets of 'places' in the relations of production. The way in which people actually experience and perceive classes and their place in them, however, is the result of political struggles which are largely about the existence, nature and significance of classes. Change is of the essence of both aspects – changes in the relations of production, and changes in the course of the class struggle.

Approached in this way, a distinctive feature of the British class system may be seen as being its archaic, caste-like character, the legacy of the distinctive and gradual path of Britain's transition to capitalism. In the period after 1945 the working class experienced a variety of changes, some of them far-reaching, in the associations of class that had characterised it for almost a century. There were changes in the

job-structure, there was increased mobility into 'middle-class' occupations for those born to manual worker parents, and there were
important changes in 'lifestyles'. The skilled manual working class in
'new tech' fields prospered under Thatcherism, while two million
workers lost their jobs and formed a potential new 'sub-working class'.[43]
The political *redefinition* or *re-formation* of the working class therefore became an important political issue. Some homogenisation
of class-ranking also occurred within the 'middle class', though this was
less significant.

To conceive classes in this way is also to recognise that political
parties are not merely instruments (or manipulators) of 'pre-given'
classes but are among the chief determinants of classes, at the same
time as they are products of them. One of the most striking dimensions
of this relationship from the mid-1960s onwards was the emergence of
new political forces that were often linked to classes, but distinct from
them. By the end of the 1970s, however, only the Conservatives had
responded effectively to these new forces, in such a way as to attract
significant new elements of the working class to Conservatism – or
more accurately, to the neo-Conservatism of the wing of the party led
by Thatcher. It might prove a temporary attachment, in party terms,
particularly since the Conservatives' economic policies had negative
effects on the incomes and job security of so many other workers; and
the new social forces to which neo-Conservatism was a reaction had an
underlying potential for radical mobilisation which had still to be
exploited. But for the time being the political potency of class, and
especially of any appeal to the working class as such, had been very
significantly reduced, as the public response to the 1984–85 miners'
strike and other episodes clearly indicated.

Notes

1 See R.T. McKenzie and A. Silver, *Angels in Marble*, Heinemann, London 1968,
   pp. 167–8.
2 The common procedure is to note the 'looseness' of ordinary usage of the term
   'class' and then to discuss how it can be made more exact, concluding with the
   adoption of occupation as the indicator closest to popular usage: see e.g., R. Rose,
   Politics in England (3rd edition), Little Brown, Boston 1980, pp. 156 ff, and J.
   Blondel, *Voters, Parties and Leaders* (revised edition), Penguin, Harmondsworth
   1974, pp. 26 ff.
3 Asa Briggs, 'The Language of "Class" in Early Nineteenth-Century England', in A.
   Briggs and J. Saville, eds, *Essays in Labour History*, Macmillan, London 1967,
   pp. 43–73, and especially pp. 52 ff.
4 W.S. Churchill, *Lord Randolph Churchill*, Odhams, London 1951, p. 565.
5 T. Nichols, 'Social Class: Official, Sociological and Marxist' in J. Irvine et al., eds,
   Demystifying Social Statistics, Pluto Press, London 1979, p. 158.

6 Nichols, p. 159.
7 V.I. Lenin, 'A Great Beginning' in *Selected Works* Vol II, Foreign Languages Publishing House, Moscow 1947, p. 492.
8 Nichols, p. 165.
9 A. Giddens, *Class Structure of the Advanced Societies*, Hutchinson, London 1973, Chapter 6.
10 Lenin, 'What Is To Be Done?', *Selected Works* Vol. I, pp. 167-77.
11 A. Przeworski, 'Proletariat into a Class', *Politics and Society*, 7/4, 1977, pp. 343–401.
12 A. Przeworski, 'The Material Bases of Consent: Economics and Politics in a Hegemonic System', in M. Zeitlin, ed., *Political Power and Social Theory a Research Annual*, Vol. 1, Jai Press, Greenwich 1980, pp. 21–66.
13 K. Marx and F. Engels, 'The Manifesto of the Communist Party', in *The Revolutions of 1848*, (ed. D. Fernbach), Penguin, Harmondsworth 1973, p. 80.
14 Giddens, pp. 107 and 110.
15 E.O. Wright, *Classes*, Verso, London 1985, esp. Chapter 4.
16 G. Carchedi, *On the Economic Identification of Social Classes*, Routledge, London 1977.
17 H. Braverman, *Labour and Monopoly Capital*, Monthly Review Press, New York 1974
18 For the radical political implications for socialist strategy which these debates entail see C. Mouffe, 'Working Class Hegemony and the Struggle for Socialism', *Studies in Political Economy* 12, Fall 1983, pp. 7–26; P. Meiksins and E. Meiksins Wood, 'Beyond Class? A Reply to Chantal Mouffe', *Studies in Political Economy* 17, Summer 1985, pp. 141–65; E. Laclau and C. Mouffe, *Hegemony and Socialist Strategy*, Verso, London 1985; E. Meiksins Wood, *The Retreat from Class*, Verso, London 1986; N. Geras, 'Post-Marxism?', *New Left Review* 163, May-June 1987, pp. 40–82; E. Laclau and C. Mouffe, 'Post Marxism Without Apologies', *New Left Review* 166, November/December 1987, pp. 79–106.
19 Butler and Stokes, p. 63. 'Middle Class' here refers to the way people described their own class membership.
20 J. Westergaard and H. Resler, *Class in a Capitalist Society*, Heinemann, London 1975. Westergaard's early critique is in 'The Withering away of Class', in P. Anderson and R. Blackburn, eds, *Towards Socialism*, Fontana, London 1965, pp. 77–113.
21 'Even in the presumably very favourable context of a period of sustained economic growth and of major change in the form of the occupational structure, the general underlying processes of intergenerational class mobility – or immobility – have apparently been little altered, and indeed have, if anything, tended in certain respects to generate still further inequalities in class chances.' J.H. Goldthorpe, *Social Mobility and Class Structure in Modern Britain*, Clarendon Press, Oxford 1980, p. 85. The evidence is summarised in Table 2.3 on pp. 60–1.
22 Westergaard and Resler, *Class in a Capitalist Society*, Part Two, Chapters 5 and 6.
23 Giddens, p. 171.
24 K. Coates and R. Silburn, *Poverty: The Forgotten Englishmen*, Penguin, Harmondsworth 1981, pp. 259–60, and *Social Trends 1979*, p. 112. Using the 'deprivation standard' of poverty Peter Townsend put the number living in poverty at 12.4m or 23% in 1968-9 (*Poverty in the United Kingdom*, University of California Press, Berkeley 1979, pp. 301–2.)
25 The seminal article on this is E.J. Hobsbawm, 'The Forward March of Labour Halted?', *Marxism Today* September 1978, pp. 279–86, reprinted in the book of the same title edited by M. Jacques and F. Mulhern, Verso, London 1981. See also J. Clarke, 'Capital and Culture: the post-war working class revisited', in J. Clarke et al., eds, *Working Class Culture*, Hutchinson, London 1979, pp. 238–53.
26 *Social Trends 1979*, HMSO, London 1979, p. 15.
27 H. Stephenson, *Mrs. Thatcher's First Year*, Jill Norman, London 1980, p. 22.
28 I. Crewe, 'Do Butler and Stokes Really Explain Political Change in Britain?', *European Journal of Political Research*, 2, 1974, pp. 47–92.

29 For a clear and helpful review of the voting literature down to 1985 see M. Harrop, 'Voting and the Electorate', in H. Drucker et al., eds, *Developments in British Politics*, Macmillan, London 1986. See also M.N. Franklin, *The Decline of Class Voting in Britain*, Clarendon Press, Oxford 1985; and Heath et al., *How Britain Votes*, Pergamon Press, Oxford 1985.

30 G. Bourque, 'Class, Nation and the Parti-Quebecois', *Studies in Political Economy*, 2, 1979, p. 130.

31 A.M. Schlesinger, Jr., *The Age of Roosevelt* Vol III, Heinemann, London 1961, p. 273, cited in G. Therborn, *What Does the Ruling Class Do When It Rules?*, New Left Books, London 1978, p. 148.

32 Przeworski, 'Social Democracy as a Historical Phenomenon', *New Left Review*, 122, 1980, p. 58.

33 See e.g., C. Offe, 'The Separation of Form and Content in Liberal Democratic Politics', *Studies in Political Economy*, 3, 1980, pp. 5–16.

34 See E. Laclau, 'Democratic Antagonisms and the Capitalist State', paper presented to the ECPR Conference, Brussels, April 1979.

35 On Gramsci's theory, see especially C. Mouffe, 'Hegemony and Ideology in Gramsci', in Mouffe, ed., *Gramsci and Marxist Theory*, Routledge, London 1979, pp. 168–204.

36 S. Hall, 'The Great Moving Right Show', *Marxism Today*, January 1980, pp. 14–20; see also his 'Thatcherism – a New Stage?', *Marxism Today*, February 1980, pp. 26–29.

37 A. Coote and B. Campbell, *Sweet Freedom*, Picador, London 1982, Chapter 4.

38 See G. Stedman-Jones, 'Marching into History?', *New Socialist*, 3, 1982, pp. 10–15.

39 S. Boston, *Women Workers and the Trade Unions*, Davis-Poynter, London 1980, pp. 284–5.

40 These data on women's employment are drawn from V. Huws, 'Women and Employment', in G. Ashworth and L. Bonnerjee, eds, *The Invisible Decade: U.K. Women and the U.N. Decade*, Gower, Aldershot 1985, pp. 50–61.

41 E. Vallance, 'Equality and the Formation of Public Policy', ibid., pp. 20–31. Thirty-two per cent of Administrative Trainees joining the Civil Service were women, and 45% of those joining the Executive grades, and so women should, by promotion, compose some 35% of the higher levels; but they have never accounted for more than 4% overall. In the 1987 election the number of women MPs rose to 41 out of 650 (6.3% – 21 Labour, 17 Conservatives, 2 Alliance, and one SNP), compared with 28 before the election. Fourteen per cent of the 2,325 candidates nominated were women (*Times Guide to the House of Commons June 1987*, London 1985, p. 281).

42 M. Prior and D. Purdy, *Out of the Ghetto*, Spokesman, Nottingham 1979, p. 97.

43 A.H. Halsey, *Change in British Society* (3rd edition), Oxford University Press, Oxford 1986, pp. 130–31.

PART III

PART III

10

The Conservative Party

Political parties are the natural victims of general crises. The Liberals succumbed – as a party of government, and for three decades as a significant political force – to the crisis of 1900–1914. Neither the Conservatives nor the Labour Party were guaranteed to survive the crisis that set in during the sixties, and any description of their main features in the late 1980s must be more than usually provisional. The Conservative Party, moreover, has been poorly served by scholarship. Material on the party's leaders and doctrines is abundant, but critical studies of its social base and political economy are lamentably scarce. Within these limitations an attempt to understand this most powerful and resilient of all European conservative parties is indispensable.

'Conservative history is a microcosm of British public history as seen from the position of the ruler.'[1] That this should be so is one of the more remarkable facts of modern party politics. The Tory Party, out of which the modern Conservative Party grew, was closely tied to landed property, which was fast being eclipsed as a significant source of wealth and power in Britain by the middle of the nineteenth century. The Conservatives succeeded in transforming themselves into a party – eventually *the* party – of industry and commerce, and then continued to dominate British politics even after the most proletarianised population in Europe (and, in trade union terms, the most unified working class) had obtained the vote. The Conservatives have been in office for 74 of the 121 years between 1867 (when male urban workers were largely enfranchised) and 1988 – and for no less than 26 out of the 43 years since 1945, when the Labour Party came into its full electoral inheritance. What made this possible?

The Conservatives' Problem

It may be objected – many Conservatives would object – that the problem as we have posed it is a false one: that the Conservative Party represents the nation as a whole, not the interests of one class (as the Labour Party initially set out to do). The party's rhetoric has always claimed this; and it is a fact that a third of all manual workers have tended to vote Conservative, while more than half of all Labour supporters approve of Conservative policies more than Labour policies.[2] However, the Conservative Party's history does not support this argument. We can follow the Tory Party's evolution into the modern Conservative Party under a succession of leaders – Peel, Disraeli, Salisbury and Baldwin, in particular – who declared more or less openly that the defence of property and the constitution which secured it was the party's prime task, and who saw the courting of the 'working man' as necessary for this purpose. The claim that, in doing so, the Conservative Party also served the interests of the workers, depends on a historic series of concessions: from the concession of cheap bread in 1846, to the acceptance of the welfare state after 1951. Of course, if measures of this kind were substantial and regular enough it would be mere prejudice to describe them as 'concessions'. Samuel Beer, in fact, argued that whatever the Conservatives' original aim may have been, they should be regarded as having become not a class party which makes concessions to the underclass but de facto a party of compromise between competing class interests.[3]

But the record does not show the Conservatives to have taken any significant initiatives on behalf of the workers except in order to preserve the party's electoral position when it was acutely threatened. After the famous year 1875, in which Disraeli's government passed a series of measures to regulate and improve workers' living standards (at the expense of the still largely Liberal manufacturers and ratepayers), Conservative social legislation was conspicuously permissive rather than mandatory, and narrow in scope. The subsequent major advances in workers' social security, health provision, conditions of work and housing were all Liberal or Labour measures, usually opposed by the Conservatives.* The Conservatives' preference has always been to improve 'the condition of the people' by a general increase in prosperity, not by legislative reforms; in hard times, they

---

* The Education Acts of 1903 and 1944 could be considered exceptions, although the latter was very much the product of the wartime coalition government and was the work of R.A. Butler, one of the Conservative leaders most alert to the risk that the party could destroy itself by not coming to terms with the popular reaction to the slump and the democratisation of British life caused by the war.

have declared reform impracticable. Andrew Boyd's judgement must be accepted:

> The Conservative party has a persisting unity denied to both the Labour and the Liberal parties. Its main purpose never changes: to preserve, as long as may be, a state of society in which private property and private enterprise may flourish.[4]

Or, in the characteristically uncompromising language of Enoch Powell in 1964 when he was still a leading Conservative:

> Whatever else the Conservative party stands for, unless it is the party of free choice, competition, and free enterprise, unless – I am not afraid of the word – it is the party of capitalism, then it has no function in the contemporary world, then it has nothing to say to modern Britain.[5]

Securing the survival of capitalism in face of a well-organised working class majority has, then, been the Conservatives' central problem. As Rose remarks, 'if the Labour Party were as successful in winning working-class votes as the Conservatives are in winning middle-class votes, Labour . . . would have a permanent electoral majority'.[6] The question to be answered is how the Conservative Party has prevented this from happening.* Furthermore, the party has had to solve this problem while also dealing with changes, and not infrequently conflicts, within its base of support. This problem is shared to some extent by any political party, but it became particularly serious for the Conservatives once they had become a party of modern capitalism, which is by its nature subject to constant changes of form and content. The Conservatives had to adapt from being a party of landowners to being a party of competitive commercial capitalism, and then adapt again to being a party of giant bureaucratic corporations. This also called for flexibility, and as Harris observed,

> When Disraeli deserted what was left of the land of the squires, when Ulstermen stood opposed to King and constitution, when the inter-war diehards went into battle in 1945 to refuse the price of the Second World War, it was certainly not a foregone conclusion that the party was capable of this 'flexibility'.[7]

---

* Of course this task does not have to be shouldered by the party alone. The power of private capital is (in Perry Anderson's words) 'polycentric'. It resides in the control of investment, in the ownership of newspapers and television companies, in its social influence within the state, and so on. None the less the ultimate guarantee that the interests of capital will be secure is that a party favourable to these interests is frequently in office; and down to the late 1970s, at least, the Conservatives have seen holding office as being very important in itself, important enough to justify the sometimes major concessions at the expense of property already referred to.

The Elements of the Problem

Andrew Gamble proposed a relatively straightforward way of analysing the Conservatives' dilemma.[8] The party has a core of interests to defend and opinions to express: the interests and opinions of capital (manufacturing, commercial and financial) and the interests and opinions of the classes allied to capital (notably, the middle classes' interests in their personal property – houses, second homes, company cars, private education and private health-service arrangements, etc.). These are 'allied' classes, in the sense that they are not themselves the principal beneficiaries of Conservative policy, but they benefit in return for the support they give to the party. The Conservative Party must resolve the conflict that arises between these elements, and between them and the workers, in such a way as to maintain their active support. Gamble calls this the 'politics of support'.

Contrasted with the politics of support are what Gamble calls the 'politics of power'. This refers to the constraints and priorities imposed on any party in office by the requirements of economic production and national security. In a capitalist country, these requirements are 'at bottom . . . a compromise between the interests of capital in accumulation and its interests in political stability'. They call for a consistent set of policy objectives: for example, 'the maintenance of free trade, economy, and the gold standard, objects of British government for so long, comprised such a set of priorities'.[9] (Later, during the 'consensus' years, the maintenance of full employment, steady prices and a positive balance of payments comprised an alternative set.) Speaking generally, the 'politics of power' means, for the Conservatives, solving problems in ways that are compatible with the economic and political requirements of capital. These requirements are evolving and changing all the time. The party leadership must constantly reassess them and find new formulae for dealing with them.

At the same time these formulae must be congruent with parallel formulae for the politics of support. For example, one of the last acts of the Macmillan government in 1964 was to pass legislation abolishing Resale Price Maintenance, which in effect restored price competition in the retail trade in British manufactures. This was judged necessary in order to restore a measure of efficiency both in retailing and in manufacturing for the home market. However, its chief effect was to encourage retail outlets with high turnover and low margins, at the expense of many small retailers who were a mainstay of the Conservative Party's constituency associations. This was a case of the politics of power incurring costs in terms of the politics of support. By contrast, Mrs Thatcher's 1979 promise to cut personal income tax was seen as consistent with both the politics of support (appealing as it did to all taxpayers, and especially those with higher incomes) and the new politics of power to which she was committed – cutting state spending and enlarging the sphere of the market. (Whether it would prove a *successful* formula for the politics of power was another matter.)

Whereas the politics of power is focused on the state, the politics of support is focused on the 'nation' (to use Gamble's term) – the social classes and other elements into which society is divided. In practice the politics of support relates to the 'nation' in three main arenas – parliament, the party organisation, and elections – but especially the last two. The Conservative leadership must satisfy the elements which finance and run the party organisation, while at the same time trying to satisfy a majority of the electorate. As Gamble points out, meeting this last requirement involves a sophisticated reconciliation between the politics of power and the politics of support, because the party's supporters do not constitute an electoral majority. The rest of the votes the party needs must be won partly by real concessions, partly by psychological inducements (appeals to patriotism, racism, social deference, and the like) and partly by appearing to have a more credible or attractive politics of power than the opposing parties – what Gamble calls the party's 'electoral perspective'.

As a party dedicated to being in office, the Conservatives have always tended – at least until the late 1970s – to subordinate the politics of support to the politics of power, or at any rate tried to adapt their politics of support to what they saw as the necessities of the politics of power. Under Thatcher, these priorities began to alter. While stressing heavily themes such as law and order, hierarchy, and individual initiative, which have traditionally expressed the interests and outlook of the party's core of support, she was studiously vague about the party's policies for dealing with the problems of the economy – so much so that some observers were misled into expecting these policies to be *less* radical than those of Heath in the years 1970–72, because Heath had heavily emphasised the formulation of detailed policies in the years before 1970.[10]

An alternative interpretation, however, is that the priorities remained the same, but that Thatcher and her closest colleagues in the leadership entertained a radically different conception of the politics of power from Heath's. On the surface, their formulae for the politics of power appear similar: a smaller state, a reduction in union power, and reliance on competition and market forces to restore efficiency and encourage new investment. But in reality they were dissimilar. Thatcher had a very different understanding of the political parameters within which such a politics of power could or should operate. She was prepared to let the 'discipline of the market' work; she was prepared to accept the unpopularity this incurred (by the end of 1981 the Conservative Party's share of popular support had fallen to 23 per cent);[11] she even seemed prepared to risk losing the next election. Unlike Heath, she conceived of a new order, for capital and labour alike, based on a return to nineteenth-century values. She did not *subordinate* the politics of power to the politics of support – she had a vision of a new politics of power, and a new electoral perspective, resulting from a new 'neo-liberal' hegemony.

These contrasting interpretations reveal the limitations of any relatively simple analytic framework. Party management and leadership remain an art, not a science, with intuition and personality playing as important a part in success or failure as analysis and organisation. None the less, Gamble's model does throw a good deal of light on the successive transformations of Conservative policy and doctrines in modern times. For example, Joseph Chamberlain's campaign for tariff reform at the turn of the century is a case of a new politics of power (protection) and a new politics of support (social reform to be financed from import duties), but it failed because the conditions were not yet ripe for either. By the 1930s, however, a number of key relationships had changed: protectionism was becoming general throughout the world, and the Conservatives had inherited the support of those elements of manufacturing capital which had been attached to the Liberals thirty years earlier. The Labour Party had been discredited by the debacle of 1931, and so protectionism as a politics of power could now be complemented by a politics of support based not on social reform but on 'safety first' – retrenchment and preservation of the status quo.

It is not entirely far-fetched to see a parallel between this and the transition to 'Thatcherism'. Heath, like Joseph Chamberlain, proposed a politics of power whose time had not yet arrived. In the early 1970s capital was not yet ready to stand by the Conservative government in its confrontation with the trade unions nor, on the other hand, to invest in manufacturing so long as the industrial balance of power remained unchanged. Heath's politics of support were also inadequate. While his doctrine of efficiency and growth (especially in its Selsdon Park version) was in tune with the sentiments of the party's activists, his technocratic approach not only failed to stress the themes through which traditional Conservative values were expressed – law and order, inequality, the family, etc. – but also led him to execute a dramatic policy U-turn when his politics of power failed. The party's supporters were thus denied even the gratification of seeing the party confirm its reputation as the natural party of 'effective government'.

It fell to Thatcher to develop a politics of support appropriate to Heath's politics of power, and to implement the latter with the necessary faith and indifference to conventional wisdom. Also, the crisis was nearly ten years older when she took office, and the CBI, in spite of some misgivings, was now desperate enough to give her government continuing support in face of policy failures for which it would never have forgiven Heath.

Reference to the CBI's misgivings serves as a reminder that neither the 'politics of power' nor the 'politics of support' is synonymous with *policies* of power or support. On the contrary, although the Conservative leader has, as we shall see, exceptional power, he or she must continually struggle to develop and maintain the chosen strategy and tactics in the face of opposition not only from the party's natural opponents, but from among its own natural supporters, and even within its own ranks. In other words, *policies* of power and support are the outcome of the *politics* of power and support. These struggles are, typically, most visible and acute between the party's activists, far removed from the responsibilities of office, and the party's leadership, which comprises a large section of the parliamentary party. When the party is in power, about one Conservative MP in three is a holder of a government position – Minister, Junior Minister or unpaid Parliamentary Private Secretary to a Minister. When in opposition, an even larger proportion are ex-members or would-be members of government. They all tend to have a national view of politics, strongly influenced by the interplay between the politics of power and their assessment of the mood of the electorate – and especially the mood of those 'marginal' Conservative voters who are near the 'centre' of the national spectrum of opinion.

Backbench MPs – particularly those with no experience of office, or no prospects of it – act as a sort of hinge between these two outlooks, and as a result backbenchers play a key organisational role in the party. Their support in the division lobby sustains the party leadership in office; their links to their constituencies make them sensitive to what their local party activists are saying.

A good example of this division of outlook occurred during the winter of 1980–81 when a series of cuts in services, flowing from the Thatcher government's spending cuts, culminated in a characteristically 'Tory' revolt. Conservative members of the House of Lords, from predominantly rural areas, declined to endorse the reduction of rural school-bus services, and some 32 Conservative MPs opposed or abstained from voting on a budget clause which further raised the price of petrol (a measure which particularly affected rural voters, on whom the party increasingly depended).

Relative Autonomy

For the Conservative Party to be able to uphold the interests of capital in face of an enfranchised working-class majority is therefore a complex task, requiring, above all, a special kind of freedom for the party leadership in carrying it out. Until about 1970 this freedom was secured in two main ways: first, a finely graduated social stratification within the party hierarchy, which insulated the leadership from its supporters; and second, a unique degree of authority vested in the leader. The finely graduated social stratification of the party was first pointed out by Jean Blondel. Drawing on a variety of sociological studies (mainly from the 1950s), he showed that as one moved up the hierarchy of the Conservative Party – from members, to constituency association officers, to parliamentary candidates, to elected MPs and finally to the cabinet – the social weight of the working class dropped, from a third of party members to zero in Conservative cabinets, by rather well-graduated stages.[12] Even more significantly, the weight of the 'lower middle class' (shopkeepers, teachers and the like, who accounted for around 16 per cent of the electorate) made up over half the membership of the Conservative Party, but only about a quarter of the local party officers. More than half of these officers were drawn from what Blondel calls the 'well-to-do' (professional people, managers), who constituted only 3 or 4 per cent of the electorate. At the level of candidates and MPs the social composition became still more rarefied. The 'lower middle class' largely disappeared, and at each level the proportion who had been educated at public school rose. 'The higher one is in the educational and occupational scale, the more one is likely to get elected for a safe seat in the Conservative party.'[13] By the time the level of Conservative cabinets was reached, the proportion who had been to public school rose to about 85 per cent and the proportion from Eton alone to over a quarter. Over two thirds had been to Oxford or Cambridge.

This structure seems to have continued essentially unchanged since the 1950s, though it seems likely that there has been some decline in the professional/upper-middle-class dominance of the leadership of the local associations, in favour of the lower-middle-class elements most committed to Thatcherism, and some decline in the proportion of MPs from public school backgrounds.[14]

The effect of this graduated social hierarcy was to *associate* the working class to some extent, and the lower-middle class quite strongly, with the party's grassroots organisation. The Conservatives have never claimed to know how many members they have; and, as pointed out by Blondel, Conservative constituency associations are indeed associations, not local parties – i.e., they are primarily social clubs, groupings of conservative-minded people, and only secondarily electoral, let alone 'policy-proposing' organisations – so it is not of great moment what precise number of working-class people are members. Rough estimates suggest that some 3–400,000 working-class people do belong, with a tendency to be concentrated in towns with longstanding traditions of working-class Conservative affiliation (such as Glossop, near Manchester, where one of the early studies used by Blondel was carried out);[15] plus perhaps three-quarters of a million 'lower-middle-class' people. These people provide the party's workers at elections, and they have some voice at the party's annual conferences; but much less than the local associations' officers, who are already predominantly drawn from higher income and status brackets, and are socially closer to the party's candidates and MPs. But even they are mostly at some social distance from those MPs who become Conservative ministers.

This graduated hierarchy, in other words, has permitted the leadership to appeal to a mass membership which has some basis in the working-class majority; to draw strength from the conservative passions of the lower middle class; but to enjoy an immunity, conferred by social distance and the respect for social status which is part of the conservative tradition, from these passions when they run counter to the requirements of the politics of power.

This versatile social chain is matched by the unique organisational independence accorded to the party leader. The main elements of the party's organisation are as set out in Figure 10.1. The Conservative and Unionist constituency associations formally comprise the National Union of Conservative and Unionist Associations and elect the bulk of the 2,500–3,000 delegates who attend the annual Conservative Party Conference. This Conference, however, is also attended by the members of the Central Council of the National Association, which meets once a year in between the annual Party Conferences and includes all Conservative MPs, members of the European Parliament, peers, prospective parliamentary candidates and the senior officials of the Conservative Central Office. The Central Office is a purely professional organisation, the party's headquarters; the Conservative Research Department and Conservative Political Centre (policy

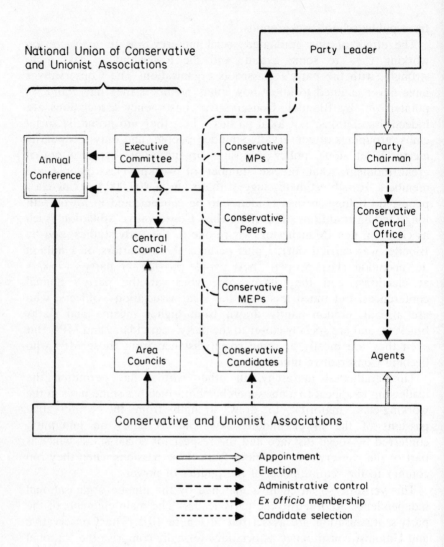

Figure 10.1 Conservative Party Organisation

making and propaganda bodies, respectively) are attached to it, but its main business is formulating electoral strategy, appointing and supervising parliamentary candidates, fundraising, the appointment of agents in the constituencies, etc.

The leader's formal position in all this is simple. Having been elected by the party's MPs, she (or he) holds office indefinitely until she resigns or is defeated at a subsequent leadership election. During this time, the leader is subject to no formal constraint or control of any kind, either from the parliamentary party or from the National Association. The Director of the Central Office is answerable to the party chairman, and both of them are appointed by the leader, who also personally appoints the Director of the Conservative Research Department, the party's Vice-Chairman and Treasurer, and other officers. The party's election manifestos, and all other policy statements, are the responsibility of the leader alone.

This organisational apartheid is very visible at annual conferences of the party (i.e., of the National Union). The leadership on the conference platform is neither elected by, nor is in any way answerable to, the party organisation represented by those on the conference floor. The leadership seek the support of conference – and usually get it, even when the mood is critical – but while leaders and supporters meet in conference, they do not transact any business together. Annual conferences pass resolutions, but the instances where these have been accepted by the leadership when they ran counter to what had previously been seen as dictated by the politics of power are so few as to be famous. One such instance was the pledge made by Harold Macmillan at the 1950 conference to accept the target of 300,000 new houses a year as government policy (a pledge later redeemed in office).

These arrangements contrast sharply with the position of the Labour Party leader, who even before the constitutional changes of 1980 and 1981 was formally bound by the policy resolutions of the Labour Party conference, and had to work with party officers elected by the conference or appointed by the National Executive Committee, none of whom was responsible to him. In addition, the Conservative leader enjoys the great power that goes with patronage – her power to appoint, and dismiss, all 130 or so members of any Conservative government.[16] The leader is thus free to adopt, adapt or drop policies according to her or his judgement of the necessary balance to be struck between the politics of power and the politics of support, to an extent not found in any other party's constitution. This freedom is the second key to the famous 'pragmatism' which the Conservatives have shown over the century-and-a-half since Sir Robert Peel first articulated the modern concept of conservatism, of continuing to conserve what is essential by accepting change in what is not.

It is striking that, with so much power, Conservative leaders have had a higher casualty rate than the leaders of other parties.[17] That is the price they have paid for not succeeding in fulfilling the party's goal of defending property to the satisfaction of their followers, above all by failing to maintain the party's hold on office. In the post-war period Churchill was untouchable because of his wartime position, and clung to office after he was no longer able to exercise it effectively; but Eden, Macmillan and Home were all forced to resign and Heath was forced to submit to re-election in circumstances which led to his defeat. The executioners of this law of failure are the Conservative MPs. This has become much clearer since Conservative MPs decided, in 1965, to elect leaders directly, and, in 1975, to oblige leaders to submit to an annual election when in opposition.

Before that, an informal process of criticism and control had been exercised by the backbenchers through the '1922 Committee', a semi-official organ of backbench opinion.* The 1922 Committee could, in effect, force the leader to take its views into account, or even to resign, by a sufficiently united and forceful expression of discontent. But it had no formal power, and a leader determined to defend himself could always hope to deflect opposition by the appeal to rank, by the use of patronage and by his strategic control of the extra-parliamentary party machine. It was to reduce the power of the 'magic circle' of rank and privilege in which previous leaders had moved that the Conservative backbenchers made these changes, making the leader directly and visibly, not indirectly and invisibly, answerable to the party in the House of Commons. These changes reflected their feeling that the style of leadership that had served the party in the interval between 1918 and the second onset of the crisis must change. In the past, it had been said that the Conservative leader 'emerged'. In absence of a 'natural leader' – and the Conservatives had known only one (Churchill) in the twentieth century – the effect of this principle was to confer the leadership on 'sound' figures at the centre of the spectrum of party opinion.

In 1964, however, the 'emergence' of Lord Home, the least divisive of the contenders for the succession to Macmillan, produced a figure unattuned to the crumbling of the consensus, a hereditary peer with virtually no experience of the Commons and little interest in domestic affairs. In sharp contrast, the leadership election of the following year led to the choice of Heath, with his clear if over-intellectualised approach to the problem of reconstructing British capitalism. Heath's policy failures (the U-turns, the unsuccessful confrontation with the miners, the imposition of direct rule in Belfast, the unpopular EEC),

---

* The 1922 Committee takes its name from a famous meeting of Conservative MPs which repudiated the decision of the party's Leader, Austen Chamberlain, to continue the coalition that the Liberal Leader Lloyd George had maintained since the end of the 1914–18 war. The committee consists of all the Conservative MPs except the leader when the party is in opposition; when the party is in office it consists only of backbenchers (the Whips attend but do not vote).

culminating in two election defeats in 1974, prompted the backbenchers to move again – this time to take routine powers to terminate a leader's tenure by means of annual elections. As the political stakes rose, the Conservative leader became more directly and visibly dependent on the parliamentary party.

Hegemony

While the relative autonomy of the Conservative leader has been necessary for Conservative success, it is not the whole explanation. Why has one worker in three regularly tended to vote Conservative? What are the positive elements which tie a major section of the working class to the Conservative Party? One surprisingly simple answer is that workers tend to agree more with Conservative than with Labour policies. Though a majority vote Labour because they see it as the party most identified with their interests, even these workers tend to hold views more in line with Conservative policies (on, for instance, education, law and order, housing or foreign affairs). What accounts for this?

The answer must be sought in the 'naturalisation' of conservative ideas that results from the penetration of all social life by the capital–labour relationship discussed in Chapter 8. This is not primarily a matter of 'indoctrination'. On the contrary, the power of the ideas implicit in the capital–labour relationship springs largely from their being *self-taught*. Paul Willis's revealing study of a comprehensive school in the Midlands in the mid-1970s showed, for example, that it was in their very rejection of the official culture of the school (with its stress on academic achievement and conformity to authority) that working-class boys *prepared themselves* for unskilled labouring jobs.[18] Their preparedness to accept a life of repetitive, low-paid work, and to accept as natural, or at least inevitable, that there should be such work and that they should do it, was largely the result of their own active contribution to a working-class counter-culture while still at school. To say that the existence of such work at one end of the scale, and of owners and managers at the other, is a 'fact of life' which is accepted as natural because 'that is the way it is', is to miss the active dimension through which – in the absence of any ideological counter-initiative – the 'victims' constantly *re-create* the social reality which victimises them. It was certainly true that the authority figures in these boys' lives – teachers, parents, police, future employers – also actively contributed, in a different way, to constructing the same social reality; and both processes continue throughout adult life.

The ideas which Willis recorded from the 'lads' at 'Hammertown Boys Comprehensive' already contained many quintessentially Conservative themes, such as the status of women, race, the value of physical labour, and the inevitability of the established order. And in another study of 'hippies' and a motorcycle 'gang', Willis noted how, with new experiences in adult life, the range of conservative political ideas expanded, even in these apparently 'deviant' working-class subcultures.[19] Nationalism, racism, the monarchy and even authority were positively endorsed.

The 'social-democratic' counter-culture of the labour movement was, by comparison, feeble, or at least feebly championed, at least by the late 1970s; such vitality as it still possessed owed more to the residual effects of the 'people's war' and the sheer scale and omnipresence of the welfare state than to any continuing effort by the Labour Party or the trade unions to develop an alternative conception of society among their members.

The Conservative Achievement 1945–70

The Conservative Party therefore appeals to a population, including its working-class majority, which tends to be predisposed to respond to conservative themes. Considered in this light, the success of the Labour Party in attracting the support of two-thirds of the working-class electorate could be said to need as much explanation as the success of the Conservative Party in retaining the support of one-third. Yet this is also a somewhat misleading way of putting the matter. The fact that a majority of workers still tend to vote Labour in spite of having more or less Conservative views on many issues, shows that voting is not a matter of policy preferences alone; the structure of people's political attitudes is much more complex. It has been shown, for instance, that people change their views on specific questions to bring them more into line with the position adopted by 'their' party.[20] What this implies for the Conservative Party is the need to maintain an 'image' capable of *activating* the conservative predispositions of the mass electorate sufficiently to offset the strength of the Labour Party's 'image' as the party of the working class.

For almost a century the Conservatives found to hand major issues which enabled them to project such an image, using and constantly adapting a limited range of traditional themes: national unity (opposition to both regional and class division), national sovereignty, the empire, the constitution (especially monarchy, parliament and the rule of law), the established Church, and last but not least, the 'conduct of the King's (or Queen's) government'. The Conservatives particularly stressed their 'competence' as the natural party of government, and attacked the Labour Party as being not merely based on 'narrow', 'sectional' (i.e., class) interests, but also as being incompetent and unfit to be trusted with the affairs of state.

For the party leadership to continue to exploit these themes, while pursuing a politics of power adapted to the greatly altered circumstances following the Second World War, tested the mechanisms of adaption outlined earlier to their limits, but with brilliant results. Two of the chief architects of what was then called the 'new Toryism', Harold Macmillan and R.A. Butler, are excellent examples of the leadership's ability to pursue the politics of power it judges necessary while at the same time disengaging the party from declining social strata and recruiting new elements of future support. After 1945, 'a vital Conservative task was to recruit professional managers in modern industry and jettison the railway stockholders and the mine owners'.[21] To enable the leadership to come to terms with the expanded interventionist and welfare state, and the new nationalised industry sector, Conservative MPs in touch with modern corporate enterprise had to replace rentiers, retired majors and landowners. The task was accomplished – gradually but thoroughly – by internal party reforms initiated after 1945. The 'new' type of Conservative MP, without large private means or a family political tradition, did not reach the ranks of the leadership until the mid-1960s, but this allowed the party to present a strong appearance of continuity with the past throughout the fifties.

As Ramsden has pointed out, the Conservatives were also helped to make this crucial transition – in effect, to come to terms with social democracy – by the fact that in the early 1950s, at least, much of the pre-war context did not seem to have changed. Apart from India, the empire was still intact; the army – so powerfully linked to the empire and the Conservatives – was larger than it had ever previously been in peacetime; the higher civil service was still largely Conservative (or Liberal) in background and outlook, as were the professions, the Church of England, most of the press and virtually all of the management of industry.[22] Secure support in these contexts allowed Macmillan not only to keep the party committed to the welfare state, but to assert his own preference for inflation over unemployment by accepting the resignation of his whole Treasury team (the Chancellor of the Exchequer and junior ministers) in 1958 when they wanted to do the opposite. (Macmillan characteristically dismissed the crisis as 'little local difficulties'.) Social services went on expanding under the Conservatives within the general lines laid down by Labour after the war. 'The Conservatives set out to prove themselves better managers of social democracy than the Labour Party, and aided by the long boom in the Western economy they succeeded beyond expectation.'[23]

This success in turn reinforced the party's image as the party of good government. By the end of the 1950s it was the Labour Party which was on the defensive, concerned that 'embourgeoisement' had made its own residual socialist commitments a liability rather than an asset among the working class. Exploiting this success, Macmillan also tackled the dismemberment of the empire (a process which Churchill had once declared himself 'not elected to preside over'), the application to enter the EEC, the abandonment of an independent nuclear capacity and the scaling down of the armed forces. Had the economy been capable of sustaining the growth of the 1950s, the Conservative Party might have survived without any more radical changes to become the dominant party of government of a prosperous middle-level European power in the last quarter of the twentieth century. But this was not to be.

The Crisis and the Conservatives

Writing in 1971 Nigel Harris observed that from the point of view of capital,

> Other things being equal, the Conservative Party could always be trusted. It might fumble, or cling to policies which aligned it with an earlier *status quo* rather than seek to accelerate the evolution of a future *status quo*, but at least it was free from those alarming adventures that occasionally afflicted Labour. Such calculations were possible provided Britain faced no crisis so great that its demands exceeded the limits of conservative 'flexibility'. It was never necessary to create a new party of the *status quo* because the Conservatives could no longer fight the fight . . . And this was so because of the sheer stability of British society . . . The social schisms never became so wide that the Conservatives could not make some attempt to straddle them. The pursuit of 'balance' was never forced to give way entirely to the struggle for 'order'.[24]

After 1970, the crisis began to exceed these limits; a growing segment of Conservative opinion began to think that the party was no longer fighting the fight. They did not turn to a new party of order, however, but sought to change the Conservative Party itself into such a party. The election of Thatcher as leader and her general election victory in 1979 were large steps in this direction, though the resistance of the 'Tory' wing of the party was not definitively overcome until 1983.

The immediate occasion of the rise of the new right within the Conservative Party was what they perceived as the growing cost of seeking trade union cooperation in the formulation and implementation of economic policy, a policy that had culminated in the concessions made to the unions under the 'social contract'. Not only did this policy seem to them to give the unions an unconscionable degree of power, it had also failed to halt the country's industrial decline. To put it in terms of Gamble's formulation, the politics of support became less and less consistent with the politics of power as Heath understood them from 1972 onwards. The mounting unrest on the Conservative backbenches was matched not only in the constituency associations – where the 'old-fashioned' right had always been strong, and where the abandonment of empire and the decline of British military power were particularly resented – but much more significantly elsewhere: for example, in the Confederation of British Industry – the organised voice of large-scale industry. There, the Director-General, after dismissing his Economic Director in 1973 for his monetarist opposition to Heath's policies, was himself obliged to quit his office in 1975, after which CBI policies swung firmly in a neo-liberal direction.[25] The fact that the civil service did not do likewise, and that the professions, the universities and the media were, by now, much less reliably Conservative (at least with a capital C) than they had been in the 1950s, heightened the sense of insecurity on the Conservative right.[26]

The electoral prospects of the party had also become increasingly bleak. Their share of the total vote cast had declined at every election since 1955, from nearly 50 per cent in 1955 to under 36 per cent in October 1974. Their grip on the all-important working-class voters had been weakening; some were abstaining, some were voting Liberal in England or Scottish Nationalist in Scotland, while in Northern Ireland the Unionists, bitterly resentful of Heath's imposition of direct rule in 1972, ended their historic alliance with the Conservatives after the February 1974 election. These losses damaged the Conservatives' image as the party of national unity as well as the party of good government. They had also surrendered sovereignty to the EEC – this, after giving up the empire.

In February 1974 Enoch Powell, a former Conservative minister, left the party and called on voters to vote Labour because Labour was opposed to the EEC; and, in October 1974, he stood as a Unionist in the Northern Ireland seat of South Down to underscore his opposition to Heath's policy of seeking an 'all Ireland' solution to the conflict in Ulster. In Scotland, the SNP offered a substitute nationalism, and in the October 1974 election pushed the Conservatives into third place in terms of votes cast. In England, too, the racist National Front won an average of over 3 per cent of the poll in the seats it contested in 1970 and in the two elections of 1974.[27] While these votes were not all gained at the expense of the Conservatives, they represented a pool of voters with whom the Conservative right felt a good deal of sympathy and whose support they would have liked to have.

What all this implied was that the Conservatives' existing politics of power could not be justified in terms of electoral success. A new 'electoral perspective' was needed too. Thatcher's contribution was to see that the new politics of power proposed by 'social market' doctrine, combined with a new politics of support based on an attack on the 'consensus', could pay electoral dividends, and she demonstrated this dramatically in May 1979. The question posed by this historic election – in which the Conservatives achieved the largest electoral swing since 1945 – is whether it marked the conversion of the Conservative Party from a dominant party of government, surviving by occupying the centre ground, into a party of order, destined to retain power only so long as no centre ground existed.

At the end of the 1980s the answer to this question lay in the future, but some signs pointed to such a change. The new leadership election process made it less likely that the party would in future be led by patricians of the Macmillan type. The internal changes inaugurated after 1945 had eventually produced a significantly different parliamentary party: 'In the seventies, for the first time in its history, the Conservative Party ha[d] more MPs from grammar schools than from Eton and half of its MPs [were] occupied in business'.[28] The significance of this shift should not be exaggerated. The Tories, or 'wets' (as Thatcher called them), were still strong, particularly among the senior ranks of Conservative MPs, and throughout the 1980s they periodically called for a return to the 'middle road'. But by the end of the decade they were increasingly a collection of former leaders without followers. The outlook of the new generation of MPs had made the parliamentary party as a whole more ideologically representative of the party's constituency activists than at any time in its history.

A similar shift also seemed to have occurred within the constituency associations. Although research is lacking, observers of annual conferences noted that the 'county' and professional middle-class element, which had tended to predominate among Conservative representatives in the past, had given way to the more aggressive accents of the lower-middle class. They also noted that the rapport between the conference rank and file and the leader (as opposed to her 'Tory' or 'wet' colleagues on the platform) was closer than at any time since 1945. Could the reduced formal autonomy of the leader have been paralleled by a process of social homogenisation in the constituency associations, thus reducing both elements of the 'insulation' which had been so important to the Conservatives' 'flexibility' in the past?

If so, the course set for the party by Thatcher might prove increasingly hard to reverse. The risks involved were signalised by the emergence in 1981 of the Liberal/SDP Alliance, whose popularity in opinion polls and at by-elections implied that the Conservatives could conceivably be reduced to a permanent parliamentary minority. At the time there was even a growing body of support within the party for proportional representation, which would almost certainly mean the end of purely Conservative governments in the future: that is to say, some Conservatives – such as those who formed the Conservative Action for Electoral Reform group – increasingly accepted that the party could no longer 'fight the fight' alone – at least, not in the way they wanted, the old Tory 'middle way' of Macmillan.

Thatcher herself was playing for higher stakes: to remain a dominant party of government in a country where 'business' could once again flourish, and where the public had returned to pre-social-democratic – if not pre-democratic – values. At the end of the 1980s it was too early to say whether her gamble had succeeded, because the election victories of 1983 and 1987 owed so much to the divisions within and between Labour and the Alliance, while the Conservative share of the poll stayed constant at 42 per cent; and because the sustainability of the economic recovery was not assured. But the signs were that the trick had been turned. The 'Tory' element in the parliamentary party was increasingly weak, and it was doubtful if either the backbenchers would elect, or the constituency parties enthusiastically support, a successor to Mrs Thatcher of the 'moderate', pragmatic kind.

Notes

1 N. Harris, *Beliefs in Society*, Penguin, Harmondsworth 1968, p. 99.
2 R. Rose, *The Problem of Party Government*, Penguin, Harmondsworth 1976, p. 309.
3 S. Beer, *Modern British Politics*, Faber, London 1965, pp. 249–51 ff.
4 F. Boyd, *British Politics in Transition 1945–63*, Praeger, New York 1964, p. 760. R. Behrens (in *The Conservative Party from Heath to Thatcher*, Saxon House, Farnborough 1980), comments that while controversy raged between the radical right and the pragmatists in the party leadership, 'there was little disagreement . . . about the importance of the rule of law, wealth and property, and aspects of Conservative policy governed by these immutable glories changed hardly at all' (p. 126).
5 Cited in A. Gamble, *The Conservative Nation*, Routledge and Kegan Paul, London 1974, p. 116.
6 Rose, p. 57.
7 N. Harris, *Competition in a Corporate Society: British Conservatives, the State and Industry 1945-64*, Methuen, London 1972, p. 259.

8 Gamble, *The Conservative Nation*, Chapter 1. Gamble's formulation is more sophisticated, though perhaps somewhat less clear, than the summary presented here.
9 Gamble, p. 5.
10 Gamble himself was momentarily deceived in this respect: see his 'The Conservative Party' in H.M. Drucker, ed., *Multi-Party Britain*, Macmillan, London 1979, p. 43.
11 Gallup poll reported in *The Times*, 18 December 1981.
12 J. Blondel, *Voters, Parties and Leaders*, Penguin, Harmondsworth 1974, pp. 96 ff and 130 ff.
13 Blondel, p. 135.
14 See D.E. Butler and M. Pinto-Duschinsky, 'The Conservative Elite, 1918–78: Does Unrepresentativeness Matter?', in Z. Layton-Henry, ed., *Conservative Party Politics*, Macmillan, London 1980, p. 195, for the class basis of Conservative Constituency parties in the 1960s; and D.E. Butler and D. Kavanagh, *The British General Election of 1983*, Macmillan, London 1984, p. 234–5, and *The British General Election of 1987*, Macmillan, London 1988, p. 202, for the public school backgrounds of Conservative candidates in these two elections (in 1983, 40% of defeated candidates and 70% of elected candidates, had been to public school; in 1987 the proportions were 41% and 68% respectively). M, Burch and M. Moran, in 'The Changing British Political Elite 1945–1983: MPs and Cabinet Ministers' (*Parliamentary Affairs* 38/1, Winter 1985, pp. 1–15) found a notable decline in the public school/Oxbridge proportion among incoming Conservative MPs in the 1979 and 1983 elections.
15 A.H. Birch, *Small-Town Politics*, Oxford University Press, Oxford 1959. *The Report of the Houghton Committee on Financial Aid to Political Parties* (Cmnd. 6601, 1979), estimated that in 1975 the Conservatives had about 1.5 million members.
16 Mrs Thatcher's government of 1979 had 86 MPs and 21 peers in paid government posts, and 20 unpaid Parliamentary Secretaries. These powers, of course, are equally enjoyed by a Labour Leader.
17 This was first pointed out by R. McKenzie in *British Political Parties*, Praeger, New York, Revised Edition 1963.
18 P. Willis, *Learning to Labour*, Saxon House, Farnborough 1978.
19 P. Willis, *Profane Culture*, Routledge and Kegan Paul, London 1978.
20 See Blondel, p. 79.
21 Harris, *Competition in a Corporate Society*, p. 264.
22 J. Ramsden, 'The Changing Base of British Conservatism', in C. Cook and J. Ramsden, eds, *Trends in British Politics Since 1945*, Macmillan, London 1978, pp. 28–46.
23 A. Gamble and P. Seyd, 'Conservative Ideology and Electoral Strategy in Britain Since 1964', paper presented to the European Consortium for Political Research, April 1979, mimeo, p. 12.
24 Harris, p. 260.
25 W. Grant and D. Marsh, *The Confederation of British Industry*, Hodder and Stoughton, London 1977, pp. 89–90, and CBI Annual Reports.
26 Gamble, 'The Conservative Party', pp. 44–5.
27 N. Nugent, 'The National Front', in N. Nugent and R. King, *The British Right*, Saxon House, London 1977, p. 183. In October 1974 the National Front ran 90 candidates.
28 Ramsden, 'The Changing Base of British Conservatism', p. 43.

The Labour Party and
the Left

The crisis affected the Labour Party even more fundamentally than the Conservatives. By the end of the 1960s the left wing of the party in the constituencies and the trade unions, and a small group of Labour MPs, had become impatient with their traditional role as the 'conscience' of the party, prominent when the party was in opposition, but disregarded by the party's parliamentary leaders when in office. From 1972 onwards they began organising to commit the party to a more uncompromisingly socialist programme; after 1979 they also mobilised to change the party constitution so as to make the parliamentary leadership more accountable to the party outside parliament.

By March 1981 the success of the 'Labour left's' campaign had precipitated a split; a small section of the parliamentary right wing, led by four ex-ministers, broke away to form a Social Democratic Party. By the end of the year, 24 sitting Labour MPs (and one Conservative) had joined the SDP, which in alliance with the Liberals had also won two by-election victories.[1] Labour's voting strongholds in the industrial cities might hold firm but there was a clear risk that the SDP/ Liberal Alliance could prevent Labour from forming another majority government – especially if the Alliance found itself in a position to secure the adoption of proportional representation. If that happened, the Labour Party could be faced with an indefinitely long period in opposition; and in that case some trade unions, already weakened by unemployment and anti-union legislation, might wish to reduce or even sever their formal links with the Labour Party – links that still formed the bedrock of the party's financial, organisational and ideological support.

The Labour Party and the labour movement were tougher, denser social forces than recognised by the media (which eagerly followed – or

promoted – the struggles within the Labour Party and the rise of the
SDP). They would not be easily separated from each other, or
displaced from the centre of the political stage. But the risk that the
crisis could effectively destroy the party was none the less real. To
assess this risk a historical understanding of the situation is essential.

Labour in Politics: The Formative Years

In 1900 two socialist parties already existed in Britain, the Independent
Labour Party (ILP), founded in 1893, and the Social Democratic
Federation (SDF), formed in 1883. Unlike their counterparts in
Germany and France, they had made very limited inroads into
working-class political consciousness. The ILP ran 28 candidates in the
1895 election; all were defeated. The SDF, a Marxist party, ran three
candidates in 1885, two in 1892 and four in 1895, all equally
unsuccessfully. The leadership of the trade union movement was
overwhelmingly Liberal in allegiance and confined itself to trying to get
a number of 'Liberal–Labour' representatives (not all of whom were
workers) adopted as Liberal parliamentary candidates. In 1895 (the
last election before the formation of the Labour Party) 24 'Lib–Labs'
were adopted and nine were elected. To appreciate the extent to which
the British labour movement was still subject to Liberal hegemony it is
only necessary to recall that, by 1912, the German Social Democrats
were the largest party in the Reichstag, while in 1910 the French
Socialists and Socialist Radicals had 42 per cent of the seats in the
Chamber of Deputies.

As we saw in Chapter 3, the trade unions' reluctant decision to seek
independent representation in parliament in order to protect their legal
rights and their members' living standards was a response to the efforts
of the employers, supported by the courts, to restore profitability by
cutting wages during the Great Depression. In 1899, the Trades Union
Congress agreed to form a Labour Representation Committee on
which the ILP, the SDF and the Fabian Society were also represented.
The 1900 election came too soon for the LRC to do more than return
two MPs, but in the 1906 election 30 LRC candidates were successful,
and joined with the 22 Lib–Lab MPs elected at the same time to form
a 'Labour Party' in the House of Commons. After 1906 the LRC and
the Labour MPs became known simply as the 'Labour Party',
supported by the network of 'Trades Councils' developed by trade
union activists in most cities during the 1890s. But it was not until 1918
that a mass base of individual members was created in 'constituency

parties' throughout the country, to complement the federal structure of 'affiliated' organisations built up by the LRC.

This delay reflected the limited conception of the LRC's founders: to establish in parliament an independent group of spokesmen for the interests of labour. The LRC rejected at the outset the SDF's proposal to make the achievement of socialism one of its objectives. The ILP, whose representative (Keir Hardie) concurred in this decision, had called itself an independent 'labour' party, not a socialist party, for the same reason: the workers did not yet support the idea of socialism. The ILP believed that once the workers supported an independent party of labour, support for socialism would grow out of the struggle for reforms. Meantime, the LRC's aims were confined to redressing the grievances of the workers within the existing order. This approach was reinforced by the Fabian Society, an organisation of middle-class intellectuals formed in 1884 and dedicated to socialist reform through 'permeation', i.e. persuading the leadership of whatever party was in power to adopt Fabian policy. At first the Fabians' hopes were pinned on the progressive wing of the Liberal Party, but they soon recognised the potential of the new Labour Party and gave it increasing intellectual support.

The LRC was also greatly assisted by a court decision in 1901 that awarded damages to the Taff Vale Railway against the Railway Servants' union after a strike, a ruling which put all trade union funds at risk in industrial disputes. The number of strikes decreased, but support for the LRC rose. Three LRC candidates were elected at by-elections in 1903. The Liberal Party's Chief Whip recognised the danger and made a secret agreement with Ramsay MacDonald, the Secretary to the LRC, to avoid the LRC and the Liberal Party competing against each other in a number of working-class constituencies. The result was a landslide victory in 1906 for the Liberal Party, combined with the remarkable success of 30 of the LRC's candidates. The Taff Vale judgement was promptly reversed by Liberals' passage of the Trades Disputes Act of 1906, which served as the legal basis of British trade union rights until the 1980s. The LRC's strategy seemed to be brilliantly vindicated.

But 'labourism' did not remain unchallenged as the policy of the party for very long. The years of industrial conflict preceding the outbreak of the First World War generated demands for more radical change. This was reflected in the party's new constitution, adopted in 1918, whose famous Clause 4 stated that the party's object was 'to secure for the workers by hand or by brain the full fruits of their industry . . . upon the basis of the common ownership of the means of production'. But these words meant different things to different people. For most of the party's leadership, and probably most of its members, the party's new programme, *Labour and the New Social Order*, also adopted in 1918, was 'a Fabian blueprint for a more advanced, more regulated form of capitalism', rather than a formula for a radically different principle of social organisation, which it was taken to be by some socialists.[2] For, by 1918, the 'labourist' conception of the party had become strongly established, and had been reinforced by two other features of the original project: its parliamentarism, and the lack of a formal extra-parliamentary base for the party in parliament.

Parliamentarism, of course, was the essence of the original proposal. The task of the LRC was to secure parliamentary representation for 'labour'. By 1918 a generation of labour politicians had been produced who saw their role in these terms. They were resistant to any proposal to use extra-parliamentary action such as strikes, boycotts or the 'blacking' of goods, in support of political aims, tactics which Conservative and Liberal MPs denounced as unconstitutional. In the earliest years, moreover, few Labour MPs had the educational or theoretical background to enable them to develop even a comprehensive set of reform proposals.[3]

The lack of a mass membership base outside parliament also gave the early Labour MPs greater autonomy. Although the authority of the party's annual conference (consisting of delegates of the trade union and other organisations which had affiliated to the LRC) and of the National Executive Committee (chosen by the conference) was acknowledged, the MPs demanded, and were in practice allowed, a good deal of freedom to go their own way. This was rationalised by saying that they must decide the 'timing and method' of implementing conference decisions in parliament: they alone, they argued, could judge the practical possibilities for action in the light of the party balance in the House of Commons, and electoral considerations. This freedom was contested from the first, but it was only after 1979 that the Labour left directed their efforts to changing the constitution so as to oblige the Parliamentary Labour Party (PLP) to carry out the policies adopted by the party conference. Before 1918, however, the question of whether the parliamentary party's de facto autonomy was compatible with socialist objectives did not arise, as socialism was not then the aim of the party, even in theory. By 1918 a large measure of autonomy for the parliamentary party had become established practice, however much it continued to be questioned.

One more development in the party's earliest years also had a major influence on later events. In 1903 the Social Democratic Federation withdrew from the LRC because of the LRC's reformist policy. At this time the SDF was a significant force, with 43 branches and a cadre of tireless propagandists who enjoyed considerable respect among trade unionists. But the Marxism of the SDF was of a very sectarian brand, and its leader Henry Hyndman had stamped on the organisation a highly autocratic mode of operation. In separating itself from the LRC, the SDF separated itself from the mainstream of working-class politics. The result was that it remained 'chronically unable to break out of its isolation, or to influence the course of history', although it continued to form an important pole of attraction for left-wing activists who became frustrated by the Labour Party's parliamentary and reformist limitations.[4] In 1913 the SDF merged briefly with some of these disenchanted activists to form the British Socialist Party, and in 1920 the Communist Party of Great Britain was formed, inheriting the role, and many of the personnel, of the SDF and BSP. The Communist Party's existence divided the left wing of the labour movement, and strengthened the hand of Labour Party leaders who adopted right-wing positions by enabling them to appeal to anti-communist sentiment.

This factor was already significant in the Labour Party's response to the wave of industrial militancy which developed from 1908 to 1913. Prices were rising while wages stayed constant (or in some industries were even cut). Trade union membership increased rapidly: more people joined unions between 1900 and 1914 than in all previous years combined, reaching a total of 4.1 million in 1914. Strike activity rose dramatically. In 1912, 40 million working days were 'lost' in stoppages, more than any year since except for 1921, and 1926, the year of the General Strike. To many contemporaries it was an extraordinary and frightening development, as the working class expressed its resentment and seemed to feel its potential strength in a way not seen since Chartism.

The Labour Party, however, and the ILP (which retained its separate existence as an organisation affiliated to the Labour Party), opposed the strikes, criticising them as 'undemocratic' – that is, as expressing grievances which should be settled through parliamentary action. The SDF, on the other hand, declared that the strikes were a distraction from the task of organising a party with a revolutionary programme. The political initiative among the strikers passed by default to the syndicalists – advocates of the direct seizure of economic control by the workers in factories. This helped to spread socialist ideas and to popularise unionism. But syndicalism had no organisational base, and the only long-run beneficiaries were the leaders of the established trade unions whose membership increased.

A few years later, during the First World War, when the trade union

BRISTOL POLYTECHNIC
ST. MATTHIAS LIBRARY
FISHPONDS

leadership agreed to an 'industrial truce' (i.e., no strikes) without first securing guarantees from the employers on job security and price controls, this was exploited by employers to raise profits at the expense of wages. As a result, the leadership of the workers' resistance (especially in the munitions industry) fell to the shop stewards in the affected factories, and a nationwide Shop Stewards' Movement developed. Its inaugural conference, held in Leeds in 1916, called for the formation of soldiers' and workers' councils (Soviets) on the Russian model. The movement collapsed, however, with the end of the war, the rise in unemployment (as soldiers were demobilised), and the end of the industrial truce. The radical impulse imparted to the labour movement by the pre-war crisis and the upheavals of wartime was thus contained and limited by the early evolution of the Labour Party and its relationship with the Marxist left.

Party Structure

The Labour Party thus emerged from the First World War with a potential mass base that had been greatly extended, even if many of the party's own leaders had not supported the popular movements which had helped to accomplish this. It was now essential for the party to take advantage of the base which had been developed. The new constitution adopted by the party in February 1918 grafted a mass individual membership, organised in 'Constituency Labour Parties', onto the network of 'affiliated' labour organisations created by the LRC, creating a unique party structure which was to persist, virtually unchanged, until the present day (see Fig. 11.1). The annual conference of the party was made formally sovereign. In contrast to the Conservatives' annual conferences it formally determines the policies which the PLP is supposed to implement. Within the conference the balance of power rests with the trade unions, because delegates cast votes in 'blocks' corresponding to the number of members in the organisations they represent (see Table 11.1). In 1982 the General Secretary of the Transport and General Workers' Union cast a 'block vote' of 1,250,000, this being the number of TGWU members whom the union had 'affiliated' to the party as having paid the voluntary 'political' levy (in addition to their union subscription).[5] By contrast the delegates from a constituency party might cast as few as 256 votes.[6]

The National Executive Committee is elected by the conference. Constituency parties' delegates vote separately from the rest of the Conference to fill 7 of the 29 NEC seats. One more member is chosen by the Young Socialist organisation and another by affiliated

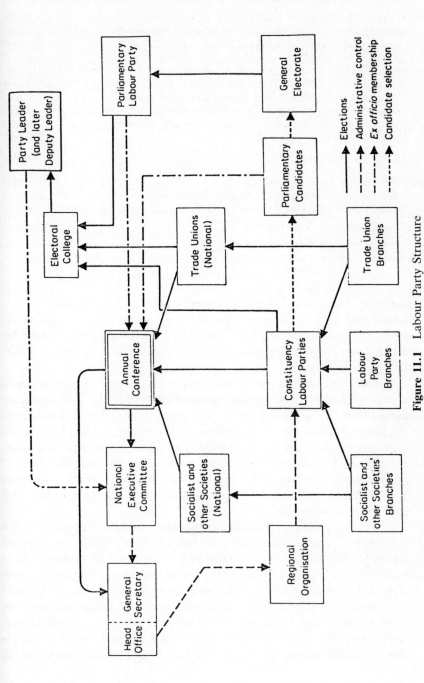

Figure 11.1 Labour Party Structure

Source: Adapted from L. Minkin *The Labour Party Conference*, Manchester University Press, Manchester.

Table 11.1   Votes at the 1982 Labour Party Conference

Transport and General Workers Union	1,250,000
Amalgamated Union of Engineering Workers Engineering Section	850,000
General and Municipal Workers Union	650,000
National Union of Public Employees	600,000
Union of Shop, Distributive and Allied Workers	418,000
National Union of Mineworkers	225,000
Union of Construction Allied Trades and Technicians	200,000
Union of Communication Workers (formerly Post Office Workers)	194,000
Electrical, Electronic, Telecommunications and Plumbing Union	180,000
National Union of Railwaymen	170,000
Total vote of 10 largest unions	4,748,000
Total vote of all other (39) unions	1,534,000
Total Constituency Parties vote (579 organisations)	602,000
Total Socialist and Co-operative Societies vote (10 organisations)	66,000
Total Conference Vote	6,950,000

Source: Labour Party Information Department; through the courtesy of L. Minkin.

socialist, cooperative and professional organisations, and the party's leader and deputy leader are members ex officio. The remaining 18 seats, however, including the 5 reserved for women, are voted for by all the delegates, so that the NEC's composition also reflects trade union predominance.

Before 1981, the formal sovereignty of the annual conference was not supported by any organisational control over the parliamentary party. If anything, power ran in the opposite direction. Constituency selection committees chose candidates for election, subject to 'official' endorsement by the NEC (which was rarely withheld), but once elected the Labour MPs alone chose a leader, who was, in practice, automatically the leader of the party as a whole, and who exercised great influence on all its parts. By 1981, however, the 'Labour left' had secured three changes.

First, sitting MPs were henceforth obliged to submit themselves for reselection prior to the next general election, rather than to be automatically reselected as in the past. The aim was to make them more representative of, or responsive to, changing sentiment within their constituency parties. The results were not dramatic. Only eight MPs were 'deselected' between the adoption of the new rules and the 1983 election, and while this was partly due to the fact that several MPs who defected to the SDP might well have been deselected, it is not the whole story: 'purges did not occur and the consequences of this reform have been much more long-term and subtle with Labour MPs having to take much more note of their local parties' opinions and modify their behaviour accordingly'.[7]

Second, the leader would in future be chosen by an electoral college in which MPs would have only 30 per cent of the votes, with 30 per cent allocated to delegates of the Constituency Parties and 40 per cent to those of the trade unions. The new procedures came into force after Michael Foot had been chosen by the PLP under the old system in November 1980, but they were applied in September 1981 to the election to the (largely symbolic) office of deputy leader, for which Tony Benn challenged the incumbent, Denis Healey. On this occasion the constituency parties' vote was overwhelmingly cast for Benn, the union vote was divided, and the outcome was settled in favour of Healey by a margin of less than 1 per cent of the total electoral college vote, primarily by the abstention of a group of MPs who were considered part of the parliamentary party's left wing but who opposed Benn and were anxious to prevent a further defection of MPs to the SDP.

Third, the final approval of the contents of election manifestos would lie with the NEC after a draft had been prepared jointly by the PLP and the NEC. In 1979, those responsible for drafting the manifesto felt that at the last minute Callaghan had arbitrarily diluted Conference commitments which had been included in the draft.

While the evidence is too limited to permit a very definite assessment of these changes, they tilted the balance of power more towards the party outside parliament, though with no decisive or early advantage to the party's left wing.

The real structure of power within the party cannot, of course, be read off from its formal constitution alone. Three other considerations are especially important. One is that the party's funds come overwhelmingly from the trade unions, partly in the form of the levy already mentioned, but also in voluntary contributions. These are of two kinds: sums donated from time to time to support the party's headquarters, and especially to meet election expenses, and funds given by individual unions to cover the constituency expenses of individual Labour MPs.[8] The unions' financial support for the party underwrites their dominant position in the party's Conference.[9]

Second, to be elected even to a constituency party seat on the National Executive Committee it is necessary to be well-known, which means that most NEC members are MPs. The PLP is thus heavily represented in the extra-parliamentary party's chief policy-making organ.

Third, and most important, most trade union delegates to Labour

Party conferences are activists; some are active in their constituency
Labour party as well as in trade union politics. Their political outlook
is affected by events in a similar way to the outlook of other
constituency party activists who, though almost always trade union
members, are active primarily in their local parties. The difference lies
in the fact that trade union delegates to the conference are elected by a
rank and file most of whom are chiefly concerned with their unions'
industrial aims, and only secondarily with the political aims of the
Labour Party. This often produces union leaders who are militantly
labourist, and lukewarm or even hostile to radical proposals for social
change. But it does not exclude the election of officials who believe
that their members' interests demand social change, or even (in some
cases) revolution.

The workers' experience of the vicissitudes of the British economy
has led them to oscillate between faith in labourism and disillusionment
with it. This is reflected, though in a very delayed and mixed fashion,
by changes in the character of the union leadership, and changes in the
power of individual leaders of the big unions. By the mid-seventies
these changes had led to a radical shift in the internal balance of forces
in the Labour Party, although its effects were temporarily held in
check by the appeal for loyalty to the Labour government between
1974 and 1979.

Also important for any analysis of the Labour Party over the years,
and for assessing its future potential, are the attitudes, conceptions,
myths and feelings that make up what Drucker has called the party's
'ethos'.[10] Drucker identified four elements in this ethos: intense loyalty
to leaders, a demand for personal sacrifice on the part of both leaders
and minor party and trade union officials, an irrational attitude to
funds (meanness and hoarding), and a deep faith in written rules. All
these traits exist, albeit to arguable degrees, and are traceable to the
distinctive historical experience of the British working class – a long
and bitter series of lessons in the essentials of class solidarity and self-
help. Drucker also notes an 'oppositional' mentality, reflecting the
workers' acceptance of their 'underclass' status, and a distrust of their
own party leaders in office, and this is also true.

But Drucker's list is incomplete, and perhaps slightly dated. For
instance, there was also an anti-intellectual tradition in the Labour
Party, reflecting distrust of the middle class from which virtually all the
party's intellectuals and most of its leaders have been drawn. In 1981 it
was still there, but a considerable proportion of the 'doctrinaire',
'polytechnic Marxists' who had been pushing the party to the left over
the previous decade were of working-class origins. So far from
becoming irrelevant, as Drucker predicted, intellectuals were becoming

more effective in the party than, perhaps, at any previous time in its history.[11] Another aspect of Labour's ethos not stressed by Drucker is the concept of the labour 'movement', i.e., the whole range of organisations and institutions through which the workers have historically expressed their interests, including not only organisations affiliated to the party but also such institutions as working men's clubs and colleges, the Workers' Educational Association, the Institute for Workers Control and even international organisations such as the Socialist International. The Labour Party has always been thought of as the political wing of this wider movement, whose traditions it shares, especially those of fraternity and democracy. This aspect of the party, it could be argued, helps to explain the strength of the swing to the left within the party after 1979, following two periods of Labour government which did not seem to have accomplished much in the interests of the labour movement.

Milestones 1918–45

Besides having these structural and cultural features the Labour Party was also the product of certain deeply formative historical experiences. The first was the formation in 1924 of Labour's first minority government, with Liberal support. In the December 1923 elections the Conservatives emerged as the largest party but with no overall majority; Labour was the larger of the two other parties which had both defended free trade, the main issue in the election campaign. In agreeing to form a government Ramsay MacDonald, the Labour leader, set three precedents: he alone chose the cabinet; he chose a strategy of trying to prove that Labour was 'fit to govern' rather than bringing forward socialist measures which the Liberals would not have supported, and then calling an election on them – i.e., an educational and mobilisational strategy for socialism; and again, he alone called an election in October 1924 on the issue of Labour's opposition to communism, not its opposition to capitalism.* All three precedents were consistent. MacDonald wanted to prove that the Labour Party was in every respect as 'constitutional' as the Conservatives and Liberals, so that middle-class voters should feel safe in voting for it. What was forfeited was the opportunity to use office to encourage the working class to believe that the 'new social order' envisaged in the

---

* The issue concerned the Attorney General's decision to withdraw the prosecution of the editor of a communist newspaper for sedition. MacDonald chose to treat the Conservatives' and Liberals' decision to set up a parliamentary enquiry into the case as an issue of confidence.

party's 1918 policy statement was something which the party could and would achieve.

The second formative event was the General Strike of May 1926, called by the TUC in support of the coalminers, who were faced with a 13 per cent wage cut and an extra hour on the working day. The Conservative government had prepared for the strike and indeed finally provoked the TUC into calling it. The TUC had no plans for sustaining a strike, let alone for seizing power if the government collapsed, and called it off unconditionally after nine days. The miners stayed out for six months, but were totally beaten. The Conservatives passed a new Trades Disputes Act in 1927 which outlawed 'sympathy strikes' and strikes intended 'to coerce the government'. They also cut at the trade unions' financial support for the Labour Party by requiring that union members should explicitly declare their wish to pay the political 'levy' to the Labour Party ('contracting in') rather than have the option of explicitly declaring their wish not to ('contracting out') as was previously the case. The Labour leaders, who had at first given lukewarm support to the TUC, and then counselled retreat, were reinforced in their fear of the consequences of extra-parliamentary action. The TUC, whose membership fell sharply, resolved in 1928 to avoid, in future, all industrial action going beyond immediate industrial disputes and to cooperate positively with management.

The third event was the collapse of the second Labour government in 1931. Once more heading a minority government with Liberal support (though this time Labour was the single largest party in the House of Commons), the Labour leadership, still under MacDonald, had no conception of a socialist approach to the economic crisis in which they found themselves after the Wall Street crash of 1929. Still obsessed with being 'responsible', they ignored the Keynesian proposals of the Liberals and of their own left wing. Instead, they accepted the need to balance the budget by cutting unemployment benefits in order to create enough confidence among foreign bankers, to whom the government looked for a loan to stem a run on sterling. After much agonising, the General Council of the TUC finally declined to endorse the cuts, and the cabinet split. MacDonald resigned, but immediately agreed to form a 'National Government' instead. Nominally this included all the parties but it actually consisted overwhelmingly of Conservatives and contained only three Labour members besides MacDonald himself. This government imposed a 10 per cent cut in unemployment benefits, devalued the pound by 29 per cent (a course which the Labour government had been advised was unthinkable), and called an election in which MacDonald appealed for a 'national' vote against his own former party. The Labour vote fell by

20 per cent, and the party was reduced to 52 seats in parliament, exactly equal to its position after 1906.

This traumatic experience, followed as it was by eight years of high unemployment, had an ambivalent effect on the party. The 1933 Conference resolved that the formation, composition and programme of any future Labour government should be subjects for determination by the party as a whole, not just the PLP or the leader; and a more explicit programme of socialist measures was adopted as party policy. But the chief political lesson drawn by the leadership (as opposed to the rank and file) was that they must, above all, become competent to master the existing system, which had twice mastered them. They found an opportunity to do this during the Second World War. As Drucker remarks, the years of the wartime coalition government in which the Labour leadership held office without fear of elections, and without the need to prove anything but their own competence (in a war economy over which the government had taken comprehensive powers), were an 'ideological holiday' for the party.[12]

As a result, the leadership was able to forget some other lessons which might have been drawn from the inter-war experience. There was no disposition on the part of most of them to envisage their next period in office as a step towards a new socialist order.[13] There was no reconsideration of the use of industrial action as an instrument to complement electoral politics. On the contrary, the party's official hostility towards communism, muted between 1941 and 1945, reached new heights with the advent of the Cold War after 1946, and this included a blanket opposition to the political use of industrial action such as the Communists then advocated. The Labour Party became even more purely parliamentary. Furthermore, having come to think of itself as a 'natural' party of government, it increasingly lost the educational or evangelical conception of its role which had previously been central to its tradition. By the 1950s most of the leadership had adopted the 'reactive' conception of policy-making of the older parties, posing the question, 'What will the voters vote for?' rather than 'What might they be persuaded to want?'

The Nature of the Labour Party

In spite of its earlier failures, the Labour Party found itself in 1945 in a position of enormous strength. Its voting support, though not its share of seats in parliament, had recovered from the 1931 debacle as early as the election of 1935. But, in 1945, after five more years of slump and five of the People's War, its share of the total vote rose from 30 per cent to 48 per cent. By 1945, trade union membership was also back to over eight million, a figure last achieved in 1921; and the party's broad programme of economic and social reforms had been legitimised by the war years. But after enacting these measures, the leadership abandoned the initiative and there followed more than a decade of opposition (1951–64) in which the party was wracked by a bitter struggle between its left and right wings, culminating in the qualified victory in 1961 of the 'revisionist' right led by Gaitskell (see Chapter 4).

The revisionist victory seemed to confirm the long-standing pattern of power inside the party, whereby the trade union leadership, through its 'block vote' on the floor of the annual conference and its dominance of the NEC, consistently sustained the parliamentary leadership in its resistance to left-wing pressure for more socialist policies. It strengthened the view, originally propounded by R.T. McKenzie and popularised by subsequent commentators, that the Labour Party's formal constitution, which made the annual conference sovereign over the parliamentary party, was incompatible with the British constitution. On this view, MPs are responsible to their constituents, not to their party. But, it was held, the real distribution of power inside the party fortunately contradicted the formal party constitution, and made the PLP in practice as free from control by the party outside parliament as the Conservative parliamentary party was.[14]

Later events were to show that this view was doubly wrong. In the first place, the 'British constitution', being unwritten, has no immutable clauses but only habitual practices with greater or less moral force, all of which are susceptible to change. If MPs became accountable to their parties outside parliament it would change the existing system but no more so than when MPs became elected on party tickets at the end of the nineteenth century.

Secondly, the support given by the trade unions to Labour's parliamentary leadership from 1945 to the end of the fifties proved to have been the product of special circumstances. The biggest unions, those of the transport workers and the engineers, were led at the time by men who endorsed the most limited version of labourism and who were also very strongly anti-communist – Arthur Deakin and William Carron. They first supported Attlee in resisting left-wing pressure for more radical policies, and then Gaitskell in moving official party policy away from its traditional commitment to socialism based on public ownership. They also supported tough procedural measures against the left wing in the party. In 1956, however, Deakin was succeeded by Frank Cousins, and in 1967 Lord Carron (as he had then become) was replaced by Hugh Scanlon. Both these new leaders were left wingers.

Under Cousin's leadership, the Transport Workers' block vote was no longer automatically cast for right-wing policies; in 1960 this led to a conference decision, carried by a small majority against the parliamentary leadership's bitter resistance, in favour of a policy of unilateral nuclear disarmament. A year later Gaitskell succeeded in getting this vote at least partly reversed, and meanwhile the Transport Workers had not opposed the adoption of a policy statement which in effect abandoned nationalisation as a goal. But 'much more than was seen to be the case, the victory of revisionism was achieved by a combination of procedural manipulation and the winning of strategically placed supporters rather than by mass persuasion of the majority of the active rank and file of the unions and the Party'.[15] The Transport Workers' vote now began to swing more and more against revisionism and, after 1967, with the leadership of the engineers, the miners, the shop workers and the post office workers also moving to the left, block votes at the conference could no longer be relied upon to support the PLP on fundamental questions of party policy.

The response of Harold Wilson, as Prime Minister after 1964, was to ignore conference decisions, with less and less pretence that he 'accepted' their authority even 'in principle'. After 1974, as the government progressively abandoned the substance of the 'social contract' in favour of deflation (see Chapter 6), conference support became less and less reliable, culminating in the rejection of Callaghan's proposed 5 per cent pay 'norm' at the 1978 Conference, and the call (after the 1979 election) to make the leader and MPs more accountable.

Following these changes, commentators who had formerly celebrated the 'good sense' of the major union leaders who had protected the party's leaders against the left wing, executed a volte-face. They suddenly discovered that the block vote was undemocratic. Union leaders, they reported, were elected by a small minority of their members but cast their entire union block vote in favour of policies which they personally favoured, regardless either of minority views or of the fact that many of their members took no interest at all in politics. The Labour Party was now urged to sever its links with the unions and the call went out for trade unions to be forced to be more democratic.

The work of Lewis Minkin put a long overdue end to this transparently ideological line of commentary. He showed that the changes in the unions' leaderships resulted from long-term shifts in rank and file opinion, which had begun to be registered at party conferences well before the leadership changes occurred. Carron, for example, who had been notoriously apt to cast the engineers' vote in favour of the party leaders' position even when a majority of the engineers' delegates opposed it (this was ironically called 'Carron's law'), was less and less able to do so in the final years of his presidency, as the left-wing tide rose. Cousins, on the other hand, did not cast the transport workers' vote against a single motion supported by the 'platform' (i.e. the mainly parliamentary party leadership) for two years after his election. When he finally did so for the first time, in 1958, it was because his personal position had by then come to be shared by a majority of his union's delegates. After 1978 the trend in leadership elections in several big unions seemed to move back again towards candidates of the right; but decisions at party conferences continued to move leftwards, because the affiliated membership of several left-oriented unions rose while that of several right-oriented ones declined.

In other words, the relation between the PLP and the party outside parliament was determined by long-term trends in which the election of particular individuals sometimes played an important part, but no more than that. It was true that only a minority of union members took part in votes for their national leaders (30 per cent to 40 per cent was common) and that certain powerful individuals – a Carron, a Scanlon or a Scargill (the left wing miners' leader who became President of the Mineworkers' Union in 1981) – could make a major impact (it was to reduce the likelihood of left trade unionists like Scargill being elected, that the 1984 Trade Union Act required them to be elected by their members directly – see p. 153 above). But the unions were not very different from most other political organisations in being run by their active minority, and those elected to leadership positions were aware of the need to stay in tune with a wider body of union opinion if their electoral base was to be kept secure. The influence of individual leaders had actually been greater in the days of Deakin and Carron, when delegates tolerated more autocratic leadership than they did later.

So the idea that the Labour Party's 'proper' functioning consists of a 'moderate' parliamentary party, sustained by 'moderate' union leaders against an 'extremist' minority, must be abandoned. The party's character has always reflected, and been a focus for, the changing relations between capital and labour. It has no immutable 'structure'; its complex organisation means that the evolving political struggle is registered in it in complex ways, after delays which vary according to the level or nature of the influence reaching it. A strong leader like Carron could delay the impact on the party of a leftward shift in a major union, while economic policies such as those of the sixties, and changes in the structure of employment, rapidly altered the voting balance by dramatically increasing the membership of some unions and reducing the membership of others.* The rhythm of change in constituency representation was different again. Individual membership declined disastrously in the disillusioning years of 1966 to 1970;[†] but the weakened constituency organisations were then more susceptible to being 'captured' by left-wing activists who moved back into party work from the early 1970s onwards.

How then should we understand the Labour Party? What determines these shifts in the balance of forces inside the party and what are their long-term implications? The interpretation of such a complex phenomenon must be tentative, but a historical view suggests the following.

Down to about 1981 the history of the Labour Party was the history of the gradual radicalisation of the labour movement. This process was not smooth or linear. At times the movement relapsed into, at most, a polite labourism, such as the 'welfare capitalism' propounded by the revisionists in the late 1950s. But over the long run it was gradually propelled away from its liberal–labourist starting point, towards the point where its demands were less and less compatible with capitalism. The evidence of opinion polls indicates that most members of trade unions did not approve of all the increasingly radical policies adopted by their leaders at both trade union conferences and at the Labour Party conferences of 1980 and 1981.[‡] The fact remains that a large majority of the people they elected, or did not trouble to oppose, had reached the conclusion that these policies were necessary and in their members' interests. The preoccupation of the press with the degree of rank and file approval for these policies was motivated partly by concern to know how far the shift of opinion in the union leaderships was reflected among the membership, but also by an awareness that, with these policies, the labour movement seemed for

* For example there was a rapid growth in the membership of the National Union of Public Employees and the Association of Scientific, Technical and Managerial Staffs, but a large drop in the membership of the National Union of Mineworkers and the National Union of Railwaymen.

† Individual membership was believed to be one million in 1952. By 1979 it was thought to have fallen to 250,000–300,000, though some observers thought even this figure was too high. The decline in membership was accompanied by a severe erosion of local party activities too (see R. Borthwick, 'The Labour Party', in H.M. Drucker, ed., *Multi-Party Britain*, Macmillan, London 1979, p. 63).

‡ By 1981 the party Conference had adopted the following policy resolutions: unilateral nuclear disarmament and the closure of all nuclear bases in Britain; withdrawal from the EEC; an Alternative Economic Strategy including reflation, restrictions on capital exports, imports controls, and a 35-hour week; extensions of public ownership and planning agreements with large private firms; the introduction of industrial democracy; repurchase at a discounted price of council houses sold to their tenants by local authorities; abolition of private schooling and private medicine; subsidised low fares for public transport.

the first time to be potentially on a collision course with British capital.

This did not mean that the leadership would persist along that course. They had backed away at the time of the General Strike in 1926, and part of the point of publishing the polling evidence of members' views was to encourage the leadership to retreat again. However, the crisis was forcing the party as a whole – not just the TUC, as in 1926, nor just the constituency activists, as critics tended to imply – to adopt a more comprehensive and consciously anti-capitalist programme than at any previous time in its history.

Although it could be readily predicted that in the medium run the leadership would moderate the programme adopted by Conference, and although the popular support that would be needed for its implementation was far from having been mobilised, both problems were being more openly confronted at the end of 1981 than ever before.* The changes in the party's constitution which had made the leadership more accountable were primarily aimed at ensuring that more uncompromising leaders would be elected in the future, while some new initiatives also tackled the task of mobilising popular support for the policies adopted at the party Conferences of 1979 to 1981.† It was true that most of these new policies – with the notable exception of the party's opposition to Cruise nuclear missiles – did not yet have majority support among the public. On the other hand, media preoccupation with the conflict between the right wing of the PLP and the party majority outside parliament, and with the rise of the SDP, tended to obscure the fact that these policies were decisions of the whole conference, not the work of an unrepresentative minority of constituency activists. They expressed the fact that those most responsible for both the unions and the party had come to see the 'centrist' options pursued by Wilson and Callaghan in the past as no longer viable, however much most Labour MPs (not to mention the SDP) still wished they were.

---

* The issue came sharply in focus in the controversy surrounding Peter Tatchell, adopted in 1981 by the Bermondsey Labour Party as their parliamentary candidate to succeed the retiring right-wing Labour ex-Whip, Robert Mellish. Tatchell had written an article calling for extra parliamentary action to complement parliamentary politics. At the instigation of the right wing of the parliamentary party, the NEC refused to endorse his candidature, initiating the most intense internal conflict over the definition and limits of parliamentarism since 1932–3.

† These initiatives were still modest and tended to be overshadowed by the internal struggles over reselection, the deputy leadership, etc. They included the launching of a new semi-popular journal, *The New Socialist*, in the summer of 1981; and the decision of the Labour Co-ordinating Committee, which had been responsible for the success of the campaign to change the party's constitution, in the autumn of 1981, to shift its activities towards popular education and agitation and to work with other movements and organisations in a variety of campaigns.

Circumstances had thus propelled the Labour Party in a gradually more radical direction. From 1900 to 1918 it had seen itself as a mere 'voice of labour' within a capitalist parliament; from 1918 to 1979 it aspired, with varying degrees of optimism and determination, to institute 'socialist' reforms within capitalism; after 1979 the question was posed – though no more than that – of whether it should (or must) aim to replace capitalism. But the party's progress through these stages was contradictory and erratic. Periods of radicalisation were followed by periods of deradicalisation, due to the oscillations of the economy, political victories and defeats, and the deradicalisation pressures experienced by all political movements which have to exist for a long time within the system they aim to replace.

In the period after 1906 the economic crisis gave rise to unprecedented industrial militancy, while the PLP's success in securing the passage of the Trades Disputes Act of 1906, combined with the Liberal outlook of most of the Labour MPs of that time, their inexperience and their concern for respectability, led in the opposite direction (a tendency in which they were reinforced by an influx into the new party of ex-Liberal intellectuals). The 1918 conference represented an attempt to bring these divergent tendencies together again. Conversely, the TUC's defeat in the General Strike, high unemployment and the collapse of the Labour government in 1931 led to a period of industrial quietism:* whereas these were also years in which Labour Party Conferences adopted more comprehensive and specific socialist policy pronouncements than ever before.[†] Experience of office during the war brought to bear on the Labour leadership the deradicalising influence of participation in the management of the capitalist state.[16] But the long-term effects of the slump and the war had made the labour movement and a significant part of the middle class more radical, to the point where the Labour leaders were obliged to commit themselves to the reforms of 1945–8.

In the 1950s, for the first time the influence of all three factors ran in the same direction – the direction of quietism. They economy enjoyed its brief post-war respite from the international effects of industrial decline, while full employment, the fruit of working-class strength due to war time mobilisation and resentment of the slump, meant that the workers enjoyed a significant share of the resulting economic gain.

---

* The average number of 'days lost' annually through strikes during the six years 1933 to 1938 inclusive was 1.9 million, compared with 4.7 million during the six years 1927 to 1932 inclusive.

[†] The 1934 Policy statement, *For Socialism and Peace*, called for the 'drastic reorganisation', in most cases involving nationalisation with a measure of workers' control, of banking and credit, transport, water, coal, gas, electricity, textiles, chemicals and insurance; and for the abolition of the House of Lords.

There was no compulsion on trade union leaders to preoccupy themselves with far-reaching radical political proposals. Increasingly severe electoral defeats in 1951, 1955 and 1959 also led to a deradicalisation of the parliamentary leadership, who after eleven years of office (1940–45 in the wartime coalition followed by the Labour government of 1945–51) had absorbed a 'governing party' perspective, primarily concerned with returning to power, and hardly at all with long-term social transformation, and especially the long-term task of political education which that would require.

McKenzie saw this combination of effects as the normal and proper situation of the Labour Party; left-wing party critics saw it as the culmination of the party's degeneration into a party of 'bourgeois politicians, with, at best, a certain bias towards social reform', who had 'no intention whatsoever of adopting, let alone carrying out, policies which would begin in earnest the process of socialist transformation in Britain'.[17] This was Miliband's judgement in 1960. In 1972 he reinforced his opinion and concluded that Labour could *never* turn into a socialist party.[18] The reasons he advanced were elaborated by others, notably David Coates, who in 1974 predicted quite correctly that the new Labour government would once again subordinate the party's promise of social reform to 'the more powerful imperatives of economic growth, capital accumulation and international payments'.[19] These judgements are evidently at odds with our general interpretation, according to which the Labour movement had been undergoing a long-term process of radicalisation, bringing it, by the end of the 1970s, close to a definite break with its parliamentarist and reformist history. Why should the negative verdict of these authorities not be accepted?

One reason is that in politics few verdicts are ever final or complete. Miliband's pessimism in 1972 seemed justified at the time, but in 1988, with the advantage of hindsight, his 1960 verdict seemed more accurate: *either* the Labour Party would become an effective socialist party, *or* it would decline. In the 1960s it did decline; but in response, a new movement developed to try to convert Labour into a socialist party. In reaction to this movement a segment of the party finally left to form the SDP, and in 1981 the SDP–Liberal Alliance appeared to have a good chance of capturing the political centre. But as events were to show, the Alliance lacked a cohesive and coherent strategy for reversing the country's industrial decline, and paid the price in electoral defeat and disintegration (see Chapter 12). Meantime, the Labour Party, shorn of many of its non-socialist MPs and members, might yet become a socialist party – even though not necessarily the kind of socialist party that Miliband had had in mind, and even though its prospects of subsequently achieving socialism were quite another matter

The Extra-parliamentary Left

It is often said that the Labour Party enjoys a degree of dominance over the British labour movement which is unmatched elsewhere in Europe. Considering that a third of all manual workers (and in the 1980s, a third of all trade union members) have voted Conservative, this claim must be qualified. What is true, however, is that in contrast to the situation in most other European countries, neither the Communist Party nor any other rival party of the left has ever been able to attract the support of a significant segment of the working class.* The reason is clearly that the trade unions came first and founded the Labour Party; they were not created by previously existing and competing parties of the left.

But the presence of other organisations on the left of the Labour Party has been politically significant, even though they have been electorally unimportant. The tendency of the SDF, and later the Communist Party, to absorb part of the intellectual and organisational talent of the left has already been noted. This has been particularly noticeable at times of disillusion with the pragmatic, accommodating policies of the Labour leadership, for instance in the 1920s when there was a steady trickle of ILP members (the most active socialists in the Labour Party) into the Communist Party; or again in the 1960s, when many activists, especially the young, never entered the Labour Party but instead joined one or other of the Trotskyist organisations.[20] And throughout the Cold War, the left wing inside the Labour Party could often be neutralised by generalised attacks on anyone who had advocated any policies which coincided with those of the Marxist left outside the party.

But the extra-parliamentary left became important in more positive ways as the party system began to break up under the stress of the crisis. Its greater importance was due partly to its near-monopoly of serious analysis of the crisis, the Labour Party having largely abandoned the task of strategic and critical thinking in favour of short-term, sectoral reform proposals.[21] It was also due to the agitational energy of the extra-parliamentary left, which gave them an impact which was many-sided and out of all proportion to their actual membership'.[22] In addition, one of the characteristics of any fundamental crisis is that it is difficult to know how to strike a balance between exaggerated ideas of possible change, and a foolish inability to anticipate enough. In a situation of rapid change and uncertainty the

---

* The Communist Party had two MPs in the 1945–50 parliament. No MPs to the left of the Labour Party were elected to any subsequent parliament.

influence of the extra-parliamentary left as a whole – its shared view of the necessity for fundamental change, as opposed to its many and often boring differences of opinion about means – could be greater than ever before. For these reasons the 'far left' cannot be altogether omitted from consideration, even though the multiplicity of organisations and the doctrinal differences among them cannot occupy us for long.[23]

The Communist Party of Great Britain (CPGB) declined, from a peak membership of 56,000 in 1942 to 18,500 in 1979, partly due to its support for Soviet foreign policies, partly because of its past tendency to Stalinism, and partly because, at least until the late 1970s, its programme seemed far-fetched to most people (it envisaged a Labour Party in power, accepting the CPGB as a 'partner', which would succeed in pushing Labour into carrying out a transition to socialism). The party remained significant mainly because of its strength in some trade unions. In its latter-day 'Eurocommunist' phase it had also become more flexible and politically creative, especially through the 'broad left' line followed by its theoretical journal, *Marxism Today*, from 1978 onwards. Until the 1970s it regularly contested 30–40 seats at general elections, and was a significant force in a number of important labour disputes; but in 1977 a split occurred, when some 700 Stalinists resigned over the adoption of a new (more Eurocommunist) programme, and in 1982 a second, much more serious split took place, this time between the traditional Leninist wing, committed to a strategy of labour militancy, and the 'Gramscian' tendency represented by *Marxism Today*. By 1987 membership had fallen to 11,000, and the number of candidates fielded at general elections had declined from the 30–40 of previous decades to 19 in the election of that year, who on average won 0.8 per cent of the votes cast.

The Trotskyist or neo-Trotskyist organisations, by contrast, probably accounted, altogether, for as many members as the CPGB, but they were shared by many different groups, and had an extremely high turnover rate. Starting from a tiny core of British supporters of Leon Trotsky, in his claim to uphold the true revolutionary tradition of Leninism in opposition to Stalinism, these groups, from the later 1950s, began to attract support from Communists disillusioned by Krushchev's secret speech of 1956 and the Soviet invasion of Hungary, and from radical activists in the Labour Party who were frustrated by its revisionism.

The Socialist Workers Party (originally the International Socialists) was at first distinguished by some interesting departures from orthodox Trotskyist ideas, and was particularly attractive to intellectuals in the late 1960s. In 1977, however, its leadership determined to convert it into a party of the Leninist type.[24] As Callaghan notes, the organisation actually reached its peak of membership and influence before this occurred. The membership never again reached the figure of nearly 4,000 achieved in 1974, and the print run of the party's weekly paper, *Socialist Worker*, only recovered its 1975 level of over 35,000 in 1983. By this time, however, the party was suffering from an acute lack of inner-party democracy, and – apart from its leading role in the Anti-Nazi League in 1977–8 – a very dogmatic 'workerist' line which (to oversimplify only slightly) saw sufficient industrial militancy as almost a sufficient condition for a revolution led by the SWP. The decline of industrial militancy under Thatcher signalled the bankruptcy of the SWP's strategy.

The Workers Revolutionary Party (until 1973 the Socialist Labour League) was the most orthodox and certainly the most dogmatic and fanatical of the Trotskyist sects. The WRP became generally known more for the fact that Vanessa and Corin Redgrave lent it their personal and financial support, than for its policies. Finally the WRP 'imploded' in a burst of splits, and the expulsion of its bizarre and autocratic leader, Tim Healy, in 1985.

The International Marxist Group, the British section of the Trotskyist Fourth International, had about a thousand members at its peak in the early 1980s. It was based primarily in white-collar sectors, with a strong focus on the new social movements in the West, and a belief that the initiative in the class struggle proper had passed to the workers of the Third World. It was the most intellectually creative of all the groupings and perhaps the least sectarian (a judgement which would not, no doubt, be endorsed by the others).[25] By 1980, after a largely abortive attempt to promote a Socialist Unity front for the 1979 elections, the IMG concentrated on support for the left inside the Labour Party, changing its name in 1982 to the Socialist League.

So-called 'entrism' proper (entering a social-democratic party to influence it from within) was most successfully practised by the Militant Tendency, a Trotskyist grouping founded in 1964 by the Revolutionary Socialist League and organised around a weekly newspaper, *Militant*. This group, which combined an admirable level of activism with a depressing dogmatism and a strong inclination to manipulation, achieved a dominant position in the Labour Party Young Socialists, thus gaining a seat on the Party's NEC, where the Young Socialists had a reserved place. The Militant Tendency was also influential or dominant in some constituency Labour parties by the time of the 1983 election (succeeding in getting two Militant members elected to Parliament, and another in 1987), and it controlled the Labour majority on Liverpool City Council following the local government elections of the same year.

By 1986 Militant claimed 8,000 members nationwide; by then, however, its manipulation of the internal democratic processes, combined with its relentlessly workerist line, had provoked a reaction within the Labour Party. Urged on by calls from the conservative media to rid the party of 'Marxist domination', Kinnock denounced the Liverpool Militants at the 1985 Labour Party Conference, expulsions took place in numerous constituency Labour Parties, and eventually two of the leading Militants on the Liverpool Council were expelled by the party's National Executive Committee. In Liverpool itself the expulsions probably helped Militant, whose politics of confrontation with the central government had eventually split its own followers and set in train a significant local backlash.[26] Yet thanks to the city's acute economic and social problems, support for the sort of intransigence on which Militant flourished could be expected to continue. Nationally, however, Militant had in the end mainly enabled Kinnock, in the name of restoring control to the party against these alien 'entrists', to assert greater power for the leader and the NEC; it had done nothing to make the Labour Party more revolutionary.

It is arguable that, whatever the significance of these parties and grouplets may have been, other 'left-leaning' movements and organis-ations have been more significant. For example, the Campaign for Nuclear Disarmament and the Vietnam Solidarity Committee were supported on a far larger scale and were themselves important sources of recruitment into the extra-parliamentary left groups in the late 1960s and early 1970s. More generally, new initiatives such as the women's liberation movement, claimants' unions, factory occupations, tenants' associations, and organisations to resist plans for new airports or motorways, undoubtedly contributed more to the development of a 'radical left' culture than any of the left parties or groups listed above. By the end of the 1980s, of all the far left organisations only the Communists seemed to be engaged in a serious effort to detach themselves from the barren legacy of the previous decades, so as to have something potentially significant to contribute to the reconstruction of the socialist project in the future.

The Future of the Labour Party and the Left

At the end of the 1970s and in the early 1980s, a keen debate took place between left and right strategists and intellectuals about the Labour Party's potential for becoming a radical socialist party, faced as it was with the increasingly obvious impossibility of continuing to manage capitalism on Keynesian lines in such a way as to satisfy the demands of the labour movement. The pessimists argued that the parliamentary leadership had become increasingly middle class, and hence increasingly apt to make parliamentarism an end rather than a means; that electoral considerations, which are central to parliamentarism, reinforce the tendency to accept capitalism as a given; that trade union leaders see their primary task as the defence of their members' short-term interests, and hence give priority to a short-term electoral perspective for the party; and that actually holding office in a capitalist state is invariably deradicalising as well. Against each of these arguments counter-arguments were advanced. The most radical party leaders in the past had also come from the middle class: the failure of parliamentarism had a radicalising effect on the rank and file and some MPs (notably Benn); as voting support declined, electoral considerations could force the party back into a long-run strategy of popular education and mobilisation of a kind not seen since the turn of the century; trade union leaders could become convinced that only a long-run political transformation could serve their members' immediate material interests; reflection on the experience of office could lead to a new priority for democratising the state.[27]

From the perspective of 1988, this debate seems to have rested on too many dubious assumptions about the medium run. By the end of the 1980s the question confronting the Labour Party was not whether it could be the vehicle of a socialist solution to the British economic crisis. That question had been superseded by Thatcher's success in imposing her solution. The question that the party now faced was: could it survive as an independent contender for power, or must it make peace with the remnants of the Liberals and elements of the SDP, now merged in the Social and Liberal Democrats? In either case, what were the implications of the fact that even in 1987, less than half of all trade unionists voted Labour, and 30 per cent voted Conservative, while a majority also belonged to unions which were not affiliated to the Labour Party – while still others belonged to unions which might well leave the TUC itself and form a separate coordinating 'central'?[28] Above all, what conception of the future – whether called 'socialist' or not – could the party now produce, that would appeal both to the employed, skilled section of the workforce which was prospering under Thatcherism, and yet also offer hope to the unskilled, unemployed, state-dependent minority of the 'north', who had become the party's vital electoral redoubt?

The 1987 election showed that in times of relative prosperity even an efficiently run campaign, with a strong show of party unity, could not win enough votes back from the competing centre parties. Too many of those who disliked Thatcherism remained unexcited or sceptical about what Labour had to offer. This was not particularly surprising. Labour had not developed a coherent policy for state-led industrial modernisation. It had failed to acknowledge that the British state was not organised or qualified to undertake this. It had not faced the need for an incomes policy of some kind in conditions of full employment, because of the trade unions' understandable bitterness about their experience of incomes policies in the past. Any reduction in the acute inequalities fostered by Thatcherism would also involve tax increases for skilled workers as well as the middle classes, while the quid pro quo of 'participation', 'open government' and the like had lost its appeal in the individualist atmosphere of the 1980s. People had been at least half-persuaded that the 'smack of firm government', disagreeable as it was, might perhaps be a necessary price to pay for long-term economic recovery. By the mid-1990s, too, the Conservatives would have sold most of the saleable public sector assets and enjoyed most of the benefit to be derived from north sea oil and gas. Altogether Labour confronted the daunting task of finding radically new expressions of the egalitarian, collective, cooperative themes in the national historical consciousness, adapted to the the 'post-Fordist' world of late-twentieth-century international capitalism, and of popularising them – while somehow maintaining itself electorally in the short term.

Its ability to do this would depend partly on factors beyond its control such as the level of international trade, the Conservatives' performance in office, and the capacity of the former Alliance forces to remain a serious electoral force (see Chapter 12). It would also depend on the reliability of the old 'hard core' of the party's electoral support: as Jessop and others noted, 'even the . . . bases of Labour's support in the seventies and eighties (in the inner cities, rainbow coalitions and social movements) could turn out to be unstable'.[29]

On the other hand a majority of the electorate had not yet accepted the Thatcherite creed. There was clearly room for an alternative and in spite of the difficulties just outlined, the Labour Party, so long as its social base in the cities endured, had in many ways the best chance of articulating it. What perhaps stood most in the way was what Wainwright has called 'A Tale of Two Parties':[30] the gulf between the new activists in the constituencies and the parliamentary and trade union leadership.

This gulf is not new, nor are its structural causes. As Cronin has pointed out, the Labour Party was formed as an extension of an already formed labour movement. It did not see its task as one of creating a new coalition of social forces, so much as one of detaching a pre-formed social class, with pre-given interests, from its earlier allegiance to the Liberal or Conservative parties;[31] nor have subsequent generations of Labour leaders seen their task any differently. Their commitment to parliamentarism reinforced the problem. They saw the party's radical and socialist wing as frightening middle-class voters whose votes were needed if the party was to win elections. This tendency remained as strong under Foot and Kinnock as it had been under MacDonald in the 1920s or Gaitskell in the 1950s. Their consistent and bitter opposition to the Labour left has meant accepting the Conservatives' definition of what is 'sound' or 'credible' and resisting rank and file initiative, and inner-party democracy, because it threatened centralised control. As Wainwright put it:

> The dilemma for the more aware and progressive amongst the Labour leadership who realised that they needed innovative thinking was that the majority of such ideas were generated by the radical left out of experiments [i.e. by Labour-controlled local authorities] which the leadership found an embarassment . . . As a result the main policies on which Labour fought the [1987] election were, with the exception of defence, policies which in effect simply defended the post-war settlement. This meant – given the desire of the Alliance leaders to return to the old consensus – that Thatcher's programme for promoting the private market and centralising public power was the only radical programme on offer.[32]

The dilemma is a real one. The short- or even medium-term electoral risks involved in envisaging the party as a democratic and pluralistic vehicle for the development and popularisation of a new 'common sense' are undoubtedly considerable. But the long-term risk involved in refusing to undertake this task could be fatal. Disraeli may have 'discerned' the Conservative working man as a sculptor perceives the angel prisoned in a block of marble, and Thatcher may have rediscerned him in the same way: but it is very doubtful if the socialist working person of the twenty-first century already exists, only waiting to be 'discerned' in the already-existing state of things by a leader of talent.

Notes

1 Shirley Williams's victory at Crosby in November 1981; by the end of 1982 a further by-election and two more defections brought the total of SDP MPs to 30: see Chapter 12.
2 R. Miliband, *Parliamentary Socialism*, Merlin Press, London 1973, p. 62.
3 H. Pelling, *A Short History of the Labour Party*, Macmillan, London 1965, pp. 19–20.
4 W. Kendall, *The Revolutionary Movement in Britain*, Weidenfeld and Nicolson, London 1969, p. 6.

5 This figure was well below the total number of TGWU members who actually paid the political levy, and substantially below the total membership affiliated to the TUC. Big unions often under-declared their affiliated membership to the party, partly so as to be free to use part of their political funds for other political purposes. On the history of the block vote see L. Minkin, 'Politics of the Block Vote', *New Socialist*, September–October 1981, pp. 52–6.

6 This was the minimum of delegates which any constituency could declare affiliated in 1980. Estimates for the 1970s suggest an average constituency affiliation of perhaps 500. See L. Minkin, *The Labour Party Conference*, Manchester University Press, Manchester 1980, p. 87; G. Hodgson, *Labour at the Crossroads*, Martin Robertson, Oxford 1981, p. 56.

7 P. Seyd, *The Rise and Fall of the Labour Left*, Macmillan, London 1987, p. 132.

8 About a third of all Labour MPs have been 'sponsored' by trade unions in the post-1945 period: see D. Butler and A. Sloman, *British Political Facts* (fifth edition), Macmillan, London 1980, p. 146.

9 On party funding generally see M. Pinto-Duschinsky, 'Trends in British Political Funding', *Parliamentary Affairs* 38/3, Summer 1985, pp. 328–47; and K. Ewing, *The Funding of Political Parties in Britain*, Cambridge University Press, Cambridge, 1987. Trade unions affiliation fees have generally accounted for 70–80% of the Labour Party funds.

10 H.M. Drucker, *Doctrine and Ethos in the British Labour Party*, Allen and Unwin, London 1979, Chapter 1.

11 Drucker, p. 120.

12 Ibid., pp. 106–7.

13 See Miliband, pp. 276–78, on how the party Conference had to force an unwilling parliamentary leadership to adopt the 1945 programme of nationalisation.

14 McKenzie, *British Political Parties* (second edition), Heinemann, London 1964.

15 Minkin, p. 326.

16 See e.g., Minkin, p. 21.

17 Miliband, p. 214.

18 Miliband, Postscript to the 1972 edition of *Parliamentary Socialism*. He also reaffirmed this conclusion in 'Moving On', *Socialist Register 1976*, pp. 128–40.

19 D. Coates, *The Labour Party and the Struggle for Socialism*, Cambridge University Press, Cambridge 1975, p. 214.

20 R. Dowse, *Left in the Centre*, Longman, London 1966, p. 206, and G. Thayer, *The British Political Fringe*, Blond, London 1965, p. 169.

21 The most notable exception to this, prior to the new infusion of left intellectuals in the 1970s, was Anthony Crosland's *The Future of Socialism*, Cape, London 1956, which set out the philosophy of 'revisionism'.

22 R. Miliband, 'Moving On', *Socialist Register 1976*, p. 137.

23 The first systematic and relatively objective study of the far left to appear is J. Callaghan, *The Far Left in British Politics*, Blackwell, Oxford 1987.

24 The name was changed from the International Socialists to Socialist Workers Party at this time. See M. Shaw, 'The Making of a Party', *Socialist Register 1978*, pp. 100–45; also I.H. Birchall, 'The Premature Burial: A Reply to Martin Shaw', *Socialist Register 1979*, pp. 26–50.

25 *New Left Review*, the most widely read and accomplished left-wing theoretical journal in English, was the work of intellectuals more or less close to the IMG.

26 See M. Crick, *The March of Militant*, Faber, London 1986, Chapters 3, 12 and 13.

27 This debate is too extensive to be referenced in a brief note; for an introduction to the arguments for a socialist Labour Party see K. Coates, 'Socialists and the Labour Party', *Socialist Register* 1973, pp. 155–78, and M. Rustin, *For a Pluralist Socialism*, Verso, London 1985; for the other side see, in addition to Miliband and Coates (notes 2 and 19 above), L.V. Panitch, *Working-Class Politics in Crisis*, Verso, London 1986, especially Chapters 1 and 4.

28 D.E. Butler and D. Kavanagh, *The British General Election of 1987*, Macmillan, London 1988, pp. 275–76.

29 B. Jessop et al., 'Popular Capitalism, Flexible Accumulation and Left Strategy', *New Left Review* 165, 1987, p. 110.
30 H. Wainwright, *A Tale of Two Parties*, Chatto and Windus, London 1987.
31 J. E. Cronin, 'Class and the Labour Party', *Studies in Political Economy* 21, Autumn 1986, pp. 107–35.
32 Wainwright, pp. 292–3.

Beyond the Two-Party System?

By 1974 popular support for the two major parties had been declining for over twenty years (see Table 5.1). Fewer people were engaged in any form of party politics: fewer voted (turnout at general elections declined from 83.9 per cent in 1950 to 72.8 per cent in October 1974); and fewer were members of any political party. Political energies flowed out of electoral party politics into various forms of extra-parliamentary politics such as claimants' unions, campaigns against new motorways or airports, or the Campaign for Nuclear Disarmament. Rank and file trade union activism also rose, drawing in new segments of the labour force, and assuming many new forms. The 1972 'work-in' at Upper Clyde Shipbuilders (a complex of four shipyards employing over 8,000 workers), for example, could not have been organised without a high order of political consciousness and local initiative.

But these were not the only alternatives to supporting Labour or the Conservatives. Voters were also drawn towards other parliamentary parties, which tried to exploit the opportunity created by the weakening of the social-democratic hegemony. These were the Liberals and the Social Democrats, the Scottish National Party in Scotland and Plaid Cymru in Wales. There was also the Irish factor. Northern Ireland returned 12 MPs to Westminster before 1979, and 17 from 1983 onwards. Since the 1880s, all but one or two of the Northern Irish seats had been safe for Unionists who for all practical purposes were members of the Conservative Party. By 1974, however, Unionist opposition to policies designed to conciliate the Catholics in Northern Ireland had forced the Heath government to suspend the Northern Irish Parliament. The Unionists dissolved into three separate organisations, the most radical of which now contemplated independence for a 'six-county' Ulster (i.e., the existing territory of Northern Ireland). In the February 1974 election the main Unionist factions formed an alliance, the United Ulster Unionists, which won eleven seats, but they no longer accepted the Conservative Whip in the House of Commons. This remained the case after the October 1974 election, when the alliance again broke up.[1] By this time, no less than 25 per cent of the votes cast throughout the United Kingdom were for parties other than Labour or the Conservatives. Together these parties accounted for 39 seats in the House of Commons, and after March 1977 (when by-election losses had destroyed Labour's slender majority) they held the balance of power (see Table 12.1).

In the 1979 election, the combined Conservative and Labour share of the vote recovered to 80.8 per cent and the number of seats won by other parties fell back to 27. But in March 1981 the formation of the Social Democratic Party (SDP) and its immediate formation of an Alliance with the Liberals again altered the situation. And while the Scottish Nationalist vote in Scotland had fallen sharply in the 1979 election its 1974 successes had taken observers by surprise after a worse electoral performance in 1970. The possibility existed of a radical change in the party system – and one which the Liberal–SDP Alliance would seek to make permanent by introducing proportional representation if it could gain sufficient parliamentary leverage to do so. In 1983, in a House of Commons enlarged by 15 seats to 650, 44 seats were won by parties other than Conservative or Labour, and in 1987, 45. The large Conservative majorities in both elections, however, and the failure of the Alliance to expand its share of the vote, meant that the threat to the two-party system was averted, at least for the time being: it was the Alliance, not Labour, which broke up. Yet the result did not indicate that the threat would never recur. The Scottish Nationalists, in particular, recovered some of the ground lost after 1979, and the potential of the merged Social and Liberal Democrats (SLD) to recover from the debacle of the Alliance remained to be seen. A short account of the strengths and weaknesses of the parties that formed the SLD, as well as of the Scottish and Welsh Nationalists, is therefore still necessary to an understanding of the future prospects of the party system.

The Liberal Party

Formed (according to convention) in 1859, the Liberal Party, after presiding over the greatest era of Victorian reform and having enlisted the support of the bulk of the newly enfranchised working class, was

Table 12.1 The smaller parties 1964–1987

	1964	1966	1970	1974 (Feb)	1974 (Oct)	1979	1983	1987
				Votes at General Elections				
Liberals/Alliance	3,092,878	2,327,533	2,117,035	6,063,470	5,346,754	4,313,811	7,780,949	7,341,290
Scottish Nationalists	64,044	128,474	306,802	632,032	839,617	504,259	331,975	416,873
Plaid Cymru	69,507	61,071	175,016	171,364	166,321	132,544	125,309	123,589
Others	214,354	232,681	421,481	881,786	800,747	848,876	951,656	857,516
			Average Percentage of votes cast per opposed candidate					
Liberals/Alliance	18.5	16.1	13.5	23.6	18.9	14.9	26.0	23.7
Scottish Nationalists	10.7	14.1	12.2	21.9	30.4	17.3	11.8	14.1
Plaid Cymru	8.4	8.7	11.5	10.7	10.8	8.1	7.8	7.3
				Seats Won				
Liberals/Alliance	9	12	6	14	13	11	23	22
Scottish Nationalists	—	—	1	7	11	2	2	3
Plaid Cymru	—	—	—	2	3	2	2	3
Northern Irish Parties*	—	—	—	12	12	12	17	17
Others*	—	2	6	2	—	—	—	—
Total	9	14	13	37	39	27	44	45

* Most of these votes were for Northern Ireland candidates (in 1987 only 124,550 were cast for 'other' candidates in Great Britain): but before 1974 Ulster Unionist voters are included with the Conservative vote, and only anti-unionist candidates with 'Others'.

Source: D. Butler and A. Sloman, *British Political Facts 1900–1979*, Macmillan, London 1980: D. Butler and D. Kavanagh, *The British General Election of 1987*, Macmillan, London 1988.

destroyed by the contradiction between the interests of labour and those of the middle classes which it represented. After 1918, its collapse was painfully complete. By 1950 it was said that the whole parliamentary Liberal Party could go to work in a taxi. Yet even at the nadir of their fortunes in 1951, when they contested only 109 seats, the Liberals won nearly three-quarters of a million votes; at the peak of the subsequent revival, in February 1974, they won six million votes (19.3 per cent of the total). In 1979 the Liberals still won 4.3 million votes (14.1 per cent). And throughout the post-war period about a third of the electorate regularly told pollsters that they would be likely to vote Liberal 'if [they] thought they would obtain a majority'.[2] Just what this means is doubtful; but there can be little doubt that the Liberals would have polled more votes at general elections had it not been for the electoral system, which reinforced the dominance of the two leading parties, and made voters feel that a vote cast for a party that could not form a government (or part of one) was wasted. Hence the Liberal Party's devotion to proportional representation.*

Up to 1956 the Liberals' survival as a parliamentary party had largely depended on an understanding with the Conservative Party. This dated from the period of 'National Liberal' participation in the Conservative-dominated national governments of the 1930s, and during the 1950s the Liberals were indeed not easy to distinguish from the progressive wing of the Conservative Party. From 1956, however, a new leader, Jo Grimond, responding to the decline of Labour in the elections of 1950, 1951 and 1955, set the Liberal Party on a new course designed to make it once more the new 'radical' party of the day, capable of displacing the Labour Party as the major party of opposition. He sought to appeal to voters who seemed increasingly to reject nationalisation, collectivism and bureaucracy, but who remained interested – as the Conservatives under Macmillan clearly were not – in further domestic reform. To implement this project the Liberal Party itself had to be radically transformed.

> Grimond encouraged the 'radicals' in the party and gave them their head, without worrying too much whether the party or he himself would agree with all they said and did. After all, there was no immediate prospect that he would have to put policies into practice; the main thing was to generate some excitement, give the impression that a new movement was growing and attract people with ideas and enthusiasm.[3]

---

* In 1929 the Liberals made the introduction of PR a condition of their support for the minority Labour government, but it was soon clear that resistance within the Labour Party, as well as on the part of the Conservatives, would have blocked the change even if the Labour Government had not collapsed in 1931.

The results were encouraging. In the 1964 election, with 361 candidates (compared with 216 in 1959) the party won 11.4 per cent of the vote and nine seats. But Labour's second election victory in 1966 made the project of displacing the Labour Party seem unrealistic (even though the Liberals won 12 seats in that year). In 1967 Grimond retired and was succeeded by Jeremy Thorpe, who saw that the Liberals' next step must be to become 'credible' as a political force capable of influencing policy. This meant the pursuit of virtually any strategy that seemed capable of broadening the party's electoral base; this included a policy of wooing 'moderate' trade unionists and – especially for younger and more radical Liberals in some of the larger conurbations in the north – the pursuit of so-called 'community politics', that is, a tireless devotion to local issues. Thorpe personally (like most of the Liberal MPs, in fact) was not radical in either outlook or style, but he accepted the radicals as necessary – even when the Young Liberals went so far as to adopt positions on race, the Vietnam War, withdrawal from NATO and worker control of nationalised industries, which had more in common with the left wing of the Labour Party than with orthodox Liberalism.

In February 1974 (after a setback in 1970) the Liberals polled their highest post-war vote and, in the south of England outside London, won more votes than Labour; but the electoral system yielded them only 14 seats. Thorpe, although invited by Heath to form a coalition against Labour, declined – Heath would not agree unequivocally to introduce proportional representation, and without this the more radical Liberals would not support Heath – and called instead for an all-party government of national unity which, however, was spurned by Labour. But in 1977, when the chance occurred to make terms over the Liberals' continued support for the Callaghan government, David Steel (who had succeeded Thorpe as leader when Thorpe was forced to resign after a scandal) exploited the opportunity by making a 'pact': Callaghan undertook to consult with him in advance on all parliamentary proposals, in return for Liberal support in the House of Commons. This policy was unpopular with many Liberals, both those who considered that the Callaghan government was in thrall to the trade unions, and the 'community politics' and Young Liberal radicals who considered the Callaghan government too conservative. The pact became unsustainable when the Labour Party refused to support the introduction of proportional representation for the election of the British members of the new European Parliament. Rank and file hostility forced Steel to give notice that the pact would lapse in the summer of 1978. But by now a clear strategy had emerged and Steel was gradually able to win a majority of the party over to it: 'to aim explicitly for the *balance* of power, to be prepared to work with either major party, and to make proportional representation the key to any such arrangement'.[4]

This strategy, with whatever 'credibility' the Liberal–Labour pact of 1976–8 may have given it, maintained the Liberal vote at 14.1 per cent of the total in 1979, with the loss of only three seats (down from 14 to 11). And with the formation of the SDP in 1981 the strategy came into its own. The SDP quickly agreed to an alliance in which the two parties would share out all the parliamentary constituencies between them, and by December 1981 polling data suggested that as much as 50 per cent of the electorate supported the Alliance.

At this point the fate of the Liberals became bound up with that of the SDP. Initially, however, both parties thought they had a strong vested interest in remaining separate. Each believed the other capable of drawing votes not necessarily available to itself. In competition, they would tend to cancel each other out; in alliance, they might, the opinion polls suggested, be able to establish a parliamentary bridgehead that could then be permanently widened by proportional representation.

What was the Liberals' chief contribution to the Alliance? Above all, it was the fact that the party had a still potent tradition, a proven core of electoral support, an organisation with some 150,000–200,000 members and exceptionally active local parties in some 20–30 constituencies.[5]

The Liberals' problem was how to expand beyond this base, which had some contradictory elements in it. Thanks to the religious basis of much of the Liberals' nineteenth-century programme, the party's support remained strongest in the non-conformist 'celtic fringe' of Wales and the highlands and islands of Scotland. At its lowest post-war ebb, the party retained three seats in Wales and one in Scotland, besides two in the northern English towns of Bolton and Huddersfield (which were only retained because of electoral understandings with the Conservatives). As the party revived it gained additional seats in the 'fringe', in 'peripheral' rural districts such as south-west England, East Anglia, and the rural areas of Scotland. In its best years, the party also advanced in some suburban constituencies, especially at by-elections. What it failed to do was to make a significant impact in urban, and especially industrial constituencies, when these were contested by both the major parties.

Where no local tradition of Liberal voting survived from the nineteenth century, support tended to be drawn rather evenly from all occupational strata – for instance in 1977–8 about 8 to 9 per cent of each socio-economic stratum declared themselves Liberal supporters. With this even spread, the Liberals had an acute problem of translating

BRISTOL POLYTECHNIC
ST. MATTHIAS LIBRARY
FISHPONDS

votes into seats. Even with nearly a fifth of the votes in February 1974, they won only 14 seats; in sharp contrast with the Labour Party, with its massive concentration of working-class votes in industrial constituencies, and the Conservatives, with their almost equally massive support in most rural and suburban seats.

Even if the Liberal vote had been better rewarded in terms of seats, the party would still have faced difficulties in maintaining its vote because it was composed of three distinct and rather contradictory elements: a more or less constant 'core' (perhaps 10 per cent of the electorate) of committed Liberals, and a 'floating' or 'protest' vote, intermittently detached from the Conservative and Labour parties, which was itself divided into two rather incompatible components.

The Liberal 'core' vote was 'radical, humanitarian, libertarian, internationalist, environmentalist and particularly interested in constitutional questions . . . the other side of the coin was its relative indifference to the major economic questions of the day',[6] This core of voters was heavily concentrated in the middle classes, who also provided almost all the Liberals' activists, as well as almost all Liberal candidates (in 1970 there was only one working-class Liberal candidate out of 332; in October 1974, there were 25 out of 619).

The rest of the Liberal vote – its 'floating' component – tended to be much more varied in character. Steed identifies two distinct elements – 'centre' voters and 'anti-system' voters – who were apt to shift their votes towards the Liberals out of frustration with one or the other of the two major parties, and especially, at least before 1974, when the Conservatives were in power. 'Centre' voters tended to be refugees from the too-explicit class character of the policies adopted by their 'normal' party – Conservatives upset by the 'unacceptable face of capitalism' (as Heath once called it) and Labour supporters upset by trade union power or state bureaucratism. 'Anti-system' voters voted Liberal 'as a generalised protest against the operation of the political system', seeing the Liberal candidate as an apparently radical alternative. Some voters of this type would even vote for the National Front (far right) or the Workers Revolutionary Party (far left) if no Liberal candidate was standing.[7]

The problem was how to retain the 'core' Liberal vote while also developing a more durable appeal to these additional elements whose outlooks appeared to be so different – both from the 'core' and from each other. The most distinctive Liberal policies reflected the traditions and interests of the party's activists, who were distinguished less by being almost exclusively 'middle class' – though that is what they were, in the sociological sense of the term – than by their dislike of being categorised as belonging to any class, and their hostility to class politics. When asked about their own social class, they tended to assign themselves to the most 'neutral-seeming' category (e.g., 'lower middle class') or said that they did not know what class they belonged to. Typical comments were: 'I do not believe in class'; 'classes are something I have never understood'; 'I don't think there is any class structure in this country except in the minds of certain politicians who use it for their own aims'.[8] This was the basis of the party's general bias, shared by its 'core' voters, in favour of non-economic policy issues. Yet it was largely economic issues, and the Conservative and Labour failures in economic policy, which were propelling the floating voters towards the Liberals.

Appealing more effectively to the 'floaters' was therefore a problem. They seemed relatively uninterested in traditional Liberal policies, remaining more favourable to either Conservative or Labour policies. And, at the same time, the reasons why they turned towards the Liberals were contradictory. The 'centre' voters turned to the Liberals because one or both of the major parties seemed to be abandoning consensus politics, while 'anti-system' voters were looking for a party which would make a still more radical break with the consensus. The most distinctive Liberal policies on economic issues – support for the EEC, an incomes policy and 'industrial partnership' between capital and labour – expressed the middle-class desire for a more harmonious society in a form which might appeal to 'centre' voters but hardly to 'anti-system' voters; while neither the 'centre' voters nor the 'core' Liberal voters could be expected to warm to anti-system policies.

The radicalism of the Young Liberals and the 'left wing' of the community action activists, though endorsed by the party's annual conferences, was largely ignored or diluted in policy statements by the leadership – a situation with obvious similarities to that of the Labour Party, and involving similar costs. In the short run, therefore, the alliance with the SDP, with its origins in the Labour Party's acute conflicts over economic issues, permitted the Liberals to continue their preferred policy of downplaying economic questions. It offered the possibility of increasing the strength of the political centre, without adding still further to the already considerable difficulty of finding common ground on which the very different elements of Liberal support could come together.

The Social Democratic Party

The SDP was officially launched at an elaborately mounted press conference on 26 March 1981, the culmination of a split within the

Parliamentary Labour Party which mirrored the division developing inside many constituency Labour parties since the early 1970s.

Two episodes in particular had been formative. One was the issue of Britain's membership in the European Economic Community. Of the four former Labour ministers who founded the SDP, Roy Jenkins had left British politics to become the first British President of the European Commission, from 1977 to 1980, and David Owen, Shirley Williams and Bill Rodgers were all also leading advocates of British membership. They had led the 89 Labour MPs who defied the party whip in order to vote for entry in 1971, and in the 1975 referendum campaign on whether Britain should remain a member they found themselves increasingly a minority in the Labour Party outside parliament, confronting an opposition led by the then Secretary of State for Industry, Tony Benn. Their differences from the anti-marketeers proved to be linked to more fundamental differences as well. Jenkins explicitly renounced 'socialism'; the others considered themselves socialists but explicitly favoured the retention of private enterprise and increasingly attacked trade-union powers.

The other primary determinant of the split was the growth of support for the Labour left in the constituencies and among trade union activists, resulting in the changes in the party constitution described in Chapter 11. These changes implied a long-term decline in the influence of centrist politicians of the type represented by the 'gang of four' (as the press dubbed the four ex-ministers) and a long-term strengthening of the party's commitment to extend public ownership, take Britain out of the EEC and give up nuclear weapons. According to Ian Bradley, active dicussion of the prospects for a new 'social democratic' party began immediately after the 1979 election among three key groups: Jenkins and his personal friends in England; the Social Democratic Association of Labour local councillors which opposed the advance of the Labour left in the constituency parties; and the 'gang of three' ex-Ministers – Owen and Rodgers in parliament, and Williams who had just lost her seat at Hertford and Stevenage. These discussions developed throughout the next 18 months as the Labour left's advance continued, culminating in the decisions of the special party conference at Wembley in January 1981 which gave the trade unions and the local Labour party membership the dominant role in the election of future party leaders. The day after the conference (25 January 1981) the 'gang' issued a statement (the so-called Limehouse Declaration) announcing the formation of a 'Council for Social Democracy'. A further 11 Labour MPs now declared their support, and two months later the Council became a party.

The new party immediately drew into it various right-wing groups

inside the Labour Party – the 'Manifesto' group of MPs, the Social
Democratic Association and the leading members of the Campaign for
a Labour Victory, all of which had been established since 1974 to
oppose the advance of the left wing led by Benn. By the end of 1981
the SDP had 27 MPs including Shirley Williams, who had re-entered
Parliament in November after a dramatic by-election victory in the
formerly safe Conservative seat of Crosby (a suburb of Liverpool).
Jenkins had also contested the safe Labour industrial constituency of
Warrington, only narrowly losing with 42.4 per cent of the vote (he
was later to re-enter Parliament after a by-election victory in Glasgow
in March 1982). In the London borough of Islington a group of 26
Labour councillors switched to the SDP and took control of the
council. A long list of prominent figures in show business and the
media, academics, lawyers, businessmen and even some trade
unionists declared their support for the new party, which by December
1981 claimed over 70,000 paid-up members.

   Thus, from its earliest days, the SDP had proved a formidable
electoral contender on the evidence of both opinion polls and by-
elections. However, the nature of the new party posed some problems.
As Bradley has pointed out, there were two very different elements in
the SDP. One was the ineffably middle-class element epitomised by
Jenkins, Owen and Williams, and by the great bulk of the enthusiastic
new recruits in the SDP membership, known in SDP parlance as the
'naives'.[9] Socially speaking, these people strongly resembled the
Liberals' core supporters (though they may well have been less
concerned to deny their own class membership), and some of them
(notably Jenkins himself) felt warmly disposed towards the Liberal
Party.* The other element was less middle class and more closely
linked to the labour movement. Prominent in this group were MPs and
councillors from safe Labour seats where the local party organisations
had previously become, to a greater or less extent, the fiefs of small
and often ageing coteries of Labour councillors plus the sitting MPs.
These were the constituencies prone to be 'taken over' by an influx of
young activists whose views were far to the left of the old guard and
the incumbent MP. As the SDP established itself, more MPs and

---

   * Among SDP members polled in November 1981, 57% were in professional and
managerial positions, while 7% were in working-class jobs and 10% in 'lower-middle-
class clerical and sales occupations. As yet it looks a distinctly middle-class club' (*The
Times*, 30 November 1981). Among SDP supporters in the electorate the middle-class
preponderance was less marked but they were older than the members; whereas most
SDP members were aged 25–34, most SDP voters were aged 35–44 – the age group 'too
young to have experienced the depression and too old to have been radicalised in the
late 1960s and early 1970s', as one activist shrewdly suggested (Ian Bradley, *Breaking the
Mould?* Martin Robertson, Oxford 1981, p. 112).

councillors of this type – the 'refugees' – joined the new party. The refugees' conception of the party was much more labourist (a 'Mark II Labour Party') than that of the 'naives', both because they had usually been in the Labour Party for a long time and because they mostly came from Labour electoral strongholds. Some of the MPs who joined the SDP did so in anticipation of not being reselected by their local parties, with whom they were in conflict. There was a wide gulf between this group and the 'naives', who seemed to constitute the majority of the SDP's activists, and had not belonged to any other party before. It was always unlikely that the euphoria of the early months, when the party was the darling of the media, would survive when these contradictory components became better acquainted.

The special role of the media in promoting the SDP also made it difficult to assess the party's longer-run significance. Its popularity was partly a result of the enthusiasm felt by so many journalists for a group of politicians who were so much like themselves – well-educated, reasonable, and equally hostile to both Thatcher and Benn.[10] The effects on the SDP of its prompt alliance with the Liberals were also hard to determine. It undoubtedly helped Shirley Williams to win a by-election at Crosby in November 1981, just as it had helped the Liberal candidate, William Pitt, to win Croydon North-West as an Alliance candidate in October. But it was not certain whether Liberal voters would all vote SDP in constituencies where a Liberal had been asked to stand down in favour of an SDP candidate; or, when the reverse was the case, that ex-Labour voters would be prepared to vote Liberal at a general election, and for mostly unknown candidates. Moreover, tensions within the Alliance over the allocation of constituencies came into the open towards the end of 1981.

The SDP's instant initial appeal was due overwhelmingly to dislike of Thatcherism in practice, and of the Labour Party's internal divisions, and to wishful thinking that the career politicians at the head of the SDP, whom the media now represented as born-again radicals, offered a new alternative. In April 1981, between 34 per cent and 68 per cent of SDP supporters polled did not know what the party stood for on any given issue. As Bradley remarked at the time, the SDP was

> in many ways a wish-fulfilment party; many of its supporters see it not as what it is but as what they think it ought to be . . . Amid the platitudes, and given the lack of hard, specific policy statements, it was easy for many voters to regard the Social Democrats as their sort of people.

But, in spite of (or because of) its vagueness on the crucial economic issues, a large part of the SDP's appeal consisted in seeming to hold out a hope of returning to a more harmonious past, free from class struggle. The key elements in SDP economic thinking were the maintenance of a 'mixed economy' combined with industrial democracy, an incomes policy coupled with curbs on union powers, and a policy of gradual but steady reflation with, perhaps, a special fund to channel North Sea oil revenues into new (private) industrial investment. There was, besides, a commitment to decentralisation; this would be difficult to reconcile with an effective national incomes policy, or with equality – for instance, in the provision of local services – which the SDP also stressed. The economic policy to which the SDP was most committed, continued membership of the EEC, was one which a majority of voters then seemed to oppose.

As David Currie pointed out, the key elements in the SDP's economic thinking were likely to be those intended to bring about a 'fundamental reform' in wage bargaining. Whichever of the schemes proposed by SDP economists was finally adopted, the SDP was clearly going to be committed to imposing on the labour movement some system of controls aimed at preventing wage demands from fuelling inflation, whereas the Labour Party's Alternative Economic Strategy seemed to reject controls without putting forward any concrete alternative for preventing inflationary wage settlements. Faced with a choice between Thatcherite deflation and Labourist inflation, voters could well feel that the SDP's approach was a new initiative which deserved a chance.[11]

None the less, gauging the electoral prospects for the SDP–Liberal Alliance was difficult. Bradley's judgement that 'it [seemed] safe to assume that the SDP/Liberal Alliance [would] do at least as well as the Liberals did in February 1974' seemed reasonable, but as he also pointed out, given the handicap of evenly distributed support (which the SDP shared with the Liberals) the Alliance would need over 30 per cent of the vote to gain a substantial number of seats.[12]

The Rise and Fall of the Alliance

In December 1981, the Gallup Poll reported, 50 per cent of the electorate declared its support for the Alliance. Twelve months later, the figure was 22 per cent. However, in the 1983 election the Alliance's actual share of the vote was 25.4 per cent; although this yielded only 23 seats, it gave hope that, especially given Labour's abysmal performance, the subsequent election might see the strategy finally pay off. But in 1987 the Alliance vote fell to 22.6 per cent, for 22 seats. It was as if the limits of what could be taken from Labour's support had been reached, while in the meantime the Alliance itself was showing every sign of stagnation and fragmentation. David Steel, the Liberal leader, had said before the election that anything less than 35 seats would count as a failure, and within a week of the result called for a merger of the two parties. It was apparent that the costs of remaining separate had become greater than any advantage it might offer, and this was the view of most Liberal and SDP activists, as well as the verdict of most political commentators.

Steel's call for a merger was supported by two of the original 'gang of four', Jenkins and Williams: David Owen, however, the SDP leader since 1983 (when he was the only prominent SDP MP to be re-elected), adamantly opposed a merger, and when a majority of SDP members voted for it nonetheless, resigned as leader, announcing that he would seek to maintain the SDP with the support of the minority of the membership who were loyal to him. Merger negotiations then ensued which eventually produced a new Social and Liberal Democratic Party. Meanwhile David Steel, injured both by his handling of some of the issues between himself and David Owen prior to the election, and by the concessions he was willing to make to the SDP during the negotiations, had used up his credit and was obliged to retire, leaving the new SLD to elect a new leader. By the beginning of May 1988 the SLD had the support of only six per cent of electors polled, while Owen's SDP had five per cent. In the local government elections that immediately followed, however, the SLD won on average 18–19 per cent of the votes, suggesting that it might re-establish itself in due course as the party of the centre if this level of support were to be replicated in general elections. David Owen's SDP candidates, however, were badly defeated.[13]

The causes of the debacle seem to lie, ultimately, in the Alliance parties' failure to offer a persuasive alternative to Thatcherism as a strategy of economic recovery. The Alliance's 1987 election manifesto was widely seen as incoherent, but the problem really lay deeper: the Alliance's appeal lay largely in the 'vague, nice' image of the Liberals, combined with the seemingly realistic, centrist economic approach of the SDP. But like the Labour Party, the Alliance did not put forward a general project for social transformation that could rival Thatcher's, and unlike the Labour Party, it did not have a solid electoral base to sustain it in spite of this deficiency. Even more than Labour, or at least more urgently, it needed to project a convincing vision of the future. But the disparate elements from which the Liberal and SDP activists were drawn did not already share such a vision (the gibe that the Alliance promised 'a better yesterday' had some force) while the party leaders – the 'two Davids' – were publicly at odds over some quite fundamental policy issues.

The one which received most publicity concerned defence. Owen was militantly pro-NATO and pro-nuclear, whereas Steel, and even more a majority of Liberal activists, were neither. Before the 1987 election Owen publicly disparaged the Liberals for, in effect, failing to meet his demands on defence policy, and by implication disparaged Steel for not being able to impose an agreed formula on his rank and file: Owen had no time for the Liberals' highly informal methods of conference policy-making. It was also apparent that Owen sympathised with Thatcher's economic strategy and felt some personal warmth for her, whereas Steel disliked Thatcher and Thatcherism and had some sympathy for the Labour leadership from whom the SDP had split. Given that the Alliance's aim was to capture enough seats to hold the balance of power, this difference was crucial – which of the two major parties would it consent to keep in power? Underlying these differences there were also, of course, personal factors. Owen's opposition to a merger could be explained partly by the fact that the Liberals, with a much larger membership, were most unlikely ever to elect him as leader of a merged party. Peter Jenkins, a political journalist very sympathetic to the SDP at its inception, summed up the truth of its leaders' situation as it was in 1987 with brutal candour:

> The Alliance's election campaign had exposed not only a lack of strategy but something much more basic. It had exposed to the protagonists their lack of real purpose and conviction. What were they offering? What exactly was their alternative? What was the nature of their project? Why were they there? It had been a noble enterprise at the beginning. . . . Yet in some way the enterprise had brought out the worst in them all. . . . Here was the stuff of tragedy. Faced with the horror of where they were, of the hollowness of their cause, most could not wait to retreat into the familiar past. Owen set off alone into the unknown future.[14]

Scottish and Welsh Nationalism

Nationalism in both Scotland and Wales corresponds to the perception by some of both countries' elites that development within the British state no longer holds out hope of progress for these 'peripheries'.[15] Instead, they propose a course of autonomous development, seeking to mobilise the Scottish and Welsh nations under their leadership.

Wales and Scotland were culturally and politically autonomous prior to their incorporation into Great Britain under English hegemony in

1536 and 1707 respectively. In both cases the landed classes moved to London and progressively lost their place in Welsh and Scottish national life. This break was especially complete in Wales, where Welsh was universally spoken (as late as 1850, 90 per cent of the population was still Welsh-speaking).[16] In Wales especially, but also to some extent in Scotland, a more democratic, more widely educated and more egalitarian society emerged than in England. Increasingly, the landowners were English, from outside local society, as were a growing proportion of industrialists, especially in the twentieth century.

Scotland, united with England later and on more equal terms than Wales, retained a substantial measure of legal, educational and religious autonomy, reinforced by a largely separate media system, football league, and other spheres of cultural independence. This was cemented by the creation in 1885 of a Scottish Office, under a government Minister (the Scottish Secretary) at Westminster; the office was elevated to the status of Secretary of State, with cabinet rank, in 1926. By 1981 the Scottish Office was located in Edinburgh and was responsible for the administration in Scotland of health, agriculture, prisons, education, trade, industry and economic planning. In addition, a Scottish Grand Committee of all Scottish MPs had been established in 1895, to which all proposed laws exclusively affecting Scotland were referred. Later, two Scottish Standing Committees were set up to consider the implications for Scotland of all other legislation, and later still a Select Committee on Scottish Affairs was created to monitor administrative policy and performance in relation to Scotland. This complex of structures catered to, and helped preserve, the distinctiveness of Scottish culture, and partly explains the relative ease with which the SNP was able to mobilise nationalist support from 1960 onwards, as the British crisis took its toll on Scotland's obsolescent textile, engineering and coal industries. A distinctive Scottish identity, once associated with Scotland's successful participation in the industrial revolution, remained intact and could be appealed to again for an independent initiative when the rewards of the industrial revolution appeared to have been exhausted.

Wales, by contrast, had been united with England earlier, a century after the defeat of the Welsh national leader Owen Glendower. What maintained a distinctive Welsh identity was not separate institutions but only the Welsh language, reinforced by the mass conversion of the Welsh people to Methodism under the impact of the industrial revolution. Between 1850 and 1901, however, compulsory primary education in English (and no compulsory education in Welsh) had reduced the proportion of Welsh-speakers from 90 per cent to 50 per cent; by 1971 the proportion had fallen still further, to 21 per cent (and only 13 per cent of Welsh people under 30). Welsh nationalism, therefore, developed as a movement to try to arrest the decline of Welsh as a spoken language, and of Welsh culture, such as choirs, the literary culture of Eisteddfodau, Welsh libraries, and so on. The movement was not originally concerned with self-government, let alone Welsh independence, but with preventing the disappearance of the basis of a national identity. Thus it was unlike Scottish nationalism, which took the continued existence of a Scottish national identity as its starting-point and sought to harness it to a new national political project. In electoral terms Welsh nationalism started out with the radical disadvantage that, by the 1920s, only a minority of Welshmen still spoke Welsh, let alone were interested in Welsh poetry. The other side of the coin of the decline of the Welsh language was the rise of the Welsh industrial working class. The dominant English-speaking majority were also overwhelmingly part of the labour movement; they belonged first and foremost to the *British* working class, and less and less to the Welsh nation.

By the late 1960s, however, the economic decline of the industrial valleys and towns of South Wales, coinciding with the nationwide reaction against bureaucracy in all spheres, stimulated a new interest in economic and administrative decentralisation. The growth of tourism was another factor; the rapid increase in the purchase, by prosperous English people, of 'second homes' in impoverished Welsh villages symbolised Welsh economic and cultural deprivation. At the same time, the Labour Party's traditional strength in South Wales had been weakened, not only by the record of policy failure on the part of successive Labour governments, but also by the existence of too many conservative, and corrupt, party oligarchies in safe industrial seats (a factor also present in south-west Scotland). These trends converged with the nationalists' growing awareness that a large measure of political autonomy was essential if Welsh culture was to be protected.

An additional factor was also at work: the 'dissolution' of the traditional working class took a particularly acute form in Scotland and Wales. Heavy dependence on the old staple industries of coalmining, steelmaking, shipbuilding, engineering and (in Scotland) textiles, meant that Scotland and Wales suffered more than England from the crisis of the economy. Unemployment rates there were 30–50 per cent higher than the British average.

In Scotland the sixties saw the start of dramatic changes in employment: ten thousand jobs disappeared every year. Out of a population of 5.1 million, nearly 300,000 emigrated during the sixties, most of them overseas; by 1981 421,000 had left within two decades, a massive share of the younger generation. For those who stayed, there was a major shift of employment into services or into new, largely foreign-owned and very large-scale consumer goods industries (some of which would also later collapse).[17]

Wales, which had enjoyed some industrial diversification during the 1940s after the catastrophe of the slump, had persistently lower living standards than England but did not experience the same degree of industrial upheaval as Scotland until the new catastrophe of the late seventies and early eighties. But for both countries the contemporary crisis was a period of accelerating disruption. Old ties of culture and place were progressively weakened.

In these conditions Scottish and Welsh voters' allegiances to the two major parties were strained too, and the appeal of an alternative *national* solution, combining economic and cultural aspirations, grew stronger. Disaffected Labour and Conservative voters, who in England gravitated towards the Liberals, tended instead to move towards the nationalists, especially in Scotland. The SNP pre-empted Liberal gains in Scotland almost completely. In Wales, the nationalist electoral achievement was much more modest, but the political potential of Welsh nationalism had probably not yet reached its full potential.[18]

The Scottish National Party

The origins of the SNP go back to the 1880s, when the Scottish economy was showing early signs of weakness. The example of the Irish nationalists led to the formation of a Scottish Home Rule association, to which both Keir Hardie and Ramsay MacDonald belonged; MacDonald was actually its secretary and London-based lobbyist. The central role later played by these two men in the Labour Party explains why Scottish nationalism did not then become a serious force: the Scottish working class, like the Welsh, played a leading, not a supporting role in the development and eventual triumph of the Labour Party. The SNP itself was formed in 1934, in the middle of the slump and after the Labour Party's crushing defeat in 1931, but it did not become a significant electoral force for another thirty years. A fresh groundswell of sentiment in favour of Home Rule arose in 1948–9, during the Labour government's 'austerity' programme. It took the form of a mass campaign to get signatures to a 'Covenant', in effect a petition for Home Rule. But the failure of this project eventually produced a reaction. In the late 1950s the SNP passed under a new leadership who were committed to the idea that Scottish independence could and must be obtained by electoral organisation.

From that moment the party increased its number of candidates, and its share of the Scottish vote, at each successive election until October 1974. Then, with 30 per cent of the Scottish vote and 11 seats at Westminster, the SNP found itself in a position to force a reluctant but thoroughly alarmed Labour government to introduce legislation for an elected Scottish Assembly with devolved powers. This was in no way a measure of independence – on the contrary it was intended by the Labour leadership to forestall further nationalist advance – but the gradualist wing of the SNP saw it as a step forward. However, opponents of devolution in the Labour Party succeeded in inserting an amendment to the Bill, which provided that the government would only be obliged to implement it if 40 per cent of the entire Scottish electorate (as opposed to a simple majority of those voting) supported it. In the referendum, held in March 1979, only 33 per cent (52 per cent of those voting) did so, and the government declined to proceed further. The 'gradualist' strategy had failed and the SNP MPs in frustration voted with the Conservatives to bring the government down. They paid a heavy price. In the May 1979 elections the SNP vote fell to 17.3 per cent of the Scottish total, and its parliamentary representation fell from 11 to 2. In its turn the SNP Annual Conference reacted by reverting to a policy of campaigning for complete independence or nothing. The 'home rulers' in the party's hierarchy were replaced, and the left wing, who wanted to commit the party to a socialist brand of nationalism, were also rejected. In May 1980 the party also lost two-thirds of its district councillors in local government elections throughout Scotland and in the 1983 election the SNP vote fell to 11.8 per cent of the Scottish total.*

To some observers the SNP therefore seemed a spent force. But the rate of decline of the Scottish economy, in combination with the appeal of nationalism, contained a permanent political potential, and the SNP was bound to revert, in due course, to a strategy of electoral gradualism. As Jack Brand commented (before the 1979 setback): 'there is no doubt that the SNP will have its ups and downs, but every downturn in the Scottish economy will turn Labour voters, and perhaps Conservative too, into the arms of the SNP'.[19] On the other hand, as Tom Nairn was to point out, the middle-class professionals who were the mainspring of the SNP's organisation were also particularly identified with the expanded Keynesian state which Thatcherism was determined to get rid of. Even if some economic recovery occurred in Scotland under Thatcherite auspices, it would not

---

* Prior to the May 1980 elections the SNP had controlled 2 of the 53 district councils and had been the largest party in another. It lost these positions and was reduced to 56 councillors out of a Scottish total of 1,121.

necessarily appease this class who, moreover, had less and less opportunity to emigrate, to England or anywhere else, as they had in the past.[20]

And in fact the SNP, after much internal convulsion, began a gradual recovery. In the 1987 election, its share of the Scottish vote rose to 14.1 per cent, resulting in the gain of one seat for a total of three, and in the May 1988 District Council elections, the SNP vote doubled, and its total number of councilors rose from about 60 to about 111, or about 10 per cent of the total.[21]

It remained difficult to assess the medium-run prospects for the SNP. It was clearly going to be very much affected by the outcome of the Thatcherite economic strategy, and the vicissitudes of the other opposition parties at Westminster. It had a problem of appealing across class boundaries in a situation where class differences were quite acute. It was now more oriented to the working class than before 1979; this involved the probable loss of some of its former middle-class support, and pitted it more against the Labour Party (which had greatly strengthened its electoral hold in Scotland, against the Thatcherite tide).

SNP candidates were still predominantly middle class, not unlike Liberal candidates. SNP activists, however, were predominantly self-employed, or were white-collar employees of small concerns. Like the SDP's new activists of 1981, most were new to politics when they joined the SNP, and as Kellas observed, such recruits tend to lack staying-power.[23] There were some signs in 1987 that a more durable core had begun to be created. The party had also possessed an active left wing, who in England would have been in the Labour left or even in the extra-parliamentary left, and who had contributed greatly to the party's intellectual calibre; by the late 1980s these too seemed to have determined to temper their aims to electoral realities.

SNP supporters resembled the floating 'centre' voters who were attracted to the Liberals in England. They were largely refugees from one of the major parties, and rather evenly drawn from all social strata.[24] Apart from by-elections, where the SNP briefly took industrial seats from Labour in the late sixties, the party was most successful in rural constituencies and in semi-urban constituencies where only a minority of the workforce was unionised, especially in the north-eastern seats of Moray and Nairn, Banff and East Aberdeenshire. The Scottish electoral map after October 1974 showed the SNP seats distributed around the periphery, very much like Liberal seats in Britain as a whole.

SNP social and economic policies also bore some resemblance to those of the Liberals, and reflected similar tensions between 'left' and 'centrist' elements. Within an independent Scotland the SNP called for decentralised government, more democratic government and more 'open' government. On the economy, the party favoured worker 'participation', but maintained that it had 'no objection in principle to either private or public enterprise', believing that 'all contributions to the success of an enterprise including capital, expertise and labour, should have a fair reward and have an effective voice in policy making'.[25]

In the 1970s, unlike the Liberals and the SDP, the SNP had had a solution to the problem of the Scottish economy – 'Scotland's oil'. In the run-up to the two 1974 elections this theme was stressed almost to the exclusion of any other. If Scotland were independent, then under international law, the SNP argued, most of the oil in the British sector of the North Sea would belong to Scotland. The government in London was extracting the oil as fast as possible, so as to maintain living-standards in England above the level that the English could afford on their own; an independent Scottish government would husband the reserves and plan their extraction in such a way as to endow Scotland with a modern industrial base. There can be little doubt that the oil issue played a large part in the SNP's 1974 election successes but the subsequent decision to support Labour's devolution bill meant that the oil theme had to be played down, because the devolution proposals left London in full control of the oil in the North Sea (and of all other revenues too, for that matter). The 'hawks' in the SNP drew their own conclusions from that result. The new SNP leader chosen in 1979, Gordon Wilson, had been closely identified with the 'Scotland's oil' strategy, and in the long run, as the life of the oil reserves was gradually seen to be longer than originally supposed, this theme could become important again, though the days when it could function as a dazzling 'instant fix' for Scottish problems were clearly past.

Plaid Cymru

The Welsh (National) Party was formed in 1925 under the leadership of Saunders Lewis, a philosopher and leader of Welsh literature. For Lewis, the new party's task was to fight for Welsh culture, but not for Welsh independence; he envisaged a world of free but federated nations. This formula had little electoral appeal. In 1945, however, the leadership passed to Gwynfor Evans, who began a gradual transformation of the party into a serious political organisation. In the early 1950s it followed the Scottish Nationalists' 1948 example, of trying to mobilise national sentiment through petitions; and in this case too, failure prompted a new, pragmatic brand of activist to try electoral organisation, concentrating especially on by-elections (at which the pull of majority-party allegiances is weakest).

The PC share of the Welsh vote grew from 0.7 per cent (for only four candidates), in 1951, to 11.5 per cent in 1970, when the party ran candidates in all 36 Welsh constituencies and won three seats. In the 1974 elections there was a slight decline (to 10.8 per cent of the total in October) but no loss of seats, and in the district council elections of 1976 the PC went on to capture control of Merthyr in the Labour-dominated industrial heartland and made significant gains throughout the mining valleys.

The growing PC threat prompted a series of administrative reforms which ultimately endowed Wales with a system of devolved administration bearing some similarity to that of Scotland. In 1964 a Welsh Office under a Secretary of State for Wales was created in Cardiff. Within six years and in face of considerable Whitehall resistance, it has assumed responsibility for health, education and agriculture throughout Wales, and established a Welsh Planning Board and an Economic Council. Welsh trade unionists, too, set up a distinctively democratic Welsh TUC (in spite of resistance from Congress House – the headquarters of the British TUC) and the Welsh Labour Party was also eventually prodded into attempting to come to terms with Welsh sentiment.[26]

These changes had a cumulative effect. The case for a more comprehensive measure of local autonomy was thrown into prominence by the inability of the Welsh people to control the branches of central government that now operated from Cardiff, and by the well-publicised findings of the Welsh Economic Council on Wales's continuing economic decline. The Labour government's Wales Act of 1978, passed simultaneously with the Scotland Act, provided for an elected Welsh Assembly with a committee system to make a policy over a wide range of devolved responsibilities. However, in the March 1979 referendum provided for under the Act, only 20 per cent of those voting (11.9 per cent of all Welsh voters) cast their votes in favour of the new Assembly. It was clear that, to the great majority of Welshmen, the Welsh language and Welsh self-government were irrelevant issues.

Plaid Cymru itself had not been strongly committed to the Assembly; its cultural wing had long argued that self-government under a predominantly non-Welsh majority in Wales would be more damaging than favourable to Wales's culture.[27] Perhaps, as a result, defeat was less damaging to Plaid Cymru than it was to the SNP. In the

1979 election the PC vote declined from 10.8 per cent to 8.1 per cent, with the loss of one seat; similar losses were experienced in the local elections held at the same time. But the strength of the cultural basis of Welsh nationalism remained, exemplified in the PC leader Gwynfor Evans's successful use of the threat to fast to death in order to force the Thatcher government to honour its 1979 election pledge to establish a Welsh-language TV channel in Wales.

With unemployment in Wales rising sharply from 1979 onwards (the official figure was 16 per cent in December 1981), the long-run possibility of a renewed nationalist advance could not be ruled out. Plaid Cymru's advance had paralleled the economy's decline, as well as the continuing encroachment of English culture through education, the mass media, urbanisation, tourism and the decline of churchgoing.[28]

However the 1983 and 1987 elections suggested that Plaid Cymru's potential was limited. Labour was the major gainer in both elections and the PC vote declined, although it gained one extra seat in 1987 thanks to a slight recovery in its rural vote.

In certain respects Plaid Cymru resembled the SNP and the English alternative parties, especially in its broad appeal to all socio-economic strata of the population. Also, like the SNP (though unlike the English alternative parties) it appealed particularly to young voters, and even more to young activists, a very large proportion of whom were students or even schoolchildren.[29] Its leaders were also overwhelmingly professional people, as were its candidates. Plaid Cymru, at least in the sixties, was 'a party strongly dominated by the middle class in Wales, with a leaven of non-manual workers drawn from the stratum of post-mistresses'.[30]

The point about these people, however, was that they were Welsh-speaking, and moreover the leaders were 'the sons and daughters of coalminers, steelworkers, shopkeepers and minor civil servants, but overwhelmingly of coalminers'.[31] Unlike the new Labour MPs from Wales, who tended to move with their families to 'prosperous parts of London', the educated miners' sons who led the PC wanted to mobilise the Welsh masses in a combined cultural and economic revival in Wales. But in spite of its 1970s advance in the industrial valleys the PC's electoral successes were confined to 'Welsh Wales' and its share of the vote remained strictly correlated with the proportion of Welsh speakers in each constituency. The scale of the PC threat was highly unlikely to lead to any new devolution measures for Wales in the foreseeable future. On the other hand, the PC vote had not collapsed, any more than had the determination of its activists. Plaid Cymru also benefited from the militant actions of the Welsh Language Society, who agitated on the language issue, through calculated attacks on property (especially 'second homes' owned by non-Welsh people) and other forms of direct action, and so publicised the nationalist cause without compromising Plaid Cymru's reformist image.

Moreover, the party's policies had evolved considerably. From its early concentration on the language issue, to the exclusion of all else, it had, by 1980, evolved elaborate economic policy proposals for Wales. Its language policy had been modified to a call for bilingualism (rather than for Welsh only), and the themes of decentralisation and democratisation fitted naturally into its communitarian philosophy, and had particular appeal in Wales. So long as the Labour Party remained unified Plaid Cymru seemed unlikely to expand significantly. If Labour were to collapse or fragment, however, the electoral potential of Plaid Cymru might become much more substantial.

The Significance of the Alternative Parties

The most obvious common feature of the alternative parties was their 'middle-class' character. Yet, although the term has been used throughout this chapter, its limitations could hardly be more obvious. Between the Welsh-speaking university lecturers and post-mistresses of Plaid Cymru in Merioneth, the pragmatic small businessmen of the SNP in East Fife, and the Oxford-educated 'gang of four' who planned the formation of the SDP in weekend cottages near London, there was in some ways little similarity. Many SDP activists may have had more in common with their Liberal counterparts, though they mostly lacked the Liberals' sometimes earnest sense of being heirs to a distinct tradition, whereas the new entrants to political activity in the SDP gave the impression of having a technocratic and somewhat superficial conception of politics. Yet in their different ways each did express an aspect of the 'new middle class' as a political factor in British politics – just as another aspect was expressed by the so-called 'polytechnic Marxists' of the Labour left from whose political machinations the former Labour MPs and local councillors in the SDP considered themselves to be refugees. This social stratum was undoubtedly playing a central role in attempts to reconstruct parliamentary party politics, though its real importance was difficult to assess.

The class character of the Liberal Party had been its Achilles heel in the past. The refusal of the middle-class members of Liberal constituency associations at the end of the nineteenth century to adopt more working-class 'Lib–Lab' candidates had helped to push the labour movement to seek independent representation, leading ultimately to the Liberals' eclipse. The modern Liberal Party had not entirely surmounted this weakness. The problem was not that middle-class Liberals lacked sympathy for the workers but that they tended to lack empathy with them.

One ALTU [Association of Liberal Trade Unionists] leader commented, not without bitterness, that while Lady Violet Bonham Carter – Asquith's daughter and a party stalwart throughout her life – had always shown concern for the problems of the working class person as an abstract part of mankind, she had never been willing to have much to do with him as an individual.[32]

The activists of the SDP had the same problem, as the tendency of the Alliance to draw more votes from Conservatives than from Labour showed. Of course the Labour Party itself was not immune to this difficulty. The increasingly middle-class character of the parliamentary party was probably responsible for the loss of some of its members and votes after 1951. It was not just the views of the left-wing constituency activists, but also the educated middle-class tones in which they were sometimes expressed, which had – ironically perhaps – precipitated the movement of some of the older working-class members out of the Labour Party into the SDP. But the Labour Party's links with the unions, which the Labour left took very seriously, made an important difference. In the Labour Party the working class still had a massive and constitutionally guaranteed presence through the trade unions.

The nationalist parties had some advantage in this respect because they explicitly appealed to a national identity common to all classes. The PC leadership's background, and the fact that it was so heavily involved in teaching (rather than in commerce or industry), gave it the fewest problems in this regard, either in relating personally to Welsh workers or in adopting broadly 'democratic-socialist' economic and social policies calling for an active and expanded – though more democratic – state sector. The SNP, by contrast, was divided into left and right wings. The party's left wing, contemplating the heavily working-class character of south-west Scotland where the population was concentrated, believed that the party must adopt democratic, socialist policies if it was ever to win power; while the right wing was opposed to socialism in principle and also judged that social-democratic policies would alienate middle-class support. Like most Liberal activists Gordon Wilson, the SNP leader from 1979 onwards, 'refused to acknowledge the existence of class problems', though after severe internal struggles the party emerged in 1987 with an explicitly left–social democratic orientation.[33] The SDP's early pronouncements did not deny the existence of classes, but scarcely mentioned them

either, except to say that the party existed 'to create an open, classless
and more equal society'.

The ambiguities of all the alternative parties on the issue of class
(with the partial exception of Plaid Cymru) expressed the classical
middle-class ambivalence towards both capital and labour – dazzled by
capital but resentful of it, sympathetic to labour but fearful of it. Yet
with the breakup of so many of the traditional connotations of capital
and labour – and especially the gradual disappearance of the
traditional industrial boss and the cloth-capped worker – it could well
be that this ambivalence would not matter electorally. In the short run
it might even be an asset. In 1981 critical commentators on the SDP
pointed to its lack of rank and file activists to get out the vote among
the workers in industrial areas. They tended to forget that Labour
Party activists had also become scarce (in 1985 Labour had some
306,000 individual members, the Liberals about 185,000, and the SDP
about 50,000),[34] that television had become the prime medium of
political communication, and that more voters than at any time since
1945 had ceased to have a routine attachment to any party.*

In any case, the class character of a party must not be identified with
the social background or even the felt interests of its activists. The
voters' initial response to the Liberal–SDP Alliance was due partly to
the fact that it succeeded in articulating new interests and appealing to
new sentiments that had been emerging in Britain during the 1960s and
1970s, to a large extent independently of class interests and sentiments.
The SNP and Plaid Cymru had also attracted a substantial block of
votes. To call all these votes 'protest votes' understates their
significance by seeming to imply that these voters were only making a
gesture *against* Labour or the Conservatives, whereas they were also
registering a positive response to some element or elements in the
'images' they had of these alternative parties. The new 'political
subjects' to whom these parties' programmes appealed were still rather
vague and certainly rather contradictory. The call made to them was
unlikely to take effect quickly, given the pull of much older
identifications. But, as the economic and social structure of the country
continued to change it seemed likely that there would continue to be a

---

* This was specially true of the working class. By 1979 fewer voters were strong
supporters of Labour than of the Conservatives, and support for Labour had declined
most of all among working-class trade unionists. Social class (in the sense of socio-
economic stratification) correlated less and less strongly with voting for the two major
parties; already by 1979 Labour's lead among manual workers who considered
themselves working class was only 20 per cent compared with 42 per cent in 1964 (R.
Rose, 'Class Does Not Equal Party', *Studies in Public Policy* 74, Strathclyde University,
1980).

process of detachment of various elements that formerly adhered to one or the other of the major parties – by the late 1980s no doubt mainly, but not exclusively, from Labour.[35] In spite of the Alliance's collapse in 1987, and the unpredictability of the electoral process in the short run, the chances of the alternative parties being able to capture the parliamentary balance of power had not been so high for 70 years.

Moreoever, the Liberals and the SDP were both committed as a matter of priority to the introduction of proportional representation, which was also supported by the SNP and – by 1988 – a significant minority within the Labour Party.* The introduction of any system of proportional representation would encourage more 'centre voters' to abandon the Conservative and Labour parties (their votes would no longer seem wasted) and give rise to permanent and substantial representation for the parties of the centre. With proportional representation, neither the Conservatives nor Labour would be likely to win outright parliamentary majorities again. The prospect would then open up of the kind of 'northern European' politics that the SDP leaders had originally had in mind:

It would have proportional representation, state-funding of political parties and possibly a federal system of government. There would be more worker participation in industry, some kind of annual agreement on incomes and more small businesses and cooperatives. Our schools and our hospitals would be more autonomous and more open institutions. Above all, perhaps, out perspective would be less insular and more enthusiastically European and internationalist.[36]

Assuming, that is, that the Thatcherite economic strategy had by then laid a 'northern European' foundation for economic prosperity and for ending the chronic poverty and dangerous hopelessness of the long-term unemployed. Otherwise multiparty, coalition government could lead in a very different, more sinister direction. As Tom Nairn pointed out in 1979, for much of the twentieth century Britain had in fact already had 'national' or coalition governments – from 1915 to 1922, and 1931 to 1945, a total of 21 years. It had, he argued, been the crucial mechanism whereby the established social order had undertaken limited, 'restorative' reconstructions of the economy and state while preserving the old balance of social and political power. 'National' governments had been necessary to effect the transition from the

---

* Before 1979 support for PR had been more noticeable in the Tory or 'wet' ranks of the Conservatives. After nine years of power, this element had become negligible whereas a growing segment of Labour Party opinion had started to favour PR both on principle, and as an opening towards coalition politics with other anti-Thatcher parties.

old Liberal hegemony to the Keynesian social-democratic order, and to secure the safe incorporation of the labour movement into the state. But if what was required – as Nairn believed it was – was something no longer restorative, but far-reaching and radical, the danger was that a national or coalition government would flounder, and give way to a 'strong man' of the far right: 'A transitional government might open the door to him, both by its general incompetence and its destructive effect on the cohesion of the old parties. And the resulting movement . . . would "normalize" UK politics with a vengeance.'[37] It may sound far-fetched to suggest that this could ever be the ultimate historical function of the 'vague, nice' parties reviewed in this chapter, but unless the problem of production and productivity is first successfully resolved, there is no reason to think that the role that such parties have played elsewhere in times of crisis could never be repeated in Britain.

Notes

1 For an introduction to the politics of Northern Ireland see L. de Paor, *Divided Ulster*, Penguin, Harmondsworth 1970; R. Rose, *Northern Ireland: A Time of Choice*, Macmillan, London 1976; M. Farrell, *Northern Ireland, the Orange State*, Pluto Press, London 1976; B. Probert, *Beyond Orange and Green*, Zed Press, London 1978; P. Bew et al., *The State in Northern Ireland; Political Forces and Social Classes*, Manchester University Press, Manchester 1979; and L. O'Dowd, *Northern Ireland: Between Civil Rights and Civil War*, CSE Books, London 1980.
2 M. Steed, 'The Liberal Party', in H.M. Drucker, ed., *Multi-Party Britain*, Macmillan, London 1979, p. 84.
3 P. Olive, 'Realignment: The Case of the Liberals', *Marxism Today*, May 1981, p. 14.
4 Steed, p. 105.
5 Olive, pp. 16–17.
6 Steed, p. 86.
7 Ibid., pp. 89–90.
8 A. Cyr, *Liberal Party Politics in Britain*, Calder, London 1977, pp. 247–8.
9 For an insight into this milieu see A. Stephen, 'The Kicking, Squealing Birth-Pangs of the SDP', *Sunday Times Magazine*, 27 September 1981.
10 I. Bradley, *Breaking the Mould? The Birth and Prospects of the Social Democratic Party*, Martin Robertson, Oxford 1981, p. 157. Or, as C. Husbands put it, 'there are numerous voters who wish or hope that there is a political Santa Claus' ('The Politics of Confusion', *Marxism Today*, February 1982, p. 12).
11 D. Currie, 'SDP: A Prop for Profits', *New Socialist*, 4, March–April 1982, pp. 9–11.
12 Bradley, pp. 155–9.
13 P. Kellner, 'Something for everyone in the local election', *The Independent*, 9 May 1988.
14 P. Jenkins, *Mrs. Thatcher's Revolution*, Cape, London 1987, p. 367.
15 This thesis is argued persuasively in T. Nairn, *The Break-Up of Britain*, London 1977, Chapter 9, 'The Modern Janus'.
16 J. Osmond, *Creative Conflict: The Politics of Welsh Devolution*, Routledge and Kegan Paul, London 1977, p. 92.

17 H.M. Drucker and G. Brown, *The Politics of Nationalism and Devolution*, Longman, London 1980, pp. 35–6, 49–50.

18 The foregoing sketch is intended to provide only the barest account of the background to the rise of the nationalist parties, and makes no pretence to do justice to the complexity of Scottish or Welsh nationalism. The literature on both nationalisms, but especially the Welsh, has lagged behind their development. For recent studies of Wales see the references to Gwyn Williams's savage survey, 'Mother Wales, Get Off Me Back?', *Marxism Today*, December 1981, pp. 14–20.

19 J. Brand, 'From Scotland With Love', in I. Kramnick, ed., *Is Britian Dying?*, Cornell University Press, Ithaca, New York 1978, p. 182.

20 T. Nairn, 'Tartan and Blue', *Marxism Today*, June 1988, pp. 30–33.

21 Including the vote cast for the candidate for the Orkney and Shetland Movement, whom the SNP did not contest.

22 *The Independent*, 7 May 1988.

23 J. Kellas, *The Scottish Political System* (second edition), Cambridge University Press, Cambridge 1975, p. 127.

24 Ibid., pp. 128, 131.

25 R. Mullin, 'The Scottish National Party', in Drucker, *Multi-Party Britain*, p. 126, quoting an SNP policy document of 1977.

26 Osmond, pp. 115–30, esp. p. 124.

27 D. Balson, 'Plaid Cymru', in Drucker, *Multi-Party Britain*, p. 134.

28 For a survey of the economic decline see A. Butt-Philip, *The Welsh Question*, University of Wales Press, Cardiff 1975, Chapters 2–3, and the references referred to in note 18 above.

29 Butt-Philip, pp. 158–9; the data, however, refer to the late 1960s.

30 Ibid., p. 168.

31 Osmond, p. 94, quoting B. Khleif.

32 Cyr, pp. 239–40.

33 Drucker and Brown, p. 12 and R. Edwards, 'A Thistle in the Flesh', *New Statesman & Society*, 23 September 1988. In November 1988 the SNP won the former Labour stronghold of Govan in a by-election on its new left–nationalist platform.

34 S. Ingle, *The British Party System*, Blackwell, Oxford 1987, pp. 132, 177, 179.

35 For a suggestive review of this possibility by a Social and Liberal democrat strategist see D. Marquand, 'Spot the Radical', in *Marxism Today*, July 1988, pp. 12–15.

36 Bradley, p. 137.

37 T. Nairn, 'The Future of Britain's Crisis', *New Left Review* 113–114, January–April 1979, p. 66.

PART IV

13

The British State

Until the mid-1970s few books on British politics, and virtually no textbooks, referred to the state. This was because the most influential theories of the state were incompatible with the tenets of pluralism. Hegel had seen the state as the embodiment of the ethical and rational principles of the nation and glorified the Prussian autocracy as its supreme expression, while Marx, on the contrary, understood it as the embodiment of the interests of the dominant class. Pluralists rejected the concepts of both nation and class. For them, 'western' societies were systems of constantly changing combinations of groups competing to control the 'institutions of government' through electoral and pressure-group activity. The 'institutions of government' were, moreover, diverse and neutral. They did not constitute a structure exerting a systematic force of any kind on political life; they were a 'dependent variable'.

The concept of the state was, however, resurrected by both left and right thinkers as a result of the crisis. On the left, in 1968 Nicos Poulantzas inaugurated a radical critique of Marxist ideas about the state from which a much more complex and subtle theory eventually emerged, and the following year Miliband published a definitive critique of the pluralist conception of the state.[1] Soon afterwards, on the other hand, neo-liberal theorists identified the 'social-democratic state' as a threat to the interests of capital. While the viewpoints of left and right theorists were diametrically opposed, they agreed in recognising what popular opinion had in any case never doubted for a moment – that the state was a massive and problematic reality.

To take Miliband first, he demonstrated that the pluralist conception of the state (shared by most social democrats) as a neutral apparatus, reflecting the changing balance of competing political forces, was untenable. He showed that in capitalist societies the state's directing echelons were staffed by people whose social background and milieu, and whose training within the state apparatus, made them see their task as that of serving the interests of capital. Moreover, even social-democratic ministers invariably saw the health of the capitalist economy as necessary to the achievement of practicable social reforms. He also showed that the pluralists' world of free and equal political competition was another myth. The independent command of economic resources by private capital made it hard if not impossible for the state apparatus to control it effectively. The withdrawal of 'business confidence' from a government that threatened business interests was frequently decisive (as in 1931 or 1964–6), and it was reinforced by the dependence of governments on external capitalist interests such as foreign banks or the International Monetary Fund. Furthermore, vis-à-vis organised labour, capital was more compre-hensively organised, less divided, better endowed, ideologically more confident, and closer to the state apparatus. The state was not neutral and the political struggle between labour and capital was not equal.

Whereas Miliband showed that the state was not neutral, Poulantzas addressed himself to the fact that it was not a mere tool of capital either. The famous dictum of Marx and Engels that the state was 'but a committee for managing the common affairs of the bourgeoisie' had long been taken by Marxists to mean that it was an agent or instrument of the bourgeoisie. This meant interpreting every state action which appeared not to be in the interests of the bourgeoisie, such as the extension of the franchise, as somehow 'in the last analysis' *really* in its interests. Poulantzas initially argued that this problem must be taken seriously, and advanced the idea that the state was 'relatively autonomous'.

First, he pointed out, it was evident that the state needed a degree of independence from the dominant class if it was to maintain the latter's long-term *political* dominance. Major concessions to working-class political strength, such as the trade union rights legislated and relegislated in Britain in 1871, 1875, 1906, 1946 and 1974 were necessary at the time in order to preserve capital from a more fundamental threat. In effect, the most important 'common affair' of the bourgeoisie was the preservation of its political power, and to 'manage' this the state needed enough autonomy *from* the bourgeoisie to be able to override its immediate economic interests if need be. Second, Poulantzas pointed out that the economic interests of different fractions of capital often conflict with each other. To reconcile, and if necessary arbitrate between them, the state must also be independent of the control of any one fraction (for instance the British state had to be able to abolish Resale Price Maintenance, which hurt many small retailers, and to take Britain into the EEC, which hurt many smaller manufacturers).

Poulantzas also suggested that the interests of the dominant class were expressed primarily in the way the state was structured and organised. He criticised Miliband for seeming to say that what makes a state capitalist is the class origin or class ties of its senior personnel. Miliband replied that Poulantzas was attributing to the structure of the state an efficacy which was ultimately mysterious. We shall comment briefly on this exchange later (see pp. 294–5); in the event Poulantzas subsequently shifted his position. In his last book, he abandoned the notion that the state is in fact always functional for capital, either in its actions or in its structure.[2] Instead he developed the idea that the state is a product – a 'condensate', in his words – of class struggles (echoing Marx's dictum that the state is an 'official résumé of civil society'). This implies not only that the structures of the state may not be functional for particular elements of capital: they may not be altogether functional for any of them. But this does not mean that the state in a capitalist society may work systematically against the interests of capital and in favour of the workers; if it did, the society would hardly remain capitalist for long. What it means is that nothing *guarantees* that the state serves the interests of capital consistently, through all changes in the nature and needs of capital, in face of all challenges – an insight of particular relevance to the British state, as we shall see.

Also of importance is the implication that the state is itself a *field of struggle*. The Leninist tradition tended to regard the state as something to be 'seized' (and then 'smashed') by the workers. Poulantzas regarded it rather as a 'field of power relations' in which elements opposed to the dominant class were also engaged. As the state had expanded, this field had been greatly enlarged, offering new opportunities to turn the state's operations against the interests of capital. A good example of this, which is very relevant to the British experience, is 'corporatism' (see Chapter 8 above).

In short, what these and other theorists did was to suggest how the state – whose political significance had become such a central fact of life in the post-war period – might be analysed without falling into the trap of reducing it to a mere reflection of the relative influence of competing groups (as the pluralists supposed) or of the interests of the dominant class (as traditional Marxists had imagined). At the same time, the new way of looking at the matter also made it clear that there is no such thing as *the* 'capitalist state'. There are only the states of particular capitalist societies, the 'condensates' of highly specific historical struggles. Once again, therefore, it is a question of trying to understand British politics – in this instance the British state – in terms of its distinctive historical development.

The Development of the Contemporary British State

The most suggestive recent work on this topic is that of Tom Nairn.[3] Nairn argued that the essential characteristics of the modern British state could be traced to the social and political context in which the industrial revolution occurred. Because the British industrial revolution was the first such revolution, the state which presided over it could be very different from those which presided over subsequent industrial revolutions in other countries. The latter all faced a common problem: how to make 'space' for, and how to protect and nurture, their countries' new industries in the face of Britain's naval power and technical and quantitative superiority in the market. This demanded a high-profile, centralised, rationalised form of state, actively clearing the way for the growth of domestic industry – a type of state which the circumstances of post-Napoleonic Europe fostered, in different ways, in both France and Germany.

By contrast, the modern British state originated in the dominance of the unique 'landed-capitalist' class which emerged from the English revolution of the seventeenth century. This, numerically small, 'patrician' class largely *was* the state – furnishing its parliamentarians, its magistrates, its militia, its policy-making bureaucracy, its military officer corps, and the clergy of its established Church. As a direct emanation of this class the British state could be highly decentralised and 'low-profile', based on strong intra-class personal ties rather than on formal and impersonal rules. In the course of the late eighteenth century, and throughout the nineteenth, this governing 'patrician' class merged with the rising class of commercial and industrial capital. As a result, the rising class had no need to attack the state; it could always be reformed to meet their needs. Steadily, corruption was reduced, and utilitarian principles were gradually extended into the staffing of the civil service and the armed forces, and into the organisation of the fiscal system and the poor law. But the essential character of the state – its informal, patrician, decentralised and above all *reactive* character – remained unchanged.

The result was a state capable of superintending the transition to commercial and industrial capitalism in the first country to make this transition: and capable of forging a new hegemony over society at large, which proved strong enough to withstand the social and economic dislocations of the transition with only a minimum resort to force. But when the competitive challenge of newer, more efficient industrial capitalisms was encountered, the same state was ill-adapted to respond as an agent of industrial reconstruction:

> emergence from the crisis demands a political break: a disruption at the level of the state, allowing the emergence of sharper antagonisms and the will to reform the old order root and branch. But in this system, possibly more than in any other, such a break has become extremely difficult. The state-level is so deeply entrenched in the social order itself, state and civil society are so intertwined in the peculiar exercise of the British constitution, that a merely 'political' break entails a considerable social revolution.[4]

Nairn's thesis is much richer than any summary, even though it is itself presented only in broad terms: a critical history of the modern British state does not yet exist.[5] But to understand the character of the British state today we need a sketch, however provisional, of the main stages of its development.

The first period, from 1832 to 1867, is, least controversially perhaps, the period of the liberal representative state. From 1832 onwards the middle classes were increasingly represented in the House of Commons, which as a result became less and less 'manageable' by the magnates of the Tory and Whig parties. It became necessary to undertake a reconstruction of the state to meet the needs of the new middle classes, including some provision for the needs of their employees. Municipal government was put on a new footing in 1835, and central administration substantially rationalised between 1853 and the 1870s. Reform of the judicature was initiated with the establishment of County Courts in 1846, and carried further (after a long resistance) in 1876. The reorganisation of the labour supply was put in hand with the 1834 Poor Law (enforced more or less generally from the mid-1850s), supplemented by a series of Factory Acts. The fiscal system was reconstructed with the abandonment of protection and the switch from tariff revenue to income tax; the Bank Act of 1844 established a central bank, and Joint Stock Company Acts of 1856 and 1862 created the legal framework for limited liability and the efficient centralisation of capital.

But the liberal–representative state was not democratic; on the contrary, it was, and actually remained, firmly opposed to democracy. By the 1860s, however, the growing strength of working-class organisation made a widening of the franchise a risk which had to be taken. Thanks to the acceptance of liberal ideas among the leaders of the labour movement at that time, it was an acceptable risk, and the next fifty years saw the construction of a state apparatus that would ensure that this change did not mean any real transfer of political power to the working class.

This phase was decisive in the development of the contemporary state: the 'historic bloc' of dominant classes and their allies now expanded and by 1918 embraced at least the male working class. The work of liberal reform was consummated in the civil service, the courts, the army, municipal and county government; and there was a great expansion of the state apparatus to meet the needs of capital as it entered the phase of monopoly and encountered rising foreign competition (for example, it had to be provided with a more literate labour force), and to meet new social demands from the working class.

The shift from the 'negative' or 'nightwatchman' liberal state of early competitive capitalism to the 'positive' state of monopoly capitalism was, however, not effected through consensus but through political struggles. The propertied classes remained nervous about what the workers might do with their vote ('a political combination of the lower classes', Bagehot had remarked, 'as such and for their own purposes, is an evil of the first magnitude'). The guiding principle of state development was the need to make those concessions to the workers which could 'safely' be made – a 'passive revolution', in Gramsci's terminology. Safety was ensured, above all, by restricting popular power to the single channel of parliamentary and local elections; by progressively neutralising the independent power of the House of Commons that had been the hallmark of the liberal–representative state; and by excluding the principle of democracy from all other spheres. At the same time, the power relations between the classes were reproduced with great precision inside the state apparatus. As a 'terrain' for working-class struggle, the apparatus of the liberal–democratic state was made as unpromising as possible. The famous Northcote–Trevelyan report of 1854, implemented in 1870, which established a career higher civil service recruited from Oxford and Cambridge and under the control of the Treasury, was a key instrument for ensuring this.[6]

This state entered into a general crisis from about 1910 onwards, a crisis resolved by the First World War and then by a transition, begun during the war, to a third phase – the Keynesian, and, eventually, social-democratic state of the post-1945 era. Apart from the reduction in the powers of the non-elected House of Lords (in 1911 and 1949) and the extension of the franchise to women (in 1918 and 1928) this phase was not marked by any major changes of formal structure. Its main features were:

1. The integration of the Labour Party into the state, on the basis of

a narrowly defined parliamentarism, through the 'controlled experiments' of the inter-war minority governments, sandwiched between two periods of 'national government'.

2. The extension of the structure of state-organised social security begun by the Liberals (old age pensions in 1908, and sickness, disability and unemployment insurance in 1911). The welfare state established by Labour in 1946–7 made comprehensive and more generous a system which had been gradually enlarged by successive governments since the First World War.

3. The enlargement of the state's apparatus for economic intervention in response to the growing problems posed by declining industries and the slump. Between the wars this branch of the state expanded fourfold.

From about 1960, however, as the new crisis set in, the state apparatus entered a fourth phase in which it began to undergo further modifications. On the one hand attempts were made to improve the performance of its existing functions – to expand its apparatus for social security, to improve its capacity to 'manage' the economy, to formalise and stabilise the 'incorporation' of organised labour and to enhance the state's popularity by means of various reforms. On the other hand, steps were taken to narrow the scope for popular control over the state; and from the mid-1970s there began a movement towards a new state-form, based less on consent and more on coercion.

In what follows, only the second and fourth of these phases will be examined: the creation of the so-called 'liberal–democratic' state – actually, the late-nineteenth-century version of the representative state – and the way in which its adaptation to civil society entrenched so many of the characteristics that are central in the present crisis; and the response of the contemporary state to the current crisis. The first of these subjects occupies the rest of this chapter; the second is the concern of Chapters 14 and 15.

The Late-nineteenth-century Liberal–Representative State

By 1900, the propertied classes' fear of democracy had been largely allayed. The labour movement had been willing to accept Liberal or Conservative leadership and to confine its demands to a relatively limited range of purely economic issues concerned with pay and working conditions. The proposition that 'a democratic political system will always seek, in the long run, to become a democratic society' did not seem to be borne out by experience.*

The middle classes were consequently all the more disillusioned and alarmed at the apparently sudden emergence of an independent Labour Party in parliament in 1906, and more so still at the mass unionisation which followed, and the explosive industrial conflict of 1911–13. Yet matters had not been left entirely to chance. The earlier fears had engendered a highly restricted conception of the political democracy which it was felt necessary to concede, and the state apparatus had been reorganised on lines which made it as far as possible immune to radical impulses of the popular will.

The 'Class-ification' of the State

After 1870 the state began what was probably the most rapid peacetime expansion in its history (before or since), dictated by the growing complexity of the economy and its growing vulnerability to German and American competition, especially with the onset of the Great Depression; and by the need to meet, as far as possible, working-class demands for improved living and working conditions and a degree of security in face of sickness, disablement, unemployment and – as life-expectancy among workers gradually rose – old age. The need to rationalise urban growth and increasingly deficient public health services, for example, led to the creation of a Local Government Board (a central government ministry) in 1871; the collapse of British agriculture from the 1870s onwards led to the formation of a Board of Agriculture in 1889. Similarly, it became clear that modern workers had to be literate and that only a national system of education could achieve this: a Board of Education was finally established in 1899. In 1873 the Board of Trade had sixty 'clerks'; by 1914 it had over 3,000. In 1871 there had been some 55,000 employees in the central civil service as a whole; by 1914 there were 280,000.[7]

Those responsible for the machinery of state during this period were fully aware of the implications of these changes, occurring simultaneously with the enfranchisement of working men. The state had to be

---

* The quotation is from Harold Laski's *Parliamentary Government in England*. Marx defined the problem in 1850 in a famous passage in 'The Class Struggles in France': 'the most comprehensive contradiction in the constitution consists in the fact that it gives political power to the classes whose social slavery it is intended to perpetuate . . . and it deprives the bourgeoisie, the class whose old social power it sanctions, of the political guarantees of this power' (D. Fernbach, ed., *Karl Marx, Surveys from Exile*, Allen Lane/New Left Review, London, 1973, p. 71).

protected from the dangerous influence of the masses. They laid great stress on 'the increasing need of voluntarily submitting the impulse of the many ignorant to the guidance and control of the few wise'.[8] Both the state apparatus and the new educational system were designed with this in view.

Robert Lowe, the politician mainly responsible for the Order in Council of 1870 which introduced competitive examinations for entry into the higher civil service, recognised that splitting the service into two separate 'classes', one to make policy and the other to implement it, would be inefficient. But like Trevelyan, the chief author of the Northcote Trevelyan Report of 1954 which the Order of 1970 put into effect, he believed it was necessary. With the rationalisation of the service and the growing control of patronage by MPs, increasing numbers of lower-class personnel could be expected to enter the lower and middle ranks of the service. Closing the policy-making ranks of the service to them, Lowe judged, was vital to secure 'that sort of free masonry which exists between people who have had a certain grade of education' and 'whose associations and ideas should belong to the class with whom they will have to deal', that is, the propertied class.[9] Consequently a policy-making 'first Division' of 'clerks' was created, and effectively reserved to the sons of propertied families by basing the entry examinations on subjects which formed the core curricula of the universities of Oxford and Cambridge.

The new educational system was conceived in similar terms. It was necessary for the ruling class to 'educate its masters' (as Lowe also remarked), but not in an uncontrolled fashion. The Education Act of 1870 which laid the basis of a national system of primary schools was, as H.G. Wells put it, 'an Act to educate the lower classes for employment on lower class lines', and secondary education was almost exclusively reserved for the children of the middle and upper classes. Some of the locally elected school boards, however, began to establish 'Board Schools' which gave a few years of secondary schooling to the ablest working-class children leaving primary school.

A witness before the Royal commission on Education in 1887 suggested that Board Schools were likely to foster socialism. Asked what he meant by socialism, he replied: 'the state of things in which there is not the respect for the classes above the children that I think there ought to be'.[10]

Concern about Britain's technological and scientific backwardness eventually prompted the Education Act of 1902, which abolished the local Boards of Education (and the Board Schools) and provided government grants to (mainly church-controlled) secondary schools. But these schools charged fees; they were not envisaged as a normal continuation of the education of children leaving primary school.

In 1906, however, the Liberals abolished fees for up to 25 per cent of the places in state-aided secondary schools, with a view to opening them up to the ablest working-class children. And in 1912 a new Division of the civil service was created, the 'Intermediate Class', in between the First and Second Division 'clerks', in order to recruit 'from among the ablest pupils of the secondary schools [those] who, for economic reasons, could not go to a university' (the idea of making university places free for such pupils was, of course, not entertained).[11]

In other words, by 1914 the essentials of a three-tier structure in both the educational system and the civil service had been established: what would later be called the 'Administrative Class', drawn from the upper and middle classes via the public schools and Oxford and Cambridge; an 'Executive Class' drawn mainly from the lower-middle class, with some working-class admixture, via the state grammar schools; and a 'Clerical Class', drawn originally from the elementary schools, and later from the grammar schools, with less emphasis on academic achievement. (Below even this tier, of course, there was yet another – the large, minimally educated stratum of messengers, filing clerks, secretaries, etc.)

This structure, mirroring the class structure as the policy-makers understood it, is one of the most characteristic legacies of the state-making of that period. It was replicated, with various nuances, in almost every branch of the central state apparatus. Up to 1871, army officers were commissioned on the basis of their ability to pay a substantial sum to the regiment concerned. A system allowing the appointment of wealthy incompetents was clearly inadequate, but the abolition of the purchase of commissions in 1871 did not throw open the officer corps to competitive examination. Instead, recruitment switched to the public schools, where 'volunteer corps' were established for boys with army careers in mind. In 1909 these became the Officer Training Corps (which have survived with various changes of nomenclature and organisation to the present), channelling boys to the Royal Military Academy at Sandhurst. Similarly for the judicial system. Solicitors, recruited through the open examinations of the Law Society, were permitted to appear in the County Courts set up in 1846, but barristers, trained in the more socially exclusive Inns of Court, retained their monopoly of the right to appear in the Crown Court, the High Court and all Appeal Courts, and only barristers could become judges.

Among the principal arms of the state only the police did not conform to the class-structured pattern. It had been laid down by the founder of the Metropolitan Police, Sir Robert Peel, that senior posts should be filled from the lower ranks in order that an adequate calibre of recruit should be attracted to what had formerly been a low-status employment. This led to a shortage of adequately educated candidates for appointment as chief constables, and a substantial minority of chief constables, and all Metropolitan Police Commissioners, were recruited from outside (normally from the armed forces). Most chief constables, however, had come up through the ranks and had working-class or (more often) lower-middle-class backgrounds.

The class-structuring of the state apparatus established before 1914 has survived in essentials, despite many changes of detail. Administrative, Executive and Clerical Classes were formally abolished after 1971, following the recommendation of the Fulton committee in 1966. Like Lowe, the Committee felt that the division of the service into separate classes was inefficient, but by now the crisis led them to give priority to efficiency over the 'freemasonry' of class and education. They recommended the abolition of the system of Classes; much greater recruitment of specialist civil servants into policy-making posts, in place of the inherited practice of relying almost exclusively on arts graduates; and the regular interchange of civil servants with business executives, especially to give civil servants more experience of the economy and society they administered.

But the system established by Lowe and his successors proved powerfully resistant to change. Ten years after Fulton the number of 'general service' classes had been reduced from 47 to 38 and the number of 'departmental' classes from 1,400 to 500. The Administrative, Executive and Clerical classes had nominally been abolished. But it was clear that no great change of practice had occurred. Graduates, predominantly with arts degrees and even more predominantly from Oxford and Cambridge, still formed the main source of recruitment for senior posts. The system of recruitment, training and promotion ensured that the class-structured character of the service remained (see Table 13.1); it is even possible that it became stronger by becoming less rigid.*

* Kelsall's work on recruitment to the higher civil service is illuminating. In 1955 he showed that the gradual shift, after 1945, from competition for entry by means of a written examination plus an interview ('Method I') in favour of a competition consisting only of a battery of skill tests and several interviews of different kinds ('Method II') had markedly shifted the balance of applications, and even more the balance of those who were accepted, away from lower-class candidates, in favour of candidates from the upper and middle classes. He also showed that in 1938 (the one year for which he was given access to the data) the effect of the final interview in 'Method I' had been that 24% of the candidates who would have been admitted on the basis of their examination results alone were replaced, in the final list of those accepted, by lower-scoring candidates of higher social status.[12] Kelsall's findings had no effect on policy and, in 1967, when another study, carried out for the Fulton Commitee, showed similar results, history, as

The record on the other Fulton recommendations was remarkably similar. No appreciable increase in 'lateral' movement of specialists into policy-making posts occurred; the recruitment of outsiders in mid-career was dropped; it was eight years before the recommendation to appoint highly trained accountants led to the appointment of a Head of Accountancy Services, and the number of trained accountants in the service which was 309 in 1965 was still only 364 in 1979; a Civil Service College was established but then marginalised, until under Thatcher it became 'a quiet Whitehall backwater'; the special advisers appointed by ministers in the 1974–9 government were effectively 'frozen out'; the new Civil Service Department established in 1968 was first deprived of real power and finally abolished in 1981. 'In virtually every area Whitehall paid lip service to the Fulton ideas, claimed in public that they were being implemented, but in practice ensured that they were not.'[16]

Information on the recruitment of army officers is hard to come by.[17] If the evidence of Simon Raven is accepted, the army officer class structure survived whatever pressure there may have been for more respresentative recruitment, with little modification, at least until the 1950s.[18] Entry from state schools had been accepted (in 1960 only 51 per cent of Sandhurst entrants were from public schools) and it seemed probable that the intellectual quality of recruitment had been raised, but an elaborate social hierarchy of regiments, and the operation of social criteria in the promotion process, appeared to have preserved the class exclusiveness of the senior ranks. In 1959, 83 per cent of the 36 most senior army officers had been educated in public schools;[19] in 1981 the proportion was 80 per cent of the most senior 50.

Kelsall remarked, repeated itself: a committee of enquiry of civil servants was set up and reported in 1969 that there was no 'acceptable evidence of social bias' in the selection procedure. Indeed, after 1969 'Method I' was abolished and was entirely replaced by 'Method II' which, as Kelsall observed, lacks 'any rigorous testing of intellectual ability in which the identity of the candidates is unknown to the examiners'.[13] Gowan notes that 'the American scholar [Robert] Moses had predicted with a chuckle before the First World War that if the right class was not being recruited through the system of written exams then the exam system would be dropped'.[14] Perhaps Moses had been reading the correspondence in *The Times* of 1905 on the selection of boys for cadetships for the navy. Lord Selbourne's new system, consisting of an interview of candidates at age 12 and a half (confined in practice to candidates from fee-paying 'preparatory' schools), followed by a non-competitive qualifying test, was hailed by *The Times* as 'a real and very valuable discovery', though it would not satisfy the 'democratic purists'. A letter from Admiral Penrose-Fitzgerald however, pointed out that Lord Selbourne's 'discovery' was a retrograde step which had replaced a system of competitive exams taken at a later age, a system which, he said, would be restored if and when the democratic purists returned to power.[15]

Table 13.1   Class and educational bias in recruitment to the Higher Civil
Service

	% of applicants	% of appointees
Father's Occupational Status	*(1971–75)*	
I and II (professional/managerial)	57.5	68.9
III (skilled)	33	24
IV (service-skilled)	4	2
V (unskilled)	1	0
Educational Background	*(1973–75)*	
Public School and Oxbridge	29.2	34.6
Public School/non-Oxbridge	8.6	21.3
	(1971–75)	
Arts graduates	42.5	56.7
	(1971: male applicants)	
Social science graduates	36	25
Science graduates	17.4	10.8

% Passing Each Stage of Selection Process, 1984*

	Qualifying Test	Civil Service Selection Board	Final Selection Board
Oxbridge	39	43	75
Other	10	22	54

* The qualifying test is written; the CSSB consists mainly of group interaction activities
in which individual performances are marked and ranked by assessors; the FSB is a
formal interview by a Board consisting mainly of senior civil servants.

Source: C. Ponting, *Whitehall, Tragedy and Farce*, Hamish Hamilton, London 1986,
pp. 74–5.

The social composition of the judiciary also remained impressively
constant. In 1967, 80 per cent of all judges and Queen's Counsel
(senior barristers from whom judges are recruited) had attended a
public school; only 12 per cent had been to a state school. In 1978, 75
per cent of High Court judges (i.e., not counting judges of the Appeal
Courts), were public-school educated, while a study of County Court
judges suggested that a similarly high proportion of them had also
been to public school.[20] In 1971 the law was changed to permit a very

BRISTOL POLYTECHNIC
ST. MATTHIAS LIBRARY
FISHPONDS

limited eligibility for solicitors to be appointed as judges, while in the meantime the social background of lay magistrates (dealing with minor offences and committal hearings) had been gradually modified so as to include a small proportion from working-class backgrounds (see Table 13.2). Here too, the class structure of the state apparatus had become more subtly graduated, without changing its fundamental character.

The police continued to provide an interesting exception to the general pattern. Between the wars there was anxiety about their political loyalty, as well as their efficiency, and from 1934 to 1939 an attempt was made by Lord Trenchard, a former Air Marshal, to introduce a class-structured system into the Metropolitan Police by recruiting university graduates earmarked for rapid promotion via a new Police Staff College. The resentment in the Police Federation against these entrants, and the outbreak of war, brought the scheme to an end. After the war a new scheme for giving university education to capable officers rising through the ranks was introduced instead. The police force remains, as a result, the branch of the state most open to talent regardless of class origin.

Meantime, large changes had, of course, occurred in the system of education. In 1944, secondary education up to the age of 14 became compulsory, and by 1973 the permissible leaving age had been raised to 16. The 1944 Act embodied the Victorian class-structuring principle by establishing, in effect, a new kind of school for the bulk of working-class children (who would now no longer leave school at age 11 or 12) – the so-called Secondary Modern schools from which most children left with few if any formal qualifications.

A small minority of working-class children were selected to join a much larger proportion of middle-class children in the state 'grammar

Table 13.2 The social background of magistrates 1966–1967

	% of magistrates	% in general population
Higher professional	21.7⎫	3.9
Managerial and other professional	55.2⎭	
Clerical	9.7	14.4
Skilled manual	12.1	49.9
Semi-skilled manual		19.9
Unskilled		8.6

Source: R. Hood. Sentencing the Motoring Offender, Heinemann, London 1972, p. 51.

schools', but the great majority 'failed' their '11-plus' examination and entered the new Secondary Moderns, which fulfilled the same role at the secondary level as the elementary schools had been intended to fulfil at the primary level in the previous century: that of providing a form of schooling adapted to the needs and expectations of manual workers.

By the end of the 1950s, however, this system no longer met the aspirations of growing numbers of parents who saw their children 'failing' at age 11 to enter a school which afforded any prospect of going on to higher education – the key to 'new middle-class' status. Growing evidence was adduced of the wide margin of error involved in selection by the 11-plus examination, and this, combined with the general meritocratic thrust of the Wilson government, led to a decision in 1965 to replace the segregated secondary school system by a single system of all-ability or 'comprehensive' secondary schools.[21]

Several features of this change should be noted. First, it was undertaken on a gradual, negotiated basis, so that the new schools would reflect the balance of opinion among local politicians, school governors and staff. This permitted prolonged resistance to the change, especially in many Conservative strongholds. As a result grammar schools survived in many places, 'creaming off' the ablest children, so that the new 'comprehensives' in these places were not really all-ability schools. It also meant that within the comprehensive schools the class structure of the wider society tended to reproduce itself, assisted in many cases by the separation of pupils into different 'streams', nominally according to ability but also according to social class.[22] Although the ideal of greater individual mobility for children between streams, compared with what was formerly possible between schools, had been partly served, for most working-class children neither personal mobility nor their general view of the system was altered.

> In the comprehensive school, as in the tripartite schools [the former division between grammar schools, secondary modern schools and a limited number of technical schools], children learn early what level they can expect to achieve in the occupational structure . . . their perceptions and evaluations of class remain unaffected by comprehensive education. There is no evidence that children come to think of the stratification system as a fluid legitimate hierarchy, rather than an inevitable and illegitimate dichotomy, as a result of comprehensive schooling.[23]

The proportion entering university from all state schools remained modest. Few university places were available (equivalent to about one

Table 13.3   The Educational System

Enrollments (United Kingdom 1985)		
State primary schools	4,624,000	pupils
State secondary schools	4,244,000	pupils
State special schools	134,000	pupils
Private primary schools	226,000	pupils
Private secondary schools	379,000	pupils
	9,607,000	

Qualifications on leaving (Great Britain 1984–85)	% Boys	% Girls
Qualifications admitting to higher education	18.8	18.5
Lower qualifications	34.2	40.9
No qualifications	47.0	40.6

Intended destinations of school leavers (England and Wales 1984–85)	% Boys	% Girls
Entering degree programmes	8.5	6.3
Entering other further education	15.7	26.6
Entering employment	75.8	67.1

Source: Education statistics for the United Kingdom 1986

for every nine school-leavers) and pupils from fee-paying schools (which by 1977, as more middle-class parents lost the option of the old grammar schools, had expanded to account for over 5 per cent of all children at school) took a disproportionate share of them.

There was no reason, of course, to have expected the post-war changes in the educational system to have had any other effect. It was prefigured in the state and educational system established at the turn of the century. It should have come as no surprise when Halsey and Goldthorpe found that whatever increase there had been in the number of working-class children reaching professional-level employment in the post-war years, it had been entirely due to the growth in such employment, and owed nothing at all to changes in the system of education.[24] The system had been made more flexible; it offered less obvious resistance to individual advance; but it effectively preserved the social hierarchy in education. And the Thatcher government's Education Act of 1988 (see pp. 124–5 above) seemed likely to reinforce this function.

The structure of the state established at the turn of the century thus proved extremely durable. In retrospect we can see that the reforms of the Victorians, sweeping as they seemed to contemporaries, actually served to preserve many aspects of the earlier state – above all, in reproducing within it the relationships of power and class in society at large. In a celebrated image, Gramsci compared the state to a possibly vulnerable outer rampart of defence against popular power, behind which lay the tougher in-depth defences of civil society: 'when the State trembled a sturdy structure of civil society was at once revealed. The State was only an outer ditch, behind which there stood a powerful system of fortresses and earthworks'.[25] In Britain one might say that the late Victorian state was less a distinct outer rampart than simply the forward line of civil society itself.

The problem remained that the higher civil service, the apex or linchpin of this structure, was not at all well suited to playing an active role in economic reform. The Benthamite poor law reformer Edwin Chadwick had foreseen this very clearly when commenting on the Northcote–Trevelyan report in 1854: the proposed higher civil service recruited directly from Oxford and Cambridge would, he wrote, select

> the gentleman who . . . wrote articles in the Reviews to show the impracticability of steam navigation across the Atlantic, and . . . [would exclude] those who accomplished the feat. [It would give precedence] for the Poor Law Service to a gentleman who could tell me the names of Actaeon's hounds, but who could not tell me the names of the chief statutes to be dealt with, and whose education had grounded him neither in the older principles of public policy nor in law or political economy applicable to them, and . . . [they] would have excluded a candidate who was pre-eminent in . . . practical administrative reform, although he had never taken an academic degree.[26]

A hundred and thirty years later Clive Ponting (the Ministry of Defence official who achieved notoriety for 'leaking' the facts about the sinking of the *Admiral Belgrano* in the Falklands War to an opposition MP in 1984) was speaking for a whole generation of modern critics when he made exactly the same point:

> The [Higher] Civil Service emerges as highly skilled in writing elegant English designed to conceal problems. It has, however, very little capability to manage complex problems, plan strategically (even if Ministers wanted to) or develop coherent integrated policies.[27]

This presented a problem for Harold Wilson's project of state-led economic modernisation in the 1960s, not to mention the Labour left's project of state-led transition to socialism in the 1970s, which was what generated the bombardment of criticism of that period and led to the Fulton Report and other proposals for reform. It presented a different problem for Margaret Thatcher's neoliberal project of economic modernisation via the market. She and her monetarist colleagues were determined to reduce the role of the state in the economy. They saw the higher civil service as incompetent at economic management, and the state as inherently inefficient in relation to productive activity. This entailed some reduction of the size and power of the civil service, including its higher echelons. But the Thatcherites also saw the civil service and its trade unions as a huge vested interest, defending some unjustified privileges and accustomed to quite excessive deference to its policy views on the part of successive governments in the past. They therefore embarked on a series of confrontations with the civil service. In 1981 the new government decided to end the system of pay awards based on keeping civil service salaries comparable with those of notionally equivalent private sector jobs. This led to a civil service strike which the government easily won. Then it abolished the Civil Service Department and in effect dismissed its Permanent Secretary, who was, formally speaking, the Head of the Civil Service. In 1984 it banned trade unions from the Government Communications Headquarters (GCHQ) at Cheltenham. And Thatcher used her powers of approval of senior appointments within the service energetically to promote activist officials who would pursue Thatcherite policies with conviction and not dilute or obstruct them.

Opinion is still uncertain as to the effects of the Thatcher government's encounters with the civil service, but on the whole it seems that the bark was worse than the bite. The government clearly wanted the service to become cheaper and more businesslike; in the view of one ex-civil servant, however, it did not get very far in this direction:

> The fundamental institutions of Whitehall have survived the Thatcher government intact. Although there has been a good deal of rhetoric about changing the culture of Whitehall, in practice little has been achieved . . . The Civil Service is certainly smaller but many of the cuts have been made by cosmetic changes and the bulk have fallen outside Whitehall and away from the elite at the top . . . There is no evidence that efficiency has been improved. Half the reductions recommended by the Rayner efficiency drive have never been implemented and Whitehall has absorbed and neutered the attempt to change the culture and make it more 'managerial'.[28]

It is probably significant that Thatcher did not follow the advice of her former adviser, Sir John Hoskyns, to abolish the career higher civil service and open up a third or more of the most senior posts to politically appointed outsiders.[29] It is not clear that Thatcher wanted any such radical opening up of the service to other influences, rather than simply to ensure that it would facilitate and not obstruct a programme of reform that was intended, in any case, to give the initiative to the market, not the state.

The 'Establishment'

In the late 1950s exasperation at the immobility and complacency of the senior levels of every sector of British society inspired Henry Fairlie to coin the expression 'the establishment'. Troubled by the seeming aptness of this label, pluralist writers subsequently devoted a lot of energy to the problem of whether there was a 'ruling elite' which governed or controlled Britain. The question was supposed to be whether they shared, and conspired to achieve, a common aim distinct from that of the rest of society, and if so, whether the evidence showed that their aims prevailed. If this could not be shown, it was argued, the term 'establishment' was no more than a pejorative word to denote those who merely happened to occupy the top places in the social, political and economic hierarchies of which any society is composed.[30] The evidence, they found, did not show the existence of a conspiracy to achieve a separate aim, and hence it followed that the 'elites' did not rule the country independently of the popular will. Yet the term stuck: it denoted something real. The problem needed to be formulated differently: what was the distinctive feature of the relation between the state apparatus and 'civil society' in Britain, which people intuitively acknowledged by persisting in the use of the expression 'the establishment'?

The question is, how many of the occupants of the top levels of non-state hierarchies have come from the same social class, have had the same socialisation, and are integrated in the same social, economic and political milieu as the occupants of the top ranks of the state hierarchy? What the term 'the establishment' suggests is that in Britain, state and non-state elites are particularly closely integrated in all three dimensions.

The evidence is fragmentary (and it is interesting to speculate why no comprehensive study based on direct observation has appeared). There are studies of the social backgrounds of particular 'elites', mostly relying on education as an indicator of social origin. Given that the cost of sending a boy (much more rarely a girl) to a public school has generally been equivalent to nearly half the average annual income of a manual worker, that the governors of public schools are drawn

Table 13.4   Social background of state and non-state elites

	% attended public school
Conservative Cabinet 1987[1]	62
Conservative junior ministers 1982[2]	88
Conservative MPs 1983[3]	70
Labour Cabinet 1979[2]	21
Labour junior ministers 1979[2]	21
Labour MPs 1983[3]	14
Higher civil servants 1976[4]	69
Senior army officers 1981[5]	80
Judges (High Court and Court of Appeal) 1971[6]	80
Ambassadors 1980[7]	70
Church of England Bishops 1971[2]	67
Directors of Big Five Banks 1980[2]	72
Chairmen of leading companies 1971[8]	74
Directors of leading industrial companies 1970–71[9]	66
Directors of leading financial companies 1970–71[9]	80
Professors, etc. in England and Wales 1967[2]	49

Sources:
1 *Times Guide to the House of Commons* 1987.
2 S. Fothergill and J. Vincent, *The State of the Nation*, Pluto, London, 1985.
3 D. Butler and D. Kavanagh, *The British General Election of 1983*, Macmillan, London 1984.
4 (Permanent and Deputy Secretaries) *Who's Who*, 1981.
5 (50 most senior generals) *Whitaker's Almanac* and *Who's Who*, 1981.
6 I. Reid, *Social Class Differences in Britain*, Open Books, London, 1977, p. 184.
7 Tessa Blackstone, BBC programme on the public schools, 1 December 1981.
8 J. Stanworth and A. Giddens, *Elites and Power in British Society*, p.90.
9 R. Whitley in ibid., p. 70.

more or less exclusively from the higher reaches of the propertied classes, and that only some 5 per cent of the population attend such schools, the indicator is not inappropriate. What Table 13.4 shows is that the majority of both the state and the non-state elite are drawn from the same extremely limited social stratum.

Although the 'density' of privilege is greater in some sectors than others, it does not correspond to the state/non-state distinction. There is rather a functional division; as more weight is given to intellectual or practical achievement, the more entrants from state schools are accepted. But nowhere do the latter predominate. Moreover, public-school background is a very conservative measure. An additional proportion of both state and non-state elites have been educated privately (e.g., by private tuition or at profit-making, fee-paying schools); while on the other hand, the great majority of recruits to the elite from state schools are also from 'middle-class' backgrounds.[31]

The overall result is that the class background of the state and non-state elites is extremely homogeneous and extremely narrow.

This is reinforced by the socialisation process of public school and university. Two points only need be made. First, the essentially closed nature of the public school world both creates social distance between its ᴏᴄᴄᴜpants and the rest of society, and creates an alternative society whose rules are familiar and to which all who have been educated to understand them automatically belong. Anthony Sampson's summary is hard to improve on:

> The Victorians used the public school to remove the sons of tradesmen from the taint of trade; and it is still often true, as G.K. Chesterton put it, that 'the public schools are not for the sons of gentlemen, they're for the fathers of gentlemen'. Most of the boarding schools were set up in the railway age, far from the main centres of population, so that the boys spend eight months a year for five years in the exclusive company of other boys; sometimes this weaning starts at preparatory (prep) schools at the age of seven . . . It was by uprooting boys from their parents and forging them into a tough society that imperial leaders were created; a boy could pass from Eton to the Guards to Oxford to the Middle Temple and still remain in the same male world of leather armchairs, teak tables and nicknames. They never needed to deal closely with other kinds of people, and some still do not.[32]

Second, the smallness of the alternative world of the privately educated deserves emphasis. In 1967, for example, there were about 10,000 pupils aged 17 or over in the private sector schools. Of these, about 1,500 will have gone on to Oxford or Cambridge, forming about 25–30 per cent of all entrants. Although they will have performed less well there than their state-school contemporaries, their public-school background will have helped those who did reasonably well to more than hold their own in the subsequent competition for jobs.[33] And within this cohort the influence of a few particularly exclusive public schools would continue to be felt in the later promotion process. In a famous 1959 study of the financial establishment, Upton and Wilson demonstrated the remarkable dominance of a mere six schools and two universities. Theirs was an extreme case, both in its focus (the City) and its timing (at the height of the Macmillan era), but as figures for 1971 (included in Table 13.5) show, a diminution of the influence of these schools in this sector seems to have been compensated for by an increase in the influence of Oxford and Cambridge.

What such data indicate is that the experience of schooling and university education is highly focused, and transcends the occupational divisions between those who have shared it, as well as the division between those in the state and non-state sectors.*

Table 13.5   The influence of six schools and two universities

	% Eton		% Eton and 5 Other Schools		% Oxford and Cambridge	
	1959	1971	1951	1971	1959	1971
All government ministers*	32.4	20.0	50.0	40.0	71	70
The 54 most senior civil servants	4.1	3.4	19.2	22.7	68	80
Directors of the Bank of England	33.3	5.5	66.6	38.9	50	61
Directors of the 'Big Five' banks	29.7	26.9	48.9	46.9	50	52
Directors of 14 major merchant banks and discount houses	32.7	23.7	43.0	36.5	35	42
Directors of 8 major insurance companies	30.7	27.3	47.0	39.8	38	39

* Cabinet and non-cabinet ministers of the Macmillan and Heath governments.

Source: Upton and Wilson, 'The Social Background and Connection of Top Decision Makers', *The Manchester School* 27/1, January 1959, pp. 30–51; R. Whitley, 'The City and Industry', in Stanworth and Giddens, *Elites and Power in British Society*, p. 70; *Dod's Parliamentary Companion* 1971; *Who's Who* 1971.

The internal relations of this world are maintained in later life by a variety of devices, such as the 'old boys' associations (Eton's had 12,000 members in 1971), interlocking directorships, membership of London clubs, intermarriage and the honours system.[34] It is no longer true to say, as Nairn did of the early nineteenth century, that the ruling class *is* the state. The state has outgrown the ruling class; the working and middle classes are not excluded from the state apparatus, but their access is progressively attenuated at each step up its hierarchy, while the operation of the 'establishment' guarantees an exceptional degree of harmony between the personnel at the top of the state apparatus and the representatives of capital, as well as of the media and other organs of class power.

This distinctive feature of the British state may well have been the

* 'Those who govern it [the British Civil Service] belong, effectively, to the same class that rules the House of Commons. Largely, they go to the same schools and universities; after admission to the same clubs. Their ideas, or rather, the assumptions upon which their ideas rest, are the same as those of the men who own the instruments of production in our society. Their success, as a Civil Service, has been mainly built upon that fact' (Harold Laski, *Parliamentary Government in England*, Allen and Unwin, London 1938, p. 316). If Laski had lived to prepare a new edition of this book in 1988 he would have had to make remarkably few changes in this argument.

root cause of one of the most celebrated features of the theoretical debate between Miliband and Poulantzas.[35] Miliband laid heavy emphasis on the bourgeois social origin and social milieu of the higher civil service, leaving himself open to the interpretation that he thought that this was the reason why the state was not neutral. Poulantzas declared that the state's bourgeois character was given by its 'objective' function in any capitalist society and that, on the contrary, 'the capitalist state best serves the interest of the capitalist class only when the members of this class do not participate directly in the state apparatus, that is to say when the *ruling class* is not the *politically governing class'*.[36]

But if Miliband was too much influenced by the British experience, Poulantzas did not take it sufficiently into account. Poulantzas's generalisation seems farfetched in relation to Britain, while Miliband's stress on the ties between the state bureaucracy and the capitalist class probably reflects unduly the British, rather than, for example, the continental experience. It is not that the connections he presents do not exist elsewhere. What is distinctive about the British situation is the directness and informality of the links, unmediated by, for example, the development of the distinctive bureaucratic profession-alism and esprit de corps characteristic of the French or German state bureaucracy. As Armstrong has noted, in Britain, in contrast with the continental experience,

> what stands out in this initial confrontation of the recruit with his new career was the continuity, the lack of traumatic new experiences . . . bucolic style, aristocratic attitude, corporate loyalty combined with easy intercourse with the general elite – all reinforced preservice socialisation patterns instead of interrupting them, as did the ENA [the Ecole Nationale d'Administration in France] and even the *Referendar* stage [in Germany]. For administrative recruits from lower-middle-class backgrounds, adjustment to the service was no doubt difficult, although their Oxbridge college experience had provided an introduction.[37]

And Griffith made the same point forcibly when comparing the British and continental judiciaries. He showed that however much the 'objective' relationship between these branches of the state apparatus and capital might be considered the same in, say, Britain and France, significant differences flow from the uniquely homogeneous 'class situation' (i.e., class origins, class milieu and class identification) of the judicial branch of the British state. In Griffith's words:

> The protection of the public interest in the preservation of a stable society is how judges see their role. The judges define the public interest, inevitably,

from the viewpoint of their own class. And the public interest, so defined, is by a natural, not an artificial, coincidence, the interest of others in authority, whether in government, in the city or in the church. It includes the maintenance of order, the protection of private property, the promotion of certain general economic aims, the containment of the trade union movement, and the continuance of governments which conduct their business largely in private and on the advice of other members of . . . the governing group.[38]

The Circumscription of Democracy

An elective element in parliament goes back to the thirteenth century. In the nineteenth century new voters were admitted to elections for MPs, and at the same time the representative principle was applied to one new state activity after another at the local level. But this was not democracy; it was a method of including the urban middle classes in the process of managing the state.

The enfranchisement of male workers after 1867, however, altered the significance of elections. It promised to give power to the demos. From then on, the tendency in local administration increasingly ran the other way. By 1940, locally elected bodies which had been established to operate schools, hospitals, poor-relief and gas and electricity supplies had all been replaced by non-elected agencies, and still further functions had been removed from the general-purpose elected local councils. Parliament also ceased to be the effective determinant of policy that it had been in the 1850s. This change was brought about by the organisation of mass parties and the imposition of discipline on MPs, and reinforced by changes in parliamentary procedure. Parliament gradually ceased in practice to belong to the 'efficient' part of the constitution. The people never in fact became 'sovereign'; they remained 'subjects'. In Britain the term 'citizen' never acquired its continental connotation of equality and political efficacy. The state remained largely non-elective, unrepresentative, unaccountable and secret.

In the first place, the elective principle was entirely confined to the House of Commons and local government. There were, and are, no elections for the Upper House of parliament, or for judges, magistrates, public utility commissioners or school boards, as there are in the USA, nor is there any popular 'initiative' as there is in Switzerland. No popular voice is heard in the selection of the board of any nationalised industry, the board of governors of the BBC or the Independent Television Authority, or of any Regional or District Health Authority, the Arts Council, the University Grants Commission, the Science Research Council, or any other of the vast penumbra of 'Quangos' (Quasi-Non-Governmental Organisations) which surround the core of the British state.

The *appointment* of such 'representatives' is not peculiar to Britain in its principle, but it is in its extent, and in the unmediated way in which it works. Numerous and powerful branches of the state apparatus have, at their head, people who are co-opted or appointed by secret processes which are informal and, it appears, subjective and arbitrary. The operative criteria of suitability and 'soundness' reflect the social and political standpoint of the co-opters or appointers as well as their professional task as state officials.* The effect is to give an appearance of representativeness – in the usual sense of reflecting the characteristics of society at large – to much of the state apparatus while actually ensuring that the real balance of experience, interests and opinions present in the community is *not* represented there. What are well represented are the characteristics and attitudes of the professional and propertied class.[39]

The secret, informal and subjective process of co-option/appointment also extends in Britain to the judiciary. Not only is 'the reliance on a very small specialist Bar for judicial candidates . . . unparalleled in any other country',[40] but those appointed are neither professionally vetted by their peers (as happens in the USA) nor given professional training as judges (as they are in most European countries). British judicial conservatism is not unconnected with this fact. Even the country's 18,000 lay magistrates are appointed, nominally by the (non-elected) Lord Chancellor, in reality by his civil servants, on the recommendations of local committees of existing magistrates – with the result that the

---

* The Treasury and the Lord Chancellor's Office, and no doubt other departments, maintain lists of potential appointees whose names and records are supplied to them from their informal contacts throughout the country. The flavour of this process as it works in relation to the quasi-judicial branch of the state which applies and interprets administrative law is conveyed (though somewhat uncritically) by R.E. Wraith and P.G. Hutchesson in their book *Administrative Tribunals* (Allen and Unwin, London 1973) Chapter 4, and in W.E. Cavenagh and D. Newton, 'Administrative Tribunals: How People Become Members', *Public Administration 49*, Summer 1971, pp. 197–218. In this sphere, the ideology in terms of which establishment criteria of 'soundness' are expressed is judicial: for example, people were excluded from becoming members of the Rent Tribunal on the basis of such comments as 'might be a tenant's man', 'inclined to be true blue', 'anti-authority?: not objective', 'no standing', 'profession would resent' (ibid., p. 201). Obviously each branch of the state has an appropriate ideological repertoire of this kind – administrative, political, social, aesthetic, etc. – to which the responsible officials must be attuned. For some light relief the reader is recommended to consult Joe Haines's excellent account of his experience as Harold Wilson's Press Secretary from 1969 to 1976, when he gained some interesting insights into the appointment/co-option process as it operated in relation to the honours system: see *The Politics of Power*, Cape, London 1977, pp. 146–9.

magistracy is only slightly less unrepresentative of the population it regulates and disciplines than are the judges (see Table 13.2 above).*

Secondly, there is virtually no accountability in any part of the state. One of the six Chartist demands of the 1830s and 1840s was for annual elections; yet significantly this is the only one that was not subsequently accepted, as it reflected the 'delegate' principle of democracy advocated by French radicals, and implied a degree of answerability to the electors. 'Representative' government was not, and was not intended to be, self-government, even when the franchise was widened to produce 'representative democracy'. As for the executive, the only mechanisms of accountability were Parliamentary Questions, the limited and ex post facto enquiries of the Estimates and Expenditure Committees, and certain other Select Committees whose efficacy is discussed in the next section. In 1967 the Parliamentary Commissioner for Administration (the Ombudsman) was appointed to investigate complaints of maladministration by the civil service: as will be seen in Chapter 15, this institution was, if not quite stillborn, born severely handicapped.

The case of the police is interesting here. The police used to be thought responsible to the 'watch' or police committee of their local authority (or to the Home Secretary, in the case of the London Metropolitan Police), but they were judicially held, in fact, not to be, and the 1964 Police Act specifically laid it down that they were not. According to the courts, they are responsible to 'the law', which in the circumstances means that chief constables have complete discretion in deciding how to enforce the law.[41] After the Brixton riots in the summer of 1981 the accumulating evidence of racial prejudice and aggression on the part of the metropolitan Police, in particular, became so strong that the issue of popular influence or control over policing policy came to the fore, and the credibility of police investigation of complaints against themselves, already forfeited among blacks, began to evaporate among the rest of the public. The Police Federation itself was finally forced to abandon its opposition to independent investigation of complaints (though it remained opposed to a restoration of local authorities' powers over policing policy). The difficulty was that if independent oversight of police conduct was not informed by the same values that inspired the repressive tasks that had increasingly been assigned to the police, it could soon give rise to a

---

* Cavenagh and Newton's study of the similarly appointed administrative judiciary (the 15,000 or so members of Britain's administrative tribunals) in two systems of tribunals in the West Midlands found that they were predominantly male (85 per cent), elderly (only 16 per cent were under 45) and Conservative (40 per cent, or two-thirds of those who declared a political orientation) ('The Membership of Two Administrative Tribunals', *Public Administration* 48, Winter 1970, pp. 449–68).

policing crisis. Eventually an independent Police Complaints Authority had to be conceded (in the Police and Criminal Evidence Act of 1986). In May 1988 the PCA reported that police officers were maintaining a 'shameful silence' to protect violent colleagues complained of to the Authority. It also emerged that the police were bringing charges against complainants to discourage people from complaining.[42]

Thirdly, any kind of popular accountability depends on information and popular understanding, and the British state is also protected from accountability by exceptionally high levels of secrecy. Secrecy is a general feature of states: it is necessary to their existence as organisations separate from civil society and effectively controlling and managing it. But secrecy conflicts with their need for popular consent, and a wide spectrum of different practices exists. At one end is Sweden, where since 1766 all citizens have had a constitutional right of access – more or less effective in practice – to all state documents other than those concerning security; and the USA, with its Freedom of Information Acts. At the other end is Britain, where not only is there no general public right to information, there are no particular individual rights enforceable through any court either. The doctrine of 'Crown Privilege' is used to protect the government and civil service from being obliged to answer any questions or produce any documents they do not wish to. All information (and disinformation) reaching the public from the state is that which the state decides to release and the evidence is that what is released excludes what would enable the public to exercise any effective control over the policy-making process.

This secrecy is justified by the doctrine that ministers are responsible for policy, and that public knowledge of how they make policy, including the information and advice tendered by civil servants, would undermine their responsibility on which the constitution rests. This justification is spurious, because the responsibility of ministers themselves cannot be enforced unless their party in the House of Commons rejects them, which hardly ever happens; and in any case the doctrine of responsibility is lifted by Prime Ministers from time to time for party purposes, without any apparent constitutional ill-effects. Moreover, ministers themselves are sometimes deliberately deprived of information by civil servants; and – the ultimate 'Catch-22' – the fact that the information on which policy is based is kept secret, makes criticism of it – let alone the enforcement of 'responsibility' by any kind of accountability – difficult.

The British obsession with secrecy is relatively modern. Before workers got the vote and could buy daily papers, and while British economic and military pre-eminence was still unchallenged, Victorian politicians and civil servants do not seem to have felt the need to be very secretive.[43] Concern with secrecy developed in the 1870s. It was integral to the class solidarity on which the new state apparatus rested, and was increasingly instilled by precept and practice from the moment a civil servant was appointed or a politician took office. The result was that secrecy eventually became a passion, which stands out strikingly in official memoirs and in the evidence of civil servants to commissions of enquiry.[44]

This passion was, however, not relied upon absolutely. It was reinforced by the Official Secrets acts. The first of these Acts was passed in 1911 in an atmosphere of German spying, and was loosely worded to make the 'unauthorised' release of any official secret, or its unauthorised receipt, a crime.[45] A former director of MI5, when asked what was an official secret, could truthfully reply: 'It is an official secret if it is in an official file'.[46] Under the acts a steady trickle of prosecutions of civil servants, ex-civil servants, and members of the public (mainly journalists) has occurred, concerning information usually (though not always) related to security but not in fact jeopardising it. The classic examples of this occurred under the Thatcher government, especially the Tisdall and Ponting prosecutions (see p. 120 above), in neither of which the government even claimed that national security was jeopardised. The number of prosecutions under the acts rose sharply as the government tried to discipline civil servants into stopping 'leaking' its neo-conservative plans (for instance, for the welfare state). The issue culminated in the long vendetta pursued by the government in the courts to prevent the publication of, or even reporting about, Peter Wright's book *Spycatcher*, the memoirs of a secret service officer. Since the book was a worldwide bestseller and could be freely imported into Britain (though not sold there) the government's aim – in which it had considerable success – was actually to secure court judgements limiting the freedom of the media to report on issues which the state decided should not be reported on.

The effect of this use of the Official Secrets Act is to make it risky for anyone but a senior official or politician to give information, because only senior officials and politicians can presumably 'authorise' its release. It also greatly reduces the chances of journalists disclosing information that the public in a democracy might well think itself entitled to know. For example, although government policy is largely determined by subcommittees of the cabinet, it is a closely-guarded secret how many cabinet committees there are, who sits on them and what they are considering.[47] In the British version of 'democracy' not even the core structures and processes of government are revealed to the electorate.*

---

* On the result of attempts to reduce secrecy see Chapter 14, pp. 284–7.

Another way in which accountability is avoided is through mystification, of which a chief form is archaism. The original archaism is the absence of a written constitution itself, which helps to preserve all the others. It would at least be harder to perpetuate the mockery of democracy just alluded to if the constitution were written. At the very least some of the quaint titles behind which the vulgar business of the state is often hidden could hardly be solemnly incorporated into a written document: for instance, the Treasurer of the Queen's Household, who is actually the government's deputy chief whip, or the Master of the Rolls, who in 1981 was the embarrassingly right-wing octogenarian president of the civil Court of Appeal.

An 'unwritten constitution' also affords scope for resistance to reform, since any unwelcome reform can be pronounced 'unconstitutional'. Making Labour Party MPs accountable to their party for pursuing its policies in parliament can be denounced as unconstitutional; making the police responsible to elected local authorities is termed unconstitutional (though Victorian chief constables do not seem to have thought it unconstitutional when their employers were Conservatives or Liberals);[48] the withholding of labour by trade unions to achieve political purposes is attacked as unconstitutional, although the withholding of investment or credit by companies or banks (as in 1964 and 1976, for example) is not. The fact that there is no written constitution allows anyone who is credited with some authority to say what it is – and such authorities concur in saying that what it excludes are actions tending towards a radical assault on private property.

After the unwritten constitution the chief fount of archaism is the monarchy. The 'convenient fiction' that the Queen rules allows the government to hide behind the 'Royal Prerogative' in refusing to give details about a large range of its actions – concerning the civil service, for example, and the conduct of foreign relations – which would hardly be tolerated if the refusal were explained as an exercise of 'Prime Minister's prerogative'. Moreover, the Royal Family and the court, financed out of public revenues on a scale unmatched by other 'constitutional monarchies', legitimate several of the more archaic elements in the culture of the British capitalist class (of which the highly publicised upbringing and eventual marriage of Prince Charles provided a paradigm): the public schools, expensive leisure activities, the empire, the ancient universities, the armed forces, the honours system and the Anglican Church.*

---

* As Nairn also pointed out, the popularity of the monarchy owes little to its antiquity: Queen Victoria was unpopular throughout most of her reign, and her predecessor still more so. Republicanism was then relatively widespread and respectable. The monarchy's modern popularity dates from the age of empire, with which it is

BRISTOL POLYTECHNIC
ST. MATTHIAS LIBRARY
FISHPONDS

Next to the monarchy the legal system is the most elaborately archaic branch of the state, helping to protect a judiciary exceptionally united in its 'tenderness towards private property and dislike of trade unions, strong adherence to the maintenance of order, distaste for minority opinions, demonstrations and protests, indifference to the promotion of better race relations, support of governmental secrecy, concern for the preservation of the moral and social behaviour to which it is accustomed, and the rest'.[49] It is hard to imagine that the British judiciary would have remained so singularly free from serious criticism were it not for the archaic and mystifying practices in which the higher courts are saturated.* Even the structure of the court system is obscure. While most British people can probably give at least a rough account of the parliamentary and cabinet system, it is doubtful if more than a tiny minority could even outline the court system, which has retained its Dickensian nomenclature and antique structure and practices to an extent that is certainly unmatched, and would probably not be tolerated, in any other branch of the state.[†]

Mystification through archaism extends also into the sphere of parliamentary politics, if less glaringly perhaps; here, however, where press attention is closer, a different form of mystification is more important – media collusion with constitutional myth. The basis of this is laid by the general absence of political education in the schools, compared with the practice of more democratic states, compounded by the uncritical approach of so many academic treatments of British politics, and sealed by the intimate dependence of parliamentary journalists on 'sources' within the leaderships of the parties. A myth of parliamentary significance is maintained, even if few parliamentary press correspondents believe in it.[‡]

---

strongly identified, and is part of the general imperial legacy 'transmitted in a thousand ways through the capillary vessels of popular culture' (T. Nairn, 'The House of Windsor', *New Left Review* 127, 1981, p. 100: a choice example of Nairn's polemical style).

* As with secrecy, however, coercion supplements mystification: anyone attempting to do work on the judicial system that is at all critical is liable to prompt judicial repression, as several researchers have found. 'The common law crime of contempt of court – insofar as anyone knows what it is – is a huge, cloudy barrier to the investigation of . . .the justice system' (D. Leigh, *The Frontiers of Secrecy*, Junction Books, London 1980, p. 71; see also pp. 71–8).

[†] Readers may ask themselves if they can distinguish between the functions of the following, and if not, whether it is sensible and appropriate that this should be so: the House of Lords, the House of Lords as a supreme court, the Judicial Committee of the Privy Council, the Court of Appeal, and the Queen's Bench division of the High Court.

[‡] The *Independent*, a daily newspaper founded in 1986, declined to become part of the parliamentary lobby system on the grounds that it compromised journalistic freedom.

Parliament

Between the mid-1840s and the passage of the second Reform Bill of 1867 a significant minority of urban constituencies had electorates that were no longer wholly under the personal influence of a large landowner or employer. These constituencies tended to return independent, and sometimes 'radical' MPs, who were also not dependent on a party 'ticket' either.[50] As a result votes in the House of Commons became unpredictable and governments were made and unmade there, so that in 1867 Bagehot quite reasonably assigned parliament to the 'efficient' part of the constitution. In that year, however, the extension of the franchise meant that it was no longer a minority, but a majority of constituencies that were now too large to be managed by a limited number of political magnates. Mass party organisations were formed, and candidates elected with their support soon became dependent on them, as electors increasingly voted for the party rather than the man. As a result, the government could increasingly rely on being able to discipline its MPs.

Parliament thus ceased to be a forum where governments were made or defeated: that function gradually passed – even if in a qualified and 'managed' fashion – to the electorate. Governments also assumed increasing powers over parliament, partly to combat obstruction by the Irish Nationalist MPs elected from the 1870s onwards, and partly to ensure the passage of the growing volume of government business. The parliamentary timetable passed under government control. The power of 'guillotine' was adopted to terminate debates on legislation. The use of 'framework' legislation, leaving important areas of subordinate legislation to be enacted, in reality, by senior civil servants, with little effective parliamentary scrutiny, became more common. The changes were gradual; like so much else, they only began to be fully apparent after the end of the First World War.

After 1906 the parliamentary parties themselves also grew more homogeneous. As the Conservatives increasingly absorbed the right wing of the Liberals, and Labour the left wing, there was less room for inter-party agreement, and so less scope for the sort of exchanges, in or outside parliament, that had been possible when both the leading parties had primarily represented (in different combinations) the same alliance of propertied classes. Edwardian politicians – Conservative and Liberal, that is – grew accustomed to deplore the decline of 'rational discussion' in parliamentary debates, and its replacement by increasingly heated exchanges of irreconcilable viewpoints;[51] though as Middlemas notes, these exchanges themselves tended to become more and more stereotyped as the parliamentary Labour Party was gradually integrated into the existing state. By contrast, the extra-parliamentary organisations of the parties were explicitly defined as lying outside the state. The reason for seeking to integrate the Labour leadership into the state was, after all, to separate it from the radical wing of the labour movement in the country. So the language of the Parliamentary Labour Party also became increasingly ritualistic, often only seeming to express fundamental class differences. At the same time there was a growing use by governments of mass communications to manage public opinion, which was increasingly closely monitored by opinion polls.

Parliament was thus placed in a paradoxical position. On the one hand it gradually ceased to be the real scene of decision-making. Even the function of representing public opinion was being usurped by opinion polls and by the government's exploitation of the mass media. On the other hand, parliament remained the focus of national political life. The fact that it was elected was the fundamental fact, giving the illusion of self-determination by the electors, legitimating their actual non-participation in government and screening out the reality of class conflict and inequality.* It is impossible to account otherwise for the way in which textbooks and the media painstakingly reproduce the myth of parliamentary power when it is so clearly mythical. This effort has some effect. Middlemas notes that in 1977, '49 per cent of [a] sample of secondary school leavers believed that the House of Commons made all important decisions about the running of the country'.[52] But in spite of these efforts the myth was increasingly undermined.

This was partly due to the incapacity of governments of either party in the 1960s and 1970s to fulfil their economic promises, leading to a general scepticism about the efficacy of parliamentary politics as a whole. The imposition of 'incomes' policies in the sixties and seventies, followed by the monetarist policies of the Thatcher government after 1979, also made it clear that the political and economic spheres are by no means separate. During the period of corporatism the close relations between governments and the CBI and TUC also cast doubt

---

* 'Parliament, elected every four or five years as the sovereign expression of popular will, reflects the fictive unity of the nation back to the masses as if it were their own self-government. The economic divisions within the 'citizenry' are masked by the juridical parity between exploiters and exploited, and with them the complete *separation* and *non-participation* of the masses in the work of parliament. This separation is then constantly presented and represented to the masses as the ultimate incarnation of liberty' (P. Anderson, 'The Antinomies of Antonio Gramsci', *New Left Review* 100, 1976–77, p. 28).

on the idea that parliament had a monopoly of the representative function. Moreover most people now followed political events primarily on television, which was excluded from parliament.* The central institution of liberal–democratic politics was thus being marginalised and ignored at the same time as the need for popular consent to government was becoming more acute.

In addition, by 1979 the House of Commons had become almost as unrepresentative of the population at large (in terms of social background) as it had been before 1900. The Labour Party had initially returned a large contingent of MPs from working-class backgrounds – an average of 72 per cent of all Labour MPs between 1918 and 1935.[53] By 1945, however, the proportion of manual workers among Labour MPs was only just over 25 per cent (107 out of 400) and by October 1974 the proportion was less than 12 per cent (38 out of 319), while the Conservatives throughout the whole post-war period never had more than one ex-worker in Parliament.[54] By 1974 the proportion of manual workers in the population as a whole was about 54 per cent; in the House of Commons it was 6.3 per cent.[55] The House of Commons had thus largely reverted to being a club of more or less exclusively middle- and upper-middle-class career politicians, as it had been before the advent of the Labour Party. (The average MP served more than ten years between 1945 and 1974, compared with 6.3 years between 1918 and 1951, and two-thirds of all MPs in the post-war period served more than 10 years.)[56] But this presented a problem because the working class was not the inarticulate and deferential mass that Bagehot had allowed himself to imagine.† That this House of Commons 'expressed the mind of the English people' (as Bagehot put it) was to say the least not self-evident.

This was the context within which a group of academics and officers of the two Houses of Parliament took an initiative to promote parliamentary reform through a Study of Parliament Group. Their

---

* The House of Commons twice rejected the televising of its proceedings (in 1978 and 1981) but finally voted in favour of it in 1987. The main ground of opposition seems to have been a fear that a discussion of 'serious issues' would be subordinated to playing to the gallery, and that television editors would be able to 'interpret' the proceedings by the way they edited what appeared on television screens. The difference between being interpreted by television editors and parliamentary press correspondents is that a) the latter interpret parliamentary proceedings in the light of their personal relationships with MPs – i.e., 'responsibly'; and b) the popular press rarely reports debates anyway.

† 'The working classes contribute almost nothing to our corporate public opinion, and therefore, the fact of their want of influence in Parliament does not impair the coincidence of Parliament with public opinion' (W. Bagehot, The English Constitution, Collins–Fontana, London 1963, p. 176).

objective was to restore to the House of Commons some of the
political centrality it had enjoyed before the age of mass parties. Most
of the subsequent literature on parliament is directly or indirectly the
product of this initiative. At its best, it presents clearly, judiciously and
meticulously the facts about parliament's negligible powers of either
legislation or detailed control of the executive, and its amateur
knowledge of, unsystematic approach to, and prevailing lack of interest
in, the detailed scrutiny of public expenditure and administration.

There is no point in rehearsing all the details so conscientiously and
clearly established by the specialists. In summary, 'the House of
Commons spends at least half its time talking about legislation'; but
'today's conventional wisdom is that . . . Parliament has relinquished
any capacity for legislative initiative it may once have possessed to the
executive' and 'in this instance conventional wisdom does accord
with the facts of life'.[57] Legislation is *government* inspired (i,e,, largely
civil service inspired); and, while it may be improved by the necessity
of undergoing scrutiny in parliament, it is seldom significantly modified
there – and then only when the government is at odds with its own
backbenchers (as for example in 1969, when the Labour government
was obliged to abandon its proposed bill to outlaw unofficial strikes,
and another bill to reform the House of Lords).

The non-specialist Standing Committees of MPs to which bills are
referred for detailed discussion are as much controlled by the
government as is the House of Commons at large. Proceedings in these
committees are frequently of a ritual nature.[58] The Minister in charge
of the bill is not infrequently persuaded to reconsider some detail, but
rarely to change his mind on any fundamental element in it. As for
private members' bills, most of them fail to become law. Of the 97
such bills enacted between 1970 and 1979 (12 per cent of all private
members' bills introduced), most were on narrow and non-controversial
questions.[59] The only controversial private members' bills for which
governments usually agree to provide sufficient time are those on
which their own parliamentary party is divided, typically questions of
public morality (Mr David Alton's 1988 bill to limit abortions to within
18 weeks of conception is a good example). All in all, the legislative
function of parliament has become largely mythical, even though it
remains ideologically central.

As for the 'power of the purse', the famous historical basis of the power
of Parliament, 'in the practical sense . . . the House has no power of the
purse' and neither debates the government's spending proposals nor shows
any serious interest in controlling spending after it is authorised.[60] Uniquely among European parliaments, the House of Commons does not discuss
tax proposals and spending proposals together; the budget is exclusively

concerned with revenue so that discussion of it is concerned only with means, rather than their relation to ends. The review of *past* spending, carried out by the Public Accounts Committee on the basis of examinations of the accounts by a large staff of accountants, is relatively haphazard, arouses little interest, and is devoid of any sanctions.

The third general function of parliament, the enforcement of 'ministerial responsibility', is equally empty. Parliamentary Questions have become a lottery. On average, only some 20–22 questions are answered each day out of 63 put down for an oral reply (plus a further 160 per day calling only for written answers). Only those which are answered orally provide an opportunity for effective pressure on the government (by means of 'supplementary' questions, which cannot be quite so confidently turned away with well-prepared answers); and as the choice of which ones are answered is largely accidental, the real function of Question Time is to provide a chance for backbenchers to speak a few words in a relatively full House – in effect to foster the myth of parliament's importance, not its substance.

The main means of control of the executive, advocated by all reformers since the 1950s, have been specialised select committees. These were introduced gradually in the sixties and seventies, and in 1979 a comprehensive system of 14 committees (and three sub-committees) was established, each dealing with a specific area of administration, having powers to call both ministers and civil servants to give evidence, and an open mandate. The Thatcher government's commitment to the new system was intended to demonstrate its enthusiasm for parliamentary sovereignty, in contrast with the sharing of power with the unions (in particular) that had characterised the years of corporatism. However, its commitment proved fairly shallow. Johnson's judgement in 1984 seems conclusive:

there is nothing for which [the committee members'] vote is needed, nothing for them to decide other than what goes into their reports. Their operating procedure remains virtually unchanged: the cumbersome hit and miss process of oral questioning, supplemented by written evidence much of which may never be read. There remains no real link between the timetable and agenda of the House (including its standing committees) on the one hand, and the often leisurely progress of select committees on the other. The attention paid by the House to select committee reports remains cursory and there is little that committees can do if Ministers and departments decline to listen to them . . . they are not important factors in what any Government understands as the management of the House.[61]

Behind the apparent failure of parliament to play a determining role in either legislation or the enforcement of ministerial responsibility lies the elementary fact of majority party government. The operative principle is that elections place a party's leaders in office. Every attempt to enforce accountability when in office is liable to weaken the governing party's electoral prospects and is resisted. Most MPs accept this. They do not protest when ministers, or even civil servants, openly disregard the myth of ministerial accountability. For example, in 1975 Mr Wilson, as Prime Minister, refused to allow the Select Committee on Expenditure to question Mr Harold Lever, the minister responsible for the government's decision to give a £162.5 million grant to the Chrysler Corporation, on the grounds that the committee could only ask ministers questions about their departmental responsibilities, whereas Mr Lever was a 'minister without portfolio'. The Committee made no protest. Nor was there a protest when the Civil Service Department told the Select Committee on Procedure, in 1970, that it would not let the Committee study the process of formal consultation between government and outside bodies in formulating legislative proposals, adding that the committee in its ignorance ('no doubt because of incomplete information') wrongly believed that such consultations were more important than they really were.[62] Similarly, no one protested when, in 1966, Mr Callaghan, as Chancellor of the Exchequer, refused to agree to a free vote (i.e., without party discipline being enforced) on the details of the new decimal currency, because various interested concerns 'had already entered into commitments', and, Callaghan said, 'you can't flop around on an issue like this with a free vote' – i.e., on an issue already secretly determined by the Government.[63] Thatcher's equivocations in the Commons over the leaked letter of the Attorney General in the Westland Helicopters affair in 1986 were no more than a continuation of this tradition.

Given that those who know parliament best find its powers so feeble, how should we account for its centrality in British political life? Part of the answer is undoubtedly that the myth of its importance is useful. If fewer people believed that the laws carried a moral sanction, the cost of enforcing them could quickly become prohibitive; the Provisional IRA's campaign in Northern Ireland shows what can happen. 'Respect for the law' is a constant theme of the comment by editors and judges on militant actions by trade unionists or anyone else who finds particular laws inequitable. Part of the effort that goes into maintaining the myth of parliament can be attributed to anxiety about what would happen if more people were to make their support for the law conditional on its merits, rather than on the fact that parliament is supposed to have made it.

The myth is also constantly refreshed by the electoral process itself, which appears to place the determination of both law and administration in the hands of the electorate. At election times, the complex reality of political power – the interposition between the voter and policy-making of the independent power of MPs and the higher civil service, the Royal Prerogative, the management of news and opinion by the state and the media, law-making by non-elected judges, law-vetoing by the non-elected House of Lords, the extra-parliamentary power of the City, CBI or the IMF – is all dissolved, leaving in sharp focus only the image of the voters, arbiters of their own fates, as they decide how to cast their votes. And the myth draws strength from the fact that people know that even this largely fictive power is better than none.

There remains, however, the fact that governments in Britain are chosen from among MPs, and they depend, in office, not on parliament but on their own backbenchers, who in turn depend for reflection, in the long run (and to a greater or lesser degree, depending on how safe their seats are) on the government's performance; while they also aspire (in most cases) to become ministers too. Parliament is the forum or cockpit of this system of mutual support and recruitment; the electoral system makes it a link between the party leaderships and constituency opinion; and the 'lobby' system makes it the source of most journalists' day to day information and opinions about party politics. Under parliamentarism – i.e. under a system which confines the democratic principle to the periodic election of representatives to parliament, and then locates real power away from parliament in the hands of the executive – the House of Commons becomes, first and foremost, a club for those who constitute and understand this system, which those excluded from membership necessarily observe with fascination – since, after all, some of the members at least know what is going on. The quip that the Commons is 'the best club in London' might well be said to capture its central, not its incidental, role in British political life.

Notes

1 N. Poulantzas, *Political Power and Social Classes*, published in English by Verso, London 1969; R. Miliband, *The State in Capitalist Society*, Weidenfeld and Nicolson, London 1969.

2 N. Poulantzas, *State, Power, Socialism*, Verso, London 1978.

3 Especially his essay 'The Twilight of the British State' (Chapter 1 of Nairn's book *The Break-Up of Britain*, Verso, London 1977).

4 Nairn, p. 45.

5 But the materials for it have recently been assembled in a number of new studies, reviewed in a powerful article by Peter Gowan, 'The Origins of the Administrative Elite', *New Left Review* 162, March/April 1987, pp. 1–34. Nairn's thesis has been subjected to extensive criticism on general theoretical grounds; some of the criticism

is justified, though without (to my mind) destroying the main force of his hypotheses. See R. Johnson, 'Barrington Moore, Perry Anderson and English Social Development' in S. Hall et al., eds, *Culture, Media, Language*, Hutchinson, London 1980, pp. 48–70.

6 See Gowan, 'The Origins of the Administrative Elite' (note 5 above).

7 K.B. Smellie, *A Hundred Years of English Government*, Duckworth, London 1950, pp. 162, 328.

8 Sir Robert Morant, author of the 1902 Education Act, cited in J. Harvey and K. Hood, *The British State*, Lawrence and Wishart, London 1958, p. 94.

9 Harvey and Hood, p. 191. Similar sentiments among senior officials are recorded in Smellie, pp. 71/4. Gowan notes that Trevelyan undertook to abolish Haileybury College, the Indian Civil Service Training school, precisely because its demanding standards and career-relevant courses were producing an outstanding administrative elite whose selection was not confined to the upper classes whose sons went to Oxford and Cambridge, and to whom Trevelyan, Jowett and their allies decided that – for political reasons – the higher civil service must in future be reserved (note 5 above).

10 K. Hutchison, *The Decline and Fall of British Capitalism*, Cape, London 1951, p. 78.

11 Smellie, p. 169.

12 R.K. Kelsall, 'Recruitment to the Higher Civil Service: How Far Has the Pattern Changed?', in P. Stanworth and A. Giddens, *Elites and Power in British Society*, Cambridge University Press, Cambridge 1974, pp. 179–80.

13 Ibid., p. 180.

14 Gowan, p. 32.

15 *The Times*, 25 and 31 March 1905.

16 C. Ponting, *Whitehall, Tragedy and Farce*, Hamish Hamilton, London 1986, p. 198. See also the *Eleventh Report from the Expenditure Committee 1976–77: The Civil Service* and *The Civil Service: Government Observations on the 11th Report from the Expenditure Committee*, Cmnd 7117, 1978. See also P. Kellner and N. Crowther-Hunt, *The Civil Servants*, MacDonald, London 1980, Chapters 4, 5 and 12; and B. Sedgemore, *The Secret Constitution*, Hodder and Stoughton, London 1980, Chapter 6.

17 A request by the author for information on the educational background of officers commissioned into the armed forces was refused by the Ministry of Defence on the grounds that it would not be meaningful.

18 S. Raven, 'Perish by the Sword', in H. Thomas, ed., *The Establishment*, Blond, London 1959, pp. 49–79.

19 C.B. Otley, 'The Public Schools and the Army', in J. Urry and J. Wakeford, *Power in Britain*, Heinemann, London 1973, p. 241.

20 J.A.G. Griffith, *The Politics of the Judiciary* (second edition). Fontana, London 1981, p. 30.

21 P. Bellaby, *The Sociology of Comprehensive Schooling*, Methuen, London 1977, pp. 44–5.

22 J. Ford, *Social Class and the Comprehensive School*, Routledge and Kegan Paul, London 1969. After the initial changeover a decline in 'streaming' was reported by the schools inspectorate, but by the end of the 1970s it was increasing again.

23 Ford, p. 120.

24 See Chapter 9, note 21.

25 A. Gramsci, *Selections from the Prison Notebooks*, Lawrence and Wishart, London 1971, p. 238.

26 Quoted in H.E. Mueller, *Bureaucracy, Education and Monopoly*, University of California Press, Berkeley and Los Angeles 1984, p. 214.

27 Ponting, p. 28. The opening broadside in this bombardment was T. Balogh, 'The Apotheosis of the Dilettante: The Establishment of Mandarins' in H. Thomas, ed., *The Establishment*, Blonden, London 1959.

28 Ponting, pp. 223–4.

29 See G.K. Fry, 'The British Career Civil Service Under Challenge', *Political Studies* 34, 1986, pp. 533–55.
30 See e.g., J. Blondel, *Voters, Parties and Leaders*, revised edition, Penguin, Harmondsworth 1977, Chapter 9.
31 For example, in 1967 the proportion of higher civil servants whose fathers had been manual workers was only 17%. At the highest levels the proportion was probably smaller still, as many of the sons of manual workers were men who had been internally promoted and such promotees rarely attained the most senior ranks. See Kelsall, 'Recruitment' (note 12).
32 A. Sampson, *The New Anatomy of Britain*, Hodder and Stoughton, London 1971, p. 132. The portrait needs updating to recognise the later tendency of many public schools to admit girls into their sixth forms.
33 H. Glennerster and R. Pryke, 'Born to Rule', in Urry and Wakeford, *Power in Britain*, p. 221.
34 Upton and Wilson and Whitley looked at the first three of these. The others have been largely neglected.
35 N. Poulantzas, 'The Problem of the Capitalist State', *New Left Review* 58, 1969, pp. 67–8; R. Miliband, 'Nicos Poulantzas and the Capitalist State', *New Left Review* 82, 1972, pp. 83–92; Poulantzas, 'The Capitalist State: A Reply to Miliband and Laclau', *New Left Review* 95, 1976, pp. 63–83.
36 Poulantzas, 'The Problem of the Capitalist State', p. 73.
37 J.A. Armstrong, *The European Administrative Elite*, Princeton University Press, Princeton 1973, p. 209.
38 Griffith, p. 240.
39 On the concept of representation, see A.H. Birch, *Representation*, Macmillan, London 1972; and R. Williams, 'Democracy and Parliament', *Marxism Today* June 1982, pp. 14–21. On patronage see R.S. Goldsten, 'Patronage in British Government', *Parliamentary Affairs* 30/1, 1977, pp. 80-96.
40 C.Campbell, 'Judicial Selection and Judicial Impartiality', *Judicial Review*, December 1973, p. 269.
41 G. Marshall, 'Police Accountability Revisited', in D.E. Butler and A.H. Halsey, eds, *Policy and Politics*, Macmillan, London 1978, pp. 51–65. The loss of power by local police committees was confirmed by the Police Act of 1964.
42 *The Guardian*, 20 and 23 May 1988.
43 H. Thomas, 'Towards a Revision of the Official Secrets Act', in H. Thomas, ed., *Crisis in the Civil Service*, Blond, London 1968, p. 112. See also the Franks Committee Report, Cmnd. 5104, 1972.
44 Also in the views of local government officials. See F. Stacey, *Ombudsmen Compared*, Clarendon, Oxford 1978, p. 209.
45 D. Williams, *Not in the Public Interest*, Hutchinson, London 1965, Chapter 1.
46 D. Leigh, *The Frontiers of Secrecy*, Junction Books, London 1980, p. 202, citing evidence given to the Franks Committee on the Official Secrets Acts in 1971.
47 B. Sedgemore, *The Secret Constitution*, Chapter 1.
48 Marshall, pp. 55–56.
49 Griffith, p. 230.
50 See A.H. Birch, *Representative and Responsible Government*, Allen and Unwin, London 1964, especially Chapter 5.
51 K. Middlemas, *Politics in Industrial Society*, Deutsch, London 1979, p. 309.
52 Middlemas, p. 380.
53 W.L. Guttsman, *The British Political Elite*, MacGibbon and Kee, London 1963, p. 105.
54 C. Mellors, *The British MP*, Saxon House, London 1978, pp. 62–6.
55 The latter figure (from Mellors) is for October 1974. M. Rush gives the proportion of workers in February and October 1974 as 13.5% and in 1979 as 14.2%. His definition of 'workers' evidently includes a number of non-manual employees: M. Rush, 'The Members of Parliament', in S. Walkland and M. Ryle, eds, *The Commons Today*, revised edition, Fontana, London 1981, pp. 49 and 61.

56 Mellors, pp. 83 and 87.
57 G. Dewry, in Walkland and Ryle, *The Commons Today*, p. 93.
58 See J.A.G. Griffith, *Parliamentary Scrutiny of Government Bills*, Allen and Unwin, London 1974, summarised and updated in his 'Standing Committees in the House of Commons', in Walkland and Ryle, especially pp. 130–1 and 136.
59 P.G. Richards, 'Private Members' Legislation', in Walkland and Ryle, p. 146.
60 A. Robinson, 'The House of Commons and Public Expenditure', ibid., p. 155.
61 N. Johnson, 'An Academic's View', in D. Englefield, ed., *Commons Select Committees*, Layman, London 1984, p. 65. See also G. Drewry, ed., *The New Select Committees*, Clarendon Press, Oxford, 1985.
62 Griffith, *Parliamentary Scrutiny*, pp. 255–6.
63 N. Shrapnel, *The Performers*, Constable, London 1978, p. 120.

14

The State and the Economy

The same circumstances that made it necessary to extend the franchise – leading to the circumscription of democracy described in the previous chapter – also necessitated the continuous growth of the state. This growth persisted and reached its apogee in the 1970s. The economic role of the state became so large that its policies profoundly affected the economy whether it sought to 'manage' the economy or not. Before 1939, economic orthodoxy in Britain largely rejected the implications of this fact. After the slump, Keynesian ideas of 'demand management' gradually gained credence and the state came to accept, in theory, responsibility for 'steering' the economy by what were seen, at least from about 1950 onwards, mainly as gentle touches on the accelerator or brakes (more often the brakes) through changes in taxation, state spending and the control of credit. As executive dominance replaced parliamentary sovereignty the 'interventionist' state replaced the 'nightwatchman' state.

In the 1960s it gradually became clear that the economy needed radical repairs, not just steering (it was in any case doubtful whether the earlier attempts at steering had done more good than harm). Meanwhile the state began to expand again, at a rate not equalled in peacetime since before 1914. Labour accepted this growth and sought to make the state into a lever of economic reconstruction. But the state apparatus, a 'condensate' of the class struggle at the turn of the century and since, was not capable of playing this role. The continued growth of the state, on the other hand, depended on continued economic growth. As economic growth declined, right-wing Conservatives responded by attacking the enlarged state itself as the prime cause of the crisis.[1] Their reasoning was faulty, but there certainly was a contradiction between a continuous rise in state spending and a continuous decline in the relative productivity of industry. The mid-1970s saw, in fact, a striking example of what James O'Connor, in a study of the American state in 1973, had identified as the 'fiscal crisis' of the state.[2]

The Fiscal Crisis of the State

O'Connor wanted to explain why on the one hand state expenditure constantly rose, while on the other hand people became less and less willing to pay taxes. The capitalist state, he suggested, spends money on two main tasks: supporting the private accumulation of capital, and maintaining popular consent to the capitalist system. These expenditures constantly expand, partly to keep pace with ever-expanding capital (more growth requires more 'infrastructures'); partly to pay for rising unemployment and absolute poverty in the 'competitive sector', caused by the introduction of labour-saving technology in the 'monopoly sector';[3] and partly because productivity in the state sector itself increases slowly or not at all, compared with the large-scale corporate or monopoly sector, whereas state sector wages tend to keep pace with those of the monopoly sector, so that the *relative* cost of state activities constantly rises. Consequently the share of GNP passing through the state's hands constantly grows.

Even in a period of boom the political system may fail to allocate either these expenditures or the taxes to pay for them in a sufficiently acceptable way, tempting the state to bridge the revenue gap by inflation. In times of depression, the problem becomes worse as few of the expenditures can be reduced, and the tax burden becomes even more politically sensitive. Companies can no longer safely pass corporate taxes on in their prices, and so they seek to transfer the tax burden to the workers, at the same time calling for more subventions for business; on the other hand the tax base is narrowed by falling production, while mounting unemployment raises the state's social security bill. The result – as events in the USA after O'Connor's study was published demonstrated – is a growing ideological attack on 'state spending', though actually only in its 'welfare' components, not on those that benefit capital, while popular support is enlisted by holding out the promise of reduced personal taxes.

The relevance of this analysis to Britain is clear. As Table 14.1 shows, by 1975 almost 58 per cent of the national income was being appropriated by the state. Half of this was 'transfer spending' – taken by the state through taxation but handed over to other individuals or companies to spend in the form of pensions, investment grants, etc.

Table 14.1 State expenditure as a percentage of National Income (1910–1975)

	1910	*1921*	*1931*	*1937*	*1951*	*1961*	*1971*	*1975*
					% of GNP at factor cost			
All Social Services	4.2	10.1	12.7	10.9	16.1	17.6	23.8	28.8
Social Security		4.7	6.7	5.2	5.3	6.7	8.9	9.5
Welfare ⎫		1.1	1.8	1.8	4.5	0.3	0.7	1.1
Health ⎬						4.1	5.1	6.0
Education		2.2	2.8	2.6	3.2	4.2	6.5	7.6
Housing		2.1	1.3	1.4	3.1	2.3	2.6	4.6
Infrastructure	0.7	0.6	1.0	1.0	3.6	4.8	6.3	6.8
Industry and Employment	1.8	4.5	3.2	2.8	6.9	4.9	6.5	8.3
Justice and Law	0.6	0.8	0.8	0.7	0.6	0.8	1.3	1.5
Military	3.5	5.6	2.8	5.0	10.8	7.6	6.6	6.2
Debt Interest and Other	1.9	7.7	8.2	5.2	6.9	6.3	5.9	6.3
Total State Expenditure	12.7	29.4	28.8	25.7	44.9	42.1	50.3	57.9
Total State Revenue	11.0	24.4	25.0	23.8	42.7	38.5	48.6	46.6
Borrowing Requirement	1.7	5.0	3.8	1.9	2.2	3.6	1.7	11.3

Source: I. Gough, *The Political Economy of the Welfare State*, Macmillan, 1979.

Table 14.2   State employment in the United Kingdom 1951–1985 (millions)

	1951*	1961	1971	1979	1985
Central government	1.9	1.8	1.9	2.3	2.4
(H.M. Forces)	(0.8)	(0.5)	(0.4)	(0.3)	(0.4)
(Civilians)	(1.1)	(1.3)	(1.6)	(2.0)	(2.0)
Local government	1.4	1.9	2.7	3.1	3.0
Public corporations	2.7	2.2	2.0	2.1	1.3
Total public sector	6.1	5.8	6.6	7.5	6.6
Private sector	17.7	18.6	17.8	17.6	17.8
Total employed labour force	20.5	24.5	24.4	25.0	24.4

* Great Britain only – excluding Northern Ireland.

Sources: Social Trends, HMSO London 1987, Table 5.8; British Labour Statistics: Historical Abstract, Department of Employment, HMSO 1971, Tables 121 and 152.

The other half was spent by the state, partly on procurements from the private sector (especially for defence, housing and the health service), and partly on the wages and salaries of state employees. Almost one person in three worked for the state (see Table 14.2). This situation had come about in three successive 'jumps' – in each of the two world wars, and then again from 1960 onwards.

Military spending accounts for rather little of the long-term increase in state spending; direct aid to industry, and infrastructure, account for rather more; but the really major growth was in social services – welfare, health, housing, education and social security. With each world war, the state was obliged to go further to meet working-class needs for social services in order to maintain popular support for the war effort. After the Second World War the need for industrial and infrastructural reconstruction caused wartime spending levels to be maintained. However, in the case of both world wars, there was, after some time, a tendency for state spending to grow less fast than national income and so to begin to decline again as a share of the total.

What is striking is that, in the sixties and seventies, without any war, the state again expanded dramatically. Gough analysed the causes of the social service component of this as: rising relative costs (for instance housing costs grew 41 per cent faster than prices generally, health and personal social service costs 13 per cent faster); demographic changes (a smaller working population relative to the number of children, and especially relative to the growing number of very old people); rising needs (for instance higher unemployment, more single-parent families depending on state assistance); and improved, or new, services.[4] Gough concluded that there had been some improvement in the quality and range of services, but that it was uncertain whether these improvements had kept pace with newly emerging needs. The expansion of the welfare state in response to political demands that had been generated (originally) in the years of the depression and the Second World War, and kept alive subsequently by electoral competition between the parties, had been resumed in the 1960s and 1970s mainly as a result of its own built-in logic, without necessarily giving added satisfaction. Rather the contrary: the chronically ill, single-parent families and the unemployed understandably found the level of state provision painfully inadequate as it fell further and further behind the standard set elsewhere in Europe.

At the same time the state was increasingly drawn into efforts to make British capital more competitive, or at least to halt its relative decline. This was reflected in the rise of state spending on industry through regional investment grants, subsidies to assist mergers, export assistance, industrial training, etc. It was also reflected in the less visible, but probably even more important 'tax expenditure' on industry (i.e., revenue foregone as a result of tax concessions) as the crisis worsened; this reached a point where, for instance, by 1977 'for the "average" industrial company mainstream corporation tax [had] effectively been abolished'.[5] Tax expenditure, of course, severely restricted the state's revenues, and the scale of tax expenditure in Britain meant that successive governments had to raise more and more tax (directly or indirectly) from personal incomes. So the 1970s saw the income tax 'net' being lowered until it caught almost the whole working population, however poor – to the point where even workers who received supplementary benefit from the state, because their earnings were below the poverty line, nonetheless paid income tax.[6] This was done by keeping the lowest tax 'thresholds' fixed while money wages rose with inflation, an inflation which was itself aggravated by government borrowing.[7]

This 'fiscal crisis of the state' – culminating in the exchange crisis of 1976 – led to the programme of expenditure cuts inaugurated by Denis Healey as a condition for the IMF loan, and to the anti-tax, anti-state reaction championed by Margaret Thatcher.*

* Real cuts were made in 1976–7, but a modest growth in state expenditure was resumed in 1978–9. However, the renewed growth was increasingly due to social security payments to the growing number of unemployed and low-paid victims of the earlier cuts, a vicious circle that was also to make the Thatcher cuts largely self-defeating down to 1983).

State Economic Management

The 'market-oriented' economic strategy of the Thatcher government was, in many respects, a reaction to the fact that the state had already proved incompetent to steer the economy, let alone reconstruct it. Thatcherism did represent strong and even doctrinaire convictions in economic matters, but it also made a virtue of necessity by adopting an economic policy in line with the balance of forces within the sectors of the state concerned with economic policy-making.

Before 1939 not even the Labour Party questioned, in practice, that the chief economic role of the state was to balance its own income and expenditure. Keynes's idea that the state could maintain effective demand by expanding its own spending out of borrowing, to compensate for falling private demand in times of depression, and repaying the loans in the subsequent years of boom, was adopted more readily abroad than in Britain. Only some Liberals, by then a dwindling minority, and Oswald Mosley, who left the Labour Party and later formed the British Union of Fascists, seriously embraced Keynes's views. By 1944, however, Keynesianism had become the new orthodoxy. Both the major parties committed themselves in a White Paper of 1944 to maintaining full employment. It was also accepted – even by a significant element within the Conservative Party – that the task of economic reconstruction could not be left to market forces. The wartime system of economic controls was kept in being for most of the period 1945–50 without occasioning much controversy.

However, subsequent events make it clear that these developments did not represent a radical or permanent change in the state's relation to the economy. Full employment was maintained after the war by the pressures of both domestic and foreign demand; there was no need to engage in deficit financing, which was fortunate since the record of post-war economic policy-making does not suggest that the Treasury or the Bank of England would have allowed deficit financing on any significant scale or for any significant length of time. The portrayal of the Treasury as predominantly 'neo-Keynesian', down to 1976, refers primarily to its acceptance of the view that it should regulate the economy, and to the periodic illusion that it did so, not to any commitment to full employment, let alone planned development.[8] The post-war apparatus of controls was seen as transitional; it began to be dismantled by the Labour government as early as November 1948 (the celebrated 'bonfire of controls' announced by Harold Wilson as President of the Board of Trade) and was finally scrapped by the Churchill government of 1951–5. The long-term economic policy pursued by state policy-makers during these years was the restoration of Britain's pre-war economy, and notably the re-establishment of overseas assets by investing British capital abroad. A good indicator of their outlook is their attempt to maintain an unrealistically high exchange rate for the pound until devaluation was forced upon them in 1949.

Under the Conservative governments of 1951–64 the state's economic role was minimised. As the recurrent balance of payments crises, which announced the return of Britain's long-term crisis of production, began to intensify during the late 1950s and early 1960s, the response of the state consisted primarily of a corresponding series of reductions in public and private demand.[9] The resistance of the Treasury to devaluation after 1964 was matched, logically enough, by the tacit abandonment of the 1944 all-party commitment to full employment; unemployment began the long upward climb which eventually brought it to 12 per cent in 1985. In other words, state economic policy after 1945 showed an underlying continuity with the past, which was reflected in the fact that, down to 1961, virtually no organisational changes were made in the economic branches of the state apparatus, except to undo the changes made in wartime.

In 1961, however, there began a series of innovations intended to deal with the re-emerging economic problem. A National Economic Development Council (NEDC) was established, representing the government, employers and unions, with a permanent staff (the National Economic Development Organisation or NEDO). There was also a set of committees for particular industries, the so-called 'little Neddies'. This was a conscious imitation of the French planning machinery which was then being credited with much of the French economy's dynamism. The idea was to achieve higher economic growth by making quantitative estimates of the implications of a higher growth target, identifying obstacles in each sector and consulting about the best means to overcome them. With Labour's return to office in 1964, on a platform of growth through modernisation and technology, this machinery was supplemented, if not eclipsed, by the creation of a new ministry, the Department of Economic Affairs (DEA); the DEA was nominally charged with 'responsibility for the management of the national economy as a whole', and immediately set about producing a five-year National Plan. Meantime, a new office had also been established to try to control wages; the National Incomes Commission (NIC, 1961–4) and its successor the Prices and Incomes Board (PIB, 1965–70) was supposed to control prices as well. There was also a new Industrial Reorganisation Corporation (IRC, 1966–70) to supervise and subsidise mergers in the interest of achieving economies of scale.

The outcome of all these initiatives has already been discussed in Chapter 5. The Treasury lost its responsibility for long-term economic strategy to the DEA but remained in charge of short-term policy. On this division of responsibility Roger Opie, an economist who worked with the DEA, cites a colleague's remark that 'no-one bothered to decide *important matters* – what always received prior attention was what was *urgent*'. Opie comments: 'The division between the Treasury and the DEA . . . exactly paralleled the division between the "urgent" and the "important" '.[10] The DEA was abolished in 1969, its purpose having already been abandoned in 1965 when growth was sacrificed to the maintenance of the exchange rate. Most of its staff were transferred to the Treasury's revived Central Economic Planning Staff, from which many of them had originally come. The PIB and the IRC were abolished by the incoming Heath administration of 1970. Of all the innovations, only the NEDC and NEDO still survived after 1979.

The importance of this episode is that it shows why the British state could not serve as an independent lever for capitalist reconstruction. The subordination of growth to maintaining the value of the pound was not a mistake, but the outcome of a sharp struggle within the state apparatus. Opposition to reversing the priority given to free trade, overseas investment and the City's interest in a strong pound was encountered at every level. Outsiders brought in to help implement the Wilson strategy met with a solid wall of resistance, reinforced by ignorance of economics and an indifference to numbers or even factual evidence, erected in defence of the trade-and-finance definition of the national economic interest permeating the Treasury, the Board of Trade and the Foreign and Commonwealth Office, not to mention the Bank of England.[11]

Having lost an initial battle to devalue the pound when the Wilson government took office in 1964, the advocates of industrial reconstruction sought to gain the necessary relief from the balance of payments crisis, which expansion would undoubtedly produce, by introducing a temporary surcharge of 15 per cent on all imports, a tax rebate on exports of goods, and restrictions on exports of capital. These measures were unpopular abroad, but in the opinion of their advocates they could be successfully defended if they led ultimately to a growth in the British economy, and they were certainly essential to growth if devaluation was ruled out. But by 1966 all these measures had been abandoned.

The new government, and its new economic advisers, were defeated by the sterling lobby. They were not defeated in the battle to control the deficit, but in the primary battle to decide how to control it . . . once the decision not to devalue had limited the room to manoeuvre drastically, each alternative measure was either destroyed where it outraged the overseas lobby, or emasculated where that lobby had to operate it.[12]

Nothing was subsequently done to make the state apparatus more adapted to the purpose of economic transformation; meanwhile, as we have seen (in Chapter 13) the Fulton reforms were largely neutralised.

If this did not present further problems it is because the 1970s were in reality a period of relatively consistent retreat from the initiatives of the 1960s, directed at state-led economic reconstruction, towards a policy of reducing the state's economic role and allowing the fate of British industry to be determined as far as possible by the forces of the international market. This trend became apparent from 1976, and was then accentuated and accelerated by Thatcher. Thanks especially to North Sea oil she was able to revert much more thoroughly to the initial policies of the Heath administration in the period 1970–2, and even to abolish exchange controls for the first time since 1945, without running into a politically unacceptable balance of payments crisis. Monetarism – carried out by public expenditure cuts and the management of interest rates – reduced the task of state economic management to one quite compatible with the organisation and orientation of the state apparatus as it had crystallised at the turn of the century, and in particular with the special place of the Treasury.

Although revenue-raising, coordination of the state apparatus and long-term policy-making for the economy are also united in one department in some other states, the centralisation of these functions in the British Treasury is peculiar in two main respects. First, Treasury control of the expenditures of other departments is exercised in such a way as to make Treasury officials quite intimately responsible for the evolution of their policies – a practice which, incidentally, was established between 1868 and 1914, as spending on social services proved impossible to control by means of purely financial limits.[13] All policy decisions, however minor, that may entail new expenditure, must have prior Treasury approval, which is granted if they conform to principles that the Treasury judges sound. A minister must seek cabinet support for any policy opposed by the Treasury, which in practice gives the Treasury effective policy-making power on all but the most contentious issues. The Treasury's 'coordination' is thus not a question of seeing that the spending departments keep within their approved estimates; it is a matter of determining the content of all future estimates, as these result from the continuous evolution of policy.

Second, the Treasury is not only, like all treasuries, hostile to increases in state spending because it is responsible for finding the revenue to pay for it; it is also hostile (for reasons we have already considered) to policies that would give manufacturing priority over trade and banking. The influence of the Treasury throughout the state apparatus reflects this bias, and is reinforced by its control of the promotion and appointment of senior personnel in all departments (a power restored to it in 1981 with the reabsorption of the functions of the Civil Service Department set up in 1968). The hegemony of banking and commerce in the economy is thus reflected in the hegemony of the Treasury in the state apparatus.

The successive spending cuts after 1976, and again after 1979, and the contraction of the industrial economy under the strategy of monetarism, were policies to which the British state was well adapted.*

Economic Policy 1979–87

The key instrument of the 'monetarist' approach to macro-economic management introduced by the Conservatives in 1979 was the Medium Term Financial Strategy. The idea was to regulate only the money supply, and with the primary objective of reducing inflation. The level of employment, and hence demand, were to be considered secondary, although 'real productive' employment would, according to the doctrine, rise in the long run, through the pressure put on firms to become efficient, and through the removal of 'supply side' obstacles to productivity growth, above all excessive trade union power. The money supply would be controlled by reducing state spending (which would also release resources for private sector expansion), and by controlling interest rates.

In practice the money supply targets were greatly exceeded in four of the first six years of the Thatcher government; the truth was that 'monetarism' cloaked an orthodox deflationary policy which would have been more politically contentious if it had been presented in orthodox terms, acknowledging that the aim was to reduce output and increase unemployment by specified amounts – let alone the very large

---

* This was conspicuous in the implementation of 'cash limits' from 1976 onwards, which made expenditure cuts much more effective than earlier public spending cuts had been. The state apparatus as a whole cannot be held responsible for all the illusions of monetary theory, but there is ample evidence of the growth of enthusiasm for monetarism in the Treasury which Keegan (the economic Editor of the *Observer*) described in 1979 as having an 'obsession . . . with financial targets as their criterion of economic rectitude' (W. Keegan and R. Pennant Rae, *Who Runs the Economy?*, Temple-Smith, London 1979, p. 209).

amounts that were actually achieved.[14] Because of the increased levels of social security payments that resulted from the rise in unemployment, total state spending initially rose as a percentage of GDP; there were also increases, as promised at the election, in real spending on law and order and defence, and further increased spending on the EEC and on agriculture (both of which the government subsequently took steps to reduce). In the three years 1980–1 to 1983–4 cuts were made in subsidies to industry, energy, transport and housing, and in a wide range of public services (mainly social services provided through local authorities). By 1987 the government was no longer aiming to reduce real public spending any further, but only to hold it constant so that its share of total GDP would fall as the the latter rose. By 1985 total government spending as a percentage of GDP had fallen slightly to 45 per cent, while the Public Sector Borrowing Requirement (PSBR), or budget deficit, was reduced and eventually eliminated by 1987 – though the figures for both total spending, and for the PSBR, were 'doctored' to some extent by setting the proceeds of asset sales (privatisation) off against total spending (reducing the apparent total spending by about 3.5 per cent in 1986–7, for example).

The short-term effect of these policies, adhered to with minimum flexibility from 1979 to 1981 in the midst of an international recession, was a dramatic drop in economic activity, and especially manufacturing, which fell by 17 per cent over those two years. The recovery which subsequently occurred was from this low base; industrial output did not recover to the level of 1979 until 1987. Keynesians argue that the net effect of the new strategy was simply to set back growth by eight years, and add a million workers to the ranks of the permanently unemployed (the total number of long-term unemployed – i.e. unemployed for a year or more – rose from about 300,000 in 1979 to about 1.3 million in 1987). The Thatcherite view is that sustained growth on the old basis has become impossible; their strategy had made it possible again because both industry and labour were being forced to become efficient, and the supply-side obstacles of the past have been progressively removed.

Of these, the most important was trade union power which as we have seen (in Chapter 8) was dramatically reduced. Minimum wages in the 'sweated trades' and retail sectors were also set to be reduced by the Wages Act of 1986, which emasculated the Wages Councils that set wages for these sectors, while enforcement was in any case made increasingly ineffective by reducing the inspectorate to a total of 119, covering 2.7 million workers in a myriad of small enterprises. The Fair Wages Resolution, requiring bidders for government contracts to pay, in effect, union wage rates, was also dropped in 1982.[15] The idea was to remove all possible lower limits to wages so that the labour market would 'clear' itself. Changes in social security provisions for young people were designed to have the same effect.

Other changes removed restraints on competition, such as those operating in the Stock Exchange, the solicitors' monopoly on convey-ancing, the use by local authorities and hospitals and other public institu-tions of their own labour forces for cleaning, catering and similar activities which could be contracted for privately, and so on. But the most publicised, if not necessarily the most important, targets in the Thatcher government's assault on the public sector were the national-ised industries.

The Rise and Fall of the Nationalised Industries

In order to appreciate the significance of this it is first necessary to understand the scope, and even more importantly, the limitations, of the nationalisation measures carried out by previous governments (including Conservative governments). What was the meaning of the 'nationalisation' of industries? How did the state deal with this large extension of its domain? And what is the significance of the sale of the nationalised industries to private capital since 1979?

By 1976, state-owned corporations accounted for some 11 per cent of total GDP and 8 per cent of total employment; the nationalised industries proper – i.e., public corporations (or publicly owned enterprises) producing all or a large proportion of the output of particular production sectors of the economy – accounted for 9.6 per cent of GDP and 6.9 per cent of employment. As Table 14.3 shows, nationalisation took place in three broad phases – before the Second World War, immediately after it, and in the 1970s.

The *first* phase comprised industries considered to be strategic at the time of their first appearance – the Post Office, electricity supplies and international air services. The *last* phase also included a similar industry – the distribution of the newly discovered oil resources of the North Sea – but otherwise comprised industries or companies that would have collapsed but for massive injections of public funds, eventually necessitating full state-ownership (Rolls Royce, British Leyland, and the shipbuilding and aircraft industries). These national-isations were far from being inspired by socialist goals; Rolls Royce was even nationalised by the Conservative government in 1971. The industries of the *second* phase, however, were taken into state ownership by the Labour government of 1945–51 (steel was denational-ised by the Conservatives in 1953 and renationalised by Labour in

1967) as a result of strong rank and file pressure within the Labour Party. This group of nationalisations is, in consequence, usually seen as falling in a different category, i.e., as a step towards the 'common ownership of the means of production, distribution and exchange' envisaged in Clause 4 of the Labour Party's constitution.

But this is a misunderstanding. The nationalisations of 1946–51 were, with partial exception of steel, responses to 'problem' industries which could no longer be run profitably in their existing form, in very much the same sense that this is true of the industries or companies taken into public ownership in the 1970s. They were run down, partly as a result of wartime exigencies but mainly due to fragmented ownership, lack of integration and a vicious circle of declining profitability and underinvestment stretching over many decades (in the case of coal, for almost half a century). Left in private hands they could only have been restructured by widespread bankruptcies, contraction and mergers. It was no longer possible to force down wages, as had been done in the coalmines in 1926; and, significantly, it was the industries dominated by the Triple Alliance of mineworkers, railwaymen and transport workers (whose solidarity had led to the General Strike) which formed the core of the 1946–8 nationalisations. In the political climate of 1945 no government could have accepted either the political cost of confronting these unions, or the economic dislocation which would have resulted from the unplanned reconstruction by 'market forces' of these basic industries. The main 1946–8 nationalisations, then, belong analytically to the same category as those of the 1970s: they represent the state intervening to prevent the market from reorganising – or in some cases perhaps eliminating – weak sectors of production, because of the economic, social and political costs this would have implied.

Once this is recognised, the subsequent history of the nationalised industries become more comprehensible. The state's intervention followed a fairly clear pattern. The coal industry and the railways were reorganised and drastically contracted; the simultaneous nationalisation of road passenger and freight transport permitted railway reorganisation, like that of the coal mines, to be accomplished in a planned fashion, avoiding redundancies (though road freight transport was partly denationalised in 1953 by the Conservatives). Tax revenues were used to compensate the former owners on generous terms and to finance large-scale new investment. Then, a process began of reassimilating the nationalised industries to the norms and requirements of the market.

This has been obscured by a large and somewhat uninspiring literature concerned with the issue of the control and accountability of the nationalised industries. This literature starts out from a distinction

BRISTOL POLYTECHNIC
ST. MATTHIAS LIBRARY
FISHPONDS

Table 14.3 Major nationalised industries and enterprises

	Shares in total UK economy in 1975 (% of total)			
	Output	*Employment*	*Investment*	*Domestic Market*
Nationalised before 1945				
Post Office & Telecommunications[1] (1635–1710)	2.8	1.8	4.5	100
Electricity Board (1926)	1.5[2]	0.7[2]	2.9[2]	100[3]
British Airways[4] (1939)	0.3	0.2	0.4	76
Nationalised 1945–64				
National Coal Board (1946)	1.5	1.2	0.9	96[3]
British Railways Board (1947)	1.2	1.0	1.0	8[5]
National Bus Company (1947)	0.2	0.3	0.1	34
National Freight Corporation (1947)	0.2	0.2	—	10
British Gas Corporation (1948)	0.8	0.4	1.7	100[3]
British Steel Corporation (1951, 1967)	0.8	0.9	2.0	56
Nine major nationalised industries	**9.2**	**6.7**	**13.6**	
Other nationalised industries	0.4	0.2	0.8	
All nationalised industries	**9.6**	**6.9**	**14.4**	
Other public corporations	1.4	1.1	4.6	
All public corporations	**11.0**	**8.0**	**19.0**	

[Nationalised after 1970 Rolls Royce (1971)[6] British Leyland (1975)[6] British National Oil Corporation (1976) British Shipbuilders (1977) British Aerospace (1977)]]

Notes: 1 British Telecommunications became a separate corporation in 1981.
2 England and Wales only.
3 In 1975 gas accounted for 22%, coal 19%, electricity 13% and oil (then still imported) 46% of final consumption of energy.
4 British Overseas Airways Corporation formed 1939; British European Airways 1946; merged 1972–74.
5 Of total passenger/km: 47% of freight tonne/km.
6 Limited liability companies wholly owned by the state.

Source: (for industries nationalised before 1970) NEDO, *A Study of UK Nationalised Industries*, HMSO, London 1976, Appendix Volume.

between 'public' and 'private' which the nationalised industries are seen as infringing. The problem is then posed as being one of how to ensure that they are accountable to parliament, since they are *publicly* owned, without this adversely affecting their performance as *businesses* (i.e., as organisms operating in the 'private' sphere). The solutions proposed concern how the chairmen of the boards of nationalised industries are appointed, what directions ministers should be able to give them, what information parliament is entitled to receive about them, what financial targets or controls should be applied to them, and so on. The distinction between public and private, however, is largely ideological. Many 'private' industries are almost wholly dependent on the state as a customer (e.g., armaments), many more have been the recipients of large grants from public funds, and virtually all have received large 'tax expenditures' from the state. What really matters are the principles on which an industry is run, not its juridical ownership. In this respect, the history of nationalisation is relatively clear.

In the first place, the boards of directors of the nationalised industries were constituted so as to provide 'the best possible collective leadership' and not, 'as in the case of comparable boards in certain other countries, to secure the representation of . . . workers and consumers'.[16] In practice, management continued to be recruited as before: there was no element of industrial democracy.* Then in 1961, when the reconstruction of coalmining and the railways was well advanced, a White Paper drew a distinction between those nationalised industry activities which were undertaken to meet 'social service' obligations, and which would be subsidised from tax revenues, and the rest, which should be made to pay for themselves. In 1967 this policy was tightened by requiring nationalised industries to charge prices equal to marginal costs and to use a test discount rate for proposed investments, to try to secure a rate of return comparable with that of private industries. In 1976 the nationalised industries' investment budgets were made subject to 'cash limits' imposed by central government – i.e., they were no longer able to spend more on capital projects than had been approved by Whitehall. And from 1978 the rate of return to be sought was laid down, and financial targets based on a three- to five-year period were required.[17] In short, to the extent that

---

* From 1935 onwards the Labour leadership, conceding to rank and file pressure, had accepted a commitment to have worker representation on the boards of future nationalised industries, though only on the basis that the trade unions would be legally entitled to *nominate* representatives from among whom the minister responsible would appoint *some* board members. At the persistent instigation of Herbert Morrison even this minimal commitment was abandoned prior to the 1945 election (see R. A. Dahl, 'Workers' Control of Industry and the British Labour Party', *American Political Science Review* 41, 1947, pp. 875–900).

the term 'mixed economy' was used to imply that the nationalised industries represented an alternative, non-capitalist or even 'socialist' principle of organisation, or economic rationality, this was an illusion.

These increasingly specific assertions of capitalist norms took place in a context of rapidly declining employment in the nationalised coalmines and railways. The number of National Coal Board employees fell from 749,000 in 1950 to 304,000 in 1977; membership of the National Union of Railwaymen (which included all the railway manual staff other than footplate workers) fell from 392,000 to 180,000 in the same period. In combination with large investments (and in spite of government-imposed additions to costs and limits on prices) this contraction increased the nationalised industries' overall productivity (measured by conventional criteria) faster than in manufacturing as a whole and, it seemed, faster than in comparable nationalised industries in other countries – in striking contrast to the view constantly reiterated in the media that the nationalised industries were inefficient.[18]

The main targets of this propaganda were the workers in the nationalised industries, who were accused of 'feather-bedding' behind the protection supposedly offered by the industries' monopoly positions in their markets. There certainly was high absenteeism among underground mineworkers and there was some overmanning on the railways, but the evidence suggests that the initial debt-burdens imposed on the nationalised industries for compensation payments, and government-imposed constraints on investment and pricing policies, played a more significant role in lowering morale and limiting productivity growth.[19] The propaganda had, however, the effect of legitimising the reestablishment of market norms for the nationalised industries. Especially after 1979, such propaganda served to justify a much narrower definition of the social costs that nationalised industries should seek to avoid – the 70,000 redundancies made at British Leyland or the 100,000 at British Steel would not have been accepted twenty or ten years earlier. It also justified the denationalisation or 'privatisation' of selected nationalised industries or parts of industries.

The subordination of the nationalised industries to the general interests of private capital also had a broader aspect, and other costs. Because they needed large-scale investments, there was constant anxiety in the Treasury lest they pre-empt investible funds, making investment more expensive for private enterprise; and in the 1960s their investment spending also began to be curtailed as part of the government's increasingly strenuous attempts to deflate the economy. They were only permitted to borrow from the Treasury, which placed them under non-market financial controls and led to successive cuts in their investment plans, in spite of the new policies which were supposed to put the nationalised industries on a more 'market' footing. The effect was to create deficits for the gas and electricity industries and the Post Office, and to increase the deficit of the railways. Then, after 1979, as part of the Thatcher government's policy of reducing state expenditure, subsidies which had been given to the nationalised industries to enable them to keep their prices down were rapidly removed so that nationalised industry prices rose much faster than the average, curtailing demand for their products.

Meantime the nationalised industries, besides being subject to central government financial controls, also remained prohibited from expanding, like private companies, into other profitable activities.[20] This meant that the nationalised industries were under constant pressure to contract, rather than expand, as the only practicable means of meeting their ever-receding financial targets. Fine and O'Donnell argue that this complemented, and perhaps accelerated, domestic deindustrialisation generally, as compared with European countries whose nationalised coal, steel and transport industries have been heavily subsidised out of general revenues as part of a strategy for industrial expansion.[21]

To summarise: the primary significance of most of the post-war nationalisations was thus to secure the reorganisation, in several cases through drastic contraction, of declining sectors, without incurring political instability. Politically this was highly successful. Apart from the coal industry, which had a high level of industrial conflict throughout most of the 1950s, nationalisation permitted contraction to be imposed without significant challenge from the labour movement during the years when full employment made the movement strong. By the end of the 1970s, on the other hand, contraction could be imposed (notably in BL, BSC and shipbuilding) much more rapidly, thanks to high unemployment and declining trade union strength. In this way, major casualties of Britain's industrial decline were prevented from becoming the focus of a potential radicalisation during the period of the labour movement's ascendancy.

Economically, on the other hand, the principles of private capitalist organisation and production were consistently asserted, not least with regard to management – but not to the point where state-owned industries were allowed to borrow, spend capital, or expand their sphere of activities like any privately owned capitalist enterprises. Not surprisingly, the economic results were frequently mediocre, where they were not altogether disastrous. This consequence took time to become fully apparent. During the 1950s and 1960s, the performance of the nationalised industries has been judged on the whole equal to that of the private sector; in the 1970s, however, they did worse.[22]

Although the evidence is limited the reason for this declining performance seems to be independent of the fact that the nationalised industries were often monopolies – such as coal, electricity, gas, the railways – and appeared instead to be traceable to inferior management, which in turn was thought attributable to lack of incentives (no risk of bankruptcy), vulnerability to the exorbitant demands of public sector unions (for the same reason), and government interference in commercial policy-making. Whatever the reasons, the long history of anti-nationalisation propaganda combined with weak performance in the 1970s to make the nationalised industries unpopular and a prime target for the Thatcherite assault.

Yet as has been widely remarked, the Conservatives did not make denationalisation a major election issue in 1979. The earliest sales of public sector assets were of relatively prosperous individual government-owned companies in competitive sectors of the economy (see Table 14.4). The contribution of these sales to reducing budget deficits encouraged the development of an expanded programme of sales. The most profitable monopolies such as Britoil and British Telecom were sold; British Gas, British Airways, and British Steel followed; the sale of British Leyland was planned for 1986 but aborted. By 1988 the sale of the Central Electricity Generating Board, British Rail, the water supply and the National Coal Board were under discussion. By the mid-1990s the 'public sector' of the economy (as opposed to central and local government services), with assets in 1981–2 of well over £80 billion, seemed likely to have disappeared almost entirely.

The monopolies were at first privatised intact, leading to a good deal of justifiable criticism, and a limited measure of competition was envisaged for later nationalisations such as the electricity industry; but on the whole neither strong competition nor strong measures of regulation were instituted. The emphasis was on privatisation, not on competition. The assets sold were deliberately undervalued, partly to ensure successful sales, and partly (later, in conjunction with other measures) to tempt 'ordinary people' into buying the shares, fostering 'popular capitalism' by offering quick profits (which, of course, led to a subsequent drastic contraction of the number of shareholders as millions of first-time shareholders took their profits).[23]* The net effect of the transactions was a gift from the population as a whole to the

---

* The number of shareholders of Amersham International fell from 65,000 to 8,000 over the two years following the initial sale: shareholders in British Aerospace fell from 158,000 to 27,000, and in British Telecom from 2.3 million to 1.7 million, in one year (C. Mayer and S. N Meadowcroft, 'Sellling Public Assets: Techniques and Financial Implications', in J. Kay et al., eds, *Privatisation and Regulation: The UK Experience*, Clarendon Press, Oxford 1986).

Table 14.4 Privatisation 1980–1987 (£ millions)

	80/81	81/82	82/83	83/84	84/85	85/86	86/87
Amersham International		64					
Associated British Ports			46		51		
British Airways							435
British Aerospace	43					346	
British Gas							2,546
British Petroleum		8		543			
British Sugar Corporation		44					
British Telecom					1,396	1,307	1,387
Britoil			334	293		426	
Cable and Wireless		182		263		571	4
Enterprise Oil					382		
NEB/British Technology Group	83	2			142	30	34
New Town Corporations and Commission for the New Towns (land sales)	52	73	1		121		
North Sea Oil Licence Premium	195		33				
Sale of Oil Stockpiles		63	33	11			
Other	32	58	41	32	40	22	16
Total	405	494	488	1,142	2,132	2,702	4,422

Source: The Government Expenditure Plans 1986/87 to 1988/89 and 1988/89 to 1990/91.

new shareholders of additional assets equivalent, in the case of the first 'tranche' of British Telecom shares, to about 80 per cent of those they actually paid for. In short the family silver was not just sold to the few family members who could afford it (to paraphrase Lord Stockton's characteristic analogy), nearly half of it was given to them free. This was done, moreover, in such a way as to give the impression that the government was actually saving money, by reducing the budget deficit. Thus the sale in 1984–5 of British Telecom shares appeared to 'raise' £1.24 billion; the true effect was a net *loss* of £1.56 billion.[24] Thus, fittingly perhaps, the illusion of the 'mixed economy' ended with an even more wonderful illusion.

Consequences of Thatcher's Economic Strategy

The acid test of the new strategy from a national (as opposed to a class) perspective is whether the evidence supports the government's view that it had succeeded in its mission to set in motion a sustained modernisation of the British economy. In 1988 the evidence was not conclusive. The spectacular jump in manufacturing productivity that occurred between 1980 and 1984 (averaging well over 6 per cent per annum) was largely a statistical effect of the closure of so many inefficient plants, and of reduced manning levels, and was followed by a decline in productivity growth to virtually nil in 1986. The productivity increases which resumed after 1986, however, which were lower but still substantial (and higher than in most other OECD countries), could not be explained in this way: the possibility existed that

> a permanent improvement [had] taken place in productivity trends . . . this would not be too surprising, since the improvement in management and working practices – which is commonly observed by company sector analysts looking at British companies – may have enabled the UK simply to catch-up with many best-practice techniques which were already in operation abroad. For example, by getting manning levels down to those which were already commonplace in other developed countries, a whole new tranche of profitable investment opportunities may have become available to UK firms . . . it seems possible that the relatively good UK productivity performance can be maintained for a prolonged further period.[25]

On the other hand, a study of the productivity challenge mounted by the fastest growing industrial economies in the post-war period shows that their productivity growth was not based on 'free market' policies but largely on long-term, large-scale, state-provided educational and other infrastructural initiatives (from large scale investments in transportation to the 'wired society'), and state-led investment and product development policies for targeted industrial sectors. Even if one accepts the Thatcherite view that the British state could never play the latter role, one may still doubt if productivity growth can be sustained for a long time without it playing the former – i.e. without large continuing investments in scientific and technical education, and in the modernisation of the increasingly archaic infrastructure in transport, health, telecommunications, etc. – to which the Thatcher government was on the whole equally firmly opposed.

Notes

1 The most sophisticated version of this argument was advanced by R. Bacon and W.A. Eltis in *Britain's Economic Problem: Too Few Producers*, Macmillan, London 1976.

2 J. O'Connor, *The Fiscal Crisis of the State*, St Martin's Press, New York 1973.

3 This aspect of O'Connor's analysis has been convincingly criticised by Ian Gough in 'State Expenditure in Advanced Capitalism', *New Left Review* 92, 1975, pp. 53–92, but without detracting from O'Connor's main argument.

4 Ian Gough, *The Political Economy of the Welfare State*, Macmillan, London 1979, pp. 84–94; see also his article cited in note 3 above.

5 S. Aaronovitch and R. Smith, *The Political Economy of British Capitalism*, McGraw-Hill, London 1981, p. 292.

6 F. Field, *Inequality in Britain*, Fontana, London 1981, pp. 105–16. Field's book is also an important source for the scope and scale of tax expenditures.

7 The threshold for the 'basic' rate of income tax was finally 'indexed' - i.e., linked to the falling value of money – as a result of the 'Rooker-Wise amendment' to the Finance Bill of 1977.

8 See W. Keegan and R. Pennant Rae, *Who Runs the Economy?*, Temple-Smith, London 1979, pp. 40–7, 94–6.

9 For this story see S. Brittan, *Steering the Economy: the Role of the Treasury*, Penguin, Harmondsworth 1971.

10 R. Opie, 'The Making of Economic Policy', in H. Thomas, ed., *The Crisis in the Civil Service*, Blond, London 1968, pp. 60–1.

11 See especially Opie, pp. 53–82; see also D. Seers, 'The Structure of Power', also in Thomas, pp. 83–109. Both authors show surprising faith in the possibility of overcoming the problem by introducing more economists into the state apparatus.

12 Opie, pp. 61–3. The last reference is to curbs on overseas investment which were supposed to be operated by the Treasury and the Bank of England and which proved ineffective in practice.

13 See S. Beer, *Treasury Control*, Clarendon Press, Oxford 1957, pp. 17–18; K.B. Smellie, *A Hundred Years of English Government*, second edition, Butterworth, London 1950; and H. Heclo and A. Wildavsky, *The Private Government of Public Money*, Macmillan, London 1974.

14 G. Thompson, *The Conservatives' Economic Policy*, Croom Helm, London 1986, pp. 22 and 29–30.

15 For these and other 'labour-market' policies of the Thatcher years see D. Deaton, 'The Labour Market and Industrial Relations Policy of the Thatcher Government', in D.S. Bell, ed., *The Conservative Government 1979–84*.

16 A. Hanson and M. Walles, *Governing Britain*, 3rd edition, Fontana, London 1980, p. 197.

17 These developments were outlined in successive White Papers, Cmnd 1337 of 1961, Cmnd 3437 of 1967, and Cmnd 7131 of 1978.
18 NEDO, *A Study of the Nationalised Industries*, HMSO, London 1976, p. 16; R. Pryke, 'The Growth of Efficiency', in L. Tivey, ed., *The Nationalised Industries Since 1960*, Allen and Unwin, London 1973, pp. 21–3. Much of the productivity growth was due to contraction which eliminated branch railway lines and some high-cost pits; and there are serious difficulties involved in using the conventional criteria of productivity in relation to large, semi-monopolistic industries such as these. The international comparisons may have some significance, but to the lay observer the most obvious feature of nationalised industries compared with those of other European countries appears to be the greater capital expenditure undertaken abroad.
19 G.L. Reid and K. Allen, *Nationalised Industries*, Penguin, Harmondsworth 1973, pp. 88–98, 119–29.
20 B. Fine and K. O'Donnell, 'The Nationalised Industries', in *Socialist Economic Review 1981*, Merlin Press, London 1981, p. 272.
21 Ibid., pp. 272–4.
22 See R. Pryke, *The Nationalised Industries: Policies and Performances Since 1968*, Martin Robertson, Oxford 1981; and 'The Comparative Performance of Public and Private Enterprise', in J. Kay et al., eds, *Privatisation and Regulation: The UK Experience*, Clarendon Press, Oxford, 1986, pp. 101–18.
23 C. Mayer and S. Meadowcraft, 'Selling Public Assets; Techniques and Financial Implications', in Kay, et al., pp. 325 and 333–4.
24 Ibid., pp. 18–25.
25 Gavyn Davies in *The UK Economic Analyst*, Goldman Sachs, London, March 1988, pp. 14–15.

15

Consent and Social Control

The state is 'hegemony protected by the armour of coercion':[1] a combination of ideological and practical measures to secure popular consent, with measures of social control. In times of prosperity consensual themes come to the fore and less control is needed. In hard times a different set of ideological themes is resorted to, some popular, some authoritarian; and – eventually – there is more reliance on coercion.

In the 1950s and early 1960s 'consumerism' served as a powerful general ideology which obscured economic inequality and legitimated the state. But even in the 'age of affluence' other contradictions emerged and other ideological themes were taken up to validate the state's activities. For example, economic growth, as interpreted by the nuclear power industry, the automobile industry, transport engineers and the airlines, obliged the state to build nuclear power stations and expropriate land for motorways and airports in hitherto middle-class 'green' areas, giving rise to new demands for popular participation in planning and a new concern for the environment. Uneven growth brought about new demands for local control, or even independence, in backward regions of the country, leading to demands for devolution or even independence. Simultaneously, new spheres of state bureaucracy – for example, in post-secondary education, social work and health services – led to demands for 'open government' and for machinery for the redress of grievances.

As the crisis set in, some of these themes became even more prominent, but they were gradually superseded by an alternative ideology of 'toughness', backed up by a franker reliance on force. Measures to strengthen social control were justified in terms of the need for 'discipline', 'the smack of strong government', and so on.

In the Wilson era – including both the 1964–70 and the 1974–6 administrations – the rhetoric of reform stressed the need for popular 'access' to and 'participation' in the state's activities, as well as the need for efficiency. As the economic crisis deepened, and as reforms aimed at efficiency seemed less and less likely to be effective, the stress on 'participation' grew. The reforms in the committee system of the House of Commons in the 1960s (to give MPs more access to government information and a sense of efficacy in making government 'responsible' to parliament) had strong overtones of both efficiency and participation. So did the measure of devolution that the Callaghan government proposed – however unwillingly – for Scotland and Wales in 1979. The Fulton proposals for reform of the civil service also equated a less exclusive administration with a more efficient one, and explicitly called for more 'openness' in public administration; and Margaret Thatcher – at first sight ironically, in view of her subsequent position on official secrecy when Prime Minister – made her parliamentary debut in 1960 by securing the passage of a private member's bill to make local government meetings open to the public.

The weakness of all these measures was, however, that while they reflected criticism of established institutions, they did not correspond to a widespread popular demand. At most, they reflected the concern of strong minorities (such as the ecology lobby or the student movement), a concern shared by a section of the press and the liberal intelligentsia and a number of MPs – so long as they remained on the benches. They were opposed by most ministers, ex-ministers and civil servants, and by many backbenchers as well. Predictably, the result was a series of reforms which it would be an exaggeration to call half-measures. Thatcher's Public Bodies (Admission to Meetings) Act of 1960 is a good example. She was 'persuaded to accept a provision allowing secrecy if [a local] council thought it would be "prejudicial to the public interest"' to meet in public, with 'no machinery to enforce the measure and no penalties for its evasion', with the result that many councils evaded it.[2] The fate of parliamentary reform, the Fulton reforms and the devolution bills have already been discussed. To bring out the common pattern, we will briefly consider here two more examples from the sixties and seventies – the redress of grievances and the issue of state secrecy.[3]

Legitimation – the 'Ombudsmen'

Unlike the French, with their comprehensive system of administrative justice, or the Scandinavians, with their ombudsmen, British citizens before 1967 who felt that they had been unjustly treated by the ever-expanding bureaucracy often had no effective means of redress. In 1967 the office of Parliamentary Commissioner for Administration was established. The model was the Scandinavian ombudsman, and the initiative came from a quarter not too far removed from the establishment: Justice, the British section of the International Commission of Jurists. When the Macmillan government flatly rejected Justice's extremely cautious proposals, the Labour Party took up the idea and legislated on it in 1967. A Health Service Commissioner was added in 1973, and Commissioners for Local Administration in 1974 (as part of the reorganisation of local government carried out in that year).* On paper, then, a comprehensive mechanism for investigating complaints of injustice by bureaucrats had been created.

But the jurisdiction and powers of the British ombudsmen (and one ombudswoman) were extremely limited – and even these powers were exercised, in crucial respects, in such a way as to reduce still further the usefulness of the institution. First of all, in deference to the supposed anxiety of MPs that their position vis-à-vis their constituents would be undermined (whether many MPs really felt anxiety was never actually tested) the Parliamentary Commissioner for Administration was only allowed to investigate complaints submitted to him through MPs. As Marshall remarks, this means that

> citizens of the United Kingdom are, in lacking direct access for complaint, denied a facility that is provided by Ombudsmen in Sweden, Norway, Denmark, New Zealand, Alberta, Ontario, New Brunswick, Quebec, Manitoba, Saskatchewan, Nova Scotia, South Australia, Western Australia, Victoria, Queensland, New South Wales, Alaska, Nebraska, Iowa and Hawaii, not to mention Uttar Pradesh and Jackson Missouri.[5]

The Parliamentary Commissioner regularly received more complaints directly, which he could not investigate, than he did from MPs (for instance in 1980, 1,194 compared with 1,031).[6]

Secondly, of those complaints passed on by MPs a high proportion fell outside his jurisdiction. The Parliamentary Commissioner was not allowed to investigate anything to do with the staffing of the civil service itself, anything to do with the nationalised industries, any contractual or commercial activities of the state, or any action involved in a police or security investigation. Similarly, the Commissioners for Local Administration could not investigate complaints about personnel

---

* A Parliamentary Commissioner for Northern Ireland, and a Northern Ireland Commissioner for Complaints (against local authorities and various other public bodies) were established in 1969.

matters in local government, or about any contractual or commercial transactions by a local authority except those relating to land. 'This means that no complaint can be investigated, for example, against the bus services run by local authorities . . . Nor can they investigate complaints about the internal management and organisation of schools or colleges'.[7] A court decision further ruled that a local authority could refuse to disclose any document to the Local Commissioners. The Health Commissioner likewise might not investigate complaints concerning the professional medical judgements of doctors, dentists, etc., or concerning the work of the Service Committees (which consist of doctors, dentists, etc., and hear complaint by patients). The areas – and the personnel – made immune to the new machinery were thus remarkably numerous.

Thirdly, the Commissioners' powers were limited to reporting on cases of maladministration. They were expressly forbidden to comment on the reasonableness of decisions. Later holders of the office of Parliamentary Commissioner have interpreted 'maladministration', on which they may comment, so as to include gross unreasonableness, and not just bad procedures. But they have done so very warily, and without any firm conviction. The ombudsmen could not say that, in their view, a civil servant had simply made a wrong or bad decision, even if he or she clearly had.

Fourthly, the ombudsmen were not entirely independent of the administrations they were supposed to investigate. They were not elected – the 'Parliamentary Commissioner' was not even elected by parliament, as he is in Sweden, but appointed, in the usual British fashion, nominally by the Prime Minister. The first three Parliamentary Commissioners were, moreoever, all former civil servants, and the first three Local Commissioners were, respectively, an ex-government minister (Lady Serota, a Labour life peer), a former civil servant and a former Town Clerk.

When Cecil Clothier retired as Ombudsman in 1984, Blom-Cooper ['a prominent public interest lawyer'] was keen to succeed him. He had been one of the earliest lobbyists in favour of importing the Scandinavian institution, and was uniquely qualified as an administrative lawyer and seasoned public enquirer. Lord Chief Justic Lane wrote to Mrs Thatcher strongly supporting him. The Whitehall mandarins were horrified. A strong-minded and knowledgeable outsider was the last person they wanted. Lane received a crisp letter of rejection from No.10.[8]

One wonders whether such appointments, supposedly to serve as public watchdogs over the executive, would have been politically credible in any other country. What is more, all the Parliamentary

Commissioner's staff were civil servants too, on secondment from their various government departments!

Fifthly, and following from this, Parliamentary Commissioners, especially, were hardly aggressive on behalf of citizens aggrieved by bureaucrats. They did not interpret their powers – though they might have – in such a way as to seek primarily a quick change of decision, where this seemed prima facie reasonable. Instead, they preferred to conduct meticulous 'ex post facto' enquiries, taking on average 12 months to complete. Moreover in their published reports on selected cases they did not name names; and as 'anonymised' reports naturally do not get much attention from the press the only effective weapon placed in the Commissioners' hands – publicity – was severely blunted.

Not surprisingly, in view of all these limitations, the public did not make much use of the ombudsmen. They – and especially the Parliamentary Commissioner – were too inaccessible (and the Parliamentary Commissioner also did not advertise his services).* In general, the Ombudsmen's jurisdiction was too restricted and they did not use the powers they had very energetically. Consequently, in 1971, the ombudsman for Denmark, with 5 million inhabitants, investigated more than twice as many cases as the ombudsmen of Great Britain, with a population of 55 million. It is unlikely that the British were twenty times better administered.[†] But the Parliamentary Commissioner 'scored one major success', Stacey noted in 1975, 'in that he has been accepted by the Civil Service'.[9] Comment on this would be superfluous.

Whitehall was, however, quite happy to see investigation of maladministration extended rather more energetically to other spheres than its own, especially local government and the National Health Service. The Local Commissioners operated under legislative provisions which went much farther than the Parliamentary Commissioner Act in making case reports locally available to the public, although their published annual reports were also 'anonymised'. In 1983–6, 6 per cent of the annual average of 4,116 complaints investigated by the Local Commissioners for England disclosed 'maladministration leading to injustice'. The Health Service Commissioner, dealing with an

---

* The Health Commissioner may be complained to directly. The Local Commissioners may also consider a complaint direct from the public if they are satisfied that a local councillor has been asked to submit it and has failed to do so. About half of the complaints submitted directly to the Local Commissioners for England and returned with a request to submit through a councillor have subsequently been so submitted.

† The annual number of complaints received by the Parliamentary Commissioner rose through the 1970s but levelled out at an annual average of 766 in the mid-1980s, when an average of 10.6 per cent were found to disclose 'maladministration leading to injustice'.

average of 848 complaints a year, and working with a significantly wider mandate, found on average that almost 29 per cent of them disclosed 'failures in service or maladministration leading to injustice'.[10] In 1981 an ombudsman for the insurance industry was created, and in 1986 one for the building societies.

Legitimation – Official Secrecy

Only slightly later than the establishment of the ombudsmen, there developed a parallel concern with state secrecy. The Fulton call for more openness was part of a gradual build-up of concern, fuelled by party rivalry and some backbench frustration, with the way the Official Secrets Act was used simply to conceal state policy-making (and incompetence) from parliament and the public, rather than to protect national security.[11] The instinct of conservatives (with a small 'c', notably including James Callaghan, Prime Minister from 1976 to 1979) was to leave the situation alone. The scope of the Act was so broad that the courts were unwilling to enforce severe penalties against journalists for 'receiving' unauthorised official information that did not in fact harm state security, even though this was illegal under the Act. But they were willing to jail civil servants, particularly junior ones, who 'leaked' any official information, however harmless to security, that their superiors wished to conceal; British judges were indisposed to back 'whistle-blowers' within the civil service. So the Act reinforced discipline within the state apparatus without, on the whole, constituting a severe threat to the press. Reformers wanted information that really related to security to be more clearly defined so that other official information could be made more freely available; while, at the other extreme, there was a call for less information to be released, a strengthening of the Act, and a more rigid enforcement against offenders.

In 1972 the Heath government, fulfilling an election pledge, appointed the Franks Committee to review Section 2 of the Official Secrets Act (the section which made all unauthorised transmissions of official information illegal). Its recommendations included a more restricted definition of what could not be divulged.[12] But, by the time it reported, the parties had become preoccupied with the economic situation to the exclusion of almost anything else, and no action was taken.

In October 1974, however, the Labour Party adopted – through the efforts of a small group of enthusiasts – a policy pledge which went much further: 'to replace the Official Secrets Act by a measure to put the burden on the public authorities to justify withholding information'

– i.e., a British version of the Freedom of Information (or 'right to know') legislation passed by the US Congress in 1966 and greatly strengthened in 1974. Meanwhile, yet a further issue became entwined with that of preventing the improper disclosure of necessary secrets or the improper concealment of facts to which the public should have access. This was, how to protect individuals' 'privacy' against invasion by the owners (state or private) of computerised data banks.[13] The stage was set for a classic exercise in the neutralisation of democratic initiatives.

Roy Jenkins, Labour Home Secretary from 1974 to 1976, visited the USA in 1975 and was readily persuaded by US officials that a Freedom of Information Act would be impossibly costly. Moreover, he subsequently declared his own opposition to conducting decision-making 'under a public searchlight'. Protagonists of change persevered, however, working on backbenchers in the House of Commons. It was difficult for the Labour government, with its rashly adopted election pledge and its growing dependence on the minority parties in parliament, to reject too openly a series of 'freedom of information' bills introduced by private members. Indeed, in 1975 the government had promised specifically to 'prepare proposals to amend the Official Secrets Act and to liberalise practices relating to official information'. As a result, one of the private members' bills, introduced by the Liberal MP Clement Freud in 1979, passed the committee stage without being wholly emasculated by government amendments. It is unlikely that the Bill would have become law, especially in view of Callaghan's personal dislike of the idea, but the question was pre-empted by the government's fall from office in April 1979.

The incoming Prime Minister Mrs Thatcher was even less sym-pathetic to 'open government' than Callaghan had been (her 1960 concern for open government in local affairs had been largely an expression of her hostility towards Labour-controlled urban councils and certainly did not extend to central government in 1979). To the contrary, her government now introduced a Protection of Official Information Bill which had been prepared by the civil service. This said nothing about the public's 'right to know'. In fact, so far from limiting the scope of the information that it would be a criminal offence to transmit, the Bill extended it. The Bill would also have allowed any minister to determine – after the event, and beyond any enquiry by the courts – whether a given piece of information was 'likely to cause serious injury to the interests of the nation'. Criticism of the Bill was widespread, but what stopped it was not criticism but the simultaneous publication of Andrew Boyle's book, *The Climate of Treason*. The facts disclosed in the book forced the government to admit that it had done a deal with a well-placed former Soviet spy who had later become Keeper of the Queen's Pictures and received a knighthood. Under the new Bill, Boyle would have been liable to a jail term for publishing this information. In the circumstances the government could only withdraw its Bill.

Still, the initiative had been decisively recaptured by the executive. The operations of the British state remained as secret as ever. An official circular of 1977 by Sir Douglas Allen, the head of the civil service, nominally laying down a policy of making more information available to the public (at the state's discretion), actually made it very clear that the object was to help forestall the introduction of legislation (such as 'the formidably burdensome Freedom of Information Act in the USA' as Sir Douglas called it)* which would oblige the state to disclose the processes through which decisions were arrived at. In practice, government departments persistently refused to make available to enquirers even the purged, sparely factual background documents envisaged in the circular, saying that there were none.[14]

Publicity for the processes of decision-making in government would, civil servants all agree, make their work more difficult: they would

> not necessarily produce worse decisions . . . but cause inconvenience . . . The unspoken heart of the argument for closed government is that private debate among civil servants and ministers produces more *rational* policies, freed from public pressure, which is assumed to be irrational.[15]

But as Kellner shows,

> Far from producing more rational government, the evidence suggests that secrecy produces more manipulative and arbitrary government . . . Officials

---

* As J. Michael has shown, this was a canard whose presence in Sir Douglas Allen's memorandum (known later as the Croham memorandum, when Allen became Lord Croham on his retirement) is exactly the sort of thing the reform is aimed to prevent. At the time when the memorandum was written there was already good evidence that the costs of the US legislation had been greatly exaggerated in the forecasts made by US civil servants before it was introduced. A year later, two civil servants from the Civil Service Department visited the USA and reached the reasonable conclusion that no one really knew what the costs of the legislation were, noting that the early estimates seemed to have been exaggerated. Had the Croham memorandum been publicly available, this inaccurate information on which its main argument turned could have been exposed. Its contents are only known because it was leaked to the press. As regards the Civil Service Department report, Michael calls it 'balanced' but later adds: 'Turning from financial costs of the US laws to other costs and benefits, the CSD report shows that impressions depend even more on who is quoted. In its balanced way, the report gave about three times as much space to those who think the laws have been a bad thing [as] to those who are in favour of them' (J. Michael, *The Politics of Secrecy*, Penguin, Harmondsworth 1982, p. 145).

are often ill-informed about the real world; ministers are often inaccurately advised by officials; Parliament often receives too little information too late from Ministers.[16]

As Lord Armstrong, another former Head of the Civil Service ('candid in retirement') admitted: 'it [secrecy] obviously is comfortable, convenient, and one has to say it allows mistakes to be covered up'.[17]

In late 1987 the issue of official secrecy was forced back on to the parliamentary agenda by a Conservative backbencher, Richard Shepherd, in the context of growing public resentment of the government's handling of the Spycatcher affair. It also emerged that the government had (secretly) widened the official definition of 'national security' in the rules governing wiretapping, so as to include activities affecting 'support of the Government's defence and foreign policies'. Mr Shepherd introduced a private member's bill (disarmingly entitled the Protection of Official Information Bill) which would have repealed Section 2 of the Official Secrets Act and made it a valid defence that it was in the public interest to disclose official information, as well as requiring the government to persuade the Judicial Committee of the Privy Council that the national interest was 'seriously injured' by the disclosure. The government imposed a three-line whip to defeat the bill, saying it would introduce its own measure later in 1988. The latter was not expected to liberalise access to official information, although the vote on the Shepherd bill indicated that in this area Thatcher did not have the full support of her parliamentary party.

Donald Rowat, a Canadian specialist on government secrecy, concluded that in a country without a strong tradition of openness government can only be expected to become more open if a radical law is passed requiring disclosure of information as the rule rather than exception, with narrowly defined exceptions, and effective enforcement by appeals to some independent arbiter. Quite apart from the unlikelihood of a measure meeting these requirements emerging from the configuration of British politics in the late 1980s, there is the more general question of how to find an independent arbiter, given the British tradition of the appointment by the state of 'independent' arbiters – whether for industrial disputes, on committees of enquiry, or as ombudsmen or judges – from within the establishment. It is difficult to share Michael's faith that either the British courts or the British ombudsmen would prove the champions of openness that judges and ombudsmen have been in the USA and Sweden respectively.[18] In short, it is difficult to see how British government can be made much more open without the British state becoming much more democratic.

To sum up what has been said in this section: it would be an exaggeration to claim that no progress whatever was made in the sixties and seventies in providing for the redress of grievances or in opening up the working of the state. However, as with parliamentary reform, civil service reform and, most visibly, devolution, the real thrust of the reformers was deflected, absorbed or in some way neutralised. In the sphere of local government, on the other hand, the tendency of reform was towards centralisation and bureaucracy, not greater democracy, even in the 1960s and 1970s, despite this being an area where great play was made with the idea of 'participation'. In contrast to the initiatives just discussed in relation to 'open government', these initiatives came mainly from within the state, and, again in contrast, they were largely successful.

The Local State

The problem of the local state – to give 'local government' a more accurate name – was that it was a good deal more democratic than the central state. The fundamental problem was that local government (here referring explicitly to its elective component, the local councils) enjoyed a 'relative autonomy from both the concerns of the central state and the impact of dominant classes. Related to this, local government is especially vulnerable to working class demands, pressures and even control.'[19] Once again we are dealing with the legacy of the informal, patrician state of pre-capitalist Britain. In most European countries which experienced the centralising and rationalising impact of the Napoleonic order, a strong measure of central control was maintained over local administration. But in Britain, as local administration in the nineteenth century outgrew the capacity of the local gentry to oversee it in their capacity as magistrates, it was generally entrusted to locally elected ad hoc commissions and boards, alongside the new municipal corporations, which were representative of the limited electorate of that time. There were elected boards or commissioners for cleaning, paving or lighting the streets, and for slum clearance, sewers, burials and water supply; as well as for administering public assistance, building and maintaining highways, and building and running primary schools.[20]

When, in 1888, a rationalised system of elected County and County Borough Councils was created, with property taxes (the 'rates') as their independent source of revenue, no general system of central supervision was placed over them.* Parliament, at the centre, established local councils by law, and by other laws laid a growing number of duties on them, and prescribed how they were to be performed; but the local accountability of locally elected councils, and a measure of financial independence, were clearly established.

> Parliament might have decided that local authorities should be elected but not have rate-raising powers, or that they should be able to raise rates without being elected. In fact Parliament has clearly established local authorities as bodies with independent sources both of democratic power and of finance.[21]

The effect was to create a potentially democratic component of the state that was to prove peculiarly susceptible to working-class influence – an influence which could not be as easily circumscribed as in the central state itself.

The majority of the working class were concentrated in the towns and cities. Nationally, this preponderance was offset by rural and suburban constituencies, where the middle classes were more numerous. However, once workers could vote, urban councils fell increasingly under their influence and eventually under Labour control. This was by no means universal, but as early as 1919 half the Metropolitan (London) Borough Councils created in 1899 were under Labour Party control, and by 1934 even London County Council was too – this at a time when the Labour Party in parliament had been reduced to a small minority. By 1939 Labour controlled, in addition, 18 County Borough Councils, 4 County Councils, and 100 District Councils (a further Act of 1894 had created a 'second tier' of Urban and Rural District Councils alongside the 'non-County' Borough Councils).

Labour control of city government was also strengthened by the exodus of the middle class into the suburbs from the end of the nineteenth century onwards, and the exodus of industrial and commercial men of property from provincial cities into the countryside. Owners of urban industrial and commercial property remained urban ratepayers and so still had votes in the towns, but they were too few to retain real power. Thus, there developed a powerful tradition of 'municipal labourism' and a significant measure of Labour moral and ideological hegemony in many cities, also reflected in a 'labourist'

---

* County Councils were made responsible for most local administrative functions, except that towns with more than 50,000 inhabitants had 'County Borough' Councils which enjoyed the same powers as County Councils and were fully independent of them. 'Non-county' boroughs had fewer powers; the County Councils of the counties within which they were situated also exercised some functions in relation to their inhabitants.

outlook among council employees, whose entire careers might be spent working for a Labour-controlled authority. In addition, local authorities did not lend themselves to the absorption of real power into the hands of an executive more or less immune to democratic control. This was partly because their functions were primarily to administer laws made by parliament, and only secondarily to pass by-laws for their areas (a fact reflected in the committee system whereby councils operated largely through committees of councillors, each committee being responsible for a separate area of administration and working directly with the responsible officials). It was also partly because the laws they administered and the services they provided dealt with local things which people experienced at first hand, and so were on the whole in a position to understand; and partly because raising revenue by rates, whatever its faults (such as that it was inelastic, uneven and regressive), is a form of taxation which, unlike the national budget, directly relates the amount of revenue demanded to the expenditure proposed, and is therefore more comprehensible.

For these reasons, Labour control of a council meant a real degree of control over the local state. The limitations of labourism itself, combined with the limited powers given to local authorities by parliament, circumscribed the political impact of this state of affairs. But as they acquired confidence, Labour-controlled councils began to exploit the powers they had been given, in addition to fulfilling the functions required of them by law: especially building houses for workers and undertaking various kinds of 'municipal trading', that is, enterprises such as public transportation, gas and electricity services, entertainments, telephone systems, docks and crematoria.

So long as central government remained under the effective control of the Conservative Party, Labour control of many of the country's city and town councils was an irritant, but not a critical one. Any new functions assigned to local authorities were determined by the central state. Extensions of municipal trading were resisted.[22] The one notable power which presented a problem during the inter-war years, the administration of the poor laws (including unemployment relief), was transferred to the central state (in the shape of a non-elective Unemployment Assistance Board) in 1934.* There were complaints about the 'calibre' of local councillors in the cities (a coded way of regretting that they only had the education provided for the working class, and were prone to set the standard of municipal services, such as council housing, above the level which middle-class ratepayers thought

* Down to 1930, poor relief in England and Wales was administered by locally elected Boards of Guardians, also often Labour-controlled in urban areas. From 1930 to 1934 it was briefly entrusted to County and County Borough Councils.

appropriate for workers).[23] But the problem was not a major one.

After 1945, however, the consolidation of the expanded welfare state greatly extended the role of the local state, since much of the expansion was in services that were already administered by local government, or led to the creation of new services that clearly ought to be. The new National Health Service was an exception; control over it was given to non-elective Regional Hospital Boards controlled by doctors, in order to help overcome their opposition to the scheme, and some 1,700 hospitals were transferred to these from local council control.[24] But the growth of the state, as measured by expenditure, was growth of the local state almost as much as of the central state. In the last pre-war year, 1938–9, local governments spent £782.8 million out of a total state expenditure of £1,801.8 million (43.4 per cent). In 1976–7 they spent £24,017 million out of a total of £63,289 million (37.9 per cent).[25] By that time they were also employing some 2.5 million people, about 10 per cent of all employees. The local state had become an immense social and economic presence. The control by Labour majorities of a large part of it was a major source of the rise of anti-state sentiment in the Conservative Party in the 1960s. Labour councils spent more on housing, education and personal-health services than non-Labour councils in areas with similar needs.[26]

This spending was covered partly by local rates, partly by revenues from services provided by the councils (e.g. rents from council-house tenants) and partly by grants from the central government to meet the cost of nationally required services administered by local authorities, and to equalise the burden of local rates between councils with differing property bases and differing social needs. By the mid-1970s central government grants accounted for about half of all local government spending (see Table 15.1). Meanwhile, ratepayers were complaining bitterly about their sharply increased rate demands (although in fact, as a percentage of total personal disposable income, the burden of domestic rates remained unchanged at 2.4 per cent of the total over the decade 1970–71 to 1980–81 – the apparent rise in the rates was an illusion entirely created by inflation).[27]* In this context the scale and spirit of the expenditures of many Labour-controlled councils became ever more unacceptable. As the fiscal crisis of the

* It is important to avoid mystification here. 'Grants' should be put in inverted commas because the term tends to connote something for nothing. 'Grants' to local government are primarily central government expenditures on nationally required tasks which are carried out locally, such as education or roadworks, for which policy is almost wholly laid down in Whitehall. Similarly with the term 'ratepayers'. It is not generally realised that tenants, including council-house tenants, pay rates just as owner-occupiers do. Commercial and industrial ratepayers, moreover, are major users of council services, contrary to the impression often given in the media.

state developed, the 'accumulation function' of the state, which was seen as calling for reduced state spending, and the 'legitimation function', which called for its maintenance, came into conflict in the local sphere.

The problem was both delicate and complex. It was delicate, partly because a solution meant reducing the degree of effective local democracy – a sensitive issue given the ideological importance of democracy in general – and partly because any such scheme promoted by a Conservative government would affect Conservative-controlled councils as well as Labour ones. On the other hand, the Labour leadership was also less than enthusiastic about local democracy because of its potential for generating more radical, extra-parliamentary forms of action.

What the Labour leadership opposed was commonly known as 'Poplarism'. In 1921 the Mayor and 29 Labour councillors of the East London Borough of Poplar went to prison for refusing to collect rates, as required by law, for any services other than those operated by themselves and the Poplar Poor Law Guardians (also controlled by Labour and largely the same people). This was a gesture aimed at forcing the government of the day to legislate so as to redistribute the cost of unemployment relief, which at that time was all borne locally. Thus ratepayers in Poplar, a poverty-stricken dockland area with 15,000 unemployed out of a total population of 160,000, were expected

Table 15.1   Sources of local government income 1961–1986 (%)

	1961	1966	1971	1976	1977	1978	1979
Central government current grants	30.6	32.2	37.8	49.4	47.7	48.4	45.9
Rates	30.8	29.8	27.6	23.7	25.8	27.1	26.0
Other	21.0	17.2	15.9	18.4	18.6	19.7	18.8
Borrowing requirement	17.6	20.8	18.7	8.5	7.9	4.8	9.3

	1980	1981	1982	1983	1984	1985	1986
Central government current grants	44.5	48.3	48.5	49.0	48.7	49.0	48.9
Rates	27.2	32.3	35.7	32.9	31.9	32.4	33.9
Other	18.4	18.1	18.2	14.8	13.8	14.8	15.7
Borrowing requirement	9.9	1.3	−2.4	3.3	5.6	3.8	1.5

Source: Social Trends.

to pay more than twice as much as the prosperous ratepayers of Westminster, where there was virtually no unemployment. In the event, the persistent and overwhelming support of the Poplar electorate over the years 1919–25 obliged successive governments to secure the release of the Mayor and councillors after a month's imprisonment, to equalise the burden of unemployment relief, to introduce a more humane system and level of poor relief, and – as a result of the gathering momentum of the cause of the Poplar leaders and the backing they received from their council employees – to accept some improvement in the real wages paid to council workers.[28]

In 1934, nine years after this protracted struggle, in which one impoverished borough forced fundamental policy changes on unwilling governments, the administration of public assistance was removed from elected councils altogether. Also significantly, the Labour Party leadership was unhappy at the way the Poplar radicals had conducted their campaign. The Labour government of 1924 had been attacked in the House of Commons for supporting 'unconstitutional' action, and the leadership saw this as partly to blame for Labour's defeat in the 1924 election.

Fifty years later, the Labour leaders were caught in exactly the same trap. In 1972 the Labour-controlled Urban District Council of the mining town of Clay Cross in Derbyshire, confronted with unemployment approaching 20 per cent due to pit closures, refused to collect an additional £1 per week in rent from the tenants of its council houses, as required by the Conservatives' new Housing Finance Act. On this occasion the government carefully avoided enforcing the law in such a way as to risk having the 11 rebel councillors sent to prison, and for two years the Clay Cross Council successfully resisted the government's efforts to collect the increased rent directly. They also raised the pay of council manual workers above the limits prescribed in the 1973 wage controls. The basis of their success was the same as that of the Poplar leaders: the solid support of a large majority in a distinctive, somewhat isolated and densely working-class area.[29]

What was significant was the reaction of the Labour Party leadership. The 1972 Labour Party Conference resolved to support any council which refused to apply the new rents, and to indemnify councillors against disqualification from office, and against any 'surcharges' which might be made on them (under the law, councillors judged by the District Auditor to have spent council funds improperly could be disqualified and billed personally to recover the sums in question). In 1924 the Labour minister concerned had promised to remit any surcharges made on the Poplar Poor Law Guardians for exceeding the legally permitted rates of relief, and this had been attacked as unconstitutional. In the Clay Cross case the Labour leadership refused to give any such promise, although without it the conference's declaration of 'support' for councils opposing the Housing Finance Act was distinctly hollow; and after Labour won the 1974 elections six of the Clay Cross councillors were allowed to be bankrupted.

The problem of Clay Cross was only resolved in a permanent manner by the abolition of Clay Cross Urban District and its absorption into the new, and much larger, District of North-East Derbyshire during the local government reorganisation of 1974. This formed part of a comprehensive reorganisation of local government, endorsed in its essentials by both parties, and designed to reduce if not eliminate the difficulty presented for the state by local democracy.

By 1961 the system of local government had remained virtually unchanged for 60 years while the social and economic structure of society had changed a great deal. However, neither party cared to impose a reform over the vociferous opposition of the members and officials of the existing local authorities (both Labour and Conservative). The most obvious anomaly was that some large and growing cities were still subordinate to County Councils while others which had declined, and were much smaller, retained their autonomous 'County Borough' status and had full responsibility for all local government functions. At the same time, it was argued that many functions could now only be efficiently performed on a larger scale than that of any existing county. But none of these arguments had been enough to carry the first proposals for change, presented by a commission in 1947.[30]

In London, however, where the anomalies were among the most severe, an opportunity existed to make a change independently of the rest of the country. London County Council (LCC) and the majority of London's metropolitan boroughs were Labour-controlled, while a Conservative government was in power at Westminster; a change could be imposed in London that would benefit the Conservatives without hurting Conservatives elsewhere. In 1963, therefore, following a special Royal Commission, the LCC was merged into a new Greater London Council (GLC) covering most of the built-up area (the LCC's boundaries having long since been outgrown), with responsibility for planning, transport policy, main roads, fire and ambulance services; while a few greatly enlarged London boroughs were made responsible for the rest (except for education in the Inner London area, which was left in the hands of an Inner London Education Authority jointly responsible to the GLC and the London boroughs).

The enlarged GLC included much more of the suburbs. This dramatically altered the electoral balance, as the Conservatives had expected. Labour continued to control the solidly working-class borough councils of East London and most of the 'inner city', but in 1967 the GLC itself and, in 1968, 27 out of the 32 new London Boroughs, passed under Conservative control, giving them overall control of London again for the first time since 1934.[31]

The example of London played an obvious part in the solution ultimately found for reorganisation elsewhere. The official argument was that larger units were much more efficient (though this was shown to be not merely not proven, but fallacious).* The tacit reasoning was that combining towns and cities with peri-urban and rural areas would also dilute areas of working-class concentration with middle-class areas. In the coded language of establishment social science, commentators noted that 'by creating areas which are rather more functionally united, but socially heterogeneous, the [proposed] structure will mean that there are fewer councils in England which are politically and socially unbalanced' – that is (in Dearlove's translation), 'it would reduce the unfettered control which working-class voters and Labour dominated councils have over the affairs of the central city'.[32]

It was again the Conservatives who, in 1972, implemented the long-delayed reorganisation. The number of counties was reduced by mergers to 47, with 333 much-enlarged District Councils within them. The conurbations outside London followed the London model, with six Metropolitan Councils – Greater Manchester, West Midlands, Merseyside, West Yorkshire, South Yorkshire and Tyne and Wear – and 36 lower-tier District Councils within them.[†] In Scotland nine regions were created, with 53 districts within them, and three virtually single-tier island councils. The new authorities were so much larger that few voters any longer had first-hand knowledge of their overall problems.

---

* The way in which the Redcliffe-Maud Commission on Local Government tried to discredit all research findings which led to this conclusion (including its own) should be an object lesson for all those who are tempted to think that making social science useful means conducting investigations into questions of interest to, or at the request of, state agencies (see Dearlove, *The Reorganisation of British Local Government,* Cambridge University Press, Cambridge 1979, pp. 68–78).

† In the 1973 elections for the new councils in England and Wales the results in terms of party control were as follows:

	Conservatives	Labour	No clear party control
Metropolitan Counties	–	6	–
Other Counties	18	11	18
Metropolitan Districts	5	26	5
Other Districts (England)	86	73	137
Other Districts (Wales)	1	19	17

Besides the enlargement of local authority areas, two other major changes also curtailed the scope of local democracy. One was the drive to assimilate local authority administration to the 'corporate' model – that is, the model of management advocated for companies. It was promoted by the central government through two enquiries, the Maud Committee of 1964–7, and the Bains Working Group of 1972.[33] The change, however, was also the product of a convergence between a new kind of councillor (Labour as well as Conservative) coming to the fore in the 1960s, and a new kind of local government official who emerged at about the same time; both were responsive to the ideology of planning, economies of scale and efficiency which were then being promoted by academic social scientists and business consultants who played an active part in local government reorganisation.[34]

Under this initiative, virtually all local authorities abandoned the practice whereby department heads (Directors of Education, of Housing, etc.) were separately responsible to corresponding committees of councillors. This was judged incompatible with integrated planning and efficient management of the councils' work considered as a whole, and – not least – considered in relation to the needs of the businesses located in their areas. Instead councils, like companies, now appointed Chief Executives, who (unlike the former Town Clerks) had formal authority over the Department Heads or Directors. The latter could, in consequence, now be grouped in a Committee of Officials (the Directors' Board was the name given to it in Lambeth, for example, who prepared agendas for a new Policy Committee, chaired by the elected Leader of the Council and consisting primarily of the chairmen of the various council committees). Although the committees still met, these changes, whatever else they may have accomplished, shifted a good deal of effective power out of the hands of the committees of elected councillors and lodged it with the Policy Committee and the Directors Board.[35] In effect, the local state was brought more into line with the structure of the central state.

The executive had been strengthened and concentrated, and the equivalent of a cabinet under the control of the leader had been created. Information was now increasingly controlled by the officials and the inner leadership of the majority party on the council, at the same time that the larger areas reduced the independent knowledge which any councillor was likely to have of the detail of any question before the council.

The second change which helped to roll back local democracy was increased financial control by central government, culminating in 1988 in the virtual elimination of the financial independence of local government. It had always been necessary for local councils to secure

Treasury permission to borrow for capital expenditure, and as the crisis developed during the 1960s and 1970s severe cuts were imposed in the building of schools, roads and houses. Local authorities were now also required to furnish estimates of their long-term future *recurrent* expenditure for inclusion in the annual projections of the Treasury's Public Expenditure Survey Committee. When monetarist policies began to be enforced from 1976 onwards, local recurrent spending also fell under the axe. Between 1976 and 1980 the percentage of local government expenditure financed by central government grants, which had risen sharply in the sixties and seventies, was cut back, as was local government borrowing (see Table 15.1), and the squeeze was even more severe under the Conservatives after 1979: local authorities were actually forced to save, not borrow, in 1982, and over the whole period from 1979 to 1987 local government spending in real terms was held absolutely constant.

At first the squeeze was accomplished by changing the terms on which the central government grants were made. In 1958, they were consolidated into a single Rate Support Grant, calculated on a very complex formula. From 1977–8 this was sharply cut back and, at the same time, any overspending by a local authority (i.e. relative to what Whitehall had approved) in one year was to be compensated for by a corresponding cut in the grant in the following year (the so-called 'cash limits'). The effect was to shift the burden of maintaining the level of local services onto the rates. Rates had already been rising in the immediately preceding years, partly as a result of the rapid growth in the demand for social services and their above-average cost increases and partly because of inflation – even though they were actually still not as high, relative to people's personal incomes, as they had been in 1939. They now rose even more sharply, thanks to the reduced grants and the high interest on the debt that many councils had felt obliged to resort to. This led in turn to a 'ratepayers' revolt' and to Conservative victories in local elections.

In effect, officials in Whitehall were now able to control in considerable detail the whole range of local government spending, and hence local government policy too. But the councils were resisting the cuts in services by means of borrowing and rate increases and in 1981 the screws were tightened further when councils were told that if they budgeted to spend more than the responsible minister approved, they would not merely lose an equivalent part of their grant the following year, they would have their grant for the *current* year correspondingly reduced. This still did not prevent councils from doing this, incurring the penalty, and making up the loss from supplementary rate demands. In some areas, of course, the rates fell heavily on businesses, and councils in these areas were tempted to follow this course in order to maintain services (and council jobs). The 1982 Local Government Finance Act closed this loophole by banning supplementary rates. This still left councils with the legal authority to levy ordinary rates and some went on levying rates well in excess of what Whitehall wanted. In 1984, therefore, following the 1983 election, the Conservatives passed a Rates Act authorising Whitehall to 'cap' the rates of selected councils – that is, to set upper limits of the rates that could be set. In 1986 this was generalised to all councils.

This prolonged process naturally had considerable costs. Policy changes following each other in rapid succession left even the most compliant councils – concerned as they were to keep local services functioning, plan ahead, be good employers and be fiscally prudent – in a state of demoralisation. In areas of severe deprivation, where there was strong and articulate opposition to the whole thrust of the government's economic and social policy, councillors were bound to resist. In Liverpool, the conurbation most seriously affected by deindustrialisation and unemployment, the Militant Tendency won enough seats in the Labour group to propel the Council on a collision course with Whitehall, culminating in a crisis in 1985 when eventually Whitehall prevailed. Even so, in spite of the errors and posturing that marked Militant's performance of this role, the government was ultimately unable to wield the full powers it had taken to deal with such a situation. More Liverpool voters blamed the government than blamed the council for Liverpool's financial problems.[36] And in the country at large surveys consistently showed that voters were more in favour of improved services, even if it meant higher taxes, than the reverse.[37]

Meantime the government had gone even further by abolishing outright the six Metropolitan County Councils set up by the Conservatives under the 1982 Act, and the Greater London Council set up (also by the Conservatives) in 1963. All seven of these bodies were irreducibly Labour-controlled, and the GLC in particular, closely followed by South Yorkshire, had been cheerfully pioneering all sorts of collective, 'progressive–populist' (i.e. as opposed to Thatcher's authoritarian variety) initiatives in the (admittedly limited) spheres of authority given to them. Although opinion polls showed that 70 per cent of Londoners opposed the abolition of the GLC, and although the ostensible reasons given for the abolition (that these councils were unnecessary, wasteful and bureaucratic) were widely disbelieved, the government pressed ahead.*

* The functions of the GLC and metropolitan councils were transferred either to the boroughs within their boundaries, or to 'residuary bodies' (in respect of functions that

The Thatcher government was animated by an open hostility towards a system of local government that it saw as having spawned a network of socialist fiefs, where property-owners' rates were spent on armies of overpaid, unionised and Labour-voting council employees, to provide expensive services to the least productive members of society. This sentiment had, thus, carried it far along the road to the de facto abolition of local government (as opposed to the local administration of central government policies), though except in relation to the metropolitan counties it had stopped short of abolishing local elections.

In 1988 it passed the new Local Government Act which finally embodied this outlook in a fully rationalised form (see Chapter 7, p. 125). The rates disappeared, being replaced by a fixed 'community service charge' payable equally by every adult, regardless of income (even people living on social security would have to pay 20 per cent of it) – the 'poll tax'. Councils would get at most 25 per cent of their revenue from this source (20 per cent in Scotland and 15 per cent in Wales). To raise their total spending by one percentage point, therefore, they would have to raise the poll-tax by at least 4 per cent. A way had at last been found, it seemed, to terminate the evil effects of the operation of the electoral principle in cities where the working class was so inconveniently numerous. The Labour leadership, which had been associated with the erosion of local democracy from at least the 1920s, was not in a strong position to object.

Law and Order

On the weekend of 10–12 July 1981 rioting broke out in more than 30 towns and cities throughout Britain. They occurred mainly in the kind of 'inner-city' areas which had been the focal points of the struggle between local democracy and centralising bureaucracy over the previous 20 years. The general cause of the riots, which sociologists and community workers had been expecting for several years, was the alienation of young people, especially blacks, caused by very high unemployment, a deprived and depressed environment, and lack of hope for the future. As we have seen, solving their problems had not been the prime object of policy with regard to local government; the prime object was to curtail local government spending. Even so, the

---

went beyond the purview of any one borough) which proved, in the end, to be necessary, wasteful and bureaucratic: see P. Hillyard and J. Percy-Smith, *The Coercive State*, Fontana–Collins, London 1988, pp. 75–7.

rioting did not happen of its own accord. Its immediate cause was the impact on these communities of a new style of policing. What the riots threw into prominence was how the state had responded to the national crisis by radically strengthening its repressive capacity.

Besides Brixton (south London) and Toxteth (Liverpool) – where the rioting was the most intense and prolonged – there were also major riots in Southall (London) and in Moss Side (Manchester). In April of the previous year, too, there had been a serious riot in the St Paul's district of Bristol. What all these areas had in common was not just inner-city deprivation and substantial black minorities, but also a recent history of exposure to a new kind of policing. They rarely, if ever, saw a local uniformed 'bobby' on a regular 'beat', who was known to and familiar with the local residents, someone who could rely on them for information and a degree of support and who was subject – even if only indirectly – to the influence of local councillors on the local police committee in matters regarding policing policy. Instead, policemen in cars and vans, acting on information from informers or from suspects' answers to questions, or on no information at all, were apt to stop and search people in social centres, such as youth clubs, discos and pubs, or on the streets. Sometimes this was done on a massive scale as part of the 'saturation policing' of an area (as happened extensively in Brixton before the riots).

Consequently, relations between the police and the local populations of these areas altered. Policemen were encountered less as 'helpers' and more as an arbitrary and often aggressive outside force, who tended to see all those who were unemployed or black, especially the young, as actual or potential trouble-makers who must be kept in their place. The evidence collected by the Commission for Racial Equality in Bristol, the Working Party on Police–Public Relationships in Toxteth and the Scarman inquiry in Brixton all showed that these confrontations were precipitated by incidents which brought hostility to the police to boiling point.[38]

The developments which lay behind this go beyond policing in the narrow sense. During the 1960s and 1970s the coercive arm of the state as a whole – the organisation and practices of the police, the secret police and the army – had undergone a qualitative change, which can be summarised as follows:

(a) the bureaucratisation of the police and the elimination of popular control;

(b) the change from 'community policing' to 'fire-brigade policing' and 'policing people' based on the doctrine of the 'pre-emption' (as opposed to prevention and detection) of crime;

(c) the development of new police technology, especially computers;

(d) the expansion of secret police surveillance of political opposition;

(e) the militarisation of policing, including the use of the army as an instrument of social control.

With the advent of the Thatcher government these changes were all accelerated, along with a major expansion of public spending on law and order, and a big expansion of police establishments.

The background to these developments (which are dealt with under separate headings below) was partly a rapid growth in crime rates. In 1900 there were 78,000 indictable offences, or 250 per 100,000 people. In 1967 there were over 3,000 offences per 100,000 people, and in 1977, 4,000 offences.[39] Such figures should be treated with great caution. Part of the increase was due to new legislation (for example, most traffic-related crimes). More importantly, reported crimes constitute such a small proportion of all crimes committed (according to all research on this question) that increases in recorded crime-rates usually tell us more about changes in reporting, recording or policing than about changes in criminal behaviour (for instance, the jump from two cases of male importuning recorded in Manchester, in 1958, to 216 by 1962, was due to an increase in police attention to the crime, ordered by a new chief constable, not an increase in male prostitution).[40] None the less, it seems clear that the incidence of crimes against property, in particular, did increase substantially. Small rural police forces, with as few as 20 or (in one case) 10 officers, were increasingly inadequate for the job of crime prevention and detection in the age of the motorway and computer fraud. Greater centralisation, specialisation and the use of new technology were necessary.* It is also clear that one or two policemen on the beat were unequal to dealing with gangs of motor-cyclists involved in mass brawls, crowd violence at football matches, or large-scale direct political action by groups such as the Committee of 100 (a section of the Campaign for Nuclear Disarmament).

However, this factor is hard to separate from at least two other developments. One was the general movement for bureaucratisation of the local state, and the elimination of control by elected local

* It is necessary to avoid the error common in much of the critical literature on the police, of falling into a naive anarchism and implicitly rejecting the need for appropriate means of enforcing social discipline. It also seems wise to be cautious in arguing for direct democratic control of the police, given that local democracy – in its admittedly often hamstrung British form – has not always led to good results in other fields such as housing: see R. Reiner, *The Politics of the Police*, Wheatsheaf/St Martins, Brighton 1985, p. 202.

BRISTOL POLYTECHNIC
ST. MATTHIAS LIBRARY
FISHPONDS

authorities. This was very clear in the attitude of chief constables towards local authority police committees, an attitude supported by home secretaries of both parties and by the judiciary. The other was a growing concern about the state's capacity to deal with extra-parliamentary political opposition, which was partly an anxiety about the growth of trade union militancy. The confrontation between 6,000 workers and 700 police at the Saltley coke depot in Birmingham during the 1972 miners' strike was a turning-point here. The police were obliged to concede to numbers and give up their attempt to protect lorries crossing the picket line. Later changes in the law on picketing (in the Employment Act of 1980) were one reaction: drastic changes in the state's capacity to deal directly with industrial mass action were another, starting immediately after the Saltley incident.

At the same time, there was a growing anxiety about 'subversion'. This was partly a response to the IRA Provisionals' bombing and shooting campaigns both in Northern Ireland and (from time to time) in England. But it was also a response to the growth of extraparliamentary radical politics generally, after about 1960: the multiplication of Marxist 'grouplets' on the left, the large increase in unofficial strikes and the emergence of community action groups of all kinds who were prepared to act directly in spheres where the parliamentary parties seemed impotent or uninterested.

Faced with these developments, successive governments expanded the definition of 'subversion'. In 1963 Lord Denning (in his report on the Profumo affair) said a subversive person was someone who 'would contemplate the overthrow of government by unlawful means'.[41] This made 'subversion' a matter of someone's ideas, but seemed to confine it to ideas about unlawful means of political action. In 1975, however, a Labour Minister of State at the Home Office said 'subversion is defined as activities threatening the safety or well-being of the state and intended to undermine or overthrow parliamentary democracy by political, industrial or violent means'.[42] This definition referred to activities, rather than ideas, but defined them so broadly or vaguely as potentially to cover almost any political action considered hostile by those in charge of the state. It remained only for a Labour Home Secretary, Merlyn Rees, to bring the two definitions together when he said in 1978 that 'the Special Branch collects information on those whom [sic] I think cause problems for the state';[43] and the evidence makes it clear that this was indeed the increasingly large task that the secret police had set themselves by this time.*

---

* And not the secret police alone. The most prominent of the new 'political' chief constables, James Anderton of Greater Manchester, said on television in 1979 that he thought that for the next 10 to 15 years 'basic crimes as such – theft, burglary, even

These institutional and policy changes, reflecting broader social and political developments, were also influenced by Thatcher's campaign for 'law and order' from the late 1960s onwards (see Chapter 7). In 1975 the Police Federation (the policemen's lobbying and negotiating organisation) broke with tradition and launched an extensive public campaign for 'law and order' as part of its efforts to raise police pay and recruitment and to make the task of the police easier. Sir Robert Mark, Metropolitan Police Commissioner from 1972 to 1977, began a new tradition of police chiefs engaging in public political discussion, with a series of attacks on the jury system and the rules of evidence. This agitation reinforced the policy trends which had developed with the support of both major parties throughout the sixties and seventies, and was energetically followed through by the Conservative government after 1979.[44] The main elements within this trend, which were listed earlier, are now considered in turn.

(a) The bureaucratisation of the Police and the elimination of democratic control

The movement to enlarge local authorities in the name of efficiency was preceded by a movement to enlarge police authority areas, which had similar motives. In 1918 a brief police strike for recognition of the Police Union frightened the authorities (Lloyd George's later remark that 'it was the nearest the country ever came to Bolshevism' shows how the strike was viewed, fantastic as the idea may be).* After the strike, the Desborough Committee initiated a process of standard- ising police recruitment, pay, training and organisation throughout the country, under Home Office supervision, beginning with the Police Act of 1919. The Committee also recommended abolishing all police forces of non-county boroughs with less than 15,000 inhabitants. This was successfully resisted by local authorities, however – a measure of their vitality and strength at that time – and the amalgamation process only began as a general policy with the Police Act of 1946.

---

violent crime – will not be the predominant police feature. What will be the matter of greatest concern to me will be the covert and ultimately overt attempts to overthrow democracy, to subvert the authority of the state and, in fact, to involve themselves *[sic]* in acts of sedition designed to destroy our parliamentary system and the democratic government in this country' (BBC 1 'Question Time', 16 October 1979, cited in *Review of Security and the State*, 1980, p. 34).

* The strike was settled with a large pay increase and an apparent agreement to recognise the Police Union when the war was over. When this recognition was later withheld the Union was skilfully divided and a second strike was quickly broken. The Police Federation, with no right to strike and with heavy over-representation of senior officers, was established by the government in place of the Union.

A Royal Commission on the Police in 1960–62 recommended carrying
the process further by amalgamating the remaining smaller forces,
but at the same time resisted proposals to create a single national
police force. A new Police Act of 1964 allowed the Home Secretary
to impose amalgamations even on forces serving populations of over
100,000. Between 1946 and 1969, the number of forces in England
and Wales was reduced from 159 to 49. In 1974, with the reduction
in the number of counties, the number was reduced still further,
to 43 (including the Metropolitan and City of London Police forces).
In Scotland, 33 forces in 1950 had been reduced to 8 by
1980. Northern Ireland (the model of 'pre-emptive' policing from
the moment of partition) had only one force (the Royal Ulster
Constabulary).

Meantime the 1960–62 Royal Commission had also redefined the
power of the once-powerful police committees of local councils as
consisting of appointing and removing chief constables (subject to the
Home Secretary's approval) and thereafter 'giving advice and guidance
to the Chief Constable about local problems'. This change was
reflected in the 1964 Police Act. 'Thus the idea of local control . . .
was set aside in a way that would have been totally incomprehensible
to most 19th-century watch committees and county justices.'[45] On the
other hand, the Home Secretary was not made formally responsible for
the police outside London, except in having to approve the
appointment or removal of chief constables, and in overseeing the
general standards of recruitment, training and efficiency. As a result,
the Home Secretary declined to answer parliamentary questions about
the conduct of provincial police forces; he also declined to answer
questions about the conduct of the Metropolitan Police, for which he
was formally responsible. With these changes, the new enlarged police
forces thus became, for all practical purposes, immune from any
control except the private influence of the Home Secretary and his
officials.[46]

This was greatly reinforced after the Saltley gates incident in the
1972 miners' strike referred to above, through the establishment of a
National Reporting Centre. Officially, the NRC is simply a communications centre linking the 43 police forces of the country so that they
can support each other more effectively in dealing with problems that
transcend the jurisdiction of any one of them. In the miners' strike of
1984–5, however, the NRC appeared to be acting as a command
centre, actively directing police operations in the coalfields from
London, and was certainly crucial in providing the basis for the central
government's political direction of the successful effort to defeat the
strike; and the chief constables of all the local police forces concerned

collaborated very closely with the Home Office, and committed the large sums of additional expenditure involved, without consulting with their local police committees.[47] Other centralising trends, strongly encouraged by the Thatcher government, included such things as making weaponry available to local police forces from a central source if local police committees (which do have powers to approve or disapprove proposed expenditures) declined to, spending heavily on computerised facilities for exchanging information on individuals and organisations between forces, and providing centralised training for the use of weapons and for Special Patrol Groups (see below).

(b) The shift to 'reactive' and 'pre-emptive' policing

Already by 1979 the new police forces had grown to a total of 126,500 officers and 47,500 civilians.[48]* Between 1979 and 1986 a fresh expansion occurred: public expenditure on 'law and order' rose by 41 per cent (more than on any other item – while spending on housing fell by 43 per cent), resulting in a further 10,000 policemen and additional civilian support staff. But as early as 1978 the Chief Inspector for Scotland had noted in his annual report that 'in effect our police force has more than doubled in the last forty years . . . and one could well ask where all the policemen have gone'.[49]

The answer was that they had been reorganised into specialised roles and into formations capable of being quickly deployed to meet threats to public order, such as from strikers or demonstrators, which were beyond the capability of the traditional police on foot patrol. The reason usually given for the absence of policemen from the streets (Whitaker records that in 1975 'there were times when none of the six stations in London's E Division could spare any man to put on the beat') was that crime-rates were outstripping police resources, but the truth was that police resources had been deliberately deployed off the streets.[50] 'Command and control' techniques, utilising computerised information on the whereabouts of the force on duty, and radio communication, imply that most policemen are in mobile units and specialised squads of various kinds. As one chief constable (a critic of the trend) summed it up, 'The car, the radio and the computer dominate the police scene. The era of preventive policing (by

---

* Excluding Northern Ireland. It is difficult to compare this with the figures for other countries. Whitaker (*The Police in Society,* Methuen, London 1919, p. 116) gives a figure for England and Wales in 1978 of 423 people per policeman, compared with 702 in the Netherlands, 533 in Canada and 323 in Belgium. The latter figures, however, are for 1972; on the other hand the British figures omit auxiliary forces such as the British Transport Police (1,900 in 1980) and the Atomic Energy Police (400).

patrolling) is phasing out in favour of a responsive or reactive police.'[51] This was only partly correct: it would have been truer to say that pre-emption was replacing prevention, as we shall see.

Again following the Saltley affair, a National Security Committee was established; and 'one of its many recommendations was that the police should revamp training in riot control and form a far closer relationship with the army'.[52] By 1980 at least 27 police forces in the United Kingdom had Special Patrol Groups (under one name or another) trained as riot control units, and all the forces had Police Support Units, notionally prepared for special security duties in the event of a nuclear attack. Hillyard and Percy-Smith estimated in 1987 that in Great Britain at least 26,000 police had been specially trained in riot control, and all forces had 'mutual aid' arrangements for this purpose. In addition, many more police had been trained in the use of firearms (an estimated 10 per cent), although it should be stressed that by international standards British policemen remained mainly unarmed.

The point is that police work in general had undergone a marked change. The new concept of policing had reinforced the distancing from the community caused by larger local authority and police force areas and the elimination of local democratic control. The outlook and experience of policemen trained more to 'contain' crime than prevent it, to deal with disorder and 'subversion' more than crime detection, tended to involve a self-fulfilling prophecy. The new 'squads' could not be put on the beat but they could be used to 'saturate' or 'swamp' a so-called 'high crime area' such as Brixton or Huyton with police for a day or a week, stopping and searching hundreds of young, unemployed or black people on the streets; or used to make 'fishnet sweeps', ostensibly to catch illegal immigrants in London, or arsonists in Wales, but actually as much to gather information and discourage or intimidate potential wrong-doers.[53] This style of policing encourages the common if not inevitable tendency of police forces to develop stereotypes of whole social categories which they see as 'naturally' prone to wrongdoing, and notably racial minorities. The racist attitudes which policemen in these formations tended to exhibit were disclosed in a number of ways during the 1970s and 1980s, and especially in a devastating report based on participant observation with the Metropolitan Police for the Policy Studies Institute in 1983.[54] While responsibility rests with the police for this state of affairs (the failure to screen out racist recruits or to discipline officers for practising, or condoning, racism) it is important to note that such a development is also a product of the situation into which the police have been thrust by the concepts of 'pre-emptive' and 'reactive' policing – and by the tendency of government policy since the mid-1970s to aggravate the problems of unemployment and inner-city deprivation.

Under the Thatcher governments police powers were also extended, police practices became more aggressive, and the courts more punitive. The Police and Criminal Evidence Act of 1984 gave the police wide powers to stop and search people, to set up roadblocks, enter and search premises without a warrant, and to detain people for up to 36 hours without charge. The Prevention of Terrorism Act of 1984 extended these powers to stop and search or arrest, if the police suspect involvement in terrorism. The Public Order Act of 1986 extended the list of possible threats to public order, required seven days notice of all marches and demonstrations, and gave the police power to impose severe restrictions on them or even ban them. The rate of arrests (as opposed to)summons) rose, and the courts increasingly remanded people in custody rather than allowing them bail, sent them to jail rather than fining them, and gave longer sentences.[55] In the miners' strike magistrates' courts frequently imposed conditions on bail for miners charged with offences in connection with picketing, which effectively barred them from further participation in the strike; in most cases, the charges were later withdrawn.

(c) The development of new technology

Apart from new weapons and equipment, from plastic bullets and CS gas to helicopters and cars specially equipped for surveillance, the main technical innovation was the computer.[56] The Police National Computer (PNC) is said to contain 50 million records of stolen or 'suspect' vehicles, all vehicle-owners, fingerprints held by the police and the names of criminals, wanted or missing persons and disqualified drivers. The nature of this computer facility, 'which is linked to every police force in the country', is a matter of public record.[57] The Metropolitan Police 'C' (Criminal) Department Computer, by contrast, is secret. It contains the records of the Central Drugs Intelligence Unit, the National Immigration Intelligence Unit, the Criminal Investigations Department and the Special Branch (the political police). By 1988 computers had been or were to be installed by most local police forces, with facilities for exchanging information with each other and with the PNC. Besides the local records that were held on these computers there was also 'intelligence'. This consisted of both factual information and hearsay and speculation about individuals compiled by officers designated as 'collators'. Some of these computers, following Northern Ireland practice, had or were intended to have comprehensive street registers, listing every house and its occupants.

The evidence suggests that by 1979 the PNC alone contained 'intelligence' (not confined to details of car ownership) on more than one-fifth of the adult population.* Telephone tapping, bugging and photographic and video technology all expanded as well during these years. The evidence suggests that it had become standard practice to tap the phones of left-wing organisations and ad hoc radical organisations such as strike committees and to photograph all participants in demonstrations.[58]

(d) The expansion of political surveillance

The Special Branch (originally the Special Irish Branch, having been, like many of the repressive aspects of the contemporary state, a response to the Irish anti-colonial struggles of the late nineteenth century) probably comprised about 1,600 officers (about 1 per cent of the total police force) by the mid 1980s. Half were in London, with the rest attached to local forces round the country.[59] The Special Branch maintained an index of some three million people, of whom files were kept on all those considered to be activists or important members of left-wing or extreme right-wing groups; and attended, or received reports from other police officers or informers about, all political meetings (apart from those of most MPs and councillors, or candidates for election to parliament or local councils). The Branch aimed to have informers in as many political organisations, and on as many university campuses, as possible, and tapped the phones of leaders of trade unions, the peace movement, the National Council for Civil Liberties and similar bodies – all of which it apparently defined, from time to time if not routinely, as 'subversive. Agents provocateurs also were employed to try – though not always successfully – to implicate 'subversives' in criminal acts.[60] The military secret service concerned with counter-espionage, MI5, worked with the latter but its work overlapped that of the Special Branch and has included spying on trade unionists during strikes. At one time MI5 even put some MPs under surveillance.[61] When two MI5 officers told a television team in 1985 that the security service had targeted and tapped the phones of various organisations such as the Campaign for Nuclear Disarmament

---

* This estimate is based on 'jury-vetting' data handed to the defence in a trial held in 1979. Out of 93 people on the jury panel, intelligence data had been provided to the prosecuting counsel on 20, of whom less than half had criminal records. The data included items (in several cases false) such as being 'believed to be a squatter' (occupying empty premises illegally) or having made a complaint against the police. The data given to the defence did not, moreover, include whatever intelligence had also been collected by the Special Branch (D. Leigh, *The Frontiers of Secrecy*, Junction Books, London 1980, pp. 171–6).

and Shelter, the government asked Lord Bridge, a judge whose job it was to review phonetap warrants, to investigate.

In just a week, including two days sitting full time in the House of Lords, he was able personally to examine 6,129 warrants signed between 1970 and 1984, decide on the merits of each warrant and conclude that not a single warrant had been improperly authorised.[62]

In 1985 after much controversy the government passed the Interception of Communications Act which established a commissioner to monitor wiretaps, and a tribunal of five lawyers to hear complaints about them. However, the tribunal was not obliged to explain its decisions and did not do so when it rejected the CND's complaint following the MI5 officers' allegations referred to above; nor could the tribunal's findings be appealed to any court.

(e) The use of the army for domestic political control

By 1988 most infantry units of the British Army had been stationed for a period of duty in Northern Ireland at some time during the past two decades, so that the military control of civilians within the UK had been their main operational experience. The lessons of this (and of earlier colonial operations) had been generalised into a doctrine of 'low-intensity operations' whose potential application on the mainland for dealing with 'nationalists' or 'industrial subversives' played an increasingly explicit part in training exercises.[63] In 1974 the army and the police jointly occupied London Airport and the surrounding area in four successive exercises. The real object, critical commentators concluded, was 'to accustom the public to the reality of troops deployed through the High Street'.[64] The army was also brought into industrial disputes in new ways, once to provide fire services during a firemen's strike in 1977-8, on another occasion to guard prisoners during 'industrial' action by prison warders in 1980. An organisational structure was created which would enable the army and the police, aided by a network of volunteer reserves totalling some 8-900,000, to operate independently in controlling the country. As the State Research group commented,

Since the early 1970s, planning for war and 'emergencies' has been treated as one problem – how to maintain law and order and the status quo *inside* Britain (whatever the source of the threat). These plans have now been far advanced with little or no democratic knowledge or debate.[65]

The results of so many far-reaching developments were complex. Civil liberties were the most obvious casualty. In 1967 the unanimity of jury decisions had already been abandoned by a Labour Home Secretary (Jenkins) in favour of majority verdicts (10 votes out of 12 became sufficient to convict). At the same time, and unknown to the public, the prosecution began 'jury-vetting' – i.e., weeding out jurors they thought likely to be sympathetic to the accused – using police, Special Branch and MI5 intelligence records.* Justified as a measure against 'disloyal' jurors in political trials (though this justification should itself be challenged), the practice was soon extended to 'major criminal' cases. The 'Judges' Rules' governing the protection of suspects' rights during police interrogation were increasingly ignored. A disturbing volume of evidence indicated that the detention and interrogation of subjects without cautioning them or informing them of their rights to communicate with a solicitor was common, that those asking to speak with a solicitor were commonly refused, and that violence was not infrequently employed. Between 1970 and 1979, 245 people died in police custody, the numbers rising in every year but one during this period; 66 of these died from 'natural causes' and 36 were suicides.[66] The Police Federation was authorised to use its funds to enable policemen to sue anyone who made a false complaint against the police, and not surprisingly, the number of complaints withdrawn rose dramatically, but not public confidence in the police. In 1985 an independent Police Complaints Authority was finally established, when public disquiet about the police investigating themselves became too widespread: it found its work obstructed by conspiracies of police silence, by a doubtfully thorough investigation on the part of the officers of one police force investigating another at the Authority's request, and by serious charges being brought against the complainants by the police force complained against.[67]

Evidence obtained by illegal means was ruled juridically admissable by the courts. The defence's right of 'peremptory challenge' of jurors in criminal cases was abolished. No effective controls existed over the use of the new police computers, and information was exchanged between them despite earlier assurances to the contrary by the government. Cases also brought to light the fact that purely speculative and sometimes false data were held on the computers, and in other

* The familiar pattern of retreating from democracy as the franchise gradually widened to include the working class was also at work here. Rate revaluations resulting from inflation gradually lowered the property qualification for jury service, leading to an almost fivefold increase in the number of eligible people between 1955 and 1964. In 1974 property qualifications for jury service were finally abolished and all voters became eligible unless they had served a prison sentence. The police and right-wing lawyers called it a lowering of standards, just as right-wing ratepayers complained of a decline in 'councillor calibre' (see Review of Security and the State 1980, p. 43, and P. Kellner, 'Deemed Unfit to Serve', New Statesman, 2 July 1982).

cases supposedly confidential data were found to have been given out to private individuals. The Data Protection Act of 1986 did not offer significant protection against this, since data certified by a minister to be relevant to national security interests were specifically excluded from the Act's protection.

These developments had not converted Britain into a police state, or even an authoritarian one; all of them were contested, and might yet be reversed. But they formed a consistent whole. The power of the central state to deal with opposition by coercion had been greatly extended, legally and practically; accountability had been reduced; the rights of individuals had been greatly curtailed; and all of these things had become to a considerable extent familiar and increasingly accepted. This represented not a step towards dictatorship, but a marked shift in the balance away from consent and popular participation towards repression and social control, a shift which Thatcher and those closest to her in the Conservative leadership believed was necessary and desirable.

Notes

1 A. Gramsci, *Selections from the Prison Notebooks*, Lawrence and Wishart, London 1971, p. 263.
2 James Michael, *The Politics of Secrecy*, Penguin, Harmondsworth 1982, p. 25.
3 For a helpful review of these and other dimensions of the British state's undemocratic character and the trend towards greater authoritarianism and social control in the 1980s, see P. Hillyard and J. Percy-Smith, *The Coercive State*, Collins–Fontana, London 1988.
4 All these institutions were scrupulously studied and assessed by the late Frank Stacey in *The British Ombudsman*, Clarendon Press, Oxford 1971, and *Ombudsmen Compared*, Clarendon Press, Oxford 1980.
5 G. Marshall, 'Parliament and the Redress of Grievances', in S. Walkland and M. Ryle, eds, *The Commons Today*, revised edition, Fontana, London 1981, pp. 277–8.
6 *Annual Report for 1980*, Parliamentary Commissioner for Administration, HMSO, London 1981.
7 Stacey, *Ombudsmen Compared*, pp. 200–1.
8 'Profile', in the *Observer*, 29 May 1988.
9 F. Stacey, *British Government 1966–1975*, Oxford University Press, Oxford 1975, p. 190. The reasons for this acceptance are apparent in the establishment prose of the Commissioners' reports, and their constant stress on the difficulties of administering a complex society such as Britain and on the need to avoid wasting 'my valuable resources' on investigating frivolous or vexatious complaints. Lady Serota's annual Reports for the English Local Commissioners, on the other hand, are refreshingly free of these characteristics.
10 *Social Trends 1988*, p. 178.
11 Michael, pp. 48–49, 194.
12 *Report of the Committee on Section 2 of the Official Secrets Act 1911*, Cmnd 5104, HMSO 1972 (the Franks Committee).
13 This was the subject of two enquiries: the *Report of the Committee on Privacy*, Cmnd 5012 of 1972 (the Younger report) and the *Report of the Committee on Data*

Protection, Cmnd 7341 of 1978 (the Lindop report).

14 A noted enquirer was Peter Hennessy of *The Times*: see P. Kellner and N. Crowther-Hunt, *The Civil Servants*, Macdonald, London 1980, pp. 269–70 and 292.

15 Kellner and Crowther-Hunt, p. 275. Chapter 11 of their book is an exceptionally cogent summary of the secrecy issue.

16 Ibid., p. 281.

17 Ibid.

18 Michael, pp. 177–8. On the attitudes of British judges on Official Secrecy see also Hillyard and Percy-Smith, *The Coercive State* (note 3), pp. 133–6, and (more generally) Chapter 4.

19 J. Dearlove, *The Reorganisation of British Local Government*, Cambridge University Press, Cambridge 1979, pp. 244–5.

20 T. Byrne, *Local Government in Britain*, Penguin, Harmondsworth 1981, pp. 27–28.

21 T. Burgess and T. Travers, *Ten Billion Pounds: Whitehall's Takeover of the Town Halls*, Grant McIntyre, London 1980, p. 18.

22 B. Keith-Lucas and P.G. Richards, *A History of Local Government in the Twentieth Century*, Allen and Unwin, London 1978, p. 40.

23 The theme of 'councillor calibre' is central to Dearlove's pathbreaking study (see note 16). See especially Chapter 4.

24 See B. Abel-Smith, *The Hospitals 1800–1948*, Heinemann, London 1964; and D. Widgery, *Health in Danger*, Macmillan, London 1979, Chapters 2–3.

25 Burgess and Travers, pp. 24–8.

26 J. Alt, 'Some social and political correlates of county borough expenditure', *British Journal of Political Science*, 1, 1971, pp. 49–62; other sources are also cited by Dearlove, pp. 234–5.

27 K. Newton and T.J. Karran, *The Politics of Local Expenditure*, Macmillan, London 1985, p. 102.

28 Keith-Lucas and Richards, *A History of Local Government*, Chapter 4; and N. Branson, *Poplarism 1919–1925*, Lawrence and Wishart, London 1979.

29 D. Skinner and J. Langdon, *The Story of Clay Cross*, Spokesman Books, Nottingham 1974. A partisan but vivid account by the leader of the Clay Cross 'rebels'.

30 The Local Government Boundary Commission Report for 1947 (the Trustram Eve Commission).

31 G. Rhodes, *The Government of London: The Struggle for Reform*, p. 108, cited in Dearlove, p. 100. Subsequently, control alternated between the two parties.

32 Dearlove, p. 103, citing M. Steed.

33 *Report of the Committee on Management of Local Government*, HMSO 1967, and *The New Local Authorities: Management and Structure*, HMSO, 1972.

34 See Dearlove, Chapters 5–6, and C. Cockburn, *The Local State*, Pluto Press, London 1977, Chapter 1. See also J. Benington, *Local Government Becomes Big Business*, CDP Publications, London 1976.

35 Cockburn, pp. 27–8.

36 M. Crick, *The March of Militant*, Faber, London 1986, Chapter 13.

37 Newton and Karran (note 27), pp. 125–26.

38 See also M. Kettle and L. Hodges, *Uprising – the Police, the People and the Riots in Britain's Cities*, Pan, London 1982.

39 B. Whitaker, *The Police in Society*, Eyre Methuen, London 1979, p. 19.

40 Whitaker, pp. 73–8 and 164; see also P. Evans, 'The Great Myth of the Detective', *The Times*, 25 March 1982.

41 *Review of Security and the State 1978*, Julian Friedman, London 1979, p. 33.

42 Lord Harris, quoted in ibid., p. 77.

43 Ibid., p. 80.

44 See M. Kettle, 'The Drift to Law and Order', *Marxism Today*, October 1980, pp. 20–7, for an excellent and balanced overview.

45 T.A. Critchley, *A History of the Police in England and Wales*, revised edition, Constable, London 1978, p. 288.

46 See *State Research Bulletin*, No. 23, April–May 1981: 'Controlling the Police? Police Accountability in the UK', pp. 110–23.

47 Hillyard and Percy-Smith, pp. 266–67; see also P. Scraton, *New State of the Police*, Pluto, London 1985, Chapter 7, esp. pp. 152–63.

48 *Review of Security and the State 1980*, pp. 146–71.

49 Cited in ibid., p. 147.

50 Whitaker, p. 88.

51 John Alderson, Chief Constable of Devon and Cornwall, 1978, cited in *Review of Security and the State 1980*, pp. 147–8.

52 Hillyard and Percy-Smith, p. 244.

53 See *Review of Security and the State 1979*, pp. 130–40 and 1980, pp. 141–2.

54 D. Smith et al., *Police and People in London*, PSI, London 1983, esp. Vol. 3.

55 Hillyard and Percy-Smith, pp. 294 and 301–2.

56 D. Campbell, 'Society Under Surveillance' in P. Hain, ed., *Policing the Police*, Vol. 2, Calder, London 1980, pp. 65–150.

57 Hillyard and Percy-Smith, p. 276.

58 *Review of Security and the State 1980*, pp. 131–6 and T. Bunyan, *The Political Police in Britain*, Quartet Books, London 1977, pp. 196–211.

59 D. Campbell and S. Connor, in *On the Record: Computers, Surveillance and Privacy*, Joseph, London 1986, p. 263, concluded that the Home Office's figure of 1,200 officers in 1984 was an understatement.

60 For examples see Bunyan, pp. 222–5.

61 Ibid., Chapter 4.

62 C. Ponting, *Whitehall: Tragedy and Farce*, Hamish Hamilton, London 1981, p. 128.

63 *Review of Security and the State 1980*, pp. 63–4.

64 The *Guardian*, cited in Bunyan, p. 273.

65 *Review of Security and the State 1979*, p. 23. For a full account of these preparations see P. Laurie, *Beneath the City Streets*, Panther, London 1979. See also D. Campbell, *War Plan UK*, Burnett Books, London 1982.

66 *Review of Security and the State 1980*, pp. 4–5 and 57–8.

67 Messrs Shaw and Logan were charged with attempting to prevent the course of justice after making complaints against the Greater Manchester police: *Guardian*, 23 May 1988.

Index